Springer Series in Supply Chain Management

Volume 19

Supply Chain Management (SCM), long an integral part of Operations Management, focuses on all elements of creating a product or service, and delivering that product or service, at the optimal cost and within an optimal timeframe. It spans the movement and storage of raw materials, work-in-process inventory, and finished goods from point of origin to point of consumption. To facilitate physical flows in a time-efficient and cost-effective manner, the scope of SCM includes technology-enabled information flows and financial flows.

The Springer Series in Supply Chain Management, under the guidance of founding Series Editor Christopher S. Tang, covers research of either theoretical or empirical nature, in both authored and edited volumes from leading scholars and practitioners in the field – with a specific focus on topics within the scope of SCM.

This series has been accepted by Scopus.

Springer and the Series Editor welcome book ideas from authors. Potential authors who wish to submit a book proposal should contact Ms. Jialin Yan, Associate Editor, Springer (Germany), e-mail: jialin.yan@springernature.com

Hau Lee • Ricardo Ernst • Arnd Huchzermeier •
Shiliang Cui
Editors

Creating Values with Operations and Analytics

A Tribute to the Contributions of Professor Morris Cohen

Springer

Editors
Hau Lee
Graduate School of Business
Stanford University
Stanford, CA, USA

Ricardo Ernst
McDonough School of Business
Georgetown University
Washington, DC, USA

Arnd Huchzermeier
WHU-Otto Beisheim School of Management
Vallendar, Germany

Shiliang Cui
McDonough School of Business
Georgetown University
Washington, DC, USA

ISSN 2365-6395 ISSN 2365-6409 (electronic)
Springer Series in Supply Chain Management
ISBN 978-3-031-08870-4 ISBN 978-3-031-08871-1 (eBook)
https://doi.org/10.1007/978-3-031-08871-1

This Springer imprint is published by the registered company Springer Nature Switzerland AG
The registered company address is: Gewerbestrasse 11, 6330 Cham, Switzerland

Preface

The field of operations management has gone through tremendous advancement in the last few decades. As operations become more globalized, the associated complexities have increased. Such complexities stemmed from the diverse geographical regions where operations occurred, the geopolitical forces impacting operational effectiveness, the increasing frequency and magnitudes of disruptions, the push for sustainability and diversity, the movement from product-based to service-based business models, and the rapid emergence of digital technologies that could change operational processes, channels, and products. These complexities have offered a rich ground for research.

In addition, operations management as a discipline has expanded its scope from production focus to end-to-end supply chain management, starting with design and new product development, supply network management, distribution, and aftersales service. Innovations in industry have taken place in new products, new processes, new services, and new business models.

This book is a collection of articles that showcase past, current, and future directions of research in some of these operations management problems. The book also serves as a tribute to honor Professor Morris Cohen. Professor Cohen has been a major contributor to advancing the research frontier of operations management, and a driving force in shaping the research directions of the field. After a very illustrious career, he has retired from the Wharton School, University of Pennsylvania, in July 2021. In a separate part, we will describe Professor Cohen's impactful career as a scholar, teacher, consultant, and entrepreneur. He has also been a mentor, professional colleague, and personal friend to many in the profession. Many of the chapters in this book were based on research that was inspired by or built upon the foundational work of Professor Cohen.

The book starts with a chapter by Professor Cohen on his perspective on the evolution of research approaches and methods in operations management. Following this chapter, the book is organized into three parts. The first part covers broad strategic issues in operations—strategies such as how the global supply chain should be designed, how a company can use business model design to gain an advantage, innovations in new product development, new product designs that go beyond the conventional profit objectives, and the treatment of fairness in the supply chain.

The second part covers breakthrough performances through smarter operations management. It starts with the use of performance-based contracts to set proper incentives, the sharing of information among supply chain partners, the consideration of corruption in operations, and advances in service parts management. The final part covers more industry-specific applications. The pandemic of COVID-19 has highlighted the importance of industries such as semiconductor, computer technology, and health care. This part covers improving operational performance of these industries, as well as the airline industry.

Our intent for this book, with coverage of strategic design issues, operations performance analysis, and industry-based practice research, is to provide the readers an exposition of some of the important advances in the field of operations management and to stimulate future research. It is our hope that, by motivating the profession to make continual advances and new discoveries, we can show our gratitude to the immense contributions that Professor Cohen has given us.

Stanford, CA — Hau Lee
Washington, DC — Ricardo Ernst
Vallendar, Germany — Arnd Huchzermeier
Washington, DC — Shiliang Cui

Achievements of Professor Morris Cohen

Morris A. Cohen has been the Panasonic Professor of Manufacturing and Logistics in the Operations, Information and Decisions Department, the Wharton School at the University of Pennsylvania. He is also Co-Director of Wharton's Fishman-Davidson Center for Service and Operations Management. He has recently served as the department editor for the *Manufacturing and Service Operations Management* journal and is a Fellow of the Institute for Operations Research and Management Science, and a Senior Fellow of the Manufacturing and Service Operations Management Society.

Professor Cohen originally came from Toronto, Canada, holds a B.A.Sc. in Engineering Sciences from the University of Toronto, and an M.S. in Industrial Engineering and a Ph.D. in Operations Research from Northwestern University.

Professor Cohen is a professor with a high standing in the profession whose accomplishments can only be described as outstanding and stellar. He has been:

- A top scholar who has made breakthrough research
- A thought leader in industry who has influenced management thinking
- An entrepreneur and industry consultant who also put theory into practice with achieved impacts
- An educator who has advised and nurtured numerous stellar scholars

Through his consulting and entrepreneurial activities, Professor Cohen has been successful in integrating practice and research. His work with industry enabled him to seed ideas and to obtain research partners for himself and for his students. At the same time, his work with companies and organizations has led to the identification of new research challenges which motivated his research. The research outputs generated from these efforts formed the basis of his industry practice.

This integration of practice and research has also influenced many of his Ph.D. students, some of whom have successfully followed his path and have become leading scholars in the operations management community.

Professor Cohen's resume contains hundreds of publications, and he is still productive. He never stops! His list of research interests and contributions is endless.

One of his greatest contributions is the realization that most economic value is created in the aftersales service in the context of supply chains. He has evolved the ideas to incorporate new technologies. From there, the buzzwords for his contributions: service supply chain strategy and solutions, machine-learning applications to supply chain planning, servitization and product-service systems, global operations strategy, benchmarking of manufacturing/logistics systems, performance-based incentives and contracting, service quality measurement, supply chain coordination, and manufacturing/marketing interfaces.

He has done consulting work in many industries: aerospace and defense, consumer electronics, healthcare technology, oil and gas, automobile, semiconductor equipment, computers, and telecommunications.

The list of awards is equally impressive:

- Advisory Board, Center for Transportation & Logistics, Massachusetts Institute of Technology, 2019
- Plenary Speaker, International Symposium, Japanese Operations Management and Strategy Association, 2019
- Teaching Commitment and Curricular Innovation Award, The Wharton School, 2015
- INFORMS Fellow, Institute for Operations Research and the Management Sciences, 2013
- Plenary Speaker, German Operations Research Society, 2008
- Inaugural POMS International Distinguished Lectureship Award, 2007
- Tibbets Award, National Science Foundation – SBIR, 2007
- Senior Fellow, Manufacturing and Service Operations Management Society, INFORMS, 2004
- Institute of Industrial Engineers Best Paper Published in IIE Transactions, 1999
- Fellow, International Academy of Management, 1998
- S.J. Hardy Award for Best Paper in Operations Management, Decision Sciences Institute, 1990
- Edelman Prize for Best Practice in Operations Research (finalist), 1990
- Lauder Institute Prize for Advances in Theory and Practice of International Management, 1989

For many of us, working with Morris has been a most enriching experience. His kindness and generosity, his insistence on rigor and quality, his humility, his ability to link management insights from model analysis, and his care for our wellbeing have had a long-lasting impact on his students.

Contents

Part I
Evolution of Operations and Analytics

Overview of Supply Chain Modeling: Steps to Nirvana

Morris A. Cohen

Abstract This chapter introduces a framework that explores the wide range of models and methods that have been used to analyze supply chains. We discuss the origins and attributes of eight different approaches, ranging from science fiction to religion. In between we consider ideas and concepts from quantum physics, engineering, management science, economics, social science, and policy analysis. We note that there is a fundamental trade-off between model fidelity and tractability, which impacts the role of the different approaches in analyzing supply chains. The paper then discusses the implementation of model-based methods and draws insights based on an application case. The application case illustrates how new technology (big data, cloud computing, and machine learning) can be combined to develop better supply chain planning solutions. The paper concludes with observations suggested by the case and the examples explored in the paper, and notes that a key requirement is to achieve robustness in the application of supply chain models to real-world planning problems. This will ensure that the output and predicted results of a model are consistently accurate even as the input variables or assumptions change drastically due to unforeseen circumstances.

Keywords Supply chain strategy · Planning models

1 Introduction

The COVID crisis has driven home the message that the management of supply chains is a critical capability that all firms and organizations must master. There is a long history in the Operations Management field of developing models and solutions to this problem. In fact, an amazing range of approaches has been used to build different supply chain models to explain or prescribe management decisions. In this

M. A. Cohen (✉)
The Wharton School, University of Pennsylvania, Philadelphia, PA, USA
e-mail: cohen@wharton.upenn.edu

H. Lee et al. (eds.), *Creating Values with Operations and Analytics*, Springer Series in Supply Chain Management 19, https://doi.org/10.1007/978-3-031-08871-1_1

paper, we will consider a framework that captures the diversity of formulations that have been adopted and highlights lessons to be learned about how to apply such models to influence management decisions.

Each modeling approach has its own advantages and disadvantages, which I have classified into eight steps in the journey to perfection, i.e., Nirvana. We will consider examples for each step to illustrate its scope, its underlying assumptions and its relevance to managers. The collection of approaches we discuss includes the underlying concepts that are relevant to supply chain modeling as well as those tools that can be used to support analysis of planning problems. We will then consider managerial insights and research implications that are suggested by the framework.

The conclusion of this review is that there is no right answer. Indeed, the appropriate choice for a modeling approach depends on the problem you want to solve. However, if the goal is implementation, then we shall see that certain approaches can be better than others. We will observe that the key is to select an approach that achieves the appropriate balance between fidelity; i.e., the accuracy of the model in predicting the consequences of selecting decisions based on the model, and the cost and difficulty in finding the best solution; i.e., its tractability for the problem to be solved.

The paper concludes with an example, based on current practice, that illustrates how the trade-off between fidelity and tractability has been fundamentally altered by the introduction of new technology, i.e., machine learning, big data, and cloud computing. The example also provides guidance for using supply chain planning to support scenario planning, which has become essential for dealing with the current environment of uncertainty and disruption.

2 Modeling Alternatives

In this section, we will discuss eight different approaches which define ways of thinking about how to model and analyze a supply chain management problem. Some of the approaches lead to specific methodologies, while others provide conceptual insights that are relevant to supply chain analysis regardless of the methodology that is being used.

The eight approaches are indicated in Fig. 1, and can be considered to be steps to reach supply chain Nirvana, where ideal decisions are made based on the recommendations of the analyst. While the approaches are listed in a sequence, we note that the sequence displayed is somewhat arbitrary. Moreover, it is by no means assured that it is possible to reach Nirvana. Rather, we will consider ways in which the approaches or combinations of approaches can be used to support a particular problem and how the attributes of fidelity and cost for each approach must be considered in doing so.

In the following sections, we will describe each step. We will observe that each can be linked to a particular mode of analysis or a perspective that is relevant to the challenge of developing policies for improving supply chain performance. We note

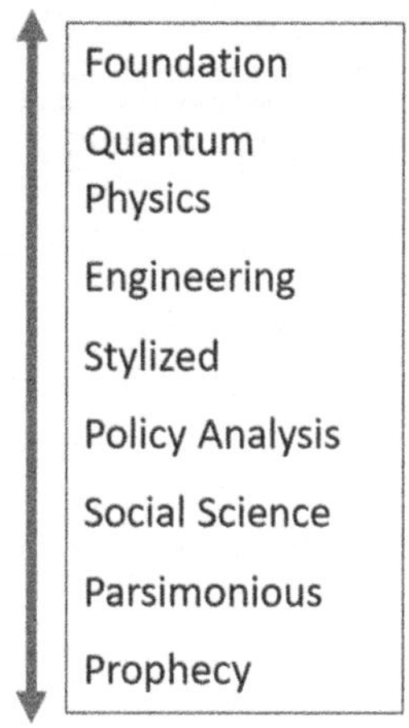

Fig. 1 Steps to supply chain modeling Nirvana

that the approaches indicated exhibit an enormous range of attributes, assumptions, and consequences.

2.1 Foundation: Isaac Asimov

This is science fiction. In the distant future technology has reached the point where it is possible to know, with certainty, how events will unfold–down to a detailed level. Leaders in the future will receive a holograph communication from the guru of the past that is meant to provide them with advice and guidance to deal with a current crisis or challenge. The holograph begins with the avatar of the guru, saying, "right now you are facing the following problem ... here is what you have to do ..." (Fig. 2).

Asimov called the method "psychohistory" (Asimov 1951) and is analogous to the kinetic theory of gases, i.e., you cannot predict individual behavior but you can predict behavior of a large number of actors, i.e., a volume of gas or a mob.

While such a tool has yet to be developed, the story illustrates the ideal goal for any supply chain planning model, i.e., to accurately predict the future and to provide a prescription for the best decision to make, which will mitigate risk and exploit opportunities.

2.2 Quantum Physics

We now know that we live in a world where parallel universes are possible. They each represent a different future that can coexist with other futures, in some mysterious fashion. This is related to "quantum entanglement" where particles can

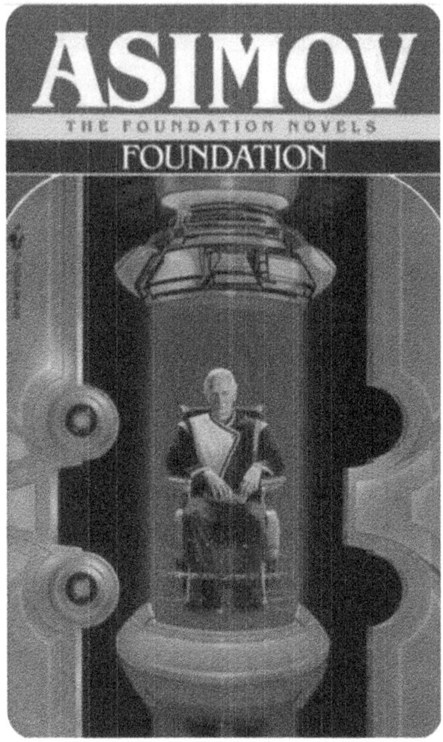

Fig. 2 The avatar of Hari Seldon, the guru in the trilogy, appears in the future to tell leaders what to do

interact instantaneously at unlimited distances. Einstein considered this idea to be spooky, and science fiction writers love it.

Schrodinger's Cat illustrated how quantum particles can exist in a superposition of states at the same time and collapse down to a single state upon interaction with other particles, i.e., is the cat dead or alive? (Fig. 3)

The mathematics to describe this phenomenon uses string theory and requires up to 26 dimensions. A recent book by Rovelli (2021) discusses the implications of quantum theory for our basic understanding of reality and suggests that the only thing that exists is the relationship between objects.

We learn from the notion of parallel universes that, in order to make plans for the future, we need to know what universe we will be living in. Today I would call this **scenario planning,** where you define a future state and come up with the "best" decision for that state. The development of quantum computing promises to expand the scope and scale of models that can be solved.

2.3 Engineering Models

This is the way I was taught to do research and solve problems. The model should be a valid and detailed representation of reality, i.e., achieve fidelity. Accurate predictions of outcomes are the goal (Fig. 4).

While having an accurate model is desirable, we discover that these models are often intractable, i.e., generating an optimal solution is not feasible or will be very difficult to achieve. Note that this illustrates the fundamental trade-off between fidelity and tractability.

Implementation of engineering models often leads to the development of heuristic algorithms to generate the near-optimal solution to the planning problem.

Fig. 3 Schrodinger's cat co-exists in two parallel universes; one where it is alive and one where it is dead

Fig. 4 Engineering models are complex and precise, like a well-oiled machine

My favorite heuristic has been the "greedy" algorithm which suits my impatient personality and tendency to make myopic decisions.

One example of this is the work I and colleagues worked on was to optimize multi-echelon inventory problems. I have been fortunate to see the results of my work in this area implemented and applied in the particular area of after-sales service/spare parts inventory management. The HBR article, "Winning in the Aftermarket" (Cohen et al. 2006), describes the strategic challenges and opportunities for using model-based tools in this area.

2.4 Stylized Management Science Models

This has become very fashionable in our field. The models provide a stripped-down representation of a real-world problem. Only those variables and decisions that are most relevant are captured. Strong assumptions are needed in order to formulate and solve these models. These models try to capture various strategic interactions among different actors (firms, individuals) with certain characteristics (e.g., self-interest, hidden information, hidden actions) and allow for the analysis of important trade-offs, risks, and constraints. They also can capture behavioral factors (Fig. 5).

Note that the stylized representation of a dragon is a far cry from reality.

This approach is desirable when the goal is to develop analytical, structural results, leading to managerial insights. Mathematics and logic are used to generate the results. Application of the insights generated by these models, however, can be a challenge and their assumptions are hard to validate. We can learn from this approach that the art of supply chain modeling requires an ability of picking the

Fig. 5 A stylized picture of a dragon

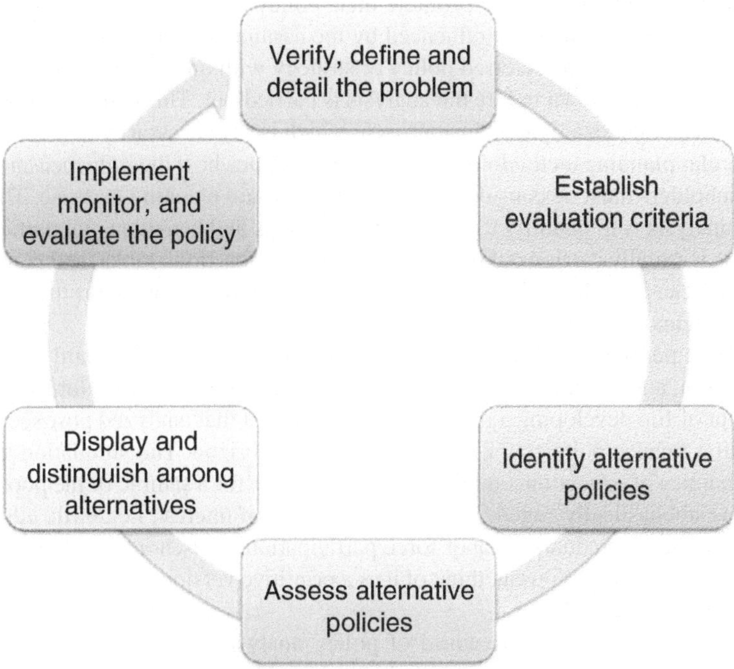

Fig. 6 Policy analysis requires multiple steps

correct assumptions and deciding on what to include and what to leave out of the model.

An example of this approach is the models I co-developed that relates to new product development and where the trade-off is between time to market, profit, and reliability (Cohen et al. 1996; Gao et al. 2021). I am impressed by the power of such basic models to communicate key ideas to managers and scholars alike.

2.5 *Policy Analysis*

This refers to the application of analytics and quantitative methods to support the development of government policy or to formulate a strategic plan for a company or organization. This is part of the political process, whereby different policies to address a particular societal challenge are developed by government and interest groups or where firms develop strategies to achieve competitive advantage. The goal of the analysis is to quantify the costs and benefits of adopting a particular policy recommendation (Fig. 6).

Since the application of models in this situation is, by definition, part of a political process, the outcome of such studies can be dictated by the particular group who are conducting the analysis to promote their policy agenda. The outcome of such studies is, of course, heavily influenced by the assumptions made in the modeling. The goal is to justify a preferred policy or strategy with quantitative results, and so the conclusion is known before the analysis is carried out. This can be dangerous!

This is another example of an approach, which is not necessarily associated with a particular planning methodology, but rather illustrates how the influence and goals of stakeholders must be considered in any supply chain planning exercise. The goal of the analysis is to quantify the distribution of costs and benefits to all parties. The analysis is usually carried out by internal policy groups, think tanks, and consulting firms and can include application of a variety of different approaches that includes simulation and analytical models.

My first permanent job was as a policy analyst at the Treasury Board in Canada, when I took a leave of absence after one year of doctoral studies at Northwestern. I had a lot of fun developing a micro-simulation model that analyzed post-secondary education finance policies for a 50-year planning horizon. The simulation tracked the dynamics of education, employment, and income for a sample of the population that was stochastically "aged" over the time period of interest, i.e., birth, education through college, graduation, labor force participation, household/family formation, retirement, mortality. You can think of it as a primitive version of psychohistory (see Cohen and Dobell 1975).

I quickly learned that the world of policy analysis was not for me, and so I returned to my doctoral studies as quickly as I could.

2.6 Social Science/Psychiatry/Empirical

The goal here is to explain human behavior. The analysis is usually empirical and the results can be controversial or unexpected (Fig. 7).

The recent controversy over "p-hacking"[1] is a good illustration of the challenges faced here. My colleagues at Wharton have pioneered the study of the p-hacking phenomenon, much to the consternation of some famous psychologists, who have seen that some of their most intriguing results could not be replicated.

Perhaps the key lesson of this approach to modeling for those of us working on operations problems is the need to apply world-class and rigorous statistical analysis methods to our empirical research. It is gratifying to see that the standard for doing so in our field has risen to the task, and now empirical supply chain research is one of the most exciting areas of our field.

[1] P-hacking is defined as: "*the misuse of data analysis to find patterns in data that can be presented as statistically significant, thus dramatically increasing and understating the risk of false positives. This is done by performing many statistical tests on the data and only reporting those that come back with significant results.*"

Fig. 7 Do macro models capture the complexity of human behavior?

One example of an empirical operations-focused research problem that I have worked on concerns the issue of information sharing between customers and suppliers in the semiconductor equipment industry. We considered the case where a major producer of semiconductor components shared information of their intent to place equipment orders in the future with suppliers. Their goal is to gain priority access to the equipment producer's capacity. We demonstrated that the sharing of information can backfire if the information that is shared is volatile and subject to change. In particular, our empirical results indicated that the lead time of a supplier is negatively correlated with the variance of the information they share with their customers. The setting was Intel and its semiconductor equipment suppliers. Intel provides a 2-year rolling horizon of "predicted" orders that is updated monthly (see Ren et al. 2005, 2010).

2.7 *Parsimonious Economic Models*

These models are very ambitious (naïve?). They typically are used to analyze macro-economic, policy questions. They have very few variables and their accuracies are not always that great. Also, their use tends to be politicized; hence we refer to economics as the "dismal science" (Fig. 8)

While I have not developed such models, I am impressed by the courage/chutzpah of using them to make decisions. We should note that much of government policy and corporate policy is dictated by the application of economic models and so their influence is profound.

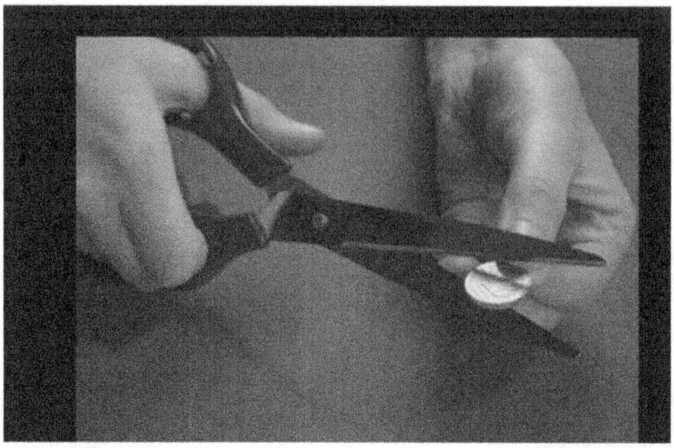

Fig. 8 Parsimony in model building requires cutting corners

Fig. 9 True believers must listen to the words of the prophet!

2.8 Prophecy

This what we find in the great religions. Prophets are inspired by God and predict outcomes that take place far into the future. The goal of the prophet is to influence the behavior of a group by telling them what is going to happen to them, unless they modify their behavior, i.e., "sinners repent" (Fig. 9).

This approach requires faith that leads to rituals where we pray to influence future outcomes. While we do not often consider the need for faith when analyzing supply chains, it is clearly required. Consider the case of Intel's "copy exactly" policy for building a new fab. Given the complexity of the production process, it typically takes a long time (i.e., a year or more) before a new fabrication process can achieve acceptable yields. There are an enormous number of variables that can influence the quality of the fab's outputs and often trial and error is used to tune the process, when a new fab comes on line,

Speed, of course, is critical in this "high clock-speed" industry where the pace of technological change is very high. Now, when it is time to add capacity by building a second fab, the approach at Intel is to copy everything, down to the most minute detail exactly (e.g., the color of the tiles in the bathrooms) in order to minimize any delay. Since we do not really understand why the process decisions we have made in building the previous fab led to a higher yield, we have to believe that what we did for the first will work for the second, i.e., we must have faith and "copy exactly."

3 Implications of the Frameworks for Implementation

So, we started with science fiction in Asimov's Foundation and we ended with faith in the prophets or in a process ("copy exactly"). Have we come full circle? Fig. 10.

Aside from science fiction, quantum physics and religion, the methods considered here have been used to solve a wide range of supply chain planning problems. Successful implementation of these model-based supply chain solutions requires an appropriate match between the model/methodology used for analysis and the problem under consideration. As we noted, there is a key trade-off between the tractability of the method, which determines the cost to implement, and the accuracy of performance metrics computed by the model, i.e., its fidelity. All models are representations of reality and all require data inputs and assumptions. Figure 11 illustrates the efficient frontier of intractability vs. fidelity, where we have restricted our attention to the five approaches that can be tied directly into a supply chain planning methodology. These supply chain analysis methods are mapped onto the frontier in positions that suggest a sequence that is consistent with the ordering in Fig. 11.

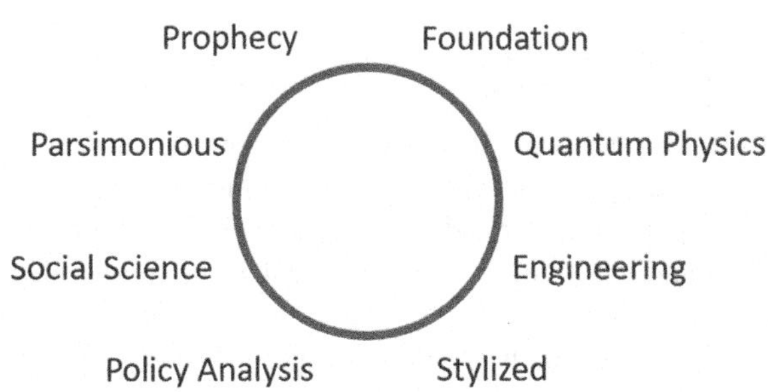

Fig. 10 The steps to Nirvana have no beginning or end

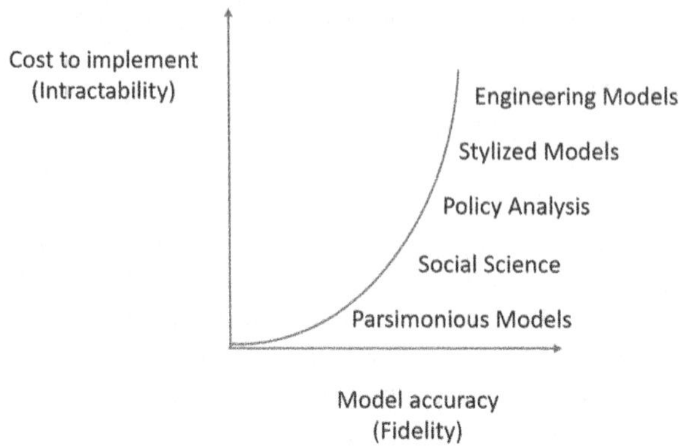

Fig. 11 The efficient frontier of supply chain model-based methodologies

As we have seen, there is a wide range of approaches that have been developed to support supply chain planning from a variety of perspectives. The question that we all face when looking to analyze and make recommendations for a supply chain problem is what approach to adopt. We note that there is no "correct" answer as to how to formulate a model. The choice is dictated by the problem at hand, which leads to conclusions on how to balance the trade-off between tractability and cost. The choice of a method to use will also be impacted by data availability and the perspectives of managers concerning the goal and scope of the problem to be considered.

In some cases, a hierarchy of models can be used, which raises the question of what is the best sequence for application of multiple approaches, i.e., top-down and bottom-up. Is it best to start with a simple model, requiring more assumptions, but which is easier to implement, and then move on to another method that provides more accuracy, but is more difficult? Or, alternatively, does one start with a detailed operational model and then move on to a simpler model which may provide insights more appropriate for strategic planning?

4 An Application Example

In the section, we consider some insights that we have developed, based on recent work we have conducted, to develop software solutions that can help managers develop strategies appropriate for today's turbulent environment. In particular, how can supply chain planning modeling support the definition of strategies to enhance agility and provide resilience? These insights will be derived from a particular example based on the management of spare parts for the after-sales support of advanced equipment used in the semiconductor industry.

I am currently involved in a new venture, AD3 Analytics, which is applying machine learning and AI to supply chain planning. It is now possible to develop detailed, scalable models that replicate reality to a high level of fidelity. This is achieved through the use of a "digital twin" of the supply chain to measure performance and the development of a detailed, granular model to find the best link between a wide range of data inputs and the specific decisions that define the supply chain strategy. The digital twin can be used to accurately evaluate performance metrics for both current and proposed supply chain decisions, either historically or looking forward through scenario planning. The detailed model can be used to determine how a wide range of data drivers can be used to define a strategy for the design and management of the supply chain. The goal is to make optimal use of extended (big) data. In our work, we are using a machine learning framework for this step. See "Agile Data Driven Decisions (AD3): Our Story" and "Agile Data Driven Decisions (AD3): Our Solution" at https://www.ad3.ai/).

Cloud computing, open source software for state-of-the-are solution algorithms and big data, which provides an unprecedented amount of data, in near-real time, from end-to-end supply chain stakeholders, are moving the tractability/efficient frontier down (as illustrated in Fig. 12). We now can solve bigger problems, faster, more precisely, quickly, and with more impact. The bottom line is that each of the various approaches we have discussed has the potential to add value, depending on the purpose and scope of the analysis. The key is to match the choice of solution method and model formulation to the problem to be analyzed in a manner that captures the key trade-offs, recognizes the principal risks, understands the limitations of available data, and captures the complexity of the underlying situation. The technology available today to support supply chain planning analysis enhances our ability to apply the methodologies depicted in Fig. 12.

The example is based on a proof of concept analysis conducted for a major producer of semiconductor equipment, that was conducted by my startup, AD3 Analytics. This example illustrates how the technologies of machine learning, cloud computing and big data can be combined to develop better supply chain planning solutions. The study focused on the company's global supply chain network for

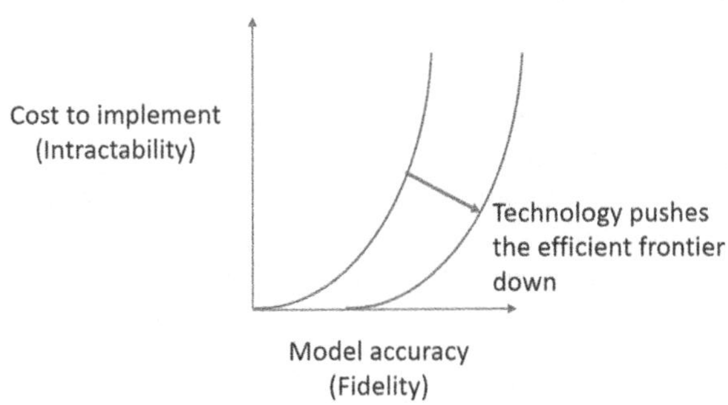

Fig. 12 The impact of technology

planning and management of parts to support after-sales service of its installed base in semiconductor fabs around the world. They manage over a billion dollars of Inventory assets for this purpose.

Before we review the results of the study, let us consider how our framework of methodologies is relevant to the analysis.

From the Foundation story, we noted that the ideal goal is to predict a future scenario with complete accuracy and then use that knowledge to support the development of a strategy that will mitigate the consequences of the scenario. The AD3 methodology is predicated on the idea that reliance on perfect forecasts is unattainable and moreover can lead to adoption of the wrong policies. The AD3 methodology uses an extended set of data coupled with optimization of the machine learning process to generate an optimal "decision function" which defines weights to be given to the various data inputs, that managers have indicated, as potential drivers of inventory stocking decisions. The underlying model is inspired by a long tradition of engineering models of the multi-echelon spare parts planning problem. Fidelity, which is achieved by having a detailed, transaction-based accounting of the impact of stocking decisions on performance metrics, is captured in the model formulation for all part-location-time period combinations. The technology advances noted previously enabled the generation of multiple solutions in a rapid and low-cost manner. This led to extensive analysis of the results in a hold-out sample, and with new data, not used in the training and evaluation steps, to test for the robustness of the recommended solution. The overall approach is inspired by the social science tradition of in-depth analysis of data generated by the application of the model.

The training of the model to produce the decision function is based on an extensive, detailed data record of past transactions and problem features. It is clear that the resulting solution will always dominate the results of any forecast/optimization model combination for the historical record. Our digital twin evaluation of the recommended solution supports this conclusion. We also note that the methodology, as implemented on the cloud, can be used to develop agile responses to new information, as it is observed, as well as definition of longer-term strategies, tied to specific, user-defined scenarios. While the methodology we used is most closely associated with the engineering model tradition, lessons learned from parsimonious and stylized models as well as policy analysis supported analysis of strategic issues, relevant to users. This can support adoption of the methodology to help managerial decision-making.

We tested AD3's methodology for robustness based on out-of-sample performance of recommended solutions as well as its ability to respond to new data and new scenarios. The results demonstrated that our solution could outperform existing software using a state-of-the-art optimization algorithm based on a complex multi-echelon inventory model, that was augmented with the company's sophisticated over-ride process. As illustrated in the efficient frontier in Fig. 13, the performance in terms of cost and service (part availability to support machine up-time) was significant. The AD3 solution also provided an enhanced capability for monitoring and updating service strategy.

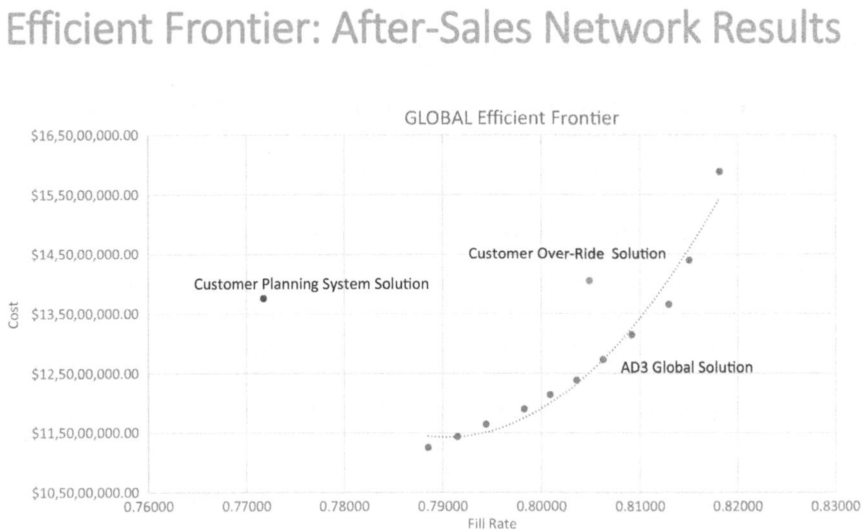

Fig. 13 Results of the AD3 proof of concept study for a semiconductor equipment manufacturer

This performance improvement was enabled by exploiting information that was ignored by the company's current solution for generating inventory stocking decisions. Predicting the demand for spare parts based on the history of machine failures is essentially impossible. Our methodology incorporated additional data, such as the dynamics of new product installations. It also used a highly accurate and detailed model of the underlying supply chain for both performance evaluation and machine learning model training. The model trained through machine learning, implemented on the cloud, enabled solutions for multiple instances of the problem that were defined by a different service metric (fill rate) target. A key insight that we developed and which distinguishes our approach is that it is not based on enhanced forecast accuracy. Rather it uses prescriptive analytics to make optimal use of past and current data and supports the definition and analysis of forward-looking scenarios.

5 Conclusions

We have reviewed the range of methods that have been used to support supply chain planning, whereas each method defines a trade-off between fidelity, (i.e., accuracy) and the cost of implementation, (i.e., tractability). The choice of method is equivalent to choosing where to make this trade-off. Every situation is different and can lead to different choices.

We then considered an example of the application of technology that promises to redefine how we can go about conducting supply chain policy studies. This technology is based on the application of machine learning to big data using the power of cloud computing and powerful commercial optimization solvers. It has the potential to enable significant changes to the practice of supply chain planning. It will do so by shifting the efficient frontier of fidelity vs. tractability down.

We conclude by noting the following observations which are illustrated in the example and are also consistent with other cases we have explored.

(a) New data sources are now available and can be exploited through the application of appropriate technology.
(b) We cannot avoid complex models if we want to get meaningful results. Large complex models can be solved accurately and quickly by using a machine learning approach, supported by cloud computing.
(c) At the same time, we must recognize the realities of addressing supply chain planning problems. It is always necessary to understand the limitations and opportunities afforded by data, the strategic goals and incentives of the stakeholders and the interplay of behavioral and analytic factors.
(d) The technology available today makes it possible to achieve more fidelity through the use of complex, realistic models and the application of a wide range of data inputs.
(e) Machine learning provides a viable way to exploit big data to address problems that are currently a principal challenge for supply chain managers. In particular, it can support more effective scenario planning that can be used to develop strategies to achieve supply chain resilience. Cloud computing and open source software have eliminated the barriers associated with solving a wide range of problem instances and contingencies.

The bottom line is that we need to achieve **robustness** in the application of supply chain models to solve real-world planning problems. Robustness ensures that the output and predicted results of our model are consistently accurate even if one or more of the input variables or assumptions change drastically due to unforeseen circumstances. As a result, the recommended decisions can be implemented and will yield the predicted result.

We are entering a new age of supply chain planning, where problems that were deemed to be intractable can be attacked with the new technology. While the fundamental trade-off between model fidelity and cost of implementation cannot be ignored, supply chain planners can approach a vastly increased range of problems and develop practical and implementable solutions by selecting from the wide range of planning tools discussed in this chapter. The combination of more data, a high-fidelity model, and the virtually unlimited compute power of cloud-based software can do the trick.

References

Agile Data Driven Decisions (AD3): Our Solution., at https://www.ad3.ai/). Accessed 13 Feb 2022

Agile Data Driven Decisions (AD3): Our Story., at https://www.ad3.ai/). Accessed 13 Feb 2022

Asimov I (1951) Foundation. Gnome Press

Cohen MA, Dobell AR (1975) Synthetic longitudinal sampling and its application to public policy analysis. In: Proceedings of the Summer Computer Simulation Conference, San Francisco, July, pp 1116–1133

Cohen MA, Eliashberg J, Ho T (1996) New product development: the performance and time-to-market tradeoffs. Manag Sci 42(2):173–186

Cohen MA, Agrawal N, Agrawal V (2006) Winning in the aftermarket. Harv Bus Rev:129–138

Gao F, Cohen MA, Cui S (2021) Performance, reliability or time-to-market? Innovative product development and the impact of government regulation. Prod Oper Manag 30(1):253–275

Ren J, Cohen MA, Ho T, Terwiesch C (2005) An empirical analysis of forecast sharing in the semiconductor equipment supply chain. Manag Sci 51(2):208–220

Ren J, Cohen MA, Ho T, Terwiesch C (2010) Information sharing in a long-term supply chain relationship: the role of customer review strategy. Oper Res 58(1):81–93

Rovelli C (2021) Helogland: making sense of the quantum revolution. Riverhead Books

Part II
Innovative Designs

New Business Models for the Digital Age: From After-Sales Services to Connected Strategies

Nicolaj Siggelkow and Christian Terwiesch

Abstract More and more firms use connected technologies to reshape fundamentally the way in which they interact with their customers. Rather than having few episodic interactions, companies are trying to create a continuous relationship with their customers that reduces friction and allows companies to anticipate the needs of their customers. In this chapter, we discuss new business models enabled by this development. We do so by reviewing some of the literature on after-sales services in general and some of Morris Cohen's pioneering research in particular. We then extend this prior work by articulating a framework of "Connected Strategy" in the form of a taxonomy of four connected customer experiences. Finally, we apply our Connected Strategy framework to the domain of healthcare delivery.

Keywords Connected strategy · Business model innovation · Healthcare delivery · Digital customer experience · Service design

1 Introduction

"Customers do not need a quarter inch drill. Instead, they need a quarter inch hole." This quote, often attributed to Marketing scholar Theodore Levitt (its origins are somewhat debated and might go back to the 1940s, see https://quoteinvestigator.com/2019/03/23/drill/), makes a simple yet powerful observation. Customers do not derive value by obtaining or owning a product (a drill), but rather from using the product to fulfill a need (creating a hole in the wall). The drill/hole example has a number of direct and indirect implications:

- Customer value or utility is not created at the time of purchasing a product, but at the time of using the product. For durable products (including a drill), this is very

N. Siggelkow · C. Terwiesch (✉)
The Wharton School, University of Pennsylvania, Philadelphia, PA, USA
e-mail: siggelkow@wharton.upenn.edu; terwiesch@wharton.upenn.edu

H. Lee et al. (eds.), *Creating Values with Operations and Analytics*, Springer Series in Supply Chain Management 19, https://doi.org/10.1007/978-3-031-08871-1_2

different from the time of sale and, thus, the value is created in the after-sales period.

- If customers derive their utility from the hole and not the drill, they might be better served by a hole drilling service provider (drill-me-a-hole.com) rather than a drill maker (Power Drills Ltd.).
- For the company that sees itself as the manufacturer of drills, the time period after the drill sale is more of an annoyance, during which its managers hope that the drill they sold is lasting and does not cause any warranty claims. Its favorite customers are those that stay away until they might need another drill. For the company that sells "hole drilling as a service," time of customer engagement and time of utility creation are much better aligned.
- Drill makers interact with their customers episodically, be that at the time when they sell the next product or when they deal with warranty issues. They are disconnected from their product when it matters the most, i.e., the point of use. This can leave them blind about how and how often the product is actually used. It is interesting to see that the most innovative drill manufacturers, including Bosch, DeWalt, and Stihl, all recently launched connected power drills that aim to overcome this blind spot.

For most of the business world, spare parts logistics and the after-sales markets rank fairly low on the totem pole of managerial importance. You have to do it in order to not upset your customers and hurt your reputation, but the focus is primarily on selling new products and services. This is true in the B2C sector—for example, in the maintenance of automotive vehicles—as much as it is true in B2B settings, including the servicing of production equipment.

One of the great accomplishments of Morris Cohen's research career has been the realization that there exist enormous opportunities for value creation in the after-sales market. Many companies, however, fail to take advantage of these opportunities. Often times, the reason for this failure is a lack of connectivity. For a company to succeed in the after-sales market, it needs high bandwidth connectivity with its customers, enabling good visibility into the product use and accurate information about the demand for spare parts. In short, Morris's research was essential in promoting a new approach to selling smart and connected products, something that, more recently, we have been referring to as a Connected Strategy (Siggelkow and Terwiesch 2019).

The purpose of this chapter is to:

- Talk about the emergence of new business models by reviewing some of the literature on after-sales services in general and some of Morris Cohen's pioneering research in particular.
- Articulate our Connected Strategy framework by first providing a taxonomy of four connected customer experiences and then explaining how firms can use business analytics to learn about their customer needs and spot future opportunities for innovation.
- Apply our Connected Strategy framework to the domain of healthcare delivery, an area where many services are delivered by providers that act like the

previously mentioned drill makers by focusing on the surgery, but ignoring the "after-sales" market when the patient has left the hospital (including problems like medication adherence and lifestyle management).

2 Winning in the After-Sales Market: Spare Parts Logistics and Performance-Based Contracts

The importance of managing after-sales services in general and spare parts inventory in particular has been discussed for a number of years. For example, Cohen et al. (2006) report that manufacturing firms make almost half of their profits from after-sales services, though these services account for only a quarter of the revenues. Moreover, the authors report that despite this financial contribution, most firms "perceive after-sales services to be a necessary evil and behave as though big business-to-business service contracts, small business-to-consumer warranties, and everything in between were–like taxes– a needless expense [Cohen et al. 2006]."

This poor management of after-sales services was first empirically documented by Morris Cohen and co-authors in a 1997 study, which showed that customer satisfaction in the after-sales market was dramatically below customer expectations in both B2C and B2B settings. Moreover, in either setting, be it customers waiting for their cars to be fixed or manufacturers waiting for a machine tool to be repaired, the costs of delays and poor quality in the after-sales market and the delivery of spare parts are much higher than during regular production. These parts typically need not only be available at the right time and location, but they also need to be handled by qualified service technicians.

Given the low demand rate, the high level of product variety, the geographic dispersion, and the increased time pressure, spare parts inventories need to be managed very differently from inventories for production parts (Cohen et al. 2006). Because of the distinctively different capabilities required in the spare parts supply chain, firms can and should design new business models which better align incentives with their customers. In most cases, this means shifting from selling them products to selling them services and integrated solutions.

The shift to services allows firms to move away from the traditional times and materials contracting. When manufacturers are compensated for the time and materials they provide ("fee for service," i.e., payments are based on the resources consumed), incentives are poorly aligned. The manufacturer gets compensated when things do not work ("pay me when it is broken"), which is not in the interest of the customer. Performance-based contracts (PBC) better align incentives by making payments contingent on uptime and availability (see Cohen 2006).

A great illustration of a transition from selling products to providing services and the associated PBC approach can be found in aircraft engine manufacturer Rolls Royce's launch of the "Power by the hour" program half a century ago, which was expanded in 2002 by its CorporateCare program. Rather than selling and maintaining jet engines, flying time is sold to Rolls Royce customers as a service at a fixed hourly rate. This aligns the incentives of Rolls Royce with the objectives of its customers (the operator of the aircraft).

Once incentives are better aligned, the airlines operating the jet engine are also willing to share data about the usage of the product and its use environments at a very high level of granularity. This not only allowed Rolls Royce to be more responsive in predicting spare parts consumption and engaging in preventive maintenance, but also to provide other services to the airline. For example, Rolls Royce now offers additional services, including engine health monitoring, optimization of engine use, and the development of digital twins. In fact, the extensive jet engine usage data that the company collects across many airlines enable high margin services such as flight optimization and fuel saving (Smith 2013, Technology Analysis and Strategic Management).

The "big data" that comes along with Rolls Royce being connected to hundreds of airplanes 24/7 also has the potential to fundamentally change some of the challenges associated with the management of spare parts inventories and inventory management in general. Cohen (2015) outlines the unique opportunities of big data in inventory management and how the service business model opens up new data flows in the interactions between manufacturers and their customers. With new forms of connectivity emerging, the manufacturer is now "in the loop" when his or her products are utilized by the customer and thus learns about product use and the environmental conditions of use. This allows the manufacturer to revisit the decision architecture of managing spare parts inventory. Rather than following the old model of data collection, forecasting parts demand, and inventory decision-making (determining quantity and location for each part), big data and machine learning now allow for automatic decision-making linking the incoming use data directly with recommendations for spare parts inventory decisions.

3 Connected Customer Experiences

Big data, machine learning, and automated decision-making—how are these technological trends impacting supply chains in the twenty-first century? In the evolution of the architectures of modern supply chains, we observe two trends across many different industries. First, companies are trying to fundamentally reshape the way they interact with their customers. Rather than having few episodic interactions, companies are trying to create a continuous relationship with their customers that reduces friction and allows companies to anticipate the needs of their customers. This has long been true for B2B settings, where electronic data interchange (EDI) platforms are common in logistics and procurement, but also is increasingly becoming the case in B2C applications. Second, many companies innovate and disrupt industries by creating new connections among previously unconnected parties in their ecosystem. The first trend we call creating "connected customer relationships," while the second is innovating on the "connection architecture" that exists in an industry.

To illustrate connected customer relationships in more detail, consider the realm of executive education, an industry that we, as business school professors, are very familiar with. As managers engage in their jobs, needs will periodically arise for skills that a manager does not possess. For instance, a production manager who is planning to suggest a capital investment may have the need (but not the knowledge) to compute an "internal rate of return." In an ideal world, the manager would like to press a "button" that would immediately deliver the precise knowledge that is needed. Companies that are able to deliver such a service have created what we call a "Respond-to-Desire" connected customer experience. In this case, customers (clients, patients) know exactly what they want. They want to listen to a particular song, for example, read a particular book, get a ride from their home to the airport, learn a particular framework, and they want their customer experience from placing the order to enjoying the product or service to be as easy and quick as possible.

A different situation might be a manager who just learned that she was promoted. In this case, the manager also needs new skills, but may not know all the relevant skills that would be useful to acquire. Companies that can help their customers to understand all the relevant options that are available to them and help them pick the best options for them have created a "Curated Offering" connected customer experience. This requires a much deeper information flow from the customer to the firm. With respond-to-desire the firm needed to know what the customer wanted (and possibly where the customer was located and how the customer wanted to pay). For a successful curated offering, a firm needs to know much more about the needs of the customer, because the customer does not know the best solution that is required.

A shortcoming of both respond-to-desire and curated offering connected customer experiences is that the customer only starts the process of looking for the development of new skills once he or she is aware of a specific need. Unfortunately, customers quite often become aware of their needs at times that are neither optimal for their own interests nor for the firms that help them fulfill those needs—if they become aware of them at all. Firms that are able to help their customers achieve goals that they have a hard time achieving themselves are creating a "Coach Behavior" connected customer experience. People want to take their medication, but they are forgetful; people want to lose some weight, but sticking to a diet is hard; people want to continue to learn and upgrade their skill set, but sticking to a curriculum is difficult. Organizations that can nudge and coach their clients by making them aware of their needs at more opportune times can create a tremendous amount of value for their customers. To pull this off, the information flow between customer and firm needs to be rich. The firm needs to deeply understand the needs of a customer, often before even the customer realizes that these needs have arisen, and then the firm needs to monitor whether the customer actually follows through with the actions that will address this need. To establish such an information flow clearly requires a tremendous amount of trust between the customer and the firm, a topic we will return to.

A fourth type of connected customer experience we term "Automatic Execution." In this case, a firm is continuously connected to a customer, detects possible needs before the customer is even aware of these needs, and then finds and executes solutions to these problems without the customer ever getting involved directly. If Tesla finds out about a possible edge case that its current automated driving software would not handle well, it can upgrade the software on all of their cars overnight via an over-the-air update without any owner ever becoming aware of the possible problem. Do learners wish they were Tesla cars, who could wake up and find that they had received knowledge and skills uploaded into their brains to help them address needs that they had not even realized would arise? Would that be magic? Or would that be creepy? Clearly both. This is an important aspect of connected customer experiences. Quite often, they operate on the fine line between magic and creepy. Different customers might have very different preferences on how much connectivity they desire and on how much they want to delegate decisions and have the environment act on them. As a result, there is no "one-size-fits-all" when it comes to connected customer experiences. Firms will have to create a whole suite of these experiences and learn over time which kinds of experiences a particular customer likes. Meanwhile, while customers may have some initial preferences, these preferences also will change over time as they have different kinds of connected customer experiences.

As the different vignettes illustrate, customer happiness is not only affected by the quality of the product or service they receive. Clearly, the quality of instruction is important, but it is not all that matters. How quickly a customer can get the instruction, how easily the most appropriate instruction can be found given the needs that have arisen, how easily the instruction can be accessed (e.g., does the learner need to travel, or is the instruction delivered in their homes), all affect the value a customer perceives. We find it helpful to think about the entire journey a customer embarks upon (see Fig. 1).

The point in time when a customer experiences the good or service a firm provides is actually fairly late in the customer journey. There are many pain points that customers might encounter before they actually enjoy the product, and each of these pain points is an opportunity for a firm to provide value to customers and to differentiate itself from its competitors.

The customer journey starts with some latent need. It is "latent" in the sense that it is always there, in the background, but not always in the mind of the customer. As an illustrative example, consider the case of executive education, an industry that as business school professors we are well familiar with. Here, the latent need is "to

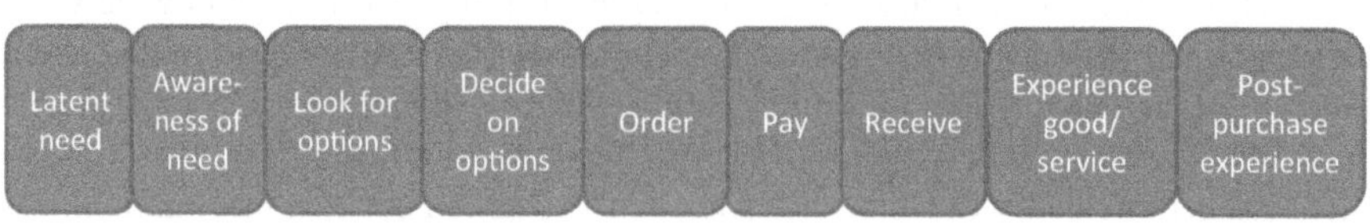

Fig. 1 Customer journey

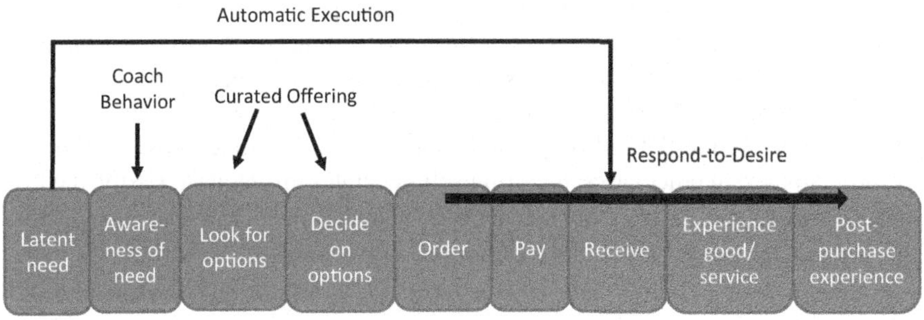

Fig. 2 Different connected customer experiences

have the right skills for whatever position I am in." Next comes the "awareness of a need." Customers are not always aware of their needs or only become aware of them at suboptimal times. Once a customer is aware of a particular need, the next steps in the customer journey are to discover all the possible options that could fulfill that need and then decide on the best solution. This can be an overwhelming step for many customers.

The World Wide Web is wonderful because customers can access the products and services of any company worldwide. But, at the same time, the World Wide Web also is horrible because now customers can access the products and services of any company worldwide. Providing customers with help at this step can remove a tremendous pain point in the customer journey. Once the customer has decided on the best solution, the steps of ordering and paying are next. In many industrial contexts, these steps can be amazingly complicated, requiring customers to create new accounts, set up bank connections, sign legal forms, wait for invoices, request invoices in different formats, and so on. Once the order has been placed and paid for, the question is: how does the customer receive the product? For instance, does the customer have to travel to the product, or does the product come to the customer? Finally, the customer can enjoy the product or service she bought. And then, as we noted above, the "post-purchase experience" begins, with its many possible value creation and appropriation opportunities.

We can now revisit the various connected customer experiences we described above and see how they act on different parts of the customer journey (see Fig. 2).

Respond-to-Desire experiences start at the "order" step of the customer journey. The customer has already worked herself through the first part of the customer journey; she knows precisely what she wants, and now she wants to press a "button" that makes the rest of the journey as smooth as possible. Curated Offering begins earlier in the customer journey. Curated Offering helps a customer understand the possible options, as well as the best option for a particular need. Coach Behavior operates even earlier: here, the firm helps customers become aware of their needs. And lastly, in an Automatic Execution experience, the firm realizes a need before the customer does and—if given permission—fulfills this need before the customer even notices it has arisen.

We find it helpful to think about three different parts of a connected customer experience. The first part is to "Recognize." The firm needs to recognize the need of a customer, or it must help the customer in recognizing a need. The second part is to translate the recognized need into a desired option that would fulfill this need and to send a "Request" for this option. In some cases, the request will be triggered by the customer; in other cases, the firm itself generates this request. Lastly, the firm needs to "Respond" to this request in a timely manner.

4 From Experiences to Relationships

Up to this point, we have been careful to talk about connected customer "experiences." We have not yet talked about the ultimate goal of creating a connected customer "relationship." To move from a series of experiences to a relationship, we need to add one more element: "Repeat." The repeat element closes the loop. By transforming a few episodic interactions that generate little information to a continuous relationship that constantly creates rich information, firms have the ability to gather more and more information which can enable it to become better and better over time in "recognizing," "requesting," and "responding" (see Fig. 3).

Indeed, it is only by "closing the loop" that we believe that firms will actually be able to create a sustainable competitive advantage using connected strategies. Many of the technologies that underlie connected strategies are available to all firms. As a result, many aspects of connected strategies will become table stakes, and imitation will be rampant. However, learning, which can accumulate over time, can create a formidable barrier to imitation. In Fig. 4, we illustrate two key learning feedback loops. If a firm, through deeper customer understanding, is able to create a better fit between the needs of the customer and the products or services it offers to the customer, then that particular customer is likely to come back to the firm. If—and this is an important "if"—the firm is able to use this next interaction to learn even more about the particular customer's current or future need, or is able to help the customer understand and express his/her needs more precisely, then the next

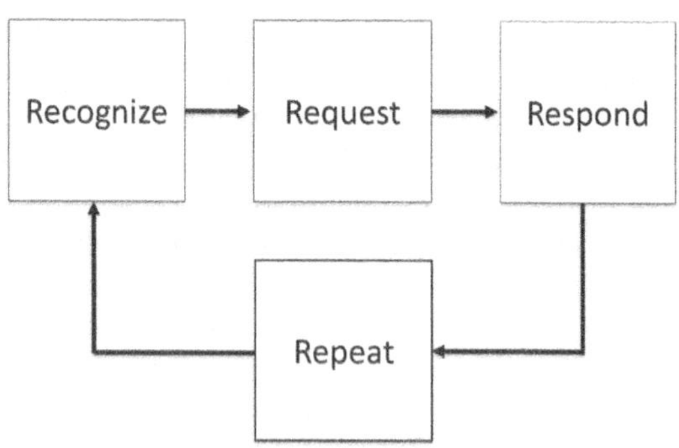

Fig. 3 The four "R"-framework of connected customer relationships

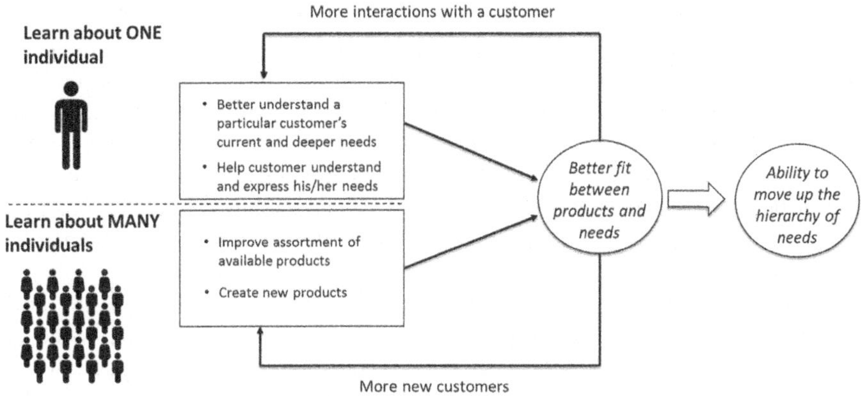

Fig. 4 Two positive feedback learning loops

time the firm interacts with the customer, there will be an even tighter fit between customer needs and the products offered. This positive learning loop (the top loop in Fig. 4) operates at the level of a particular individual. However, it often solves only half of the problem. Now a firm knows precisely what a particular customer wants. The challenge remains whether the firm has the required product available. Since firms usually can stock/provide only a finite number of different products, a second learning loop becomes important. Therefore, the firm also needs to learn about "customers like the focal customer," i.e., it has to engage in meta-learning at the level of the (sub-)population level. If a firm is able to generally provide a better fit between needs and products than its competitors, then it will also attract new customers (the bottom loop in Fig. 4). If the firm uses the information it gathers on all "similar customers" to the focal customer, it can over time improve the assortment of its products and even create new products that allow it to create a very tight fit between needs and available solutions, attracting yet more customers. Lastly, if a firm is able to delight customers repeatedly over time, and if the firm learns more deeply and broadly about the needs of a customer, a firm will be able to move up the hierarchy of needs of a customer. Rather than being simply a provider of the knowledge of how to compute an internal rate of return, a firm can become the "trusted partner in education" for a customer. At that point, a firm has truly created a connected customer *relationship*. Once a firm has been able to achieve this status, it is much harder to dislodge it from that position, and its competitive advantage has become much more sustainable.

5 Applications to Healthcare Delivery

The management of healthcare delivery is facing many of the challenges we discussed in conjunction with the after-sales market. First, consider the challenge of dealing with repair requests in the field. Traditionally, healthcare systems did not pay a lot of attention to what happened to their patients while they were outside the walls of the hospital (Asch et al. 2012). During the episode of a hospital stay, clinicians would do anything they could to help the patient. After discharge, however, the patient was left mostly alone, disconnected from the healthcare system. This disconnect comes at substantial economic and medical expense, as even very sick patients spend the majority of their time outside the hospital. It is at this time when crucial decisions relating to lifestyle, medication adherence, and home care are made.

A second similarity between spare parts logistics and healthcare is the poor alignment of incentives. Traditionally, healthcare systems were compensated on a fee-for-service basis. When a patient was readmitted to the hospital, which resembles a warranty case in manufacturing, the hospital was able to bill for additional services. More recently, hospitals are creating value-based payment models for procedures such as hip replacements, which display a remarkable similarity to performance-based contracting in logistics.

Third, and finally, technology has the potential to create new business models, similar to what we have seen in the Rolls Royce example and the four vignette cases in our executive education example. As technology advances, a number of connected care devices have launched, including:

- Secure messaging and text- and email-based communication between patients and providers
- Video conferencing technology allowing for video-based consultations instead of office visits
- Connected pill bottles that monitor medication compliance
- Pills with embedded signal transmitters that connect to a mobile device indicating that they have been swallowed and digested
- Connected devices that track breathing problems and provide asthma medication
- Wearable trackers such as the ones made by Fitbit, Apple, or Whoop that monitor heart rate variability, breathing patterns, and sleep

With all of these new technologies, it is now possible to create patient journeys that go beyond the episodic care model of the twentieth century. But what might these new journeys look like? Below, we build on our Connected Strategy framework and the four connected user experiences described above to articulate four ways to serve patients using connected health technologies.

5.1 Respond-to-Desire Patient Experience

Consider the case of the respond-to-desire connected customer experience first. Most of us have experienced the need of reaching a clinician in a timely manner. More often than not, fast access to the care team has been difficult and associated with travel time, substantial waiting times, and other forms of inconvenience. Nor surprisingly, the field of healthcare operations has put a great emphasis on studying patient wait times (e.g., Batt and Terwiesch 2015) and has shown that friction points such as poor access are associated with inferior health outcomes and lost revenue for the healthcare system. A number of prescriptive models have looked at optimal policies for patient scheduling (Zacharias and Pinedo 2013), panel sizing (Green et al. 2007), and the management of provider capacity (Green et al. 2013).

As much as creating easier access to healthcare is a noble objective worthy of academic investigation, it is associated with a potential downside. Most operations models treat patient demand as exogenous—following some stochastic arrival process capturing how patients fall sick and require care. But, is demand for care truly exogenous? When determining whether or not to seek healthcare, rational patients not only look at the potential benefits of care (hopefully, in the form of medical recovery), but they also look at the associated transaction costs in the form of waiting times, travel times, and medical expenses (e.g., co-pays).

If new technologies reduce some of these transaction costs, they have the potential to increase the overall patient demand. A driver of a car is unlikely to dramatically change her driving behavior knowing that vehicle repair is quickly and conveniently available. In contrast, a patient, who detects an abnormality in her skin, might not be sufficiently concerned about skin cancer to justify making a dermatologist appointment three months into the future, requiring a 30 min drive, and being associated with a $50 co-pay. If, however, that same patient were given the opportunity to take a photo of her skin and submit it directly to a dermatologist in an almost frictionless experience, she would decide to seek care.

This convenient customer experience has empirically been connected with two sets of problems. First, there is the effect of induced demand. Bavafa et al. (2018) show how demand for care in a healthcare system increased once patients were allowed to directly message their care teams through a secure patient portal. Though this increased demand also increased system revenue for patients insured in a fee-for-service agreement, it does consume more provider capacity. Since provider capacity is limited, congestion increases and some patients are crowded out. The authors show that this is especially hurting the opportunities for access for new (as opposed to existing) patients.

A second set of problems relate to the work hours of the providers. In traditional outpatient services, the clinical hours of healthcare providers were well structured and followed traditional business hours of operations (say from 8 am to 5 pm). However, when work for providers does not come in the form of patients but digital patient requests, taking care of patients becomes a 24 h operation with no respect for weekends, holidays, or vacations. Bavafa and Terwiesch (2019) show how the introduction of patient messaging technology has dramatically increased the number of hours a week providers spend on taking care of their patients. Again, incentives need to be put in place to compensate providers for their increased and less structured work schedule, especially given the current situation of provider burn-out.

5.2 Curated Offering

In most cases, patients do not want to see a specific doctor, but are interested in seeing a doctor that is right for them. If the patient is facing a new medical condition, she or he is especially unlikely to know which doctor is the right one to see. For example, the patient might want to see a dermatologist, but has no idea whether or not to see Dr Jones or Dr Zheng. Moreover, scheduling an appointment in the not too distant future at a time that fits the patient's busy schedule can be a major challenge.

The curated offering approach that has emerged in response to this problem is one of demand aggregation and guided navigation through the inventory of available appointments. What OpenTable is for restaurants, ZocDoc is for clinicians. As a two-sided market, it matches patients with providers. Beyond providing scheduling information, it also helps the patient community crowdsource physician reputation based on posted reviews. In the field of Dermatology, Smith and Lipoff (2016) have investigated patient reviews on ZocDoc and Yelp and how they impact demand for future care.

5.3 Coach Behavior

Most patients intend to live a healthy life, especially after encountering major health challenges such as a heart attack. However, myopia and inertia oftentimes get in the way of following through on these intentions. For example, it is a well-known fact in the healthcare community that medication adherence is poor, even for patients discharged from the hospital following major complications such as myocardial infarction.

In a large-scale, randomized control trial, Volpp et al. (2017) provided electronic pill bottles to newly discharged patients and engaged them through a battery of reminders and incentives. These ranged from simple automated text messages ("you have not taken your medication today") to incentives (lottery enrollments upon being compliant with medication regimen for a given duration) all the way to clinical interventions (a call from the nurse). In a follow-up study, Cohen et al. (2006) developed a machine learning method to allocate the capacity of the reminder resource to the patients that seem to benefit the most for them. The study showed that better health outcomes (fewer readmissions) can be achieved with the same level of clinical effort.

Such nudging, or as we refer to it, such behavior coaching, has been shown to be effective in a number of clinical domains, ranging from smoking cessation (Volpp et al. 2009) to weight loss (Volpp et al. 2008). As sensor technology becomes more and more sophisticated, it becomes easier to take an action without waiting for the patient to take the initiative. Though there clearly exist ethical concerns about monitoring the patient 24/7 (recall our earlier point of the tension between magic and creepy), we propose that patient inertia and myopia can justify the use of connected healthcare technology and support the interest of the patients. For example, just as connected devices such as Fitbit or Apple Watch can remind a patient to get up from their chair and move, connected pill bottles can alert patients when it is time to take their medications. In fact, the drug Abilify is now combined with a connected delivery model in which each pill includes a small transmitter that connects with a patch the patient is wearing on the skin and that sends a signal once the pill reaches the gut.

5.4 Automatic Execution

As magical as coach behavior experiences might be, they still rely on the patient or the provider to eventually take an action. However, there might arise a situation in which the patient is simply not capable of taking an action. Consider the examples of implanted defibrillators as well as fall sensors. Patients that are at risk of sudden cardiac death due to ventricular fibrillation can benefit from the implantation of a cardioverter-defibrillator. This device is capable of automatically detecting abnormal heart rhythms. Upon detection of such an event, the device does not prompt the patient to seek the help of a cardiologist (that would be a coach behavior customer experience), but, instead starts pacing the heart by automatically initiating electric stimulation.

Similarly, patients that are at risk of experiencing a fall can benefit from wearing a fall sensor. The sensor, similar to sensors that activate an airbag in an automotive vehicle, detects a potential fall and automatically issues a 911 call without the patient being in the loop.

6 Conclusions and Opportunities for Future Research

In this chapter, we discussed a powerful trend that is reshaping many industries. More and more firms use connected technologies to reshape fundamentally the way in which they interact with their customers. Rather than having few episodic interactions, companies are trying to create a continuous relationship with their customers that reduces friction and allows companies to anticipate the needs of their customers.

The increase in connectivity also opens up many opportunities for future research in Operations Management:

- The continuous data exchange between firm and customer leaves an electronic fingerprint behind (sometimes referred to as digital exhaust, Terwiesch 2019), which can be econometrically analyzed to test hypotheses from theoretical models of Operations Management (see Cohen et al. 2003 for an example of this in semiconductor equipment procurement).

- The massive data streams also allow for the deployment and advancement of machine learning methods, allowing for a better integration between forecasting inventory management decisions (Cohen 2015).
- The value that is created by the improved connectivity needs to be shared among the parties in the ecosystem, requiring the development of novel contracts and revenue models such as proposed by Kim et al. (2007a, b).

As predicted by Morris Cohen's research many years ago, the growing connectivity increases the importance of a deeper and higher bandwidth customer-firm relationship. In such a connected world, value is created continually, and the distinction between products and services loses its meaning. This paradigm shift in thinking about supply chain relationship opens up many opportunities for research, many of which will be the intellectual offspring of Morris's pioneering work.

References

Asch D, Muller R, Volpp K (2012) Automated hovering in health care — watching over the 5000 hours. N Engl J Med 367(1):1–3

Batt RJ, Terwiesch C (2015) Waiting patiently: an empirical study of queue abandonment in an emergency department. Manag Sci 61(1):39–59

Bavafa H, Terwiesch C (2019) Work after work: the impact of new service delivery models on work hours. J Oper Manag 65(7):636–658

Bavafa H, Hitt LM, Terwiesch C (2018) The impact of E-visits on visit frequencies and patient health: evidence from primary care. Manag Sci 64(12):5461–5480

Cohen MA (2015) Inventory management in the age of big data. Harv Bus Rev. Digital article

Cohen MA, Whang S (1997) Competing in product and service: a product life-cycle model. Manag Sci 43(4):535–545

Cohen MA, Ho TH, Ren ZJ, Terwiesch C (2003) Measuring imputed cost in the semiconductor equipment supply chain. Manag Sci 49(12):1653–1670

Cohen MA, Agrawal N, Agrawal V (2006) Winning in the aftermarket. Harv Bus Rev 84(5):129

Green LV, Savin S, Murray M (2007) Providing timely access to care: what is the right patient panel size? Jt Comm J Qual Patient Saf 33(4):211–218

Green LV, Savin S, Savva N (2013) "Nursevendor problem": personnel staffing in the presence of endogenous absenteeism. Manag Sci 59(10):2237–2256

Kim SH, Cohen MA, Netessine S (2007a) Performance contracting in after-sales service supply chains. Manag Sci 53(12):1843–1858

Kim SH, Cohen MA, Netessine S (2007b) Reliability or inventory? Contracting strategies for after-sales product support. In: Proceedings of 2007 International Conference on Manufacturing & Service

Siggelkow J, Terwiesch C (2019) Connected strategy: building continuous customer relationships for competitive advantage. Harvard Business Press, Boston

Smith D (2013) Power-by-the-hour: the role of technology in reshaping business strategy at Rolls-Royce. Technol Anal Strat Manag 25(8):987–1007

Smith R, Lipoff J (2016) Evaluation of dermatology practice online reviews: lessons from qualitative analysis. JAMA Dermatol 152(2):153–157

Terwiesch C (2019) OM Forum—empirical research in operations management: from field studies to analyzing digital exhaust. Manuf Serv Oper Manag 21(4):713–722

Volpp KG, John LK, Troxel AB, Norton L, Fassbender J, Loewenstein G (2008) Financial incentive–based approaches for weight loss: a randomized trial. JAMA 300(22):2631–2637

Volpp KG, Troxel AB, Pauly MV, Glick HA, Puig A, Asch D, Galvin R et al (2009) A randomized, controlled trial of financial incentives for smoking cessation. N Engl J Med 360(7):699–709

Volpp KG, Troxel AB, Mehta SJ, Norton L, Zhu J, Lim R, Wang W et al (2017) Effect of electronic reminders, financial incentives, and social support on outcomes after myocardial infarction: the HeartStrong Randomized Clinical Trial. JAMA Intern Med 177(8):1093–1101

Zacharias C, Pinedo M (2013) Appointment scheduling with no-shows and overbooking. Prod Oper Manag 23(5):788–801

New Product Development: Trade-offs, Metrics, and Successes

Teck-Hua Ho and Dayoung Kim

Abstract This chapter reviews Morris Cohen's scholarly contributions to new product development (NPD) and the other areas at the interface of marketing and production. Specifically, we examine how Morris and his co-authors' pioneering work in NPD has generated follow-up work by a number of scholars, demonstrating the frequent tension between the marketing and production functions. The authors provide rigorous support for performance metrics used by practitioners in the NPD process. Their work on a data-driven decision support system shows the usefulness of their research to industry. In summary, this work on NPD reveals who Morris Cohen is as a scholar—someone with the rare ability to link rigorous research with practical implementation.

Keywords New product development (NPD) · Marketing-operations interface · Time-to-market · NPD metrics · Forecasting

1 Introduction

New product development (NPD) is central to the success of any product or service company. This chapter describes Professor Morris Cohen and his co-authors' scholarly contributions to NPD, a field of study that lies at the interface between marketing and production. This review is not comprehensive; it is intentionally restricted to work done by Morris Cohen and his co-authors. In addition, we focus on work done by Teck-Hua Ho, which has been influenced by Morris Cohen's work.

T.-H. Ho (✉)
National University of Singapore, Singapore, Singapore

D. Kim
Global Asia Institute, National University of Singapore, Singapore, Singapore

Department of Management, California State University at Fullerton, Fullerton, CA, USA
e-mail: dayoungkim@nus.edu.sg

H. Lee et al. (eds.), *Creating Values with Operations and Analytics*, Springer Series in Supply Chain Management 19, https://doi.org/10.1007/978-3-031-08871-1_3

We apologize in advance to authors who feel their work has not been included or mentioned.

The chapter is organized into three sections:

1. Trade-offs, which reviews studies on the trade-offs that arise at the interface between marketing and operations, paying specific attention to NPD and how Cohen et al. (1996) have shaped research on NPD.
2. Metrics, which reviews metrics used by firms and how the metrics can be understood within a rigorous modeling framework.
3. Successes, which reviews two prevailing forecasting approaches used by firms for new product successes: (a) data-driven statistical methods and (b) prediction markets.

2 Trade-offs

Matching demand and supply in a dynamic and uncertain market is challenging and can create tensions between a company's marketing and production functions. Frequently, marketers focus on *maximizing demand from customers* while production managers focus on *minimizing production costs to meet a demand.* Sombultawee and Boon-itt (2018) provide a recent review of the literature on the interface between marketing and production, while Tang (2010) systematically documents the models that researchers have developed to analyze the trade-offs that arise from coordinating marketing and production. Some of these trade-offs are discussed in detail in Eliashberg and Steinberg (1987, 1993), Porteus and Whang (1991), Karmarkar (1996), Kulp et al. (2004), Yalabik et al. (2005).

Shapiro (1977) provides a good overview of these tensions, outlining eight areas where coordination is necessary between marketing and production. In this section, we focus on four of those areas: (a) capacity planning and sales forecasting, (b) the breadth of the product line, (c) service quality assurance, and (d) NPD. Note that these tensions are still relevant in many operations management settings. The development of new technologies and the outbreak of the Covid-19 pandemic have shifted emphasis somewhat towards capacity flexibility and operations innovations in order to respond to rapid disruptions in supply chains.

2.1 *Capacity Planning and Sales Forecasting*

Since it can take time for a firm to adjust its manufacturing capacity for a new product, it is crucial that the firm obtain accurate long-term demand forecasts. Marketers frequently use the celebrated Bass diffusion model (Bass 1969) to estimate such demand. Thorough reviews of the use and extension of the model in marketing contexts are given in Mahajan and Muller (1979) and Mahajan et al. (1990). One of the practical limitations of early Bass-related models is their assumption that firms have unlimited capacity to fulfil any level of demand. This assumption often does not hold because firms have a fixed manufacturing capacity which can lead to supply constraints, backorders, and lost sales.

Consequently, several operations researchers incorporated supply-side constraints into the Bass diffusion model to make it more realistic. For example, Ho et al. (2002) endogenize demand dynamics to study how a firm should plan its capacity for a new product with backlogs and lost sales. Kumar and Swaminathan (2003) extend the Bass model to capture the effect of lost sales (due to supply constraints) on future demand and show that if a firm wants to maximize total sales during the lifecycle of a product, a myopic marketing plan that maximizes sales at each instance is not optimal.

These revised Bass diffusion models have been made more realistic by removing the assumption that customers generate positive word-of-mouth. This is particularly relevant in the age of social media, where word-of-mouth communication and real-time consumer reviews (i.e., social learning) can have a huge effect on sales. Hu et al. (2016) and Davis et al. (2021) investigate the influence of social learning on stocking (capacity) decisions, while Feldman et al. (2019) investigate the influence of social learning on optimal product design and pricing. This line of work is important and likely to generate much follow-on research.

2.2 *Breadth of the Product Line*

Marketers often want to extend a product line to satisfy customers' heterogenous needs and/or customers' variety-seeking behavior. Extending a product line comes at a cost. For example, broadening a line may incur setup costs, and as a consequence, reduce effective capacity. Similarly, a wider product line requires higher levels of inventory and transportation costs. These tensions are discussed in the book *Product variety management: research advances* (Ho and Tang 1998), which collects articles by a group of leading interdisciplinary researchers, including economists, engineers, marketers, and operational management researchers. The early chapters of the book explain what motivates a firm to broaden its product line, while the later chapters examine leading industry practices to manage product variety in terms of design, pricing, and manufacturing.

The book led to several streams of research. Kim et al. (2002) extend the standard choice models used in marketing by allowing for multiple varieties of a product to be bought at the same time. Cachon et al. (2005) consider how a firm should optimize its product assortment when a customer exhibits heterogenous behavior. Gaur and Honhon (2006) and Kök and Fisher (2007) investigate the same assortment problem when consumers can substitute for a product that is out of stock, a similar product that is available. Alptekinoğlu and Corbett (2008) discuss the implications of an extremely large product line (i.e., mass customization) with price competition. Broda and Weinstein (2006) use trade data from the USA to show how increasing the product line by importing a variety of products has contributed to national welfare gains in that country.

2.3 Service Quality Assurance

Service quality assurance is another area where marketing and production must align their decisions. Guaranteeing a high level of customer service requires balancing (a) the service capacity and the speed at which service is provided and (b) the customers' degree of preference for service quality. So (2000) and Ho and Zheng (2004) examine the effect of guaranteeing customer delivery times under competitive rivalry. So (2000) considers an oligopolistic scenario where firms compete on a delivery time guarantee. If firms are heterogenous in capacity, larger firms tend to offer a shorter delivery time guarantee. Ho and Zheng (2004) consider a duopoly scenario where firms choose delivery time guarantees to influence customer expectations. They show that the optimal guarantee requires a balance between service capacity and customer sensitivity to the guarantee. So and Tang (1996) consider a setting where firms can choose both the number of servers and a service guarantee. The authors quantify the benefits of dynamically adjusting the number of servers and evaluate the interactions between the number of servers and the level of guaranteed service.

2.4 NPD

The pressure on firms to develop and launch new products rapidly has intensified because product life cycles have become significantly compressed. As a consequence, the decisions on *when* to introduce the new product and *what* its performance level should be, cannot be overemphasized.

Until the early 1990s, little attention was devoted to analytically modeling the trade-offs between time-to-market and product performance. Cohen et al. (1996) was the first to present a comprehensive model of the complex NPD process by analyzing trade-offs that arise within a fixed NPD time horizon. The authors demonstrate how firms should strike a balance between time-to-market, product performance, and cost in order to maximize lifecycle profits. The proposed model allows for product performance to be enhanced over multiple stages. The authors show that the optimal NPD policy is for firms to concentrate efforts on the most productive stage of the multistage NPD process. The paper generated much follow-up work and significant interest among practitioners. As of October 4, 2021, it has been cited 674 times on Google Scholar.

Indeed, a review paper on product development decisions, Krishnan and Ulrich (2001), evaluated the main contribution of Cohen et al. (1996) as "sorting the relative priority of development objectives" and "showing that performance measures are often traded off against one another." Tatikonda and Montoya-Weiss (2001) also added how Cohen et al. (1996) created new avenues of research by examining "the advantages and disadvantages of being first (or faster) to market, depending on demand, product life cycle, growth stage, competitive context and behavior, consumer behavior, and elements of the marketing mix." Table 1 is a summary of papers that build on Cohen et al. (1996) and which have received more than 250 citations on Google Scholar. In these papers, the term "product performance" and "product quality" are used interchangeably.

3 Metrics

To help NPD teams to make optimal decisions and maximize the chance of a new product's success, quantifiable metrics must be developed and used. Bill Hewlett, co-founder of Hewlett-Packard (HP), once said, "You cannot manage what you cannot measure." House and Price (1991) describe how HP used quantifiable performance metrics[1] such as break-even-time to maximize the chance of a new product's success.

Similarly, leading Japanese companies use target unit cost as a tool to manage NPD teams (Cohen et al. 1996). The target costing approach provides a structured way to constrain the NPD process so that the new product will not be too costly to produce by quantifying the cost of the potential new product early in the development process (Cooper and Slagmulder 2017). As a consequence, NPD teams avoid developing low-margin products and bring only highly profitable products to market. Cooper and Chew (1996) provide a successful application of the target costing approach at Olympus, a market leader in single-lens reflex (SLR) cameras in 1980s. The company had no competitors in Japan until the early 1980s but began to lose market share and money when competitors produced a compelling alternative. In response, Olympus adopted the target costing approach to drive NPD, with the NPD team having to measure the cost of adding a new feature. Using this process, Olympus reduced its production costs by about 35% in the 1990s (Cooper and Chew 1996). Note that target costing may mitigate the level of product performance and lengthen the time to market.

Cohen et al. (1996, 2000) provide an integrated framework for analyzing the implications of using simple and measurable performance metrics in NPD. Cohen

[1] HP successfully reduced break-even-time by one-half for new products through the effective use of metrics. Four key metrics they adopted are break-even-time (BET), time-to-market (TM), break-even-after-release (BEAR), and return factor (RF). BET is a measure of the total time until the break-even point on the original investment is reached. TM is the total development time spent from the start of product development to manufacturing release. BEAR is the time from manufacturing release to when project investment costs are recovered in the form of profit from a product. RF is a calculation of profit dollars divided by investment dollars at a specific point in time after a product has moved into manufacturing and sales.

Table 1 Papers that have expanded on the research in Cohen et al. (1996)

Method	Bibliography	Description	Relevance to Cohen et al. (1996)
Empirical investigation	Shankar et al. (1998), *Journal of Marketing Research*	Empirical analysis of 13 brands across two ethical drug categories suggests a trade-off between innovativeness and entry timing. The authors identify the mechanism through which innovative late movers can outsell pioneers and suggest new strategies for late entry.	The authors use the same assumption as Cohen et al. (1996), that firms often have conflicting objectives in terms of cost, timeliness, and innovativeness. They also focus on how different metrics such as time-to-market and cost are often traded off against one other.
Empirical investigation	Moorman and Slotegraaf (1999), *Journal of Marketing Research*	Controlling for the effects of external market information, the authors investigate the relationship between a firm's organizational capabilities and NPD outcomes. They find that marketing and product development capabilities jointly influence the speed of product development.	The authors include product development cost as a variable in the model to control for the trade-off between the efficiency of development and cost, as discussed in Cohen et al. (1996, 1997).
Empirical investigation	Tatikonda and Montoya-Weiss (2001), *Management Science*	Using the data from 120 development projects for assembled products, the authors find that an organization's information processing factors and capabilities are associated with the speed of NPD. As a result, the factors and capability are linked to achieving a target for product performance, unit cost, and time-to-market.	The authors consider time-to-market, cost, and product performance to be key objectives for NPD. They demonstrate that achieving the time-to-market objectives improves customer satisfaction and product success.
Framework for new service development	Menor et al. (2002), *Journal of Operations Management*	The authors provide a review of research areas in new service development (NSD), highlight areas for further refinement and exploitation, and identify areas for new study and discovery.	The authors devise performance metrics for NSD and highlight that total development cost, as suggested by Cohen et al. (1996), is important for managing NSD.

(continued)

Table 1 (continued)

Method	Bibliography	Description	Relevance to Cohen et al. (1996)
Model application in different industry	Plambeck and Wang (2009). *Management Science*	The authors use a stylized model to investigate the impact of e-waste regulation on introducing new products in the electronics industry. Specifically, they explore the effects of e-waste regulations on the NPD process, the quantity of e-waste generated, social welfare, consumer surpluses, and manufacturer profits.	As in Cohen et al. (1996, 2000), the standard Cobb–Douglas production function was used to formulate the relationship among expenditure, speed, and quality in NPD. Manufacturers choose the development time and expenditure for a new product, which together determine its quality.
New framework and empirical validation	Pavlou and El Sawy (2011), *Decision Sciences*	The authors propose a structural model where dynamic capabilities influence product success by reconfiguring existing operational capabilities in the context of NPD. Dynamic capabilities were found to be important for higher environmental turbulence.	As in Cohen et al. (1996), the authors view NPD success as the achievement of product performance (quality, innovativeness) and process efficiency (time-to-market, low cost).

et al. (2000) generalize the modeling framework from Cohen et al. (1996) by allowing the level of resources used in NPD to vary over time. Cohen et al. (2000) rigorously analyze the pros and cons of setting a target on each of the three simple and measurable metrics: (1) time-to-market, (2) product performance, and (3) total development cost. The authors derive optimality conditions to enable firms to become aware of the potential impact of setting a target on one of these metrics. For example, the paper shows that setting a compressed time-to-market target can lead to downward bias in product performance and suboptimal product success. The authors demonstrate that the target total development cost approach can also result in a similar bias. Finally, the target total performance approach was shown to lead to extended development times and a shorter sales cycle.

The approach of using the above-mentioned NPD metrics has been expanded in several ways. Researchers in operations management have started to focus on developing resilience in capacity planning in anticipation of unforeseeable market shifts and technology disruptions. Such resilience-oriented metrics will cost more and take longer to develop but will be meaningful additions to the above-mentioned NPD metrics. These new metrics extend the existing framework by allowing for a longer time horizon and more variability and disruption in demand conditions (Steenburgh and Ahearne 2018).

4 Successes

In this section, we describe two methods of new product success forecasting. The first is based on well-established statistical methods used in marketing (e.g., econometric analyses, probabilistic models, individual choice models), and the second is based on prediction markets.

4.1 Statistical Methods

Since the 1980s, marketing researchers have advanced the statistical models used in demand forecasting (Hogarth and Makridakis 1981; Makridakis et al. 2008). Guadagni and Little (1983) created a fundamentally new approach to demand forecasting by pioneering the use of panel-level scanner data to develop individual choice models. For a review, see Rossi et al. (1996), and for two well-known applications, see Erdem and Keane (1996) and Erdem and Winer (1998). Individual choice models have also been used to forecast the success of new products in the market (Neelamegham and Chintagunta 1999). To address a challenge posed by product categories that have hundreds of stockkeeping units (SKUs), Ho and Chong (2003) developed a parsimonious model to forecast demand at the SKU-level.

Cohen et al. (1997) demonstrate how statistical methods can be used in the NPD process in practice. The authors develop a decision support system based on an analysis of historical data from 51 new products launched at a major food manufacturer. The system evaluates the financial prospects of extending a new product line and provides shipment forecasts at various stages of the NPD process. The authors demonstrate how taking a "product line" perspective system (instead of a "product" perspective) can improve the success of new products.

Another method of forecasting new product success is the Bass diffusion model (Bass 1969). Srinivasan and Mason (1986) show that this model can be advanced to forecast new product diffusion in retail, industrial technology, and durable consumer goods among others. See Mahajan et al. (1990) for a comprehensive review of this stream of literature.

The strong emphasis on empirical analysis in marketing has significantly influenced the development of the field of operations management. In the 1990s, academics in operations management began to place strong emphasis on empirical analysis. For example, they frequently use the random utility model (Ben-Akiva and Lerman 1985) to capture demand substitution within a product assortment. As a consequence, researchers can now analyze how inventory stocking and pricing decisions change as a result of demand substitution (e.g., Vulcano et al. 2012; Fisher and Vaidyanathan 2014; Rusmevichientong et al. 2014). For comprehensive reviews, see Ho et al. (2017) and Fisher et al. (2020).

4.2 Prediction Markets

A separate and complementary stream of research focuses on using prediction markets to predict the success of new products. Ho and Chen (2007) describe a market-based method of demand forecasting to leverage on the "wisdom of the crowd" in a so-called prediction market. A prediction market is a price-discovery mechanism designed to aggregate information by allowing a large group of individuals to bet on possible outcomes in the form of shares. The authors describe the history and the scientific foundations behind the prediction market and present step-by-step approaches for setting one up. They show how a prediction market can be used in the motion picture, information technology, and healthcare industries, all of which involve high uncertainty in demand and a short product lifecycle.

The prediction market has been used to improve prediction accuracy in presidential elections (Snowberg et al. 2007; Chen et al. 2008) and the seasonal influenza epidemic (Polgreen et al. 2007; Tung et al. 2015). More recently, it has been used to predict the progression of the Covid-19 pandemic (Ho et al. 2021), demonstrating that a prediction market can be a promising forecasting tool, even in the case of one-off, disruptive events. However, prediction markets only work well when participants in the market have experience or knowledge of the topic being forecasted and have views that are sufficiently independent (Ho and Chen 2007).

5 Conclusion

This chapter focuses on Morris Cohen's contributions to the marketing-operations interface, specifically in NPD. Cohen and his co-authors pioneered research in this area and laid some of the foundations for subsequent work. They demonstrate how a combination of rigorous modeling, empirical analysis, and practical insights can help to shift the development of research not only in operations management but also at the interface between marketing and production.

Personal Note
I (Teck-Hua Ho) have had the great privilege of working on NPD with Morris (production/operations) and Professor Jehoshua (Josh) Eliashberg (marketing). Both of them are giants in their fields and I benefitted enormously from collaborating with them. They have been great mentors, ardent supporters, phenomenal cheerleaders, and, most importantly, true friends. I am forever grateful to them.

References

Alptekinoğlu A, Corbett CJ (2008) Mass customization vs. mass production: variety and price competition. Manuf Serv Oper Manag 10(2):204–217
Bass FM (1969) A new product growth for model consumer durables. Manag Sci 15(5):215–227
Ben-Akiva M, Lerman SR (1985) Discrete choice analysis: theory and application to travel demand, vol 9. MIT Press
Broda C, Weinstein DE (2006) Globalization and the gains from variety. Q J Econ 121(2):541–585
Cachon GP, Terwiesch C, Xu Y (2005) Retail assortment planning in the presence of consumer search. Manuf Serv Oper Manag 7(4):330–346
Chen MK, Ingersoll JE Jr, Kaplan EH (2008) Modeling a presidential prediction market. Manag Sci 54(8):1381–1394
Cohen MA, Eliasberg J, Ho TH (1996) New product development: the performance and time-to-market tradeoff. Manag Sci 42(2):173–186
Cohen MA, Eliashberg J, Ho TH (1997) An anatomy of a decision-support system for developing and launching line extensions. J Mark Res 34(1):117–129
Cohen MA, Eliashberg J, Ho TH (2000) An analysis of several new product performance metrics. Manuf Serv Oper Manag 2(4):337–349
Cooper R, Chew WB (1996) Control tomorrow's costs through today's designs. Harv Bus Rev 74(1):88–97
Cooper R, Slagmulder R (2017) Target costing and value engineering. Routledge
Davis AM, Gaur V, Kim D (2021) Consumer learning from own experience and social information: an experimental study. Manag Sci 67(5):2924–2943
Eliashberg J, Steinberg R (1987) Marketing-production decisions in an industrial channel of distribution. Manag Sci 33(8):981–1000
Eliashberg J, Steinberg R (1993) Marketing-production joint decision-making. Handbooks Oper Res Manag Sci 5:827–880
Erdem T, Keane MP (1996) Decision-making under uncertainty: capturing dynamic brand choice processes in turbulent consumer goods markets. Mark Sci 15(1):1–20
Erdem T, Winer RS (1998) Econometric modeling of competition: a multi-category choice-based mapping approach. J Econ 89(1–2):159–175

Feldman P, Papanastasiou Y, Segev E (2019) Social learning and the design of new experience goods. Manag Sci 65(4):1502–1519
Fisher M, Vaidyanathan R (2014) A demand estimation procedure for retail assortment optimization with results from implementations. Manag Sci 60(10):2401–2415
Fisher M, Olivares M, Staats BR (2020) Why empirical research is good for operations management, and what is good empirical operations management? Manuf Serv Oper Manag 22(1):170–178
Gaur V, Honhon D (2006) Assortment planning and inventory decisions under a locational choice model. Manag Sci 52(10):1528–1543
Guadagni PM, Little JD (1983) A logit model of brand choice calibrated on scanner data. Mark Sci 2(3):203–238
Ho TH, Chen KY (2007) New product blockbusters: the magic and science of prediction markets. Calif Manag Rev 50(1):144–158
Ho T-H, Chong J-K (2003) A parsimonious model of stockkeeping-unit choice. J Mark Res 40(3):351–365
Ho TH, Tang CS (eds) (1998) Product variety management: research advances, vol 10. Springer Science & Business Media
Ho TH, Zheng YS (2004) Setting customer expectation in service delivery: an integrated marketing-operations perspective. Manag Sci 50(4):479–488
Ho TH, Savin S, Terwiesch C (2002) Managing demand and sales dynamics in new product diffusion under supply constraint. Manag Sci 48(2):187–206
Ho TH, Lim N, Reza S, Xia X (2017) OM forum—causal inference models in operations management. Manuf Serv Oper Manag 19(4):509–525
Ho TH, Jin L, Kim D (2021) Using wisdom of crowd to predict COVID-19 cases and deaths. Working Paper
Hogarth RM, Makridakis S (1981) Forecasting and planning: an evaluation. Manag Sci 27(2):115–138
House CH, Price RL (1991) The return map: tracking product teams. Harv Bus Rev 69(1):92–100
Hu M, Milner J, Wu J (2016) Liking and following and the newsvendor: operations and marketing policies under social influence. Manag Sci 62(3):867–879
Karmarkar U (1996) Integrative research in marketing and operations management. J Mark Res 33(2):125–133
Kim J, Allenby GM, Rossi PE (2002) Modeling consumer demand for variety. Mark Sci 21(3):229–250
Kök AG, Fisher ML (2007) Demand estimation and assortment optimization under substitution: methodology and application. Oper Res 55(6):1001–1021
Krishnan V, Ulrich KT (2001) Product development decisions: a review of the literature. Manag Sci 47(1):1–21
Kulp SC, Lee HL, Ofek E (2004) Manufacturer benefits from information integration with retail customers. Manag Sci 50(4):431–444
Kumar S, Swaminathan JM (2003) Diffusion of innovations under supply constraints. Oper Res 51(6):866–879
Mahajan V, Muller E (1979) Innovation diffusion and new product growth models in marketing. J Mark 43(4):55–68
Mahajan V, Muller E, Bass FM (1990) New product diffusion models in marketing: a review and directions for research. J Mark 54(1):1–26
Makridakis S, Wheelwright SC, Hyndman RJ (2008) Forecasting methods and applications. John Wiley & Sons
Menor LJ, Tatikonda MV, Sampson SE (2002) New service development: areas for exploitation and exploration. J Oper Manag 20(2):135–157
Moorman C, Slotegraaf RJ (1999) The contingency value of complementary capabilities in product development. J Mark Res 36(2):239–257
Neelamegham R, Chintagunta P (1999) A Bayesian model to forecast new product performance in domestic and international markets. Mark Sci 18(2):115–136

Pavlou PA, El Sawy OA (2011) Understanding the elusive black box of dynamic capabilities. Decis Sci 42(1):239–273

Plambeck E, Wang Q (2009) Effects of e-waste regulation on new product introduction. Manag Sci 55(3):333–347

Polgreen PM, Nelson FD, Neumann GR, Weinstein RA (2007) Use of prediction markets to forecast infectious disease activity. Clin Infect Dis 44(2):272–279

Porteus EL, Whang S (1991) On manufacturing/marketing incentives. Manag Sci 37(9):1166–1181

Rossi PE, McCulloch RE, Allenby GM (1996) The value of purchase history data in target marketing. Mark Sci 15(4):321–340

Rusmevichientong P, Shmoys D, Tong C, Topaloglu H (2014) Assortment optimization under the multinomial logit model with random choice parameters. Prod Oper Manag 23(11):2023–2039

Shankar V, Carpenter GS, Krishnamurthi L (1998) Late mover advantage: how innovative late entrants outsell pioneers. J Mark Res 35(1):54–70

Shapiro BP (1977) Can marketing and manufacturing co-exist. Harv Bus Rev 55(5):104

Snowberg E, Wolfers J, Zitzewitz E (2007) Partisan impacts on the economy: evidence from prediction markets and close elections. Q J Econ 122(2):807–829

So KC (2000) Price and time competition for service delivery. Manuf Serv Oper Manag 2(4):392–409

So KC, Tang CS (1996) On managing operating capacity to reduce congestion in service systems. Eur J Oper Res 92(1):83–98

Sombultawee K, Boon-itt S (2018) Marketing-operations alignment: a review of the literature and theoretical background. Oper Res Perspect 5:1–12

Srinivasan V, Mason CH (1986) Nonlinear least squares estimation of new product diffusion models. Mark Sci 5(2):169–178

Steenburgh T, Ahearne M (2018) How to sell new products. Harv Bus Rev 96:92–101

Tang CS (2010) A review of marketing–operations interface models: from co-existence to coordination and collaboration. Int J Prod Econ 125(1):22–40

Tatikonda MV, Montoya-Weiss MM (2001) Integrating operations and marketing perspectives of product innovation: the influence of organizational process factors and capabilities on development performance. Manag Sci 47(1):151–172

Tung CY, Chou TC, Lin JW (2015) Using prediction markets of market scoring rule to forecast infectious diseases: a case study in Taiwan. BMC Public Health 15(1):1–12

Vulcano G, Van Ryzin G, Ratliff R (2012) Estimating primary demand for substitutable products from sales transaction data. Oper Res 60(2):313–334

Yalabik B, Petruzzi NC, Chhajed D (2005) An integrated product returns model with logistics and marketing coordination. Eur J Oper Res 161(1):162–182

Product Design with the Triple Bottom Line

Fei Gao and Shiliang Cui

Abstract The triple bottom line, coined by the famed business writer John Elkington, consists of three elements—profit, people, and the planet. It maintains that companies should commit to focusing as much on environmental and social issues as they do on profits. This chapter reviews existing literature that focuses on the financial and environmental impacts of product design and presents recent work to motivate research needs on the social impact of product design. It also includes a general demand model that can serve as a starting point for future researchers to develop methodologies to help companies address product design issues with the triple bottom line.

Keywords Product design · Triple bottom line · Sustainable operations management

A Tribute from the Authors Professor Morris Cohen has made important contributions to many research areas in our field. His 1996 *Management Science* paper "New Product Development: The Performance and Time-to-Market Tradeoff" (co-authored with Jehoshua Eliasberg and Teck-Hua Ho) has made a significant impact on the product design and innovation literature. As his former students and co-authors, the authors of this chapter are indebted to his mentorship, support, and encouragement especially during their early academic careers. Morris has continuously inspired the authors to learn, to think, to conduct meaningful research, and to become better people.

F. Gao
Kelley School of Business, Indiana University, Bloomington, IN, USA
e-mail: fg1@iu.edu

S. Cui (✉)
McDonough School of Business, Georgetown University, Washington, DC, USA
e-mail: shiliang.cui@georgetown.edu

H. Lee et al. (eds.), *Creating Values with Operations and Analytics*, Springer Series in Supply Chain Management 19, https://doi.org/10.1007/978-3-031-08871-1_4

1 Introduction

Product design is crucial to a company's success and has drawn large amounts of attention to research in the Operations Management literature. The literature has traditionally focused on studying how a firm should manage its product design decisions to maximize financial impact (see Krishnan and Ulrich 2001 for a review). These include product quality, price, and time-to-market decisions. In addition, quality of a product covers multiple dimensions such as product performance and product reliability (Gao et al. 2021). We refer to the function or features of a product as *product performance* (see, e.g., Krishnan and Gupta 2001), and whether a product will perform its function or fail to perform as *product reliability* (see, e.g., Baiman et al. 2000).

While the traditional product design decisions (product quality, price, time-to-market) continue to be important, customers are now increasingly concerned about the environmental and social impact of products which affect their purchasing decisions (Business Wire 2019; CDP 2019; eMarketer 2018). The triple bottom line (TBL), coined by the famed business writer John Elkington, maintains that companies should commit to focusing as much on environmental and social issues as they do on profits (Elkington 1997). The TBL consists of three elements—profit, people, and the planet—corresponding to financial, social, and environmental performance of a company. Consequently, the TBL is commonly used to gauge a company's commitment to corporate social responsibility (CSR).

There is a growing literature that studies the impact of product design on the environment, namely green product design (see Agrawal et al. 2019 and Atasu et al. 2020 for recent reviews). Contrarily, research on product design with (non-environmental) social impact has been very limited, even though social issues generally are becoming a mainstream research area in the Operations Management field (Lee and Tang 2018; Plambeck and Ramdas 2020). In this chapter, we will first briefly review the existing streams of the product design literature that focuses on the financial and environmental impacts, respectively. Then, we call for research needs on the social impact of product design by describing the latest work on a specific topic (namely, cause marketing). Finally, we propose a general demand model which provides future researchers with a starting point as they begin to study product design issues in the TBL context.

2 Financial Impact of Product Design

The traditional product design literature focuses on a firm's profit-maximizing product quality, price, and time-to-market decisions, and the internal trade-offs between them. For example, there is an extensive literature that examines the trade-off between product performance and time-to-market for a firm (see, e.g., Bayus 1997; Cohen et al. 1996, 2000; Klastorin and Tsai 2004; Özer and Uncu 2013; Souza et al. 2004). Especially, a product with higher performance (which corresponds to a positive effect on demand) has a longer development time which thus, lengthens the product time-to-market. However, this also leads to delays of the product launch (which has a negative demand effect). A related stream of papers research on firms' sequential innovation decisions over time with one (see, e.g., Bhaskaran and Ramachandran 2011; Jain and Ramdas 2005; Krishnan and Ramachandran 2011) or multiple product generations (see, e.g., Bhaskaran et al. 2021; Lobel et al. 2015; Morgan et al. 2001).

Gao et al. (2021) add in the product reliability perspective in designing an innovative product, which is not explicitly considered in the above-mentioned papers. In particular, while a more innovative product may deliver better product performance, without sufficient development time, the product may not be as reliable given that innovations require a time buffer to conduct many iterations of product testing and improvement. Daughety and Reinganum (1995) also study the trade-off between development expenditure and product reliability (more R&D leads to a safer product), but do not consider product time-to-market or treat demand as a function of product performance. Arora et al. (2006) show that a software vendor has incentives to release a buggier product early and patch it later in a larger market. Thus, the authors study the trade-off between product reliability and time-to-market decisions that can be characterized as "rush and be wrong or wait and be late" (Loch and Terwiesch 2005).

3 Environmental Impact of Product Design

In the literature of sustainable and environmental Operations Management (see recent reviews by Agrawal et al. 2019; Atasu et al. 2020; Bouchery et al. 2016; Girotra and Netessine 2013; Kalkanci et al. 2019; Lee and Tang 2018), there is a growing interest in studying the product design perspective. Agrawal and Ülkü (2012) study the modular upgradability decision of a product as a green design strategy. Kraft et al. (2013) and Kraft and Raz (2017) study firms' replacement strategies of potentially hazardous substances in their product. Yenipazarli and Vakharia (2015) considers a firm's decision to expand a "brown" product line with a new green product. Agrawal et al. (2015) and Örsdemir et al. (2019) consider product durability decisions as a sustainable product feature. Bellos et al. (2017) find that car sharing can increase green product designs because it is optimal for automakers to increase the fuel efficiency of the vehicles used for car sharing. Peng et al. (2021a,b) focus on product packaging design and study a firm's green packaging decisions when consumers may choose to bring their own containers to consume the product. While most of the above-mentioned papers focus on the setting of a monopolist, Cohen et al. (2019) capture market competition by allowing two competing firms to make product design decisions for their green products.

There is also a stream of literature that studies the role of government policies in the stimulation of green product design and sales which dates back to Fullerton and

Wu (1998). In this space, Plambeck and Wang (2009) study the effects of e-waste regulations of a government such as "fee-upon-sale" versus "fee-upon-disposal" on new product introduction timing and expenditure decisions. Many other papers have considered the impact of Extended Producer Responsibility (EPR)-based take-back legislation on product design and green supply chain, see, e.g., Alev et al. (2020); Atasu and Subramanian (2012); Atasu and Van Wassenhove (2012); Atasu et al. (2009); Chen and Sheu (2009); Esenduran and Kemahlıoğlu-Ziya (2015); Esenduran et al. (2017, 2020); Gui et al. (2015, 2018); Huang et al. (2019). Murali et al. (2019) study the impact of voluntary ecolabels and mandatory environmental regulation on green product development among competing firms. Chen (2001) (resp., Bellos et al. 2017) considers the impact of environmental quality regulations (resp., standards) on green product design and the environment.

4 Social Impact of Product Design

Social impact design can be defined as "design that seeks to solve humanitarian issues such as improving living conditions for its beneficiaries" (Curry Stone Foundation 2021). In practice, firms can use product design as a method to solve various social needs and problems. For instance, Microsoft has developed a free app called Seeing AI that narrates the visual world for the blind and low vision community, which has an estimated size of 2.2 billion people according to the World Health Organization (2021) but is oftentimes underserved by the current technology.[1] This app, which is available in 70 countries and a number of languages, uses AI technology not only to recognize and read short text passages, documents, product labels, and so on but also describe people and scenery captured by a mobile phone camera (Tezuka 2020).

Another example of product design for social impact is HopeLab who developed a video game called Re-Mission, which has been associated with improved health outcomes for young cancer patients.[2] In addition, Prevention through Design (PtD), a concept related to social impact design, focuses on "design out" or minimize occupational hazards, with an emphasis on optimizing worker health and safety throughout the life cycle of work materials and processes. The interested reader is referred to the National Institute for Occupational Safety and Health (NIOSH), a large contributor to PtD efforts in the United States, for more information on this topic.[3]

Although the business world is paying more and more attention to the social impact of product design, the efforts of academia seem to be lagging behind, at least in our Operations Management field. Lee and Tang (2018), Kalkanci and Plambeck

[1] https://www.microsoft.com/en-us/ai/seeing-ai.

[2] https://hopelab.org/product/re-mission/.

[3] https://www.cdc.gov/niosh/topics/ptd/.

(2020) and Plambeck and Ramdas (2020) provide excellent reviews of our recent research on socially responsible practices, however, the research reviewed focuses on non-product-design contexts. To motivate research needs on the social impact of product design, we will now present recent research on one specific example of social impact design, namely cause marketing (CM), which is the practice of donating proceeds from product sales to designated charitable causes (Varadarajan and Menon 1988).

According to the Independent Evaluation Group (IEG), corporate cause sponsorship spending in North American was \$24.2 billion in 2018 and had been increasing over years (IEG 2018). In practice, however, different firms have different product line design strategies when it comes to implementing their CM campaigns. For instance, companies such as Apple and Gap have chosen to develop new products (i.e., iPhone (PRODUCT)^{RED} and Gap (PRODUCT)^{RED}) and donate a portion of the sales from those special-edition products to the Global Fund to fight AIDS, malaria, and tuberculosis in Africa. Meanwhile, other companies such as Warby Parker and TOMS make donations without introducing any new product; both companies promise to contribute to a social cause from the sales of all their products. For the rest of this section, we present a simple model framework based on Gao (2020) to study how a firm should make its product design decisions in a CM campaign.

Suppose a firm sells a product with unit cost c_1. Besides the product price p_1, the firm also decides the donation amount, k, for each unit sold in the CM campaign (if $k = 0$, CM is not implemented). For simplicity, we assume there are two types of customers in the market, non-prosocial and prosocial customers. *Non-prosocial customers* have valuation $v > c_1$ for the product, and they do not care about the product's social impact. Therefore, regardless of the donation amount k, non-prosocial customers' utility from purchasing the product is $u_n = v - p$. *Prosocial customers* have the same valuation v for the product; in addition, they obtain an extra positive utility $s(k)$ from purchasing the cause-linked product when they know that the firm will donate k to the social cause, due to the warm-glow effect (Andreoni 1989). Therefore, prosocial customers' utility function from buying the product is $u_p = v + s(k) - p$. The function $s(k)$ measures prosocial customers' social preference and it satisfies $s' > 0$ and $s'' < 0$ because Koschate-Fischer et al. (2012) find empirically a positive and concave relationship between consumers' willingness to pay and the donation amounts. Note that $k = 0$ corresponds to the case when there is not any donation to the cause, and thus $s(0) = 0$. In addition, we assume $\lim_{k \to \infty} s'(k) = 0$, i.e., the impact of additional increase in donation value k on consumer shopping behavior is minimal when it is already high enough.

Without loss of generality, we normalize the total number of customers in the market to 1. Denote the fraction of the prosocial customers in the total population as $\alpha \in [0, 1]$; the rest $(1 - \alpha)$ fraction are non-prosocial customers. The interaction between customers and the firm can be modeled as a sequential game. First, the firm announces product price p_1 and unit donation amount k. Then, customers purchase the product if their utility (i.e., u_n or u_p) is nonnegative. Thus, the firm's profit function can be expressed as the following:

$$\pi(p_1, k) = (p_1 - c_1 - k)\left(\alpha I_{u_p \geq 0} + (1-\alpha) I_{u_n \geq 0}\right),$$

where I_A is an indicator function and $I_A = 1$ (or $= 0$) if event A is true (or false).

So far, we have assumed that the firm relates the sales of the existing product to the social cause in its CM campaign (if any); this resembles the Warby Parker and TOMS examples given earlier. Next, we extend the model above to study the case where the firm designs a special version of the product and links it to the social cause (the iPhone 12 (PRODUCT)^{RED} example). For the regular product, the production cost (c_1) and consumers' valuation (v) remain the same as before. For the special product, the production cost is denoted as c_2, which could be greater than the regular product's (i.e., $c_2 \geq c_1$), due to the potential change of product design and manufacturing process. Consumers' valuations for the special product continue to be $v > c_2$, since the basic functions of the product remain unchanged from the regular counterpart (e.g., the iPhone 12 (PRODUCT)^{RED} has the same features as the regular iPhone 12). The key difference between the two versions of the product is that only the sales of special product contribute donations to the social cause.

The firm decides the price for each product (p_1 for the regular version and p_2 for the special version) and the unit donation amount k for the special product. Consumers decide whether to purchase a product and which product to purchase. Table 1 summarizes consumer utility functions from buying each version of the product. Note that prosocial customers enjoy the warm-glow effect (i.e., $s(k)$) only if they purchase the cause-linked special product which triggers donation.

Therefore, the firm's profit is given as follows:

$$\begin{aligned}\pi(p_1, p_2, k) = &(p_1 - c_1)(\alpha I_{u_{p1} > u_{p2}, u_{p1} \geq 0} + (1-\alpha) I_{u_{n1} \geq u_{n2}, u_{n1} \geq 0}) \\ &+ (p_2 - k - c_2)(\alpha I_{u_{p2} \geq u_{p1}, u_{p2} \geq 0} + (1-\alpha) I_{u_{n2} > u_{n1}, u_{n2} \geq 0}),\end{aligned}$$

where the first (resp., second) part represents profit from the regular (resp., special) product. Note that the firm incurs the donation cost k only for the sales of the special product.

The firm can choose to implement CM with or without a special product. By comparing the firm's equilibrium profits in different scenarios, we can identify the firm's optimal product (line) design decisions in the following proposition (which is Proposition 6 in Gao 2020). The interested reader is referred to Gao (2020) for the proof of the result.

Table 1 Consumer utility functions with extended product line

	Non-prosocial customer	Prosocial customer
Regular product	$u_{n1} = v - p_1$	$u_{p1} = v - p_1$
Special product	$u_{n2} = v - p_2$	$u_{p2} = v + s(k) - p_2$

Proposition 1 *There exist thresholds* $\bar{\alpha}^*, \bar{\bar{\alpha}}^* \in [0, 1]$ *such that*

(i) *if* $\alpha \leq \bar{\alpha}^*$, *the firm does not link its product to the social cause;*
(ii) *if* $\alpha \in (\bar{\alpha}^*, \bar{\bar{\alpha}}^*]$, *the firm extends its product line and links the special-version product to the social cause;*
(iii) *if* $\alpha > \bar{\bar{\alpha}}^*$, *the firm links its existing product to the social cause.*

Proposition 1 shows that the optimal product design decision depends on the size of the prosocial segment (i.e., α) in the firm's target market. If the majority of customers are not concerned about social impact (i.e., $\alpha \leq \bar{\alpha}^*$), then there is little benefit for the firm to engage in CM because it is costly. Otherwise (i.e., $\alpha > \bar{\alpha}^*$), it is optimal for the firm to implement CM because of the warm-glow effect it generates among the prosocial customers. However, it needs to balance the production and donation costs in deciding whether to design a special version of the product or not. In particular, if the size of the non-prosocial segment is intermediate (i.e., $\alpha \in (\bar{\alpha}^*, \bar{\bar{\alpha}}^*]$), the firm should introduce a special product in the CM campaign to induce non-prosocial customers to buy the regular product, saving donation costs. If prosocial customers account for a significant portion of the market (i.e., $\alpha > \bar{\bar{\alpha}}^*$), then the firm can simply link their existing product line to the social cause without incurring additional costs to introduce a new version of the product.

As documented in many studies (see, e.g., Business Wire 2019; Cone Communications 2014; Nielsen 2021), the number of prosocial customers is growing in today's market. As a result, more and more companies have implemented CM, albeit in different ways. Proposition 1 could shed light on not only the increasing popularity of CM in the corporate world but also the heterogeneity with respect to firms' product design choices. When Apple released the (PRODUCT)^{RED} edition of iPhone 12 in October 2020, it chose not to include any CM campaign for the more high-end iPhone 12 Pro. Proposition 1 provides a possible explanation for Apple's strategy. Piff et al. (2010) empirically find that people of higher social status tend to be less prosocial. If this is true, the value of α at Apple might not be very large because many of Apple's customers are in the upper social class (Frick and Berinato 2014). According to Proposition 1, Apple should have a special product if the company chooses to implement CM. This explains the release of the special-edition iPhone 12. Compared to the iPhone 12, the iPhone 12 Pro attracts more upper-social-class customers (i.e., α is smaller). Therefore, by Proposition 1, Apple should not implement CM on the iPhone 12 Pro. In contrast, our other examples Warby Parker and TOMS have adopted a different strategy by implementing CM without introducing special products, as their primary customer segments are young and socially conscious (i.e., large α). This is also consistent with the prediction of Proposition 1.

5 A General Model for Product Design

As we have demonstrated in the chapter so far, when it comes to product design, firms should not only consider the traditional financial impact but also the product's environmental and social impacts, especially when customers are increasingly concerned about them when making their purchase decisions (Business Wire 2019; CDP 2019; eMarketer 2018). In this section, we provide a general demand model to capture this shift in consumer preferences and hope that this simple model framework can help future researchers study product design issues in the TBL context.

Let us first use three vector variable, $\boldsymbol{q_f}, \boldsymbol{q_e}, \boldsymbol{q_s}$, to represent a firm's decisions over the product's $f$inancial, $e$nvironmental, and $s$ocial impact, respectively. For instance, vector $\boldsymbol{q_f}$ could include traditional product design decisions such as quality and time-to-market (Gao et al. 2021); vector $\boldsymbol{q_e}$ could include product carbon footprint at different levels of a supply chain (Gao and Souza 2022); and vector $\boldsymbol{q_s}$ could include the donations to a social cause (Gao 2020) or the product's impact on consumer health (Brox et al. 2011). Then, for a consumer i, her utility function can be expressed as follows.

$$u_i = V_{f,i}(\boldsymbol{q_f}) + V_{e,i}(\boldsymbol{q_e}) + V_{s,i}(\boldsymbol{q_s}) - p, \tag{1}$$

where the three non-decreasing functions $V_{f,i} \geq 0$, $V_{e,i} \geq 0$ and $V_{s,i} \geq 0$ measure customer i's preferences for the product itself, the product's environmental impact, and the product's social impact, respectively, and p denotes the product price.

Given consumers' utility function above, we can derive the demand for the product as

$$D(p, \boldsymbol{q_f}, \boldsymbol{q_e}, \boldsymbol{q_s}) = \sum_i I_{u_i \geq 0}$$

where the function I_A is the indicator function with $I_A = 1$ (resp., $= 0$) if A is true (resp., false). The firm's product design decisions $(\boldsymbol{q_f}, \boldsymbol{q_e}, \boldsymbol{q_s})$ not only impact the unit production cost of the product $c(\boldsymbol{q_f}, \boldsymbol{q_e}, \boldsymbol{q_s})$, but can also have implications on fixed cost denoted as $f(\boldsymbol{q_f}, \boldsymbol{q_e}, \boldsymbol{q_s})$. For example, the fixed cost may include R&D expenditure (Gao et al. 2021) and/or adoption of green manufacturing technologies (Gao and Souza 2022). As a result, the firm's general optimization problem can be formulated as follows:

$$\max_{p, \boldsymbol{q_f}, \boldsymbol{q_e}, \boldsymbol{q_s}} [p - c(\boldsymbol{q_f}, \boldsymbol{q_e}, \boldsymbol{q_s})] D(p, \boldsymbol{q_f}, \boldsymbol{q_e}, \boldsymbol{q_s}) - f\left(\boldsymbol{q_f}, \boldsymbol{q_e}, \boldsymbol{q_s}\right) + M(p, \boldsymbol{q_f}, \boldsymbol{q_e}, \boldsymbol{q_s})$$

where the last term $M(p, \boldsymbol{q_f}, \boldsymbol{q_e}, \boldsymbol{q_s})$ indicates the environmental or social mission that can be potentially achieved (Chen et al. 2021).

As we have reviewed in Sect. 4, the literature of product design has long focused on studying how a firm can manage its traditional product decisions $\boldsymbol{q_f}$

to maximize its financial performance while assuming customers are not concerned about the product's environmental and social impacts (i.e., $V_{e,i} = V_{s,i} = 0$ and $M(\cdot) = 0$). In recent years, given the monumental shift in public engagement around climate change, a growing stream of literature (as shown in Sect. 3) examines green product design issues and incorporates the term $V_{e,i}(\boldsymbol{q_e})$ in the analysis. In contrast, the third element in the above demand model (1), i.e., $V_{s,i}(\boldsymbol{q_s})$, has not received much attention in literature. We hope the simple model framework we proposed in Sect. 4 can be used as a starting point to inspire more future research to study how companies should make product design decisions for social impact.

Note that the general demand model (1) above can capture the heterogeneity with respect to consumers' preferences over the product itself, the product's environmental impact and the product's social impact, because the valuation functions $V_{f,i}$, $V_{e,i}$ and $V_{s,i}$ are all consumer specific. Moreover, this general demand model allows for the possibility that a consumer's preferences for different product impacts are correlated, a phenomenon largely ignored in literature but rather common in practice. Here, we present two illustrating examples:

- Millennials are more generous when giving to charities (Watt 2017) and are more likely to buy items associated with a cause than previous generations (Boston Consulting Group 2012). Meanwhile, millennials are most willing to pay a premium for healthy food (Nielsen 2015) and they become less interested in fast food restaurants like McDonald's (Jargon 2014). Given the said empirical evidence, we can conclude that consumers' preferences for a product itself and its social impact, namely $V_{f,i}$ and $V_{s,i}$, are more likely to be positively (resp., negatively) correlated for healthy food chains such as Panera Bread and HoneyGrow (resp., fast food restaurants such as McDonald's).
- Women are more likely to believe in climate change and are more concerned about how warming will affect the planet than men (Maron 2010). Thus, consumers' preferences for a product itself and its environmental impact, namely $V_{f,i}$ and $V_{e,i}$, are more likely to be negatively correlated for products that are valued more by male consumers, such as smart home devices (PwC 2017). By the same token, the two types of consumer preferences are more likely to be positively correlated for products that are valued more by female consumers, such as small SUVs and compact cars (MarketWatch 2016).

One way to evaluate this preference correlation is by conducting a survey in the firm's targeted market, asking people how they like the product itself and the social/environmental issues and using statistical methods to calculate the relevant metrics, e.g., the Pearson Correlation Coefficient (Lee Rodgers and Nicewander 1988). Firms could also use consumer demographics (e.g., age and gender) as mediator variables to estimate the correlation between consumers' preferences for the products and for social causes, as discussed above. In Gao (2020) and Gao and Souza (2022), both of which use a simplified variation of the general model (1), it is found that such consumer preference correlation has significant implications for both for-profit firms and non-profit non-governmental organizations (NGOs). Here, we simply present one result from each paper and refer the interested reader to Gao (2020) and Gao and Souza (2022) for more detailed discussions.

- Implications on NGOs who seek corporate partners to run a CM campaign (Gao 2020): If prosocial customers value the product more than non-prosocial customers (i.e., $V_{f,i}$ and $V_{s,i}$ are positively correlated), then an NGO should always work with downstream retailers in a supply chain to raise more funds in a CM campaign. In contrast, if non-prosocial customers value the product more than prosocial customers (i.e., $V_{f,i}$ and $V_{s,i}$ are negatively correlated), then it may be beneficial for the NGO to collaborate with upstream manufacturers in the supply chain.
- Implications on firms who consider buying offsets in a voluntary carbon market (Gao and Souza 2022): If eco-unconscious customers value the product more than eco-conscious customers (i.e., $V_{f,i}$ and $V_{e,i}$ are negatively correlated), then the firm should always offset more of its greenhouse gas (GHG) emissions as the carbon offset price decreases. In contrast, if eco-conscious customers value the product more than eco-unconscious customers (i.e., $V_{f,i}$ and $V_{e,i}$ are positively correlated), then it may be profitable for the firm to offset a lower share of its emissions in response to a decrease in offset price.

The results above highlight the importance of incorporating the correlation between consumer's product and social/environmental preferences in future studies of product design with the TBL objective. We hope to stimulate more empirical efforts in collecting relevant data and developing econometric methodologies to estimate said correlations between consumer preferences. At the same time, we call for more research on analytical modeling to incorporate the empirical findings to generate managerial insights (e.g., through stylized models) and provide actionable guidance (e.g., through engineering models) on how to design products in the face of environmentally/socially conscious consumers.

6 Concluding Remarks

The goal of this book chapter is to promote research needs on product design in the triple bottom line (TBL) context. In other words, the general goal of a company's product design strategy should have a positive impact on the environment, society, or both, while also benefiting the firm's profitability. Our research efforts in the Operations Management community to date have been mainly focused on product design with financial and environmental consequences, rather than social consequences. However, as the business world is paying increasing attention to the social impact of product design, we as the academics need to step up our efforts in studying the relevant problems. In order to help the readers understand the current progress, in this chapter we have provided references to representative research conducted on the financial and environmental impacts of product design and showcased latest research on the social impact of product design. We have also proposed a general demand model which can be used as a starting point for future researchers to continue this line of research.

While there are many research opportunities ahead for studying product design issues with the TBL objective, there are also difficulties. For one, it may not always be easy to define a firm's objective function. This is because unlike financial impact which can be measured by the firm's profitability, environmental, or social impact of a particular product design may be difficult to measure/quantify. Additionally, it may be challenging to properly measure or separate consumers' preferences for the product itself, the product's environmental impact, and the product's social impact. As a result, it can be a daunting task for the firm to estimate product demand. Last but not least, there is a high degree of uncertainty in demand as consumers' environmental and social preferences can be affected by unpredictable events (e.g., an earthquake or a terrorist event can stimulate people to buy cause-marketing products as they become more willing to donate for relief efforts).

However, as Operations Management researchers, we have tools readily to solve these problems. We are capable of designing surveys or field/lab experiments to understand people's pro-environmental and prosocial behaviors. We can employ machine learning techniques to help companies predict their product demand. We can build and optimize analytical or data-driven models to capture the various trade-offs. Yet this is not enough of what we should do. As demonstrated in Sect. 4, an environmental or social impact product design does not always hurt a firm's profitability, that is, the objectives of the TBL are not directly opposite each other but when done correctly they can bring a better profit, a better planet and a better society. This is something that relevant stakeholders (firms, consumers, investors, workers, NGOs, governments) should all be informed of. Opportunities abound, and it is a good idea to start with talking to our students, who will one day become the mainstream of society.

References

Agrawal VV, Ülkü S (2012) The role of modular upgradability as a green design strategy. Manuf Serv Oper Manag 15(4):640–648

Agrawal VV, Kavadias S, Toktay LB (2015) The limits of planned obsolescence for conspicuous durable goods. Manuf Serv Oper Manag 18(2):216–226

Agrawal VV, Atasu A, Van Wassenhove LN (2019) OM Forum—New opportunities for operations management research in sustainability. Manuf Serv Oper Manag 21(1):1–12

Alev I, Agrawal VV, Atasu A (2020) Extended producer responsibility for durable products. Manuf Serv Oper Manag 22(2):364–382

Andreoni J (1989) Giving with impure altruism: Applications to charity and ricardian equivalence. J Polit Econ 97(6):1447–1458

Arora A, Caulkins JP, Telang R (2006) Research Note—Sell first, fix later: Impact of patching on software quality. Management Science 52(3):465–471

Atasu A, Subramanian R (2012) Extended producer responsibility for e-waste: Individual or collective producer responsibility? Product Oper Manag 21(6):1042–1059

Atasu A, Van Wassenhove LN (2012) An operations perspective on product take-back legislation for e-waste: Theory, practice, and research needs. Product Oper Manag 21(3):407–422
Atasu A, Van Wassenhove LN, Sarvary M (2009) Efficient take-back legislation. Product Oper Manag 18(3):243–258
Atasu A, Corbett CJ, Huang X, Toktay LB (2020) Sustainable operations management through the perspective of manufacturing & service operations management. Manuf Serv Oper Manag 22(1):146–157
Baiman S, Fischer PE, Rajan MV (2000) Information, contracting, and quality costs. Management Science 46(6):776–789
Bayus BL (1997) Speed-to-market and new product performance trade-offs. J Product Innovat Manag 14(6):485–497
Bellos I, Ferguson M, Toktay LB (2017) The car sharing economy: Interaction of business model choice and product line design. Manuf Serv Oper Manag 19(2):185–201
Bhaskaran S, Erzurumlu SS, Ramachandran K (2021) Sequential product development and introduction by cash-constrained start-ups. Manuf Serv Oper Manag 23(6):1505–1523
Bhaskaran SR, Ramachandran K (2011) Managing technology selection and development risk in competitive environments. Product Oper Manag 20(4):541–555
Boston Consulting Group (2012) The millennial consumer Accessed 14 Feb 2022. https://www.bcg.com/publications/2012/millennial-consumer
Bouchery Y, Corbett CJ, Fransoo JC, Tan T (2016) Sustainable supply chains: A research-based textbook on operations and strategy, vol 4. Springer
Brox E, Fernandez-Luque L, Tøllefsen T (2011) Healthy gaming–video game design to promote health. Appl Clin Inf 2(2):128–142
Business Wire (2019) Consumers expect the brands they support to be socially responsible Accessed 14 Feb 2022. https://www.businesswire.com/news/home/20191002005697/en/Consumers-Expect-the-Brands-they-Support-to-be-Socially-Responsible
CDP (2019) Top FMCGs in race to keep up with conscious consumers Accessed 14 Feb 2022. https://www.cdp.net/en/articles/media/top-fmcgs-in-race-to-keep-up-with-conscious-consumers
Chen C (2001) Design for the environment: A quality-based model for green product development. Management Science 47(2):250–263
Chen L, Kim SH, Lee HL (2021) Vehicle maintenance contracting in developing economies: The role of social enterprise. Manuf Serv Oper Manag 23(6):1333–1682
Chen YJ, Sheu JB (2009) Environmental-regulation pricing strategies for green supply chain management. Transp Res E Logist Transp Rev 45(5):667–677
Cohen MA, Eliasberg J, Ho TH (1996) New product development: The performance and time-to-market tradeoff. Management Science 42(2):173–186
Cohen MA, Eliashberg J, Ho TH (2000) An analysis of several new product performance metrics. Manuf Serv Oper Manag 2(4):337–349
Cohen MA, Cui S, Gao F (2019) The effect of government support on green product design and environmental impact. Working Paper, The University of Pennsylvania
Cone Communications (2014) 2014 Cone communications digital activism study Accessed 14 Feb 2022. http://www.conecomm.com/research-blog/2014-cone-communications-digital-activism-study
Curry Stone Foundation (2021) What is social impact design Accessed 14 Feb 2022. https://currystonefoundation.org/what-is-social-impact-design/
Daughety AF, Reinganum JF (1995) Product safety: Liability, R&D, and signaling. Am Econ Rev 85(5):1187–1206
Elkington J (1997) Cannibals with forks: The triple bottom line of 21st century. Oxford, Capstone
eMarketer (2018) Consumers want brands to take a stand Accessed 14 Feb 2022. https://www.emarketer.com/content/consumers-want-brands-to-take-a-stand
Esenduran G, Kemahlıoğlu-Ziya E (2015) A comparison of product take-back compliance schemes. Product Oper Manag 24(1):71–88

Esenduran G, Kemahlıoğlu-Ziya E, Swaminathan JM (2017) Impact of take-back regulation on the remanufacturing industry. Product Oper Manag 26(5):924–944
Esenduran G, Lin YT, Xiao W, Jin M (2020) Choice of electronic waste recycling standard under recovery channel competition. Manuf Serv Oper Manag 22(3):495–512
Frick W, Berinato S (2014) Apple: Luxury brand or mass marketer? Harvard Business Review Accessed 14 Feb 2022. https://hbr.org/2014/10/apple-luxury-brand-or-mass-marketer
Fullerton D, Wu W (1998) Policies for green design. J Environ Econ Manag 36(2):131–148
Gao F (2020) Cause marketing: Product pricing, design, and distribution. Manuf Serv Oper Manag 22(4):775–791
Gao F, Souza G (2022) Carbon offsetting with eco-conscious consumers. Management Science. Forthcoming. https://doi.org/10.1287/mnsc.2021.4293
Gao F, Cui S, Cohen M (2021) Performance, reliability, or time-to-market? Innovative product development and the impact of government regulation. Product Oper Manag 30(1):253–275
Girotra K, Netessine S (2013) OM Forum—Business model innovation for sustainability. Manuf Serv Oper Manag 15(4):537–544
Gui L, Atasu A, Ergun Ö, Toktay LB (2015) Efficient implementation of collective extended producer responsibility legislation. Management Science 62(4):1098–1123
Gui L, Atasu A, Ergun Ö, Toktay LB (2018) Design incentives under collective extended producer responsibility: A network perspective. Management Science 64(11):5083–5104
Huang X, Atasu A, Toktay LB (2019) Design implications of extended producer responsibility for durable products. Management Science 65(6):2573–2590
IEG (2018) What sponsors want & where dollars will go in 2018 Accessed 14 Feb 2022. http://www.sponsorship.com/IEG/files/f3/f3cfac41-2983-49be-8df6-3546345e27de.pdf
Jain S, Ramdas K (2005) Up or out—or stay put? Product positioning in an evolving technology environment. Product Oper Manag 14(3):362–376
Jargon J (2014) McDonald's faces 'millennial' challenge. The Wall Street Journal Accessed 14 Feb 2022. https://www.wsj.com/articles/mcdonalds-faces-millennial-challenge-1408928743
Kalkanci B, Plambeck EL (2020) Managing supplier social and environmental impacts with voluntary versus mandatory disclosure to investors. Management Science 66(8):3295–3798
Kalkanci B, Rahmani M, Toktay LB (2019) The role of inclusive innovation in promoting social sustainability. Product Oper Manag 28(12):2960–2982
Klastorin T, Tsai W (2004) New product introduction: Timing, design, and pricing. Manuf Serv Oper Manag 6(4):302–320
Koschate-Fischer N, Stefan IV, Hoyer WD (2012) Willingness to pay for cause-related marketing: The impact of donation amount and moderating effects. J Market Res 49(6):910–927
Kraft T, Raz G (2017) Collaborate or compete: Examining manufacturers' replacement strategies for a substance of concern. Product Oper Manag 26(9):1646–1662
Kraft T, Erhun F, Carlson RC, Rafinejad D (2013) Replacement decisions for potentially hazardous substances. Product Oper Manag 22(4):958–975
Krishnan V, Gupta S (2001) Appropriateness and impact of platform-based product development. Management Science 47(1):52–68
Krishnan V, Ramachandran K (2011) Integrated product architecture and pricing for managing sequential innovation. Management Science 57(11):2040–2053
Krishnan V, Ulrich KT (2001) Product development decisions: A review of the literature. Management Science 47(1):1–21
Lee HL, Tang CS (2018) Socially and environmentally responsible value chain innovations: New operations management research opportunities. Management Science 64(3):983–996
Lee Rodgers J, Nicewander WA (1988) Thirteen ways to look at the correlation coefficient. Am Stat 42(1):59–66
Lobel I, Patel J, Vulcano G, Zhang J (2015) Optimizing product launches in the presence of strategic consumers. Management Science 62(6):1778–1799
Loch CH, Terwiesch C (2005) Rush and be wrong or wait and be late? A model of information in collaborative processes. Product Oper Manag 14(3):331–343

MarketWatch (2016) Women are more likely to drive these cars Accessed 14 Feb 2022. https://www.marketwatch.com/story/women-are-more-likely-to-drive-these-cars-2016-03-02
Maron D (2010) Women more likely than men to believe the science on global warming. Scientific American Accessed 14 Feb 2022. https://www.scientificamerican.com/article/women-more-likely-than-men/
Morgan LO, Morgan RM, Moore WL (2001) Quality and time-to-market trade-offs when there are multiple product generations. Manuf Serv Oper Manag 3(2):89–104
Murali K, Lim MK, Petruzzi NC (2019) The effects of ecolabels and environmental regulation on green product development. Manuf Serv Oper Manag 21(3):519–535
Nielsen (2015) We are what we eat Accessed 14 Feb 2022. https://www.nielsen.com/wp-content/uploads/sites/3/2019/04/Nielsen20Global20Health20and20Wellness20Report20-20January202015-1.pdf
Nielsen (2021) Attracting multicultural consumers: Does corporate social responsibility matter? Accessed 14 Feb 2022. https://nielseniq.com/global/en/insights/analysis/2021/attracting-multicultural-consumers-does-corporate-social-responsibility-matter/
Örsdemir A, Deshpande V, Parlaktürk AK (2019) Is servicization a win-win strategy? Profitability and environmental implications of servicization. Manuf Serv Oper Manag 21(3):674–691
Özer Ö, Uncu O (2013) Competing on time: An integrated framework to optimize dynamic time-to-market and production decisions. Product Oper Manag 22(3):473–488
Peng Y, Gao F, Chen J (2021a) Green packaging and communication: The implications of bring-your-own-container. Kelley School of Business Research Paper
Peng Y, Gao F, Chen J (2021b) Green product and packaging design with consumer engagement. Kelley School of Business Research Paper
Piff PK, Kraus MW, Côté S, Cheng BH, Keltner D (2010) Having less, giving more: the influence of social class on prosocial behavior. J Personal Soc Psychol 99(5):771
Plambeck E, Wang Q (2009) Effects of e-waste regulation on new product introduction. Management Science 55(3):333–347
Plambeck EL, Ramdas K (2020) Alleviating poverty by empowering women through business model innovation: Manufacturing & Service Operations Management insights and opportunities. Manuf Serv Oper Manag 22(1):123–134
PwC (2017) Smart home, seamless life Accessed 14 Feb 2022. https://www.yumpu.com/en/document/read/57359318/smart-home-seamless-life-unlocking-a-culture-of-convenience
Souza GC, Bayus BL, Wagner HM (2004) New-product strategy and industry clockspeed. Management Science 50(4):537–549
Tezuka K (2020) Seeing AI empowers people who are blind or with low vision for everyday life Accessed 14 Feb 2022. https://news.microsoft.com/apac/2020/12/03/seeing-ai-empowers-people-who-are-blind-or-with-low-vision-for-everyday-life/
Varadarajan PR, Menon A (1988) Cause-related marketing: A coalignment of marketing strategy and corporate philanthropy. J Market 52(3):58–74
Watt H (2017) Millennials give more generously and carefully to charity, study finds. The Guardian Accessed 14 Feb 2022. https://www.theguardian.com/money/2017/dec/18/millennials-give-more-generously-and-carefully-to-charity-study-finds
World Health Organization (2021) Blindness and vision impairment Accessed 14 Feb 2022. https://www.who.int/en/news-room/fact-sheets/detail/blindness-and-visual-impairment
Yenipazarli A, Vakharia A (2015) Pricing, market coverage and capacity: Can green and brown products co-exist? Eur J Oper Res 242(1):304–315

Fair Price, Fair Trade, and Fair Pay in Supply Chains

Li Chen, Hau Lee, and Christopher S. Tang

Abstract The COVID-19 pandemic has not only caused unprecedented disruptions of global supply chains but also exposed unfair supply chain practices including unfair pricing, unfair trade, and unfair pay. Despite these unfair incidents, we observe that new industry initiatives have been developed to address various supply chain fairness issues. In this chapter, we discuss the notion of supply chain fairness as well as its strategic values and historical movements. We further outline the challenges of putting fairness to practice and various research opportunities in this area.

Keywords Social responsibility · Supply chain management · Fairness · Transparency

This chapter is an abbreviated and adapted version of an article (Chen et al. 2022) to be published in *Production and Operations Management*.

***A Tribute from the Authors*:** Professor Morris Cohen has been a major pillar in the research of global supply chains, and his influence has also been extended to practitioners and business executives. The authors of the current chapter are indebted to his contributions, and the subject of fairness is motivated by the general global supply chain research of which Cohen was a key part of.

L. Chen (✉)
Samuel Curtis Johnson Graduate School of Management, Cornell University, Ithaca, NY, USA
e-mail: li.chen@cornell.edu

H. Lee
Graduate School of Business, Stanford University, Stanford, CA, USA
e-mail: haulee@stanford.edu

C. S. Tang
Anderson School of Management, UCLA, Los Angeles, CA, USA
e-mail: chris.tang@anderson.ucla.edu

H. Lee et al. (eds.), *Creating Values with Operations and Analytics*, Springer Series in Supply Chain Management 19, https://doi.org/10.1007/978-3-031-08871-1_5

1 Introduction

Environmental and social responsibility have been percolating as a major part of a firm's supply chain strategy in recent years, but the COVID-19 pandemic of 2020 has brought various ***supply chain fairness issues*** to the forefront. Because unfair practices can be exposed more easily in normal times, businesses and individuals are more restrained from doing so in fear of reputational damage. However, during challenging times such as the COVID-19 pandemic, businesses and individuals can justify their unfair practices under the pretense of unforeseeable market forces. By noting that supply chain fairness issues become more prevalent during these trying times, we examine these issues more formally in this chapter with the hope to stimulate further discussion.

The pandemic of COVID-19 has exposed many seemingly unfair supply chain practices. Consumers have found unfair pricing, such as the surge of personal protective gears, toilet papers, or cleaning supplies at the peak of the pandemic. The scarcity of these supplies has enabled price gouging by some suppliers. Unfair trades also surfaced when many brand owners, faced with plummeting demands from store closures in 2020, dealt a blow to their factory suppliers. Orders were canceled, even shipments of completed products were rejected, payment terms were unilaterally extended, price concessions were demanded, or outstanding balances were flatly refused, in the name of *force majeure* (Tang and Yang 2020). The factory owners, in turn, delayed wage payments to workers, laid off workers without full severances, or asked for wage concessions. Some governments provided subsidies to businesses in such tough times, but then the subsidies, in many cases, did not get passed onto workers.

As the global economy started to recover in 2021, the surge in demands of container shipments, coupled with the reduced capacity at ports in both the USA and China, created excessive delays for the loading and unloading of cargoes at ports. Ocean liners raised the container shipping prices to an unprecedented level (Page 2021). These price hikes were not just due to the increasing costs of running container ships, as shipping lines like Maersk have since then earned skyrocketing profits (Dean 2021). The result was higher and higher inflation in prices of consumer goods everywhere.

Fairness in supply chain practices has been under greater and greater scrutiny. Social responsibility has already been a subject of intense research in recent years (Sodhi and Tang 2014; Lee and Tang 2018). Fairness is an added dimension of such responsibility issues. This is the focus of this chapter.

The rest of the chapter is organized as follows. In Sect. 2, we discuss the definition of fairness and unfair practices, as well as the strategic values and historical movements of fair supply chain practices. Section 3 highlights some of the operations challenges and potential opportunities for firms to achieve various fair practices. We propose some Operations Research (OM) research questions for further examination in Sect. 4. Section 5 concludes this chapter.

2 Fair Price, Fair Trade, and Fair Pay

2.1 Fairness and Unfair Practices

Fairness is closely related to "equity" and "justice." Oxford Dictionary defines fairness as "*to be impartial and just treatment or behavior without favoritism or discrimination*." Similarly, equity is defined as "*fair and reasonable; treating everyone in an equal way*." According to the organizations and psychology literature (e.g., Colquitt 2001; Hornibrook et al. 2008), fairness can be further divided into three types: fairness of outcome distributions, termed as *distributional fairness*; fairness of processes that lead to such outcomes, termed as *procedural fairness*; and fairness related to individual's reactions to decision outcomes and the information provided regarding the outcomes or procedures, termed as *interactional fairness*. In the OM literature, fairness in services often refers to non-differential treatments in servicing customers (e.g., Avi-Itzhak and Levy 2004; McCoy and Lee 2014).

In the supply chain context, fairness is more related to the distributional and procedural fairness in the literature, as it reflects how the supply chain partners are treating each other. Our focus is therefore centered on the supply chain processes and the practices that lead to fair or unfair distributional outcomes. Figure 1 presents an illustration of supply chain fairness, where we have consumers, buyers, suppliers, as well as the employees of the buyers and suppliers. There are three fairness concerns in this illustration: "fair price" between consumers and buyers, "fair trade" between buyers and suppliers, and "fair pay" between buyers/suppliers and their employees. The bi-directional arrows in the figures highlight the fair treatment between entities can go both ways.

By using the framework as depicted in Fig. 1, we now use case examples to illustrate unfair price, unfair trade, and unfair pay practices that occurred in different supply chains amid the COVID-19 pandemic. First, we have observed unfair pricing practices that exploited the vulnerabilities of desperate customers during the pandemic. There was widespread price gouging over supplies in shortage. For example, a dozen of N95 face masks was once offered by a seller for $3799 on

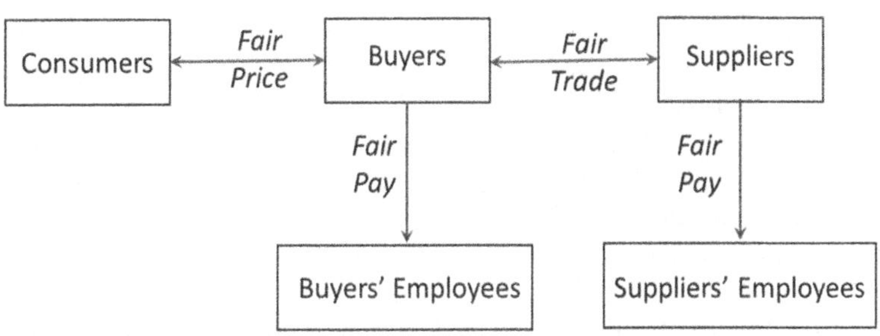

Fig. 1 Fair price, fair trade, and fair pay (Source: Chen et al. 2022)

Amazon, and a pack of 36 rolls of toilet paper was priced at $79.99 by a store in Florida.

Second, unfair trade took place in many supply chains as a result of the disruption caused by the pandemic. For example, the apparel supply chain was hit heavily by the pandemic due to the closures of retail stores and consumers curtailing their spending. Many major retailers (e.g., Neiman Marcus, JCPenney, and J. Crew) filed for bankruptcy in 2020. Other cash-strapped retailers rushed to cancel their orders with suppliers on a short notice. Some of them delayed or defaulted payment on existing invoices from their suppliers. Chua (2021d) reported that about 40% of suppliers in the garment industry received delayed payments from the buyers beyond the usual 60 days. Due to the canceled orders, many upstream suppliers were put in a dire financial situation with excess materials or components. Such trade practice was clearly unfair.

Third, the unfair trade practice caused a cascading effect of unfair pay. Consider the case when the upstream suppliers did not have enough funds to pay their workers due to the unfair trade practice as explained above. Since 2020, many garment workers were fired without proper severance compensation, and this form of "severance theft" was estimated to be over $500 million in the global garment industry during the pandemic (Corbineau 2021).

2.2 *Strategic Values of Fairness*

Despite the existence of unfair supply chain practices, as discussed in Sect. 2.1, many leading firms have tried to maintain supply chain fairness. These firms viewed fair supply chain practices as part of their competitive positioning, creating strategic values.

First, fair supply chain practices can be used as a defensive strategy to help firms to mitigate risks and strengthen their supply chain resilience in the following three areas:

1. **A risk-hedging strategy.** Due to the heightened awareness of social responsibility issues in supply chains, most firms have strived to comply with environment, safety and health regulations established by the local government (Chen and Lee 2021). These regulations often align with fair treatments of consumers, employees, and trading partners. Therefore, firms can hedge against regulatory risks by improving their fair supply chain practices. Moreover, fair practices (e.g., fair trade and fair treatment to workers) can complement the auditing and contracting mechanisms designed to hedge against the collateral reputational risk from suppliers' violations in environmental and social standards (Chen and Lee 2017; Chen et al. 2020).
2. **A sustainable supply chain strategy.** Fair supply chain practices help strengthen relationships inside a firm as well as between the firm and its trading partners. Strong relationships make the supply chain more sustainable, with better capac-

ities to withstand external shocks. For example, Starbucks long-term success depends on having a stable and sustainable supply of high-quality coffee beans sourced from farmers in developing countries. These small-hold farmers are often vulnerable to price fluctuations or natural disasters. To ensure that the farmers can sustain their farm operations to provide a sustainable coffee supply, Starbucks' Coffee and Farmer Equity (C.A.F.E.) purchase program and its Fair Trade certification guarantee qualified coffee farmers a fair price (Lee 2008).

3. **A resilient supply chain strategy**. Fair supply chain practices can also help firms to become more resilient. Fair pay can bring "positive reciprocity" from workers to firms (Akerlof 1982; Fehr et al. 1993). During the COVID-19 pandemic, a leading automotive manufacturer in Wuhan, China, was reported to achieve a 6% increase in annual production in 2020 after a two-month lockdown (Liu et al. 2021). It was found that the firm paid their workers with full wages during the lockdown period. After the lockdown ended, workers made voluntary efforts and sacrifices to expedite the firm's recovery operations, contributing to the overall productivity post-recovery. Similarly, fair trade can create positive reciprocity as well. Putre (2020) argued that the positive reciprocity could enable an original equipment manufacturer (OEM) to recover faster in the post-COVID era, especially if the OEM treated its suppliers fairly with trust and transparency.

Second, as an offensive strategy, fair supply chain practices can enable firms to gain competitive advantage as follows:

1. **A branding strategy.** From the marketing perspective, fair supply chain practices can help firms to build a brand that attracts the Millennials and Gen Zs. For example, Everlane, a startup in the apparel sector, uses cost transparency and fair price to gain brand awareness from conscious consumers (Lim et al. 2021). JD.com, one of the leading ecommerce platforms in China, ensured fair pricing and fair fulfillment of products during the pandemic to gain consumer trust and further enhance its brand (Shen and Sun 2021).
2. **A differentiation strategy.** Patagonia is known for differentiating itself from competition by being an environmentally and socially responsible apparel firm. Its commitment to fair pay, i.e., paying living wage to workers at its suppliers' factories, further differentiates itself from competition and helps to justify its premium retail prices. In Zambia, COMACO markets its food products by showcasing its fair treatment of farmers. Such fairness-based differentiation strategy helps enhance a firm's brand equity.
3. **A socially responsible strategy.** To strengthen its social responsibility commitment in developing countries, Unilever launched the living wage initiative in 2021. This initiative is intended to pay living wages to all workers in Unilever's global supply chains by 2030. In a similar vein, the intent of Nestle's "Creating Shared Value" initiative is to provide economic and social support to all workers along its global supply chains (Tang 2018). These "do good" supply chain initiatives are certainly costly, but they can help these two firms to build up new consumer bases in the long run (Karnani 2007).

2.3 Fair Supply Chain Movements

According to Britannica, there is no consensus regarding a starting date of the fair trade movement. However, many attributed to Edna Ruth Byler during her 1946 visit to a women's sewing group run by the Mennonite Central Committee (MCC) in Puerto Rico. Byler began selling the group's crafts to friends and neighbors in the USA and paid MCC a fair price. To enable customers to know whether the sellers had treated the producers fairly, Fair Trade USA created the mechanism and standards for monitoring the trade transactions across the globe since 1990 (Shoenthal 2018). Specifically, Fair Trade reviews its certification standards and its fair prices (for standard quality) and "extra premium" (to support the community of the producers) to ensure fair trade between suppliers and buyers. In addition, Fair Trade conducts independent audits to ensure all Fairtrade transactions comply with the Fairtrade Standards. Clearly, the origin of the fair trade movement is to make sure that the smaller businesses are treated fairly in trade with large firms. Nevertheless, such fair supply chain practices need not be limited to commodity trades such as coffee, cacao, and crops. In our subsequent discussion, we shall broaden its meaning to any fair practices in a supply chain (Fig. 1).

In the same spirit, fair price (Fig. 1) is about treating downstream consumers fairly. Clearly, to persuade consumers that a firm's retail price is fair, the firm needs to reveal its cost first. However, cost transparency is rare because firms are fearful that consumers may refuse to purchase their products once they learn about their profit margins (Sinha 2000). Interestingly, Mohan et al. (2020) found that cost transparency can induce trust that can stimulate sales. For example, Everlane reveals materials cost, labor cost, transportation cost, and duties as well as average price markup by others for similar items sold in the market. Cost transparency is essential to establish the notion of fair pricing, which can generate sales from consumers who find the price to be fair (Li and Tang 2021).

Fair pay is the flip side of fair price. As more conscious consumers care about workers being paid a fair living wage for their work (Hackenberg 2021), fair pay has become a recent industry movement (as illustrated in the Unilever's living wage initiative above) that promotes fair practices between firms and their employees (Fig. 1). To ensure fair pay, monitoring is key. In Asia, Esquel tracked the payments of their factory workers, compared with the country's minimum wage and living wage requirements (Lee 2021). Besides fair wage, non-monetary fair treatment to workers is also important, if not more. Such treatment includes living conditions (crowdedness of worker's dormitory), work hour restrictions, employee benefits, and working conditions, which all affect how workers perceive fairness of being treated at work. Some of the issues, such as working long hours, have been addressed as supply chain compliance issues; and others have been addressed through extra compensation.

We refer the interested reader to Chen et al. (2022) for a more comprehensive review of the fair supply chain movements in industry. Table 1 summarizes the relationship of treatment and measures for fair price, fair trade, and fair pay.

Table 1 Fair pay, fair trade and fair price

Fairness issue	Relationship of treatment	Primary fairness measure	Secondary fairness measures
Fair price	Seller to consumer	Price charged for products or services	Conditions of transactions, auxiliary charges, authenticity of products or quality of service, etc.
Fair trade	Buyer to supplier	Contract price charged for products or services	Trading terms and conditions, timeliness of payments, process for product/service acceptance, etc.
Fair pay	Company to employees	Compensation paid for work or services	Benefits, work conditions, timeliness of payments, termination treatments, etc.

3 Putting Fairness to Practice

Despite the potential strategic values of fairness, putting them into practice is far from easy. Myopically, there might be short-term gains to a firm to engage in unfair practices. There are therefore challenges that range from organizational self-interests, infrastructural limitations, and institutional barriers to collaboration. These challenges, which lead to potential opportunities, can be classified into two groups: building the foundation and practicing fairness in action.

3.1 Building the Foundation

There are two aspects to building the foundation. First, we need to have a common understanding of what fairness means, as well as the appropriate measurement mechanisms in place. Second, we need interconnected data systems that would enable the visibility and monitoring of fairness provided for the right members in the supply chain.

While it is difficult to define fair price, fair trade and fair pay in absolute terms, one can develop a simple definition that is perceived to be fair. For example, Unilever defines a living wage as one that gives people enough to provide for their family's basic needs for food, water, clothing, housing, education, transportation, and healthcare. It also allows for some discretionary income and includes enough provision to cover unexpected events. In terms of measurements, developing an objective measurement of fair price and fair pay with an independent and trusted agent can be useful. For example, Unilever worked closely with an independent NGO, the Fair Wage Network (FWN), to develop an objective external source of the living wage amount for each of the countries where they had employees. Similarly, Patagonia worked with the Fair Labor Association (FLA) to develop living wages in 20 countries by using the Anker Method, which estimates local costs of a basic but decent lifestyle for a worker and their family within a specific area.

Besides prices and wages, there are many other fairness elements to consider. For example, if a seller imposes certain sales restrictions and different terms of sales, fairness can be compromised. For example, during the peak of the COVID-19 pandemic, US consumers have faced prolonged shortages of cleaning wipes and hand sanitizers, even though manufacturers were producing at full capacity. There were questions about whether the manufacturers had treated their customers fairly, as the bulk of the supply was sent to big corporate customers like airlines and merchants like Amazon.com. Even when customers can buy the product, what kind of return and refund policies would be considered fair? Although price fairness is critical, we should be aware of the other dimensions of fairness to customers.

Regarding fair trade, the terms of trade are what made up whether the trade was fair or not. There were many examples during the COVID-19 pandemic when firms unilaterally canceled orders, forced suppliers to take returns, accepted only partial products, extended payment terms, or even forced suppliers to give deep discounts. These practices had implicit price/cost implications, which affected fairness in trade.

In addition to wages paid to workers, fair pay should also include living conditions in the workers' dormitory, employee benefits, work conditions, forced overtime, etc. Another question is what constitutes a living wage, which is tightly linked with the problem of overtime. Due to the ebb and flow of orders coming in from buyers, factory owners tend to keep a base level of workers and rely on the use of overtime to meet peak demands. To keep this cost within control, workers might not be paid at the minimum wage during regular working hours, but when supplemented with overtime payments, the factory could show that the minimum living wage had been met (Kuruvilla 2021). Excessive overtime, of course, is a labor compliance problem by itself, and it is deemed unfair because it deprives a worker's personal leisure time.

These challenges can be addressed through technology innovations, such as designing data collection toolkits to measure supply chain fairness. For example, FLA has created a "fair compensation dashboard" and wage data collection toolkit to allow buyers and factories to measure and track worker pays. Deepening organizational collaboration can also help develop objective measures. For example, in addressing the worker overtime problem, Chintapalli et al. (2017) show that suppliers can offer discounts to entice customers to place their orders during non-peak periods, so as to reduce the reliance on excessive overtime.

Even with good intentions, implementing fair supply chain practices can be challenging, especially when the firm does not have supply chain visibility. In this context, supply chain visibility includes the identity of each business entity and each person (consumer or worker) in the supply chain as well as the financial transactions between two business entities (or between a business entity and a person). Payments to workers in many developing countries are opaque. For example, to sustain the operations of factory owners in South and Southeast Asia during the pandemic, brand owners such as H&M and Levi Strauss have claimed that they had paid their (contract) factory owners in full. Despite good intentions, 1.6 million workers were laid off, and many did not even get the wages owed to them (Chua 2021a). In many instances, financial payment records can be deceptive. For example, UK's online fashion retailer Boohoo has found some of their suppliers required the workers to give some portion of their wages back to the firm to circumvent the minimum wage requirement (Chua 2021b).

True supply chain visibility is necessary for implementing fair supply chain practices, and advanced technology such as blockchain and AI can help. For example, Denver's Coda Coffee partnered with a startup, Bext360, to develop a blockchain application to track the process flow in every step: collecting, washing, drying, milling, export, and roasting of beans through retail operations. Smallholder farmers in Uganda can deposit their coffee beans into a "bextmachine" that uses machine vision technology to determine the quantity and quality of the coffee beans and then issues a receipt, so that the farmers can collect their fair payments from trusted financial institutions.

Besides coffee, various Chinese firms are leveraging advanced technology to improve fair practices. Chinese fintech startup JDH leveraged mobile and blockchain technology to track financial transactions of suppliers several tiers deep into various electronics manufacturing supply chains (Tang and Yang 2020). In the same vein, Serai created a network-based digital business-to-business platform that provided a traceability solution to enable apparel firms to track cotton and other raw materials, ensuring fair treatment of workers in Xinjiang, China (Taylor 2021).

3.2 *Practicing Fairness in Action*

Even if and when a firm can gain true supply chain visibility, implementing fair supply chain practices can be challenging unless the firm is vertically integrated for the following reasons. First, if the focal firm is decentralized, then its upstream suppliers serve many other firms. As different firms trade with these suppliers under different contract terms, it is impractical to expect these suppliers to pay all workers according to the living wage specified by the focal firm.

Besides organization structure, supply chain partners are reluctant to implement fair practices because they are concerned that they would be taken advantage of by yielding visibility or giving up some proprietary practices. To foster collaboration, some proven win-win benefits can be helpful. For example, through Nike's equitable manufacturing initiative, Nike showed that all partners can see improvements like quality, employee morale, turnover reduction, productivity increases, and higher employee motivation (Chen and Lee 2021). Thus, benefits accrue to Nike, factory owners, and the workers. Win-win benefits for all entities and workers along the supply chain have been shown through Nestle's "Creating Shared Values" initiative (Lee et al. 2013a).

Another difficulty in implementation is that there can be potential mislabeling or misinformation in the supply chain. The most recent debate on what constitutes "organic cotton" is one example. While companies might want to buy organic cotton, and consumers might think that the premium price of the products that they paid for were made from organic cotton, Wicker et al. (2022) found that a lot of the organic cotton was not truly organic. Fair trade and fair price have been compromised. Yet Friedman (2022) reported that industry associations have disputed such claims. In truth, a company or a consumer could not find out the true status of fairness in the supply chain.

It is even more challenging to put supply chain fairness in action when enforcement is weak. For example, the milk formula scandal in China and the collapse of Rana Plaza exposed weak local government enforcement in developing countries (Tang and Babich 2014). As ocean shipping freight skyrocketed during the COVID-19 pandemic, some shipping lines failed to honor the contracted volumes of shipping slots at pre-negotiated prices to shippers, forcing the shippers to use the much higher spot prices. Similarly unfair reneging practices also occurred toward the shipping lines in the past when some shippers found cheaper spot prices. Such unfair trade practices from both sides can be attributed to the lack of contract enforcement.

In many developing countries, there is a lack of whistleblower protection laws, so that workers in supplier factories are reticent out of fear of retaliation from their employers. Consequently, some contract manufacturers in Asia may achieve the living wage requirements through excessive overtime by force. To overcome this challenge, Unilever conducts internal audits annually to ensure that all Unilever employees receive livable compensation without the need to work excessive hours, that employees' full pay is delivered correctly and on time in every country, and that there is no unequal pay between genders. In addition to annual audits, some firms (such as Nike) have partnered with outside agencies (such as MicroBenefits) to allow workers to provide direct feedback to brands through mobile applications. App-based iCare solutions developed by MobiVi in Vietnam record workers' pay and working hours, enabling brands to monitor and detect unfair practices such as excessive overtime for the factory to meet the wage standards (Lee et al. 2013b).

4 Research Opportunities

As we described in Sect. 3, there are indeed significant challenges for fair practices to be more widespread, while unfair practices could be contained. Some of the examples show how some innovative companies have been able to overcome such challenges, which provides ideas for operations management researchers to pursue. These ideas are presented below.

4.1 Understanding Key Relationships

Understanding some key relationships would enable better policies and instruments to be designed. The prevalence of potential unfair practices can be highly dependent on the industry characteristics. Understanding the link between the industry characteristics and the incidences and the nature of fairness issues can enable government policy makers or industry associations to focus on these characteristics to make improvements. For example, in industry sectors where the supplier base is concentrated in a few key firms and the supplier substitutability is low (such as the electronic manufacturing services or automobile manufacturing industries), the buyers and the suppliers usually engage in a long-term strategic partner relationship. As a result, there have been fewer supply chain fairness incidents reported in those industries. On the other hand, in industry sectors where the supplier base is highly fragmented and when the suppliers are easily replaceable (such as apparel and footwear industries), the bargaining power disparity between the buyer and the supplier is usually large. As such, supply chain fairness incidents appear to be more prominent as evidenced. Research based on empirical data could help to establish such linkages.

Another relationship to explore is the link between fair trade and fair pay. The consequence of a firm being unfairly treated by its trading partner could be that the firm would then not pay its workers fairly. Kuruvilla (2021) found that buyers' purchasing practices were a contributing factor to low wages and high overtime in the garment industry. In 2020, the Fair Wear Foundation led the Sustainable Textile Initiative: Together for Change (STITCH) initiative that brought European fashion brands and trade unions in garment production countries to work together. The underlying principle of the STITCH initiative is that, when the brands trade fairly with their suppliers, the suppliers will pay their workers fairly. Does fair trade positively link to fair pay? If not, what kind of mechanism is needed to ensure positive changes along the supply chain?

As discussed earlier, workers may not just care about their pay but also other benefits and work conditions. In developing countries where many are struggling to make a living, pay is crucial. Besides pay, fair treatment of employees is equally important. In many economies, workers care about other elements beyond pay for their work. What are the elements that would create and sustain a motivated and therefore loyal and productive workforce? Nike's Equitable Manufacturing initiative went beyond pay, and aimed at empowering workers, providing training, and supporting their lives inside and outside of the factory. Pilots were encouraging, but more research is needed to show how these efforts can be linked to productivity and quality improvement, better morale, and less turnover. Apparel maker Esquel created a new factory campus in Guilin that is environmentally enticing and ergonomically pleasing and provided workers with health-focused diets and work processes. Would this make workers happier, leading to the other benefits for the workers and the firm?

Finally, the relationships between the values derived from fairness, and the costs caused by unfairness, need to be established. Fair supply chain practices certainly can have strategic values, but there have not been rigorous empirical studies that quantified such benefits, in the form of increased sales, better margins, or higher shareholder returns. In the context of social responsibility, Kraft et al. (2017) conducted different laboratory experiments to show that consumers' valuation (in terms of willingness to pay) increased with a higher level of supply chain visibility (in terms of the visibility of the firm's payment to the worker) when workers were disadvantaged. How much premium would consumers be willing to pay for products made by firms that have fair trade, fair pay, and fair price? On the cost side, we need to quantify the costs of unfair practices. Unfair practices may allow a firm to have short-term gain at the expense of either their consumers, trading partners, or employees. But what about long-term cost implications of such practices? Empirical studies to demonstrate how unfair practices could eventually bring harm to the firm in its sales, profitability, employee loyalty, consumer trust, stock prices, supply chain relationships, operating costs, and penalties to or reduced support from the government, would be valuable.

4.2 *Instruments Used to Improve Fairness*

There are instruments used to improve fairness, and research is needed to assess the effectiveness of these instruments. One of the instruments used to foster fairness has been industry consortiums as a platform to accelerate implementation. A firm in a supply chain often has to deal with multiple suppliers or multiple buyers who may have different standards and practices. With a diversity of standards and expectations, especially if they may not have always been consistent with one another, it is doubly difficult for a firm to improve its fairness practices. Implementation of fair trade and fair pay in a supply network with complex buying and selling relationships can therefore be challenging (Kuruvilla 2021). In such a situation, having an industry consortium to come up with a more uniform standard could be helpful. One prominent example is the ACCORD, an agreement based on consortiums of firms that established safety standards, audit processes, and collective penalty schemes, to address fire and building safety in Bangladesh (Caro et al. 2018). In September 2021, The Sustainable Terms of Trade Initiative (STTI) published a white paper that outlines the "core principles" of commercial compliance for fair trade (Chua 2021d). An industry consortium has potential, but its sustainability is questionable. ACCORD was in the blink of collapsing in early 2021 when various members were hesitant to renew their commitment: some brands were doubtful about its value, and factory owners in Bangladesh felt their interests were not well represented (Sani 2021). ACCORD survived only when big brand owners such as H&M and Inditex renewed their membership in August 2021. Due to the self-interest of multiple stakeholders, this episode exposed the challenges of using consortiums as a means to improve fairness. Indeed, forming a consortium is difficult, but sustaining it is even harder. What are the mechanisms for sustaining the effort of a consortium?

As discussed earlier, having supply chain visibility is a prerequisite to improve fairness, and yet most firms lack such visibility. Transparency is needed for a firm to know who their supply or customer network is, and it is needed for the public interested in supply chain fairness. To gain visibility, a firm can invest in data integration with its partners and convince the partners to allow for such transparency. Traditionally, supply chain opacity provides a competitive advantage for a firm by keeping its low cost supplier identity as a secret weapon (Sodhi and Tang 2019). Some global firms, such as Nike, Apple, Patagonia and Boohoo, have started disclosing their tier-1 suppliers to the public. There are many open questions: What are the best ways to increase transparency? Certainly, there has to be demonstrated benefits to the parties that are disclosing such information. Should firms self-disclose their cost structure to the public? Should firms disclose compensation to their employees? Would compensation transparency improve perceived pay fairness?

Certification has also been used as a means to ensure fair trade and fair pay practices. To compete for environmentally and socially conscious consumers, the number of certification labels has mushroomed over the years. When consumers suffer from *label fatigue,* the differentiating value of Fair Trade has diminished. Consequently, some firms refused to pay the extra premium as explained earlier and developed their own in-house certification. For example, Mondelez (parent company of Cadbury and Toblerone) shifted away from Fair Trade certification and developed its in-house certification scheme called "Cocoa Life" in 2017 after Nestlé launched its own "Cocoa Plan" in 2013. Not satisfied by Fair Trade's certification which does not address environmental concerns, Starbucks created their own C.A.F.E. program to certify their suppliers. Without an independent agent to establish fair supply chain practices, there is concern about self-interest after the public was shocked to learn that Boeing self-certified its own planes (Tang and Zimmerman 2009). When can self-certification work? How does its effectiveness differ from external certification? Will consumer care and trust self-certification?

Monitoring and tracking a firm to see if it provided fair pay is not sufficient. It may be best supplemented by incentive solutions. Long-term contractual commitments or more generous contract terms from buyers can also help promote fair pay practice at the factories (Kuruvilla 2021). The Starbucks C.A.F.E. practice provided incentives, in the form of premium pricing and training, for farmers who complied with the sustainable farming practice. Tang et al. (2016) showed that incentives can entice farmers to comply with sustainable farming practices in Italy. Similarly, Maxport's factory in Vietnam was able to work with trade union representatives to modify worker' incentives and bonuses, and the resulting productivity improvements boosted the take-home pay of workers by 21% year after year (Chua 2021c). Negative incentives, in the form of penalty, can also be used. In June 2021, Germany's parliament passed a supply chain act that is intended to penalize firms (up to 2% of their annual global revenue) if their supply chain partners at any level violated human rights and environment regulations (Dai and Tang 2021). The challenging research questions are: what kind of incentive schemes work well, should governments be involved, and what are the mechanisms in which the incentive schemes can be fairly applied?

Table 2 summarizes the research topics and the research questions for each of the topics.

Table 2 Research topics and questions

Broad issues	Research topics	Research questions
Understanding key relationships	Fairness and industry characteristics	• What industries exhibit more unfair practices? • What kind of unfair practices were observed in different industries? • What are the characteristics of the industries that led to the above differences? • What kind of policies or measures can be inferred as potentially useful for the different industries?
	Expanded view of fair pay	• What would increase the morale and satisfaction of a workforce besides pay? • In what ways can the expanded elements of fair "pay" be delivered? • What are the links between satisfied workforce and productivity?
	Linking fair trade and fair pay	• Is fair trade positively linked to fair pay? • What specific unfair trade practices would lead to the worst unfair pay practices? • Are companies that practice fair pay also sound fair trade partners?
	Values and costs	• Can we quantify, empirically, the different dimensions of the strategic value of fair supply chain practices? • What are costs of unfair practices? • What is the time frame when values and costs can be observed?
Instruments to improve fairness	Consortium for implementation	• What are the nature of the consortiums that seemed to be more effective in improving fairness practices? • Why were some agreements by consortiums short-lived, or some lasted longer?
	Increasing transparency	• What are the best ways to increase transparency? • Should firms self-disclose their cost structure to the public? • Should firms disclose compensation to their employees? • Would compensation transparency improve perceived pay fairness?
	Certification	• What are the comparative effectiveness of external vs. self-certification? • When can self-certification improve fairness? • Will consumer care or trust self-certification?
	Use incentives to encourage fair pay	• What kind of incentive schemes work well to induce fair pay? • Can an incentive scheme create unintended consequences that may lead to other positive or negative behaviors? • Should governments be involved?

5 Conclusion

In this chapter, we have examined fair price from the perspective of the firm's treatment of consumers, fair trade from the perspective of the buyer treating its suppliers, and fair pay from the perspective of the firm's treatment of employees. We have described some potential definitions and measurements of fairness and discussed the underlying challenges and opportunities for firms that are committed to improve supply chain fairness. Also, we have proposed various open research questions for further exploration.

In addition to the issues discussed in the chapter, there are other perspectives that we have not considered. First, fair price is about whether the merchant sets a fair price to the consumer. The opposite perspective is whether the consumer has treated the merchant fairly. Second, while we focus on whether buyers have treated suppliers fairly, suppliers can also treat their buyers unfairly and even unethically. Third, fair pay is about how employers treat their employees. On the other hand, disgruntled employees may treat their employers unfairly by making unfounded negative claims or accusations (see Chen et al. 2022 for a detailed discussion on these issues).

Finally, we have focused on the fairness issues in the traditional supply chain context. Our proposed framework can nevertheless be extended to study the fairness issues in service industries, such as unfair treatment of platform workers (Feng 2020) and unfair labor scheduling in food services (Kamalahmadi et al. 2021), to name a few. We hope that this chapter could serve as a catalyst to initiate and stimulate more follow-on discussions and studies on fair price, fair trade, and fair pay in supply chains as well as in service industries, leading to positive changes that benefit all stakeholders involved.

References

Akerlof GA (1982) Labor contracts as partial gift exchange. Q J Econ 97(4):543–569

Avi-Itzhak B, Levy H (2004) On measuring fairness in queues. Adv Appl Probab 36:919–936

Caro F, Chintapalli P, Rajaram K, Tang CS (2018) Improving supplier compliance through joint and shared audits with collective penalty. Manuf Serv Oper Manag 20(2):363–380

Chen L, Lee HL (2017) Sourcing under supplier responsibility risk: the effects of certification, audit, and contingency payment. Manag Sci 63(9):2795–2812

Chen L, Lee HL (2021) Supply chain compliance. In: Daniel Sokol D, van Rooij B (eds) Cambridge handbook of compliance. Cambridge University Press, Cambridge

Chen L, Yao S, Zhu K (2020) Responsible sourcing under supplier-auditor collusion. Manuf Serv Oper Manag 22(6):1234–1250

Chen L, Lee HL, Tang CS (2022) Supply chain fairness. Prod Oper Manag. Forthcoming

Chintapalli P, Disney SM, Tang CS (2017) Coordinating supply chains via advance-order discounts, minimum order quantities, and delegations: the case of two manufacturers. Prod Oper Manag 26(12):2175–2186

Chua JM (2021a) Pandemic cuts put garment workers through "unimaginable human sorrow." Sourcing Journal. July 22

Chua JM (2021b) Boohoo suppliers "getting creative" in hiding pay abuses. Sourcing Journal. August 5
Chua JM (2021c) How two factories achieved a "living wage" for supply chain workers. Sourcing Journal. September 2
Chua JM (2021d) Purchasing practices need to change, suppliers say this is how. Sourcing Journal. September 16
Colquitt JA (2001) On the dimensionality of organisational justice: a construct validation of a measure. J Appl Psychol 86(3):386–400
Corbineau G (2021) Garment workers' "severance theft" exceeds US$500m. Just Style. April 12
Dai T, Tang CS (2021) Integrating ESG measures and supply chain management: research opportunities in the post-pandemic era. Service Science. Forthcoming
Dean S (2021) A broken supply chain isn't a problem for the logistics industry. It's a money making opportunity. Los Angeles Times. November 26
Fehr E, Kirchsteiger G, Riedl A (1993) Does fairness prevent market clearing? An experimental investigation. Q J Econ 108(2):437–459
Feng E (2020) For China's overburdened delivery workers, the customer - and app - is always right. NPR. https://www.npr.org/2020/12/01/938876826/for-chinas-overburdened-delivery-workers-the-customer-and-app-is-always-right. Accessed 25 Nov 2021
Friedman A (2022) GOTS challenges NYT expose on role in India's organic cotton scandal. Sourcing Journal. February 15
Hackenberg J (2021) Brands, you need to listen to the conscious consumer of the future. Forbes. April 29, 2021. https://www.forbes.com/sites/jonquilhackenberg/2021/04/29/brands-you-need-to-listen-to-the-conscious-consumer-of-the-future/?sh=73cbdadc1d46. Accessed 17 July 2021
Hornibrook S, Fearne A, Lazzarin M (2008) Exploring the association between fairness and organizational outcomes in supply chain relationships. Int J Retail Distrib Manag 37(9):790–803
Kamalahmadi M, Yu Q, Zhou Y-P (2021) Call to duty: just-in-time scheduling in a restaurant chain. Manag Sci 67(11):6751–6781
Karnani A (2007) The mirage of marketing to the bottom of the pyramid: how the private sector can help alleviate poverty. Calif Manag Rev 49(4):90–111
Kraft T, Valdes L, Zheng Y (2017) Supply chain visibility and social responsibility: investigating consumers' behaviors and motives. Manuf Serv Oper Manag 20(4):617–636
Kuruvilla S (2021) Private regulation of labor standards in global supply chains: problems, progress, and prospects. Cornell University Press, Ithaca, NY
Lee HL (2008) Embedding sustainability: lessons from the front line. Int Commer Rev 8(1):10–20
Lee HL (2021) Supply chain with a conscience. Prod Oper Manag 30(3):815–820
Lee HL, Tang CS (2018) Socially and environmentally responsible value chain innovations: new operations management research opportunities. Manag Sci 64(3):983–996
Lee HL, Over K, Tang CS (2013a) Creating shared value at Nestle, Supply Chain Management World Case Study. Stanford University and UCLA Case
Lee HL, Tang CS, Masood J (2013b) MobiVi: establishing credit lending, micro donations, and allied services in Vietnam using telecom technologies. Stanford Graduate School of Business Case #: GS82-PDF-ENG
Li Q, Tang CS (2021) Unlocking the value of innovative selling: information and options. Manag Bus Rev. Forthcoming
Lim WS, Mak V, Tang CS, Raghabendra KC (2021) Adopting cost transparency as a marketing strategy: analytical and experimental exploration. Working paper, UCLA Anderson School of Management
Liu X, Luo L, Chen L, Choi T (2021) Recover to discover the new normal: a case study of automotive supply chain restoration after a complete shutdown due to COVID-19. Working paper. Cornell University
McCoy JH, Lee HL (2014) Using fairness models to improve equity in health delivery fleet management. Prod Oper Manag 23(6):965–977

Mohan B, Buell RW, John LK (2020) Lifting the veil: the benefit of cost transparency. Mark Sci 39(6):1105–1121

Page P (2021) Container shipping prices skyrocketed as rush to move goods picks up. Wall Street Journal. July 5

Putre L (2020) Which automotive OEM is in the best position for recovery?, July 24. https://www.industryweek.com/supply-chain/media-gallery/21134925/which-automotive-oem-is-in-the-best-position-for-recovery. Accessed 4 Sep 2021

Sani M (2021) Why global unions are severing ties with Bangladesh RSC. Sourcing Journal. May 14

Shen M, Sun Y (2021) Strengthening supply chain resilience during COVID-19: a case study on JD.com. Working paper, University of Hong Kong

Shoenthal A (2018) What exactly is fair trade, and why should we care? Forbes. December 14, 2018. https://www.forbes.com/sites/amyschoenberger/2018/12/14/what-exactly-is-fair-trade-and-why-should-we-care/?sh=e499de07894c. Accessed 17 July 2021

Sinha I (2000) Cost transparency: the net's real threat to prices and brands. Harv Bus Rev. March–April Issue

Sodhi M, Tang CS (2014) Supply chain research opportunities with the poor as suppliers or distributors in developing countries. Prod Oper Manag 23(9):1483–1494

Sodhi M, Tang CS (2019) Research opportunities in supply chain transparency. Prod Oper Manag 28(12):2946–2959

Tang CS (2018) Socially responsible supply chains in emerging markets: some research opportunities. J Oper Manag 57(1):1–10

Tang CS, Babich V (2014) Using social and economic incentives to discourage Chinese suppliers from product adulteration. Bus Horiz 57(4):497–508

Tang CS, Yang A (2020) Financial supply chain in the Covid-19 pandemic: fuel or wildfire? Forbes. April 30, 2020. https://www.forbes.com/sites/lbsbusinessstrategyreview/2020/04/30/financial-supply-chain-in-the-covid-19-pandemic-fuel-or-wildfire/?sh=730211ea6346. Accessed 18 July 2021

Tang CS, Zimmerman J (2009) Managing new product development and supply chain risks: the Boeing 787 case. Supply Chain Forum: Int J 10(2):74–86

Tang CS, Sodhi M, Formentini M (2016) An analysis of partially-guaranteed-price contracts between farmers and agri-food companies. Eur J Oper Res 254(3):1063–1073

Taylor G (2021) Serai debuts supply-chain traceability solution amid Xinjiang scrutiny. Sourcing Journal. January 28

Wicker A, Schmall E, Raj S, Paton E (2022) That organic cotton T-shirt may not be as organic as you think. The New York Times. February 13

Part III
Breakthrough Performances

Performance-Based Contracting: Past, Present, and Future

Sang-Hyun Kim, Jose A. Guajardo, and Serguei Netessine

Abstract In commemorating Morris's illustrious research career, in this chapter, we examine the genesis and legacy of the research on Performance-Based Contracting, the subject Morris focused on in the years since 2004. Based on the written notes and voice recordings from the early days of research, we provide first-hand accounts of how the research got its start, memorable anecdotes, and the process through which research was developed and conducted. We then discuss the impact of our early research effort by reviewing some of the relevant articles that have appeared in the operations management literature since our collaboration started. The chapter concludes with a discussion of the current state of performance-based contracting in practice, how it may evolve in the future, and what we learned in the process of developing this project.

Keywords Aerospace and defense · Performance-based contracts · Product-as-a-service · Servicization · Spare parts inventory

1 The Beginning

It was fall of 2004 when we had the first discussion about a new research project on Performance-Based Contracting (PBC) which, unbeknownst to us at the time, led to a journey that proved to become a major part of our academic careers and which had a significant impact on the academic literature in operations management (OM).

S.-H. Kim (✉)
Yale School of Management, Yale University, New Haven, CT, USA
e-mail: sang.kim@yale.edu

J. A. Guajardo
Haas School of Business, University of California at Berkeley, Berkeley, CA, USA
e-mail: jguajardo@berkeley.edu

S. Netessine
The Wharton School of Business, University of Pennsylvania, Philadelphia, PA, USA
e-mail: netessin@wharton.upenn.edu

H. Lee et al. (eds.), *Creating Values with Operations and Analytics*, Springer Series in Supply Chain Management 19, https://doi.org/10.1007/978-3-031-08871-1_6

Back then, Morris was splitting his time between the Wharton School and MCA Solutions, a software company based in Philadelphia that he had co-founded with Vipul Agrawal, one of many distinguished students that Morris advised over the years at Wharton. Serguei was into his third year as an assistant professor, and Sang had just completed his first year of his doctoral program. Jose joined the research team a couple of years later.

Morris first learned about the concept of PBC through his contacts at Lockheed Martin, one of MCA Solutions' customers. Lockheed was using MCA Solutions software system that analyzed and recommended spare parts usage and procurement, based on the multi-echelon, multi-indenture spare parts inventory optimization algorithms that he, Vipul, and others had developed based on their research and prior projects. Lockheed management was grappling with the implications of a new Department of Defense (DoD) initiative called Performance-Based Logistics (PBL; because of its importance in military procurement, "logistics" replaced "contracting"). PBL was to become the standard protocol for materials procurement in after-sales repair and maintenance services. The core premise of PBL was that the DoD would pay a contractor for actual mission-readiness performance, such as realized uptime or availability of an aircraft fleet, instead of the resources (like spare parts) consumed to deliver performance. Stakes were high for Lockheed, as it had been recently selected as the system integrator ("prime") for the Joint Strike Fighter (JSF) program under which the next-generation stealth fighter jet F-35 Lightning II was to be designed, produced, and maintained by Lockheed and its subcontractors. As JSF was the first major DoD program that required PBL for after-sales product support, there were many unknowns and speculations.

Serguei had heard about PBL from Morris in passing, but it did not occur to him initially that the idea could be converted to academic research, although it seemed more like an interesting application. Sang, after completing his first year summer paper with Serguei on a procurement problem based on game-theoretic analysis, was on the lookout for a new project with direct practical relevance, given his industry experience before enrolling in the PhD program. So when the subject of PBL ("something about contracting in the defense industry") came up during a conversation between Serguei and Sang, it sounded like an opportunity worth exploring.

Soon afterwards the three of us sat in Morris's office. Morris was familiar with Sang's summer research, and the conversation started with how the model was developed and how it could be improved. Morris also had an opinion on the style of research:

> Morris: [Your approach to this problem has been] trying to find a situation where the model could point you towards looking at a real-world problem that has some of these features and probably other features that you haven't thought about. So, in a sense, you guys invented this problem out of thin air.
>
> Serguei: Well . . .
>
> Morris: I'm being harsh! [I know] you invented it based upon the literature. You read the literature, and said, this and this have never been put together, and if you put all that together,

that's new, therefore it's innovative, therefore it's a contribution. And a priori it seems interesting because it does relate to, in a general way, the stuff that people have talked about, and it's managerially relevant, so let's do it. And voila, you did it! That's one way to go, and you could continue it that way. But another way is to say, well, there are other problems, something like this that are out there, that are not just thought about but actually exist. And if we go look at those problems, what do we see? I will make a prediction that you won't see exactly this model, but you will see something that maybe inspires to you to come up with a related or new model... That line of research is also a possibility. But it has to be something that you are interested in doing.

Sang: Well, for me, I'd be most interested in the problems that come up in the real world. I guess one hurdle that we've faced was how we get those stories [that lead to research problems].

Morris: You mean access to them.

Sang: Yes.

Morris: That's not a problem.

(With laughter) Serguei: It's not a problem for Morris!

Morris went on to describe what he had heard from Lockheed and some of the features that he thought could be developed as a formal model. He specifically mentioned the pricing mechanism called Cost Plus: a supplier is guaranteed to be paid a price that is equal to the cost of providing a product or a service plus some margin, negotiated up front with a buyer. In essence it is a reimbursement mechanism, widely used in government procurement and healthcare. The problem with Cost Plus, Morris explained, is that it provides a supplier with little incentive to be efficient in its operations: "depending on how the contract is written, the supplier may like to increase its cost." Despite its bad reputation, Cost Plus is widely used in environments where cost is difficult to measure because, for example, of uncertainty related to development of new or very complicated products. Many DoD contracts are based on Cost Plus precisely because of this reason, especially for newly developed weapon systems.

PBL, on the other hand, had potential to alleviate the incentive issue that plagues Cost Plus and other traditional contracting approaches (see Fig. 1; this point will be elaborated below), but in order for PBL to become a practical contractual mechanism, there should be a good estimate of system characteristics such as failure rate and cost of repairs that serve as a basis of performance-based payments. Unfortunately, these can be estimated only *after* the system has been in operation for a number of years and the fleet size has been expanded to provide enough data points; for a completely new program like JSF, Lockheed lacked such information that would allow for structuring a performance-based contract, despite the DoD's mandate for PBL. Morris's idea was that the ideal contractual relationship between Lockheed and the DoD could be some combination of Cost Plus and PBL, with the former more emphasized during the initial phase of the program when there is great cost uncertainty, transitioning toward the latter as the program matures.

These insights offered a starting point, but it was clear that more information needed to be collected. Thus, the conversation shifted to how it could be done. The

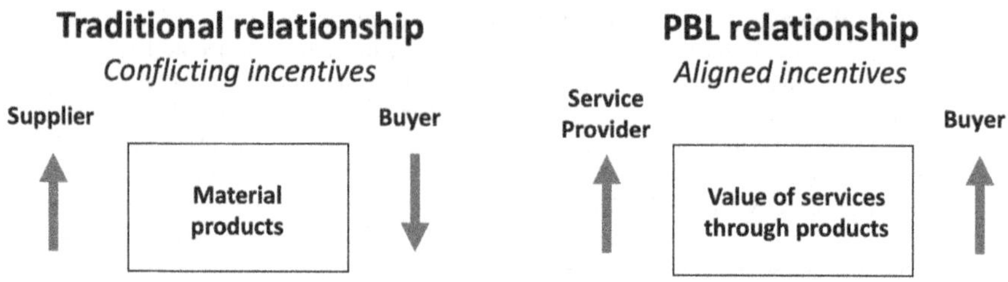

Fig. 1 Incentive alignment under PBL

model that Morris had in mind was the experience of Justin Ren, at that time the most recent doctoral student of his, who had spent 9 months at an Intel facility in rural part of Arizona collecting data on demand forecast sharing between a supplier and a buyer which ended up providing Intel's senior management with managerial insights for policy implementation, while at the same time resulted in an academic paper. "We don't want to be consultants, but we want to get our hands dirty with data," said Morris. Sang, being single and enjoying the city lifestyle, privately dreaded the suggestion of potentially spending months in a remote location.

In the following months, we engaged deeply with Lockheed management. With other commitments on both ends the progress was slow in the beginning, until March 2005 when the representatives from Lockheed's aftermarket division paid a visit to Wharton and presented their business challenge to us. The following is the description of "business case" identified from that meeting:[1]

> Under PBL, the customer determines contract terms based on the usage of an aircraft (which could include a component base on $ per flying hour) subject to a performance target (e.g., % availability). This overall aircraft usage, however, is linked to a variety of heterogeneous usage metrics that apply at the subsystem and component levels. For example, avionic system performance is measured in power on time, whereas engine performance is measured in engine cycles. Lockheed is interested in a methodology that allows for the breakdown of overall aircraft usage into sub-system and component usages, which in turn can be used as a basis for determining the system price in combination with suppliers' price/cost/performance information.

The problem statement sounded daunting, especially from a modeling perspective. There were too many moving parts: usage allocation, risk sharing, availability constraint, heterogeneity, multi-echelon structure, pricing, etc. (see Fig. 2). How do all of these fit into the stylized optimal contracting framework developed by economists? How does the contracting dimension fit into the spare parts inventory optimization framework that Morris has focused on in his research and his work at MCA Solutions? To collect relevant data, where should we look and who do we talk to?

[1] Meeting log "Problem statement based on discussion with Lockheed Martin, 3/28/05."

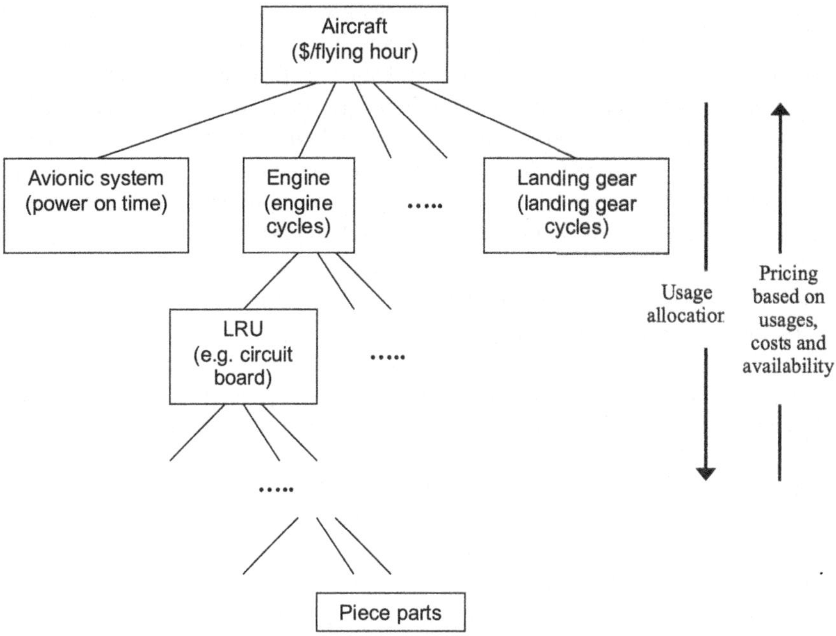

Fig. 2 Description of "business case" identified in the meeting with Lockheed Martin representatives in March 2005

2 Model Development

From the beginning, the focus was on collecting data. Through MCA Solutions, a limited set of operational data were available, but a meaningful analysis would require information on contracts and other parameters that defined the problem. Numerous follow-up meetings with Lockheed took place, which every time led us to different parts of the company to inquire. Because PBL was so new and so entangled with many different aspects of the weapon system procurement business, it was difficult to access someone with enough knowledge that could help us advance the project. Sensing that data collection would be a time-consuming process (that might press against the timeline for Serguei's promotion and Sang's job market plans down the road), while waiting for the data we decided to go ahead and develop a theoretical model that captures key features of the problem we were told by then. Although we were deviating from Morris's initial suggestion to "go where data would lead you to," we felt that enough good stories emerged from the conversations that could become a basis of an interesting paper.

It is important to recall the backdrop that gave rise to our approach to modeling. The field of OM went through a major transformation at the turn of the new millennium. A new breed of researchers armed with the tools and ideas imported from microeconomics started reinterpreting the traditional OM research topics through the game-theoretic lens, shifting focus toward issues such as competition among firms, incentive design, contracting, and information asymmetry. This was a departure from the single-entity (monopolistic), tactical-level optimal decision-making paradigm that dominated the field in the preceding decades. Gerard Cachon and Martin Lariviere wrote pioneering articles that laid the foundation for countless other works that appeared afterwards. Such a seismic change was later followed by the introduction of econometric analysis of operational problems which eventually led to an exponential growth of empirical research in OM. Much of the innovations in these new research directions were taking place at Wharton. Game-theoretic analysis was en vogue, and it was the perfect tool for investigating our problem because the role of incentives was at its core.

The key challenge was how to "marry" two very distinct modeling frameworks that were simultaneously important in analyzing the problem. To represent the traditional business logic of managing assets for after-sales support for products like aircraft, models developed for spare parts inventory optimization were the most relevant. The natural starting point was the METRIC (multi-echelon technique for recoverable item control) model, developed in the 1960s by Craig Sherbrooke for the U.S. Air Force. Not surprisingly, the model lacked any element of incentives or contracting, an essential feature of our problem. Those elements would have to come from the economics literature, in particular the principal–agent framework built on the idea of designing an optimal contracting mechanism. The two frameworks could not have been farther apart: in contrast to the METRIC model that was developed to compute item requirements for thousands of spare parts across multiple layers of locations in a dynamic, stochastic environment (but without considerations of how prices are determined in a supplier–buyer relationship), the usual variants of principal–agent (moral hazard) model wrapped all such complexities in a single stylized random variable while highlighting how a buyer could devise a utility-maximizing contract that shapes the incentive of a supplier to elicit the desired level of "effort." Reconciling the two frameworks required compromises on both sides, in the name of mathematical tractability. This meant adopting a barebones version of the METRIC model, stripping away the multi-echelon aspects and other complexities but retaining the essential features like system availability constraint, and tweaking the model to include cost uncertainty and a measure of risk aversion that would allow us to incorporate the notion of risk sharing under Cost Plus contracting, while adding the incentive compatibility and individual rationality constraints.

The outcome of this Frankenstein-esque effort was a highly stylized yet rich enough (and also "cute") model that allowed us to analyze and answer key questions that we set out. In particular, the model predicted that the optimal contract would evolve from Cost Plus to PBL as the program matures, exactly as hypothesized by Morris in our first meeting. It also offered a conceptual framework for how to structure a PBL contract and how to allocate system-level availability constraints into subsystem-level requirements under PBL. Most importantly, the model highlighted the incentive alignment advantage of PBL. The work, titled

"Performance Contracting in After-Sales Service Supply Chains," was eventually published in *Management Science* (Kim et al. 2007).

Although the output of this paper was not as prescriptive as we had originally hoped—as articulated in our "business case" document—the managerial insights derived from the analysis seemed to resonate with Lockheed management and other stakeholders in the defense industry. In February 2006, we presented the findings of the paper in the Wharton-Stanford Service Supply Chain Forum, a practitioner-oriented conference that Morris and Hau Lee organized every year. In the audience were representatives from commercial and defense aerospace companies as well as military generals (who particularly enjoyed learning about military contracts from a guy with a strong Russian accent). Our presentation generated healthy conversations with not just Lockheed but also other defense and commercial companies who were interested in collaborating with us for joint studies. This set off our journey in search of PBC research data.

3 Planes, Trains, Automobiles, and Aircraft Engines

Inspired by the JSF project, starting in summer of 2006, we engaged with other major players in the aerospace and defense industry, including: BAE Systems, Bell Helicopter, Boeing, Rolls-Royce, Sikorsky, and the U.S. Navy. These activities were supported by a rather large grant from the US Air Force which we received in collaboration with the University of Tennessee which has large military educational and research projects. We made numerous visits to their offices in Dallas Fort-Worth, Indianapolis, Philadelphia, and Washington D.C., presenting the findings of our research and exchanging ideas on how PBC would impact their businesses. It was an exciting time. Three of us drove to Washington D.C. in Serguei's minivan (after dusting off cheerios on the seats left by his daughter) for a follow-up meeting with Lockheed. Amtrak rides to the D.C. area enabled our engagement with Boeing. On our way to a meeting at the Naval Inventory Control Point outside of Philadelphia, Serguei and Sang found out that Morris liked to drive fast in his BMW. In that meeting we also learned that government organizations like the U.S. Navy had a mindset very different from that of commercial enterprises: "It is illegal for us to go bankrupt," we were told. We flew together to Indianapolis to meet with managers at Rolls-Royce, complemented with a tour of the company's aircraft engine factory where we witnessed Toyota manufacturing principles in action. Sang spent a few days in Fort-Worth at a Bell Helicopter office, confined in a cubicle except for bathroom breaks (due to security clearance restriction) rummaging through the company database for PBC-related contract clauses. By the time we completed 2 or 3 trips, we became accustomed to introducing ourselves as a team of researchers with suspicious backgrounds for a defense-themed project: one from Korea, another from Russia, and the other one from Canada.

We approached the organizations with a grand vision of the study we aimed to conduct. We prepared a 7-page document that included questionnaires on how each organization's PBC program was structured and a list of desired data fields that could be plugged into our empirical analysis. After spending weeks and months speaking with different managers and examining numerous spreadsheets, we were left with a dejected feeling: the information we had gathered did not point to a well-defined research problem. In some cases the data were not adequate enough to test our hypotheses, and in other cases the stories that data seemed to be telling us were not academically interesting ones. But in most cases the data were not tracked at all. As the Government Accountability Office concluded a bit later (U.S. Government Accountability Office 2008), the implementation of PBL contracts in the Defense industry was not supported by data because suppliers did not bother to track data at a level that was detailed enough.

These setbacks led us to, once again, develop new theoretical models in parallel with the efforts for data collection. Even though our push for data analysis was going slowly, a big benefit of engaging with practitioners to get data was we were hearing many stories that inspired new ideas for analytical models. Often, 15 min with practitioners was enough to come up with an idea. Among them was the issue of how PBC implementation impacted product reliability. In most of the models addressing spare parts inventory management, including METRIC, product/component failure rates were assumed to be given exogenously because they are regarded as input parameters for computing inventory levels, the main decision variable of interest. Under the PBC environment, however, the altered incentive structure impacts not only the decision on inventory levels but what gives rise to the need for inventories in the first place, namely the reliability decisions that determine the rate of failures. Reliability can be set during a product design phase (which fits Lockheed's situation because F-35 was being prototyped at that time) or through product reengineering during deployment. Enhancing reliability requires significant investments and has ramifications to after-sales product support planning; therefore, it was not a simple matter of "the higher the reliability, the better."

What was unique about the reliability angle was that, when coupled with inventory consideration, it shed a light on a skewed incentive inherent in the product support business model. Because the companies in this industry—in the pre-PBC environment—generated most of their revenue by selling expensive spare parts and maintenance services that are needed after product malfunctions, their revenue would grow if the product to be serviced failed more often. In other words, the incentive was put in place so that product support service providers preferred a less reliable product. Since in many cases it is the same company that designs the product which also provides after-sales services (due to near-monopoly for services for specialized products in the aerospace and defense industry), in theory, it would offer the least reliable product to its customers who would then have to spend excessive amount to acquire spare parts inventory to meet its product availability requirement. Worse yet, because a significant part of the fleet would always be "out of order," more products would have to be acquired to maintain proper fleet availability.

This insight led to another modeling effort. The analysis showed that PBC had the potential to bring a win–win outcome that benefits both the service provider and the buyer by incentivizing the provider to design a reliable product that fails

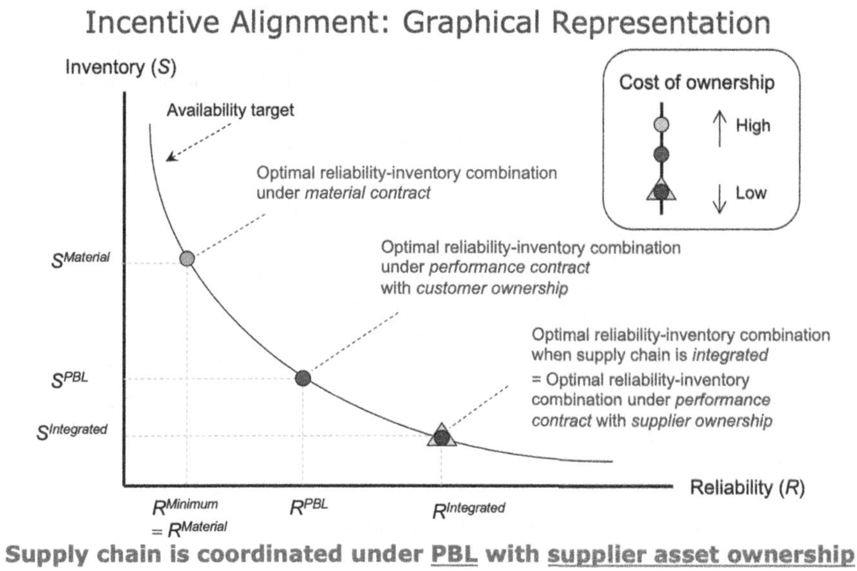

Fig. 3 Graphical illustration of optimal reliability-inventory investments and the total cost of ownership under the traditional ("materials") contract vs. PBC

less often, which in turn lowers the expenditure on spare parts (Kim et al. 2017). An additional dimension was the question of who has ownership of spare inventory assets: if it is the provider that owns and manages spare parts—hence converting the service provider into a "total solution provider"—our analysis predicted that the first-best outcome can be attained. (See the summary of insights in Fig. 3, which illustrates how the traditional contractual mechanism ("materials contract") and PBL under different assumptions about asset ownership structure give rise to different combinations of reliability and inventory investments.) Perhaps not surprisingly, the suggestion that an organization like DoD could achieve better efficiency by transferring at least some of its asset ownership to suppliers was controversial among the industry participants of the 2007 Wharton-Stanford Service Supply Chain Forum, where we presented our theoretical findings. Despite that concern, the presentation generated many conversations that eventually led to our insights featured in a report by the U.S. Government Accountability Office that evaluated the PBL programs run by the DoD at that time (U.S. Government Accountability Office 2008).

As luck would have it, while we were focusing on the reliability-inventory angle of PBC, a dataset that suited to the subject became available, but not exactly where we were looking, namely, military suppliers. It came from the civil part of Rolls-Royce, which provided us with years' worth of data on its aircraft engine maintenance and overhaul history. Each engine unit was associated with either traditional Time and Materials Contracts (T&MC) or the Power by the Hour contract (the term trademarked by Rolls-Royce, designating its PBC program). The dataset did not reveal spare parts usages, but it was rich enough for us to test the base hypothesis that products under PBC exhibit higher reliability, as predicted in our theoretical model. The timing was also right to add a new member to our group, Jose, then a doctoral student at Wharton with extensive experience in empirical methods already.

In the Rolls-Royce dataset for commercial aircrafts, there were two different types of contracts: T&MC and PBC. The main distinction between the two was the basis of compensation to the supplier (Rolls-Royce). Under PBC a customer agrees to pay a fee in proportion to aircraft flying hours, which in turn is affected by the availability of all major aircraft subsystems (including engines). Flying hours—a key measure of product utilization in the aerospace industry—depends heavily on subsystem reliability as well as other factors such as the stocking levels of spare parts inventory and the speed of repair at maintenance depots. Under T&MC, in contrast, the supplier is compensated for the amount of resources consumed (such as spare parts and labor) whenever product maintenance is required. The ultimate impact of contract choices on engine reliability was far from obvious, however.

The dataset included records of engine removals (the event that signifies a major repair or maintenance) over a five-year period, including both planned and unplanned removals. The removals served as a proxy for the variable of our interest, product reliability. In developing our econometric model, the main challenge was to account for the endogeneity of contract choices. Indeed, contracts are not randomly assigned; instead they are chosen as a result of decision-making. Hence, ignoring such endogeneity would lead to biased estimates. To account for this we developed a two-stage econometric model in which, in the first stage, a contract choice model was estimated, and in the second stage, the impact of contract choices on product performance was estimated, with the first-stage results incorporated.

Our results would ultimately illustrate the importance of accounting for the endogeneity of contract choices: we found product reliability to be higher by 25%–40% under PBC compared to under T&MC, but this effect was only present when the endogeneity of contract choice was taken into account. We presented these results to practitioners on a number of occasions. Oftentimes, explaining the "endogeneity" component would occupy a significant part of the conversation. For example, in our 2008 report to Rolls-Royce, the first key finding from the statistical analysis we reported was as follows: "Endogeneity is present since contract choice by the customer and various attributes that are related to engine reliability are related. The results indicated that ignoring such interactions can lead to erroneous conclusions concerning the impact of contract type on reliability."

The work, titled "Impact of performance-based contracting on product reliability: An empirical study," was eventually published in *Management Science* (Guajardo et al. 2012).

4 Continuation and Impact

By many measures, our research on PBC turned out to be highly impactful and became a significant part of our research careers. According to Google Scholar as of September 2021, with the citation count of 641, our first paper on PBC published in *Management Science* in 2007 is ranked No. 4 among Morris's all-time publications in refereed journals, and No. 1 among the publications by Serguei and Sang. The empirical paper published in *Management Science* in 2012 has a citation count of 262, and is ranked No. 11 among Morris's publications, No. 9 in Serguei's, No. 2 in Sang's, and No. 1 in Jose's. These papers helped Sang and Jose win numerous awards, including Dantzig Dissertation Award (2008) and Juran Dissertation Fellowship Award (2010), not to mention their academic placements at Yale and UC Berkeley. More importantly, our works generated interests among other scholars in OM and related fields, attested by over a thousand publications in various journals from *Management Science* to *Technology Analysis & Strategic Management* that cite our papers on PBC. In this section we review selected articles on PBC that have appeared in the OM literature since we first started our PBL project with Lockheed Martin. (Note this is not meant to be a comprehensive literature review; the articles we review in this section are the ones that, in our view, are most directly related to the spirit and tradition of our research and which developed it in new directions.)

The literature includes the articles whose scopes coincide with our original PBC research, namely those that examine the incentive role of PBC in the context of after-sales maintenance services. A few of them were authored by us in collaboration with colleagues. Kim et al. (2010) focus on another unique feature of the product repair and maintenance businesses: product failures, which drive all service activities, occur sporadically. At a component level of industrial equipment, it is common to encounter at most one occurrence of failure in a year. The intermittency and randomness bring challenges to performance measurements and resource planning, which are exacerbated in the PBC environment because supplier compensation requires unambiguous evaluation of performance outcome. The analysis demonstrated that the seemingly equivalent contract mechanisms, one based on sample average of product downtimes and the other based on cumulative downtimes, may diverge in their influence on the supplier's incentive and that the incentive issue becomes magnified if the product is highly reliable, thus highlighting the importance of agency cost in a nontrivial setting where business activities are driven by infrequent product failures. Bakshi et al. (2015) examined a related issue but from a different perspective. The main focus of this paper is how PBC can be used to alleviate the impact of information asymmetry, in particular how a supplier can signal product reliability to a buyer when the product is so new that the best the buyer can do is to infer the reliability by observing the supplier's spare parts inventory investments in response to contract terms. The authors document conditions under which over- or underinvestment in inventory will arise.

Jain et al. (2013) are one of the closest to our research in terms of the modeling approach and the problem addressed. Like in our papers, the authors of this article studied PBC in the context of equipment repair and restoration. While spare parts inventory was not part of the consideration in this model, it included novel features such as the use of stochastic financial distress model to represent a service provider's contract risk and double-sided moral hazard, i.e., both a service provider and a buyer deal with unverifiable decisions by one another which give rise to the dynamics absent in earlier works. Under these assumptions, the authors concluded that PBC with tiered structure outperforms linear PBC in aligning the incentives. Li et al. (2020) studied the issue of information asymmetry in maintenance contracting, in a manner similar to Bakshi et al. (2015) but in a screening rather than a signaling setting, and found that the lack of access to certain information about the operating environment may give rise to the advantage of implementing the traditional contracting approach as opposed to PBC. In addition, Huber and Spinler (2014) demonstrated the significance of learning effects in maintenance contracting in their numerical study of data from an equipment manufacturer.

Beyond the practices in the aerospace and defense industry from which we got the inspiration for our early research, contracting issues in repair and maintenance come up often in other areas such as healthcare. Chan et al. (2019) evaluated performance of maintenance contracts for medical equipment, based on service records of more than 700 diagnostic body scanners. This empirical study used matching to deal with endogenous contract selection, finding that moving the equipment operator from a basic, pay-per-service plan to a fixed-fee, full-protection plan not only reduces reliability but also increases equipment service costs. They showed that a basic pay-per-service plan can improve performance and reduce costs, in contrast with the findings of our own empirical study (Guajardo et al. 2012). The main difference is that the contract in Guajardo et al. (2012) is based on performance, whereas the one in Chan et al. (2019) is simply "fixed fee" but does not depend on performance. This difference highlights the importance of explicitly tying the contract to performance. In addition, Guajardo et al. (2012) studied both planned and unplanned maintenance events, while Chan et al. (2019) only observed unplanned "reactive" maintenance events. In another healthcare setting, Chen et al. (2021) analyzed the vehicle maintenance contracting practice of Riders for Health, a social enterprise operating in sub-Saharan Africa to deliver healthcare products and services to remote regions. Among the innovations brought by Riders for Health was its use of PBC for repair and maintenance services for the fleet of motorcycles owned by local governments, the main means of deliveries. The authors combined the theory of optimal maintenance with the principal–agent analysis to bring insights into the advantages and disadvantages of different modes of PBC that Riders for Health experimented with. PBC has been used in healthcare not only for maintenance contracting but for general medical services as well. Focusing on patient waiting time as the outcome metric, Jiang et al. (2012) set up a queuing model that incorporates both moral hazard and adverse selection considerations to evaluate the performance of PBC in clinical settings. Also in the healthcare domain, Aswani et al. (2019) studied the Medicare Shared Savings Program (MSSP), which was created under the Patient Protection and Affordable Care Act to control escalating Medicare spending by incentivizing providers to deliver healthcare more efficiently. They used a data set containing the financial performance of providers enrolled in the MSSP, which together accounts for 7 million beneficiaries and more than $70 billion in Medicare spending. Based on maximum likelihood estimation, the authors estimated that introducing performance-based subsidies to the MSSP can boost Medicare savings by up to 40% without compromising provider participation in the MSSP.

PBC has caught the attention of the spare parts inventory optimization community as well. Mirzahosseinian and Piplani (2011) analyzed a repairable spare parts inventory system under PBC with capacity-constrained repair processes. Based on the observation from numerical analyses, the authors concluded that a service provider's focus should be on reliability improvement and repair efficiency instead of inventory investment. Öner et al. (2010) devised an algorithm for optimal component reliability and inventory levels under PBC, demonstrating that it resulted in significant cost reduction compared to non-integrated optimization methods that focus only on inventory levels. The same authors also investigated a component upgrading policy designed to enhance reliability under PBC (Öner et al. 2015). Jin and Tian (2012) similarly investigated the optimal reliability and inventory level optimization under PBC, but for a situation where the size of installed base increases over time which introduces non-stationary dynamics. Nowicki et al. (2012) focused on improving the computational efficiency of the METRIC model-driven approach to meet the requirements from increased adoption of PBC. At the other end of the product lifecycle spectrum is a paper by Hur et al. (2018), who studied the problem of aircraft spare parts management under PBC during the end-of-life phase of fleet operations. For inventory systems other than spare parts, Liang and Atkins (2013) embedded the elements of common service-level agreements (SLA; a form of PBC) in a periodic-review inventory model to analyze how different approaches to configuring SLAs shape strategic behavior, concluding that proportional penalties outperform lump-sum penalties.

On the economics-oriented side of OM studies, our PBC research has been associated with the literature on strategic sourcing management. In their game-theoretic analysis, Roels et al. (2010) examined the environmental characteristics that determine which among fixed-fee, time-and-materials, and performance-based contracts is preferred when a buyer and a vendor produce output through "collaborative services." Sieke et al. (2012) analyzed service level-based supply contracts, evaluating the relative performance of fixed penalty and per-unit penalty schemes and suggesting how to structure the optimal contract parameters. Ning et al. (2018) empirically analyzed contracts for managed print services, using a structural model to conclude that the service provider exhibits significant risk aversion. MacCormack and Mishra (2015) empirically analyzed the interplay between PBC and R&D, using primary data collected from 172 R&D projects. They studied how a contract choice (fixed price, T&MC, and PBC) influenced the relationship between partner integration and partnering performance in R&D projects, finding that greater partner integration is associated with increased project costs for all contract choices but with increased product quality only when using more flexible T&MC or PBC. Their results suggest that while PBC is viewed as a more flexible type of contract, they behave in a manner distinct to other contract types, leading the authors to conclude that the optimal choice of contract in a project may be a hybrid type. Other notable works in this stream of literature that are related to our PBC research include Li (2013) and Zhang et al. (2018).

Finally, our PBC research has brought awareness among scholars and practitioners about the "servicization" business model that underpins PBL, Power by the Hour, and other outcome-driven practices, which hold potential to fundamentally reshape the business relationship between a buyer and a service provider. The idea of servicization is captured by our earlier observation that a win–win outcome can emerge from the use of PBC, in particular with a supplier transformed into a total solution provider who creates value by selling functionality of a product rather than the product itself, shielding its customers from the complexities of delivering services such as management and ownership of inventories. A business model perspective of the insights from our PBL research was discussed in an article titled "Power by the Hour: Can paying only for performance redefine how products are sold and serviced?" (Knowledge@Wharton 2007), which also became a part of the book by Girotra and Netessine (2014) as one example of "business model innovation." Among the quantitative analyses that examine the servicization business model is Kastalli and Van Looy (2013), who presented empirical evidence that a firm adopting the model may face hurdles in translating the immediate efficiency gain from servicization into long-term profitability. In another study, Korkeamäki et al. (2021) categorized firms as an outcome-based service provider if the firm's description includes related terminology (e.g., "power by the hour," "pay for performance," "as-a-service") and found that firms using outcome-based contracts have better profitability than those who do not. One particular feature of servicization that is often studied is its environmental impact, guided by the notion that selling service rather than product should be beneficial to the environment. While Avci et al. (2015) dispute this assertion in the application to electric vehicles, Agrawal and Bellos (2017) and Örsdemir et al. (2019) provide a more nuanced view by identifying the conditions under which it can both enhance profitability and reduce environmental footprint.

5 Recent Developments and Future Directions

As the literature review of the last section shows, PBC has become an established topic of research in the years since we first engaged in our collaboration with Lockheed Martin. In this section we comment on some of the recent developments and opine on the future of PBC research.

One of the most notable developments is a broader acceptance of PBC and the servicization model in a digitally-driven business environment. It is not uncommon these days to hear the terms "outcome-based contract" or "outcome-based pricing" and the Product-as-a-Service (PaaS) business model, a contemporary reincarnation of the servicization idea with an emphasis on digital delivery and management via technologies such as cloud computing and Internet of Things (IoT). The idea has gained much attention as one of the most key enablers of the Industry 4.0 movements.

PaaS was derived from Software-as-a-Service (SaaS) business model that became popular over the last decade as many organizations transitioned from in-house data warehousing to cloud-based solutions, with the advent of services such as Amazon Web Services and Azure by Microsoft. Companies like Salesforce, ServiceNow, Box, and Shopify thrived in this environment, delivering software solutions in the cloud and charging customers on a subscription/usage basis. PaaS is enabled by either offering value-added services for existing fleet of equipment or products that customers own (e.g., General Electric's Predix system that offers remote sensing through IoT devices and analytics capabilities for industrial equipment such as wind turbine) or leasing products with bundled services as a package, as available from many car companies (e.g., Care by Volvo program that offers monthly subscription of selected Volvo models with maintenance and insurance included in one pricing package). Clearly, there are several challenges associated with applying the same concept behind SaaS to physical products. Because physical presence and characteristics may matter as much as the functionalities provided by the product depending on product category, a careful assessment is needed to determine the degree to which PaaS can be pushed. For example, there is a big gap between offering PaaS for a consumer electronics product versus for industrial equipment; the proportion of value derived from functionality alone is likely to be much higher with the latter, making it a better candidate for the PaaS model. Another issue is that subscription pricing is not straightforward because, unlike software, a durable hardware loses value over time and the obsolescence cost would have to be taken into account. Yet another challenge is that companies considering PaaS—many of them traditional manufacturers in B2B space—would have to go through the transition of going from selling products to designing and offering product-service bundles, shifting focus from quarterly revenue generation to customer relationship management by tracking new performance measures like net promoter scores and customer lifetime value. Such a transition impacts not only the revenue model but also internal organizational incentives (e.g., performance of a salesforce team is evaluated on customer churn rate instead of quarterly sales), which many organizations find challenging to deal with.

In many cases PBC is an integral part of PaaS implementation. GE, for example, sets its IoT monetization strategy around outcome-based contracts, creating additional value by optimizing usage efficiency of equipment installed at customer sites using the IoT-enabled sensor data collected in real time, and sharing the gains from efficiency improvements with customers. (Not surprisingly, GE's strategy was modeled after Rolls-Royce's Power by the Hour program; General Electric 2017.) The concept behind PBC has received traction in the insurance industry as well. With increasing availability of data on usage patterns of millions of drivers through smartphones and in-car telematics devices, auto insurance companies are now able to analyze the risk factors more accurately and offer personalized products tailored to each individual, going beyond the traditional demographics-based product offerings (Wall Street Journal 2020). Metromile is one such company that pioneered usage-based car insurance (based on miles driven). Most large insurers now offer discounts to drivers able to demonstrate good driving habits, whereby data is obtained from mobile phones. The same mobile phone devices can be then used to improve driving behavior through tips, nudges, and other short messages that drivers receive in real time (Choudhary et al. 2021). Solar energy is another sector in which PaaS has gained significant popularity, where the model is commonly referred to as third-party ownership (TPO). Adopters of solar energy can opt for direct ownership or TPO, which takes different forms such as leases and power purchase agreements (the latter based on performance). Interestingly, this sector is often subject to state subsidies, which sometimes are also performance-based. One example is the California solar initiative, which for the non-residential sector considered subsidies directly dependent on performance. Guajardo (2018) analyzed how the ownership structure affects the performance of solar energy systems in this setting, showing that operational performance—as measured by yield of each solar system—is superior under TPO. This study illustrates the importance of considering the interplay between public policy (e.g., subsidies) and the inherent incentives in contract design, a notion that is applicable in many other sectors.

The increasing availability of granular data also facilitates the implementation of data-driven decision-making in contract design applications related to PBC. This is illustrated by Deprez et al. (2021), who used data analytics to determine how to price full-service maintenance contracts. Their framework first considers a prediction model based on simulated data, which, in combination with data on the history of product failures, preventive maintenance, and their respective cost, can then be used to find out the break-even contract price and evaluate different tariff plans.

6 Concluding Remarks

In this chapter, we documented the journey that we went through during our early careers working on PBC research and discussed its impact and legacy. While the "PBC era" represents only one part of Morris's illustrious career, the backstories and anecdotes told here offer a window into the mind of a pioneer whose curiosity and passion inspired many colleagues and the younger generation of researchers. In closing, we summarize the lessons we learned during our journey that have served us well throughout our careers.

First, we learned that interesting and impactful projects come from practice. As Karl Ulrich at Wharton once put it, "nothing interesting happens in your office." One must get out into the field and talk to practitioners, asking what bothers them and then come up with answers that speak to them. This key learning was shaped by watching how Morris interacted with companies, helping us structure our own interactions with practitioners. This early experience also led to our belief that research we conduct should address needs beyond our need to publish, and that it should include stakeholders beyond academia including the society as a whole (Netessine 2021).

Second, our interactions with companies taught us about the challenges and opportunities of doing "real world research" with field data. We learned that this kind of research is time-consuming, and that it is more of an exception than a rule that an engagement with companies leads to a paper. We had companies promising us data but never delivering it (even when they were compelled to share it by the US government at one point); we had companies delivering us "data" that turned out to be unusable; we had a point person inside a company showing interest and sharing decent data then moving onto another job before we could publish results. Challenges similar to these are common. Yet, the potential reward is enormous once they are overcome, and it is heartening to see the OM community developing appreciation for this type of research.

Third, we learned that an academic can wear many hats and that his or her career becomes more fulfilling when the hats help each other. We watched Morris establishing contacts and engaging with companies for data as a professor and as a CEO, setting up teaching collaborations and inviting them to the conferences he organized to gain insights that would help our modeling effort, and enabling our research by convincing them to support the Wharton Fishman-Davidson Center he directed.

The approach of creating this "virtuous cycle"—research feeding into teaching, then to consulting, then to research funding—has been the model of our pursuit to become impactful researchers.

References

Agrawal VV, Bellos I (2017) The potential of servicizing as a green business model. Manag Sci 63(5):1545–1562

Aswani A, Shen Z-J, Siddiq A (2019) Data-driven incentive design in the Medicare shared savings program. Oper Res 67(4):1002–1026

Avci B, Girotra K, Netessine S (2015) Electric vehicles with a battery switching station: adoption and environmental impact. Manag Sci 61(4):772–794

Bakshi N, Kim S-H, Savva N (2015) Signaling new product reliability with after-sales service contracts. Manag Sci 61(8):1812–1829

Chan TH, de Vericourt F, Besbes O (2019) Contracting in medical equipment maintenance services: an empirical investigation. Manag Sci 65(3):1136–1150

Chen L, Kim S-H, Lee HL (2021) Vehicle maintenance contracting in developing economies: the role of social enterprise. Manuf Serv Oper Manag 23(6):1333–1682

Choudhary V, Shunko M, Netessine S, Koo S (2021) Nudging drivers to safety: evidence from a field experiment. Manag Sci, forthcoming, 2021, 29, 9

Deprez L, Antonio K, Boute R (2021) Pricing service maintenance contracts using predictive analytics. Eur J Oper Res 290(2):530–545

General Electric, The outcome as a service model is on the rise in the power sector. https://www.ge.com/power/transform/article.transform.articles.2017.oct.the-outcome-as-a-service-model. Accessed 4 Mar 2022
Girotra K, Netessine S (2014) The risk-driven business model: four questions that will define your company. Harvard Business Press, Cambridge MA
Guajardo JA (2018) Third-party ownership business models and the performance of solar energy systems. Manuf Serv Oper Manag 20(4):788–800
Guajardo JA, Cohen MA, Kim S-H, Netessine S (2012) Impact of performance-based contracting on product reliability: an empirical study. Manag Sci 58(5):961–979
Huber S, Spinler S (2014) Pricing of full-service repair contracts with learning, optimized maintenance, and information asymmetry. Decis Sci 45(4):791–815
Hur M, Keskin BB, Schmidt CP (2018) End-of-life inventory control of aircraft spare parts under performance based logistics. Int J Prod Econ 204:186–203
Jain N, Hasija S, Popescu DG (2013) Optimal contracts for outsourcing of repair and restoration services. Oper Res 61(6):1295–1311
Jiang H, Pang Z, Savin S (2012) Performance-based contracts for outpatient medical services. Manuf Serv Oper Manag 14(4):654–669
Jin T, Tian Y (2012) Optimizing reliability and service parts logistics for a time-varying installed base. Eur J Oper Res 218(1):152–162
Kastalli IV, Van Looy B (2013) Servitization: disentangling the impact of service business model innovation on manufacturing firm performance. J Oper Manag 31:169–180
Kim S-H, Cohen MA, Netessine S (2007) Performance contracting in after-sales service supply chains. Manag Sci 53(12):1843–1858
Kim S-H, Cohen MA, Netessine S, Veeraraghavan S (2010) Contracting for infrequent restoration and recovery of mission-critical systems. Manag Sci 56(9):1551–1567
Kim S-H, Cohen MA, Netessine S (2017) Reliability or inventory? An analysis of performance-based contracts for product support services. In: Ha A, Tang C (eds) Handbook of information exchange in supply chain management. Springer
Knowledge@Wharton (2007) 'Power by the Hour': can paying only for performance redefine how products are sold and serviced? https://knowledge.wharton.upenn.edu/article/power-by-the-hour-can-paying-only-for-performance-redefine-how-products-are-sold-and-serviced/. Accessed 4 Mar 2022
Korkeamäki L, Kohtamäki M, Parida V (2021) Worth the risk? The profit impact of outcome-based service offerings for manufacturing firms. J Bus Res 131:92–102
Li C (2013) Sourcing for supplier effort and competition: design of the supply base and pricing mechanism. Manag Sci 59(6):1386–1406
Li D, Mishra N, Netessine S (2020) Contracting for product support under information asymmetry. Working paper
Liang L, Atkins D (2013) Designing service level agreements for inventory management. Prod Oper Manag 22(5):1103–1117
MacCormack A, Mishra A (2015) Managing the performance trade-offs from partner integration: implications of contract choice in R&D projects. Prod Oper Manag 24(10):1552–1569
Mirzahosseinian H, Piplani R (2011) A study of repairable parts inventory system operating under performance-based contract. Eur J Oper Res 214(2):256–261
Netessine S (2021) A vision of responsible research in operations management. Manuf Serv Oper Manag 2021(4):8
Ning J, Babich V, Handley J, Keppo J (2018) Risk-aversion and B2B contracting under asymmetric information: evidence from managed print services. Oper Res 66(2):392–408
Nowicki DR, Randall WS, Ramirez-Marquez JE (2012) Improving the computational efficiency of metric-based spares algorithms. Eur J Oper Res 219(2):324–334
Öner KB, Kiesmüller GP, van Houtum GJ (2010) Optimization of component reliability in the design phase of capital goods. Eur J Oper Res 205(3):615–624
Öner KB, Kiesmüller GP, van Houtum GJ (2015) On the upgrading policy after the redesign of a component for reliability improvement. Eur J Oper Res 244(3):867–880

Örsdemir A, Deshpande V, Parlaktürk AK (2019) Is servicization a win-win strategy? Profitability and environmental implications of servicization. Manuf Serv Oper Manag 21(3):479–711
Roels G, Karmarkar US, Carr S (2010) Contracting for collaborative services. Manag Sci 56(5):849–863
Sieke MA, Seifert RW, Thonemann UW (2012) Designing service level contracts for supply chain coordination. Prod Oper Manag 21(4):698–714
U.S. Government Accountability Office (2008) Defense logistics: improved analysis and cost data needed to evaluate the cost effectiveness of Performance Based Logistics. https://www.gao.gov/assets/gao-09-41.pdf. Accessed 4 Mar 2022
Wall Street Journal (2020) Driver data is a help and a hazard for auto insurers. https://www.wsj.com/articles/driver-data-is-a-help-and-a-hazard-for-auto-insurers-11606729983. Accessed 4 Mar 2022
Zhang H, Kong G, Rajagopalan S (2018) Contract design by service providers with private effort. Manag Sci 64(6):2672–2689

Corruption in Large Government Projects Not Only Inflates the Budget But Reduces Managerial Effectiveness

Jimoh Ibrahim, Christoph Loch, and Kishore Sengupta

Abstract Research on operations analytics has focused on the design and execution of processes and projects. For projects in particular, the emphasis is on factors such as plans, stakeholders, and uncertainty; and their effects on the outcomes of projects. Little attention is paid to a variable of considerable importance: ethical behaviour, particularly corruption in large projects. This matters because studies of corruption have shown that corruption inflates project budgets (by sometimes 30%) and thus imposes an unproductive tax. This chapter builds on an original dataset of 38 very large government projects in Nigeria to demonstrate that corruption not only inflates project budgets but also distorts decisions, rendering other project management success drivers less effective. The chapter demonstrates that corruption has negative interactions with the positive effect of project success drivers and illustrates on a detailed case example what these interactions look like in practice.

Keywords Project management · Megaprojects · Government projects · Corruption

1 Introduction

Corruption can be defined as "the sale by government officials of government property for personal gain" (Shleifer and Vishny 1993, p. 599) or "the abuse of entrusted power for private gains" (Adeyemo and Amade 2016, p. 1). Corruption is one of the key issues in public policy. It is a major impediment to the economic development of emerging countries (Loosemore and Lim 2015; Tabish and Jha 2011; Treisman 2007). Corruption is pervasive in large public projects such as the development of infrastructure or social institutions—not only in developing countries, but also to an extent in developed countries.

J. Ibrahim · C. Loch (✉) · K. Sengupta
Cambridge Judge Business School, University of Cambridge, Cambridge, UK
e-mail: ifj21@cam.ac.uk; c.loch@jbs.cam.ac.uk; k.sengupta@jbs.cam.ac.uk

H. Lee et al. (eds.), *Creating Values with Operations and Analytics*, Springer Series in Supply Chain Management 19, https://doi.org/10.1007/978-3-031-08871-1_7

There is a parallel to complex supply chains, where corruption is certainly also highly significant. As in project management, excellent work has focused on system design and operations analytics (the topic of this book), but Cohen and Lee (1989) conceded that one of the key drivers of supply chain design decisions were cultural, language, and skill differences (which includes corruption), and Hausman et al. (2013) indicated that the World Bank's corruption index was a key factor in affecting a company's sourcing or trading decisions.

Corruption is not easy to diagnose without going deep into project documents—interviewees tend to avoid the topic because it is uncomfortable to discuss. Indeed, corruption is difficult to pin down precisely because it is, by definition, opaque, which is exacerbated by the potency of corruption claims (or the dismissal thereof) as a political weapon (Elinoff 2017, p. 588).

Many studies of the effects of corruption in projects have focused on the "extra cost" of bribes. For example, a classic theoretical analysis (Shleifer and Vishny 1993) compared corruption to a "tax". This study concluded that corruption, because it is illegal and secretive (as its proceeds benefit a special interest group rather than the public), is much more costly and damaging than taxes; moreover, weak governments that do not control their agencies tend to suffer more from corruption than strong governments with transparency and processes in place. In an empirical study, Locatelli et al. (2017) examined corruption in large rail projects in Italy, and while the effect of corruption is difficult to quantify, they found strong evidence that it causes additional budget and schedule overruns.

These "cost inflation effects" are certainly important, and they are consistent with our observations—we conducted one interview with a senior project manager of a major contractor (who spoke on the condition of guaranteed anonymity). This person estimated that corruption adds, on average, 30% to the budget of a large government project. This is roughly consistent across studies in multiple countries, such as Olken (2006) or Reinikka and Svensson (2006).

This would be bad enough, but if this were all it would perhaps be a small price to pay if by paying some people off one could assure the smooth execution of the project otherwise. However, the *nature* of corruption can have a significant impact on the economic damage caused by that corruption, above and beyond the financial losses. Bribery payments which are made to unblock projects and services (that are otherwise sound) at inflated prices may be far less damaging than corrupt activities which impact the quality of delivery or the type of projects undertaken (Kenny 2006, p. 17). "The incentives to spend money on building infrastructure rather than operations and maintenance, the incentive to build poor quality infrastructure in the wrong place and the incentives to poorly operate it probably account for the bulk of the negative development impact of corruption" (Kenny 2006, p. 18) (This is also observed by Adeyemo and Amade 2016). Kenny and Søreide (2008) detail evidence of the distinction between "petty corruption" ("small" cost increases from bribes) versus "grand corruption", or the large-scale distortion of decisions because of influencing for private advantage.

In other words, corruption is even more corrosive than its direct effects on budgets because it also *distorts decisions*. For instance, some project goals are downplayed, which benefits the goals of the briber; some stakeholders may be frozen out because others have bribed; and the project design may favour some performance dimensions, which are in the interest of the bribers, over other dimensions. As a result, public projects affected by corruption will drift away from the public benefit purposes that they are supposed to serve; as a result, their value will diminish, resistance from left-out stakeholders may increase, projects become more likely to fail. If they do succeed, they will provide fundamentally diminished value to the public.

This paper develops systematic evidence (not just in case studies but across many projects) for the corrosiveness of corruption, which has been proposed by Kenny (2006), in the context of Nigeria. In 2012, a government study commissioned by President Goodluck Jonathan found that since 1970, 11,886 out of (an estimated) 19,000 government-owned projects had been abandoned across the majority of the 36 states of the federation. This represents an abandonment rate of 63%, or almost two-thirds (Abimbola 2015). While megaprojects are prone to cost overruns of almost 50% across the world (Flyvbjerg 2007, 2014), outright abandonment rates are normally much lower.

In order to examine the reasons, including corruption, the authors have constructed a unique database based on detailed questionnaires from 3 respondents each from 38 large public projects in Nigeria. The 114 detailed questionnaire responses were accompanied by in-depth qualitative case studies on some of the projects. This paper reports on the effect of corruption on project decisions via econometric analysis, identifying interactions between corruption and other success drivers. Finally, the study shows what corruption looks like in one in-depth case study, the Ajaokuta Steel Project.

2 Methodology

Constructing a database of large government projects that enables a systematic comparison of successes and failures is difficult. No data are available in Nigeria, in official databases or in accumulated reports from the press. In the absence of systematic data (the commission that found a 63% abandonment rate of large government projects did not publish a list!), the projects had to be identified and paired for comparison, and the representatives of the abandoned projects had to be convinced to provide responses.

This took significant effort, time, and investment of social capital. Organizations (even more than individuals) loathe speaking about their failures because they fear damaging their external image. Add to this the pressure on large government projects in Nigeria from the press and the public, and the reader may understand why no one has yet constructed this kind of data—not because no one cared but because it is difficult to do.

The authors collected detailed data on 19 completed and 19 abandoned projects (38 of the targeted 40). While this sample is to some degree "opportunistic" (limited by finding project participants to share information, even anonymously), it is well structured for making comparisons: it consists of matched pairs, a pair belonging to the same sector, having a similar budget size, and, if possible, having been carried out by the same contractor (which was possible to engineer in around a third of the cases). Collectively, this sample covers key sectors of government investment—roads, airports, power stations, ports, housing, ICT systems, waste management, hospitals, education, and social projects (the full sample is shown in Appendix 1).

Each project had a questionnaire answered by three respondents: an owner (senior civil servant), a supervisor (mid-level civil servant), and a project manager from the contractor company. All respondents were guaranteed anonymity, and a research associate sat with them and helped to interpret and answer the questions. The questions used a seven-point Likert scale because the concepts probed for were mostly not readily available in any quantitative format, and getting answers at all required allowing the respondents to make qualitative estimates. The use of multiple respondents allowed us to control for respondent bias, while testing for legitimate differences in what the different categories of project players perceived. Therefore, data analysis was carried out with all 114 questionnaires as separate data points (while also doing analysis by respondent category to check for result robustness. These checks can be found in Jimoh et al. 2022). The questions are listed in Appendix 2.

The survey questionnaire contained 41 variables (corruption, plus 40 other success driver variables, which were identified from a literature survey of previous studies of large public projects). The 41 variables and their rooting in previous project literature are not of primary interest in this chapter—for the discussion of corruption, this chapter focuses on 4 condensed success factors that were distilled from the variables (see Sect. 3). The details of the success driver framework and the 41 variables are reported in Jimoh et al. (2022).

As predefined questions only capture certain types of information, possibly missing additional issues that did not fit the assumed structure of the problem, we added a second method by writing detailed case studies, telling the causal stories of what actually happened, for 11 of the 38 surveyed projects (Jimoh et al. 2022). One of the case studies is reported in full in Sect. 4 of this paper—the Ajaokuta steel project, which is highly visible in Nigeria and was plagued by corruption over two phases of its life cycle.

3 Statistical Results: How Corruption "Poisons" Decision-Making

In the questionnaire, groups of the 41 variables "are related" and "get at" the same underlying characteristic of how a project was managed. The questionnaire started with three variable groups—*governance*, *initiation*, and *execution*—and then multiple questions explored each area. The reason for the overlaps is reliability of getting at the underlying concepts—a respondent may misinterpret or wrongly fill out a single question, but if we "get at" a managerial characteristic with multiple questions, there is a better chance that the responses will be stable and reliable.

When a group of variables contains information on a similar theme, we can extract the theme by condensing related variables via factor analysis. In essence, this is an exercise in testing for commonalities among groups of variables. A factor is an unobserved underlying force, and each variable that is measured in the questionnaire is treated as if it were a linear combination of multiple underlying factors: where in our primary data table, each data point (each questionnaire) is represented by 41 numbers (values on the 41 variables), we now want to represent the questionnaire as a representation of a smaller number of factors. We do not know a priori how many factors will emerge: while we started out thinking it might be three (based on previous literature, we structured the questionnaire into sections initiation and planning, governance, and execution), the exploratory factor analysis proposed 4 factors.

This four-factor solution (Table 4) was validated through confirmatory factor analysis and was statistically robust with strong factor loadings. The set of identified factors also turned out to be meaningful: the factors cut across our three "pre-named" categories but each had a clear interpretation (the details of the factor analysis are shown in Jimoh et al. 2022). The emerging factors were the following. The four factors plus corruption represent the five variables with which the effects of success drivers on project completion and success were then statistically estimated.

- **Factor 1: Contractor Selection.** This factor captures variables connected to contractor selection and qualification. It includes items such as: appropriate selection process, contractor capability, contractor experience, experience considered in selection, collaboration between contractor and supervisor, capability of sub-contractors.
- **Factor 2: Project Goals.** This includes business goals as well as societal goals. Items include the extent to which goals were understood, measured, and prioritized, the extensiveness of a business case, clarity of benefits to business and society, and risk analysis of goals.
- **Factor 3: Resources and Planning.** The third factor collects variables that relate to resources (adequacy of funding, funding renewal, availability of personnel, logistics support) and planning (stakeholder interests plans, timelines, and risks).
- **Factor 4: Supervision and Stakeholders.** The fourth factor captures elements of the supervision structure (whether it gave clear guidance, was involved and informed, and uncovered difficulties) and stakeholder involvement (the extent to which the public could ask questions, whether stakeholders had visibility and were heard, whether their views were taken into account). The reader might wonder whether it would be better to split this factor in two, one on supervision and one on stakeholders. However, it turned out that such a five-factor solution was less statistically robust and had more cross-loadings; in other words, the

data suggests that supervision and stakeholder management capability tended to go together.

- **"Factor" 5: Corruption.** Corruption ("a significant presence of *gratification* in any form was present in the project") was a single question in the survey, and it was treated as a separate concept. The rationale is that corruption is the phenomenon of interest here; it is not fully under managerial control in the project but partially driven by the project environment.

Armed with the composite factors, or underlying management characteristics, we can now attempt to *detect causal patterns* that explain why projects were abandoned, and what their budget and schedule performance was for the half of the sample that were completed. The analyses shown are all based on 114 questionnaires (three data points per project); however, we performed the same analyses separately for each of the three respondent groups for robustness, obtaining consistent results (albeit at lower significance levels because of the smaller sample sizes).

3.1 Econometric Prediction of Project Completion

Here, we predict the probability of project completion in a probit regression—completion is a zero-one variable, so we cannot use a normal linear regression, which requires a continuous dependent variable. The dependent variable in the probit regression is the logarithm of the probability of a project being completed.

We add one more variable into this probit regression. The reader may recall that we treat the three responses related to one project (owner, supervisor, and contractor) as three different data points. We include a measure of how much the three respondents on one project disagree: if the three respondents disagree strongly, this may reflect problems (for instance, in working together, in agreeing on plans, or in agreeing on goals). For any of the variables, respondent disagreement is measured as follows:

1. For each project and variable, take the three responses and average them to create a baseline.
2. For each respondent, take the *absolute value* of the difference from the baseline (the average of this variable). This is the disagreement for a variable for each respondent, and the average over the three respondents' disagreement scores is this variable's disagreement score; averaged over all variables, we get the project's respondent disagreement score.

The set of analyses shown in Table 1 predicts the logarithm of the probability of project completion as the dependent variable, with the independent variables discussed earlier.

Table 1 suggests that the high rate of project abandonment in Nigeria is not mysterious and can be explained by the managerial characteristics of the projects: all four factors are strongly significant (at the 5% level or better), and their coefficients

Table 1 *Probit* regressions of the probability of project completion

	Factor 1: contractor selection	Factor 2: project goals	Factor 3: resources and planning	Factor 4: supervision and stakeholders	Corruption	Respondent disagreement	Constant
Coefficients	1.40***	1.01***	0.99***	1.03***	−0.97 * *	−0.89 * *	−13.27**
Standard errors of coefficients	0.43	0.31	0.50	0.62	0.72	0.42	

Note: (McFadden's) Pseudo-$R^2 = 0.58$; significance levels are indicated as ****: $p < 0.001$; ***: $p < 0.01$; **: $p < 0.05$

are of a similar size, which means that no one factor dominates but they all have important influence. In addition, corruption is as important as each of the four other factors even when only considering its direct effect on completion (neglecting interactions). Finally, disagreement among the respondents (in their answers) is also a significant factor, as it captures the potential for tensions and misalignments among their actions.

All variables are statistically significant, being combined in one model, which implies that they measure different aspects of the project. The model offers a level of explained (pseudo-)variance of 58%. This suggests that the project characteristics that we have measured do not merely capture small influences, but our variables together explain a large part of the probability of a project reaching completion or being abandoned during execution.

In order to examine the robustness of the model, we added two additional control variables: first, we counted how many times the president and thus the government changed during the life of a project (this varied between zero and, for three projects, 12 times). The idea behind this variable is that each government change carries with it the danger of disruption and discontinuity. However, this control variable is not statistically significant (neither alone nor when included together with the other variables), and we therefore do not show it in the reported tables. The effect of discontinuity, while plausible, is so noisy that it cannot be reliably identified in an econometric analysis.

Now we turn to the managerial meaning of the parameters in Table 1, which represent a "model" that predicts the completion probability of a project depending on its scores of the factors and the corruption and disagreement variables. We show some elements of this model in graphical form in Fig. 1, *which shows by how much the completion probability changes if the two most influential variables change by one score point up or down.* The midpoint of the x-axis in the graph is the completion probability when all factors are at their average—it is 55%.[1] The two curves show how the completion probability changes when one variable changes while the other variables are held constant (we chose the two variables/factors with the largest and smallest regression parameter because they have the greatest effects; the effects of the other variables lie in between).

The two curves in the graph demonstrate powerfully how large the effects of the variables are: if the corruption score can be reduced by *one score point* from its average (which is 4.89, in a range between 1 and 7) to 3.89, the completion probability increases from 55% to 88%! If, in contrast, corruption deteriorates to a score of 5.89, the completion probability diminishes to 20%. This represents the first piece of clear evidence that corruption, in its main effect, does not just increase project costs but can actually destroy the chances of completion. The effect

[1] The average completion probability of our 38 projects is, of course, 50%, because that is how the sample was constructed. However, as our regression is not linear, the success probability of the average parameter values is not the same as the average success probability; it is slightly offset.

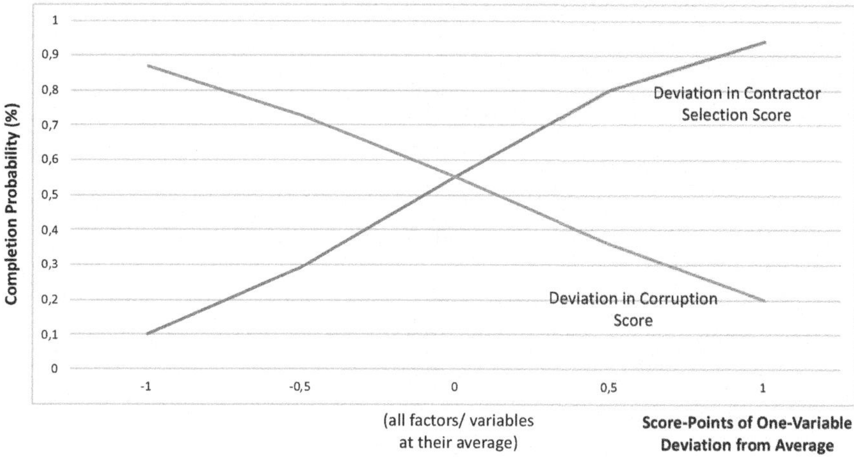

Fig. 1 Change in completion probability if factor score points change

is literally huge—a 30% completion probability increase for a \$1B project translates into an expected cost of \$300M (assuming the whole budget is spent)!

Similarly, a one-score-point improvement in the contractor selection score, from its average of 4.74 to 5.74, increases the probability of completion to 95%. Again, we could not demonstrate more powerfully the importance of contractor selection.

Thus, the econometric analysis shows clearly how important it is to manage the success variables that we have identified and measured. Specifically, our data demonstrates that corruption causes projects to fail, and that achieving even a moderate reduction of corruption can have a very large effect.

3.2 *Econometric Prediction of Cost and Schedule Overruns for Completed Projects*

We now examine whether the condensed factors also predict schedule and cost performance for the set of completed projects. We conduct this examination using linear ordinary least square regressions.

Table 2 shows the regression results of how our variables predict cost overruns (measured as a percentage of budget, which normalizes the absolute budget size away). As in the prediction of project completion, we again find that the factors matter, all reducing budget overruns (the signs of their coefficients are negative). All variables are statistically significant, and they explain not just some but a large fraction of the variance in the cost overrun performance measure (69% for the full model). Not only is the explained variance high, but the model overall is also highly statistically significant (the F-statistic for the model is $F = 14.612.\ p < 0.001$).

Table 2 Regression of cost overruns (% of budget) for completed projects

	Factor 1: contractor selection	Factor 2: project goals	Factor 3: resources and planning	Factor 4: supervision and stakeholders	Corruption	Respondent disagreement	Constant
Coefficients	−505.1**	−311.9**	−351.0**	−412.1**	321.0**	−312**	9936***
Standard errors of coefficients	695	71	412	702	401	701	

Note: Explained variance $R^2 = 0.52$; significance levels are indicated as ****: $p < 0.001$; ***: $p < 0.01$; **: $p < 0.05$

As in the prediction of project completion, the coefficients of the five factors, including corruption, are of a similar size. This strengthens the finding of the regression on completion: corruption as an individual variable is important for the project's budget compliance—corruption directly inflates the project budget.

Interestingly, respondent disagreement reduces budget overruns. Disagreement increases the chance of the project of being abandoned (Table 1), but given that the project was completed, disagreements among respondents are associated with lower overruns. The most plausible explanation of this is that, given that the project was completed rather than abandoned, there is a "luxury of different views" associated with lower overruns: when the project goes badly (overruns are high), everyone has to agree that it goes badly. When the project is proceeding adequately ("it is OK"), things are possibly more ambiguous in the sense that people might disagree how well (or badly) things are going.

Two additional control variables were added into this regression: first, the number of government changes during the life of the project (the same variable is in the project completion regression), and again, this variable turns out statistically insignificant. Second, the initial *budget size* of the project was included (we could do this only in the regression with the completed projects as we did not have reliable total budget estimates for the abandoned projects). The initial budget size is a measure of complexity and therefore project difficulty, and one might expect that (percentage) overruns are worse for larger projects. However, this turns out to not be the case—the budget size is again statistically insignificant. One interpretation is that all the projects in the sample are large enough to be difficult, and the forces that cause them to encounter difficulties are unrelated (or not consistently related) to size.

Similar to Fig. 1, Fig. 2 demonstrates that the variable effects are large enough to be of strong economic significance. The average budget overrun of the 19 completed projects is 760% (of the overrun, as a percentage of the original budget). This drives home the point that "completed" is not the same as "successful"—an almost eight-fold overrun is not a great performance. However, not all projects had such large overruns, and the econometric model from Table 2 predicts that the budget performance can be greatly influenced if the success factors can be changed.

The two curves in the graph again powerfully demonstrate how large the effects of the variables are: if the corruption score can be reduced by 1 from its average of 4.4 (while holding the other variables unchanged), the overruns can be almost halved (however, if the corruption score deteriorates by 1, the overrun increases by almost 50%, to 1100%). Reducing the budget overrun by half is worth $370M, on average, over the 19 completed projects! The contractor score has a similar effect. The impacts of the other variables are in between (closer to the contractor selection variable).

We now turn to the schedule overruns among the completed projects. Table 3 shows the regression results (measured as a percentage of planned project duration). As for budget overruns, we again find that our factors matter, all reducing schedule overruns as well (the signs of all coefficients are negative). All variables are statistically significant, and they explain not just some but a large fraction of the

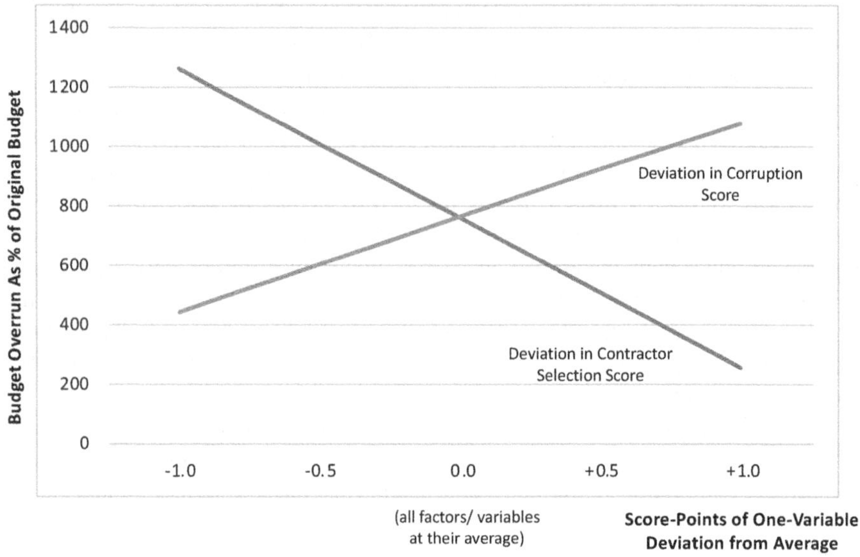

Fig. 2 Change in budget overruns if factor score points change

variance in the cost overrun performance measure (49% for the full model). Not only is the explained variance high, but the model overall is also highly statistically significant (the F-statistic for the model is $F = 9.41$ $p < 0.05$).

We again demonstrate the economic significance of our success drivers (factors and variables) in graphical form in Fig. 3. The *average* schedule overrun among the 19 completed projects was 134% (of the originally planned duration). The highest impact on the schedule lies in project goals and supervision (and we can see in Table 3 that the stakeholders' factor is almost as important): if we could improve the project goals and supervision factor by 1 score point (from its average of 6, while holding the other variables constant), the schedule overrun would be reversed to a schedule *acceleration* of 50%! This is, of course, not a "prediction" but an artefact of a linear extrapolation pushed further than is realistic. Once the schedule has been achieved, further improvements will not improve the schedule further, as the pressure to do so disappears. Whatever slack one has created will then be used to improve quality, reduce cost, or increase profit. This limit of linear extrapolation is, of course, the reason why we show only "one-score-point changes" in the graphs in the first place. However, the linear regression model still provides an estimation of how powerful the difference made by small improvements can be.

Corruption is less important for schedule adherence in comparison to the other variables than for budget adherence—its coefficient is only the 4th-largest. This is instructive—it gives us tangible evidence that the direct effect of corruption is relatively most damaging for the probability of completion (Fig. 1) and budget inflation (Fig. 2).

Table 3 Regression of schedule overruns (% of planned duration) for completed projects

	Factor 1: contractor selection	Factor 2: project goals	Factor 3: resources and planning	Factor 4: supervision and stakeholders	Corruption	Respondent disagreement	Constant
Coefficients	−18.5**	−191.1***	−9.2*	−188.0***	34.1**	16.8**	2547***
Standard errors of coefficients	70	69	10	63	53	61	

Note: Explained variance $R^2 = 0.40$; significance levels are indicated as ****: $p < 0.001$; ***: $p < 0.01$; **: $p < 0.05$

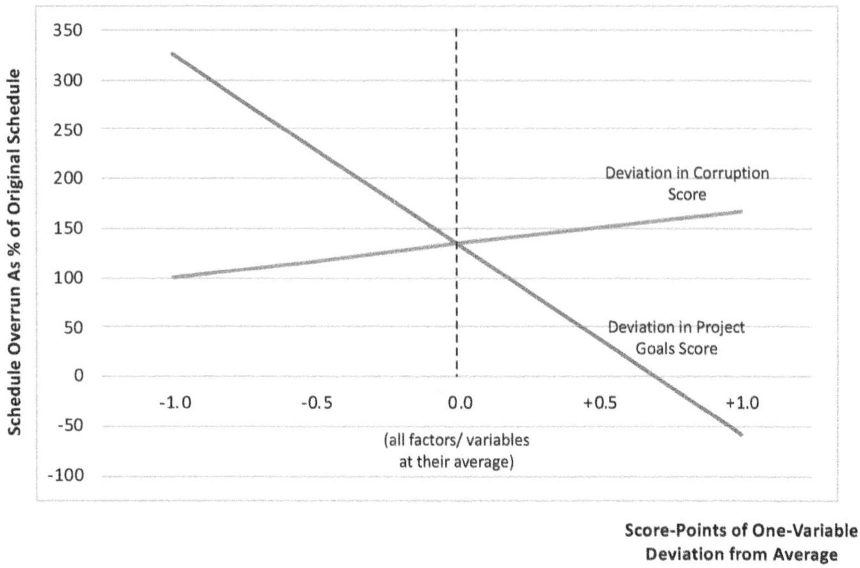

Fig. 3 Change in schedule overruns if factor score points change

3.3 *The Negative ("Poisonous") Side Effects of Corruption*

Our statistical analysis strongly demonstrates that all five success factors matter, and specifically, corruption has a large direct effect on completion probability and budgets. We now turn to the "side effects" of corruption, our prediction that corruption not only inflates the budget but also reduces the effectiveness of management (represented her by the other success factors).

In order to examine this, we include not only corruption in the project completion regression, but also an *interaction term*, the *product* of *(Factor x) X (Corruption index)*. If this product is significant in the regression, this means that the effect of Factor x will be changed (get larger or smaller) as the extent of corruption changes.

The interactions are not statistically significant in the Completion probability regression: corruption directly reduces the completion chance of a project but does not influence the effects of the other variables. However, the interactions *are* econometrically visible in the cost overrun regression for the completed projects. The result is reported in Table 4. Because of the small size of the dataset, we could not simply add the interactions into the full regression without losing significance; instead, the table elaborates elements of Table 2, showing each factor and its interaction with corruption one at a time.

Table 4 Regression of the effects of interactions between corruption and other variables on cost overruns (% of planned duration) for completed projects

Model	Factor coefficient (standard error)	Corruption coefficient (standard error)	Interaction of corruption with this factor coefficient (standard error)	Constant	Explained variance (R^2)
Factor 1 only: contractor selection	−572**(631)	370**(401)	260**(391)	8117***	0.37
Factor 2 only: project goals	−272**(364)	361**(472)	260**(391)	8591***	0.32
Factor 3 only: resources and planning	−287**(472)	350**(406)	249**(306)	8072***	0.36
Factor 4 only: supervision and stakeholders	−364**(429)	371**(510)	142*(412)	8356***	0.29

Note: significance levels are indicated as ****: $p < 0.001$; ***: $p < 0.01$; **: $p < 0.05$, *: $p < 0.10$

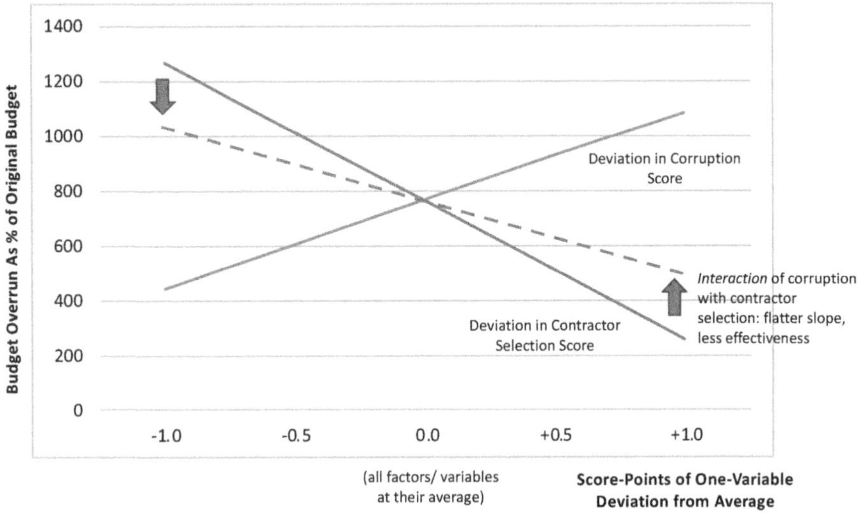

Fig. 4 Corruption through interaction weakens contractor selection effectiveness

As in Table 2, the coefficients of the factors are negative, which means that increasing the index of, for instance, contractor selection *reduces* the predicted amount of budget overrun. In contrast, the coefficients of corruption (in each partial regression) are positive, which means that an increase in the index of corruption *increases* the predicted budget overrun, as its main effect.

The focus of this table is the coefficient of the interaction term (Factor x) × (corruption index). This coefficient is positive (and significant) in all four partial regressions. This coefficient means that if the corruption index increases, then the overrun-reducing effect of the factor is weakened. In other words, increasing corruption weakens the budget-overrun-reducing effects of contractor selection, project goals, resources and planning, and supervision & stakeholder relations. This is graphically illustrated in Fig. 4, which adds the interaction to the main effects of Fig. 2: an increase in corruption flattens the regression coefficient, and thus the slope of the regression curve, of contractor selection

This illustrates that the corrosive effect of corruption on the important project decisions and practices can be econometrically measured—corruption does not "merely" inflate budgets but weakens the effectiveness of project management practices throughout the project. This is the sought direct evidence of Kenny's (2006) theoretical proposition that corruption negatively effects project management, in addition to its direct effect of inflating budgets.

4 Case Study Example: Ajaokuta Steel Company

4.1 *Project Initiation*

The idea of large-scale national steel production first arose as early as 1958 among the soon-to-be rulers of an independent Nigeria when regions were identified with significant amounts of iron ore (Matusevich 2003, p. 191). The official view became that "No country can talk about power status and the defense of national interests (...) without a well-established, integrated, fully operational native steel industry" (Unongo 1980, p. 7).

Between 1961 and 1965, several proposals were invited for the construction of an integrated iron and steel complex, but the result was that the (Western) suppliers did not believe this could be done economically using local raw materials. In 1967, discussions about a possible contract were initiated with the Soviet Union in response to Western countries criticizing Nigeria's civil war. Gaining a relationship foothold in the largest African country was important for the Soviet Union; soon after, a team of Soviet steel experts recommended a blast furnace/basic oxygen facility (using the technology that Russia excelled in rather than the upcoming direct reduction technology that used gas rather than coke); as a result, the Russian firm Technoexpert was awarded a contract in 1970 to examine the quantity and quality of Nigerian ore and coal.

The year 1971 saw the creation of the Nigerian Steel Development Authority (NSDA) to carry out surveys and research and to plan, construct, and operate steel plants. Difficult negotiations took place between the Nigerian government and the Soviet contractor, Tyajz Prom Export (TPE) among unease about deepened relationships with the Soviets (Alli-Balogun 1988, p. 195), but a contract for the construction of a plant was finally signed in 1979 (just before the military president handed over to the first civilian government). A few months later, the new civilian Shagari Administration declared steel to be a high priority and created a ministry for steel. The contract foresaw an initial phase with a plant of 1.3M tons of annual production capacity, for a sum of $2B (with Nigeria also covering 50% of the cost of transporting and housing 7000 Soviet technicians and their families on-site).

The choice of location was difficult and ultimately "non-optimal". A place close to the available ore and coal deposits had to be found, and while Ajaokuta was one of the candidates, Onitsha was closer to both deposits. However, economic optimality was trumped by political justifiability (in 1974, just four years after the civil war, awarding a strategically important project to one of the strongholds of the rebelling state was not considered prudent) (Oyeyinka and Adeloye 1988, p. 26).

Moreover, much has been made of the raw materials dilemma: Nigeria had large ore deposits (albeit with low iron content, below 40%) but a paucity of coking coal, while there was an abundance of gas (from oil production). Therefore, the choice was between a (old technology) blast furnace process, with a relatively cheap upgrading (of iron content) of local ore, and a modern direct reduction process using cheap gas for heating, as well as iron reduction, but requiring higher-grade ore (of around 80%, which would have to be imported because an intermediate step to upgrade the local ore would have been prohibitively expensive). In the end, the blast furnace process was chosen (pushed for by TPE), but coking coal would have to be imported at least initially, because the local coking-ready coal from Lafia/Obi had excessive ash and sulphur content, as well as structural mine problems (Olatunji 2018).

Therefore, the plant would require a dedicated 66 km rail line to transport ore from the mine at Itakpe, in addition to a river port to receive imported coking coal. Thus, it was clear from the outset that the economics of the plant would not be straightforward. Nonetheless, all of these problems ultimately had solutions and were known to the decision-makers, and none were "showstoppers".

However, another aspect of Nigeria's grand steel ambition was more insidious: Ajaokuta was not the only project in the pipeline. Nigeria's industrialization was believed to require a portfolio of steel mills (and a portfolio of supplier countries): 1977 saw the signing of a contract with a consortium of 10 German and Austrian firms to construct a 1M ton direct reduction plant, Delta Steel; and 1979 witnessed contracts (with Japanese and German companies) for three rolling steel mills of 200K tons per year in Katsina, Jos, and Oshogbo to produce bars and wire rods (based on the steel output from Ajaokuta and Delta). More plants were foreseen.

Although Delta was commissioned in 1982, it never produced more than 200K tons per year, and even this declined because of rampant corruption (for instance, paying inflated prices for materials), which led to declining production and, finally, an end to its operations in 1995, which, in turn, shut down the rolling plants (Amzat 2018). More generally, undertaking these overly ambitious projects at the same time turned the steel dream into a nightmare for Ajaokuta (Oyeyinka and Adeloye 1988, p. 15): there simply was not enough money, or talent, to carry out all these projects.

4.2 Project Construction and Cessation by 1988

In 1980, the FSDA became defunct and was replaced by specialized companies, one of them being the Ajaokuta Steel Company. TPE had originally been expected to deliver the project in 1989 and to deliver half the capacity as output by 1983. TPE had a track record of on-schedule, on-cost delivery of steel projects, including in Brazil, South Korea, and China. However, the Soviets wanted to focus on the steel mill, so Western contractors had to be found for the civil works. Furthermore, disputes arose (with the Soviets withholding personnel because their accommodation had not been built), tensions arose between Soviet and Nigerian personnel (because the Soviets were perceived to be receiving astronomical salaries, among other things, see Alli-Balogun 1988, p. 632), and delays and overruns accumulated. By the end of 1983, all work had to be halted because, being in an economic recession, the government ran out of money and stopped paying the contractors. The civil works contractors withdrew their personnel, blocking TPE's work (Matusevich 2003, p. 214), and work essentially stopped.

At the end of 1983, the military deposed the civilian Shagari government and installed General Muhammadu Buhari as a military president. Within days, the Canadian-educated general manager of Ajaokuta was in jail, along with 12 fellow senior managers, accused of "stupendous dishonesties" (corruption and mismanagement), and all work at Ajaokuta was halted. In addition, relationships with the Soviets became so frosty that Nigerian officials accused the Soviets of wanting to bring more "technical personnel" than was necessary, with the Nigerian embassy refusing visas to 500 Russians who wanted to enter Nigeria in 1987.

Discontinuity across administrations was (as in other cases) a factor in this tale. Of course, every administration had its own view. Here is the view of (former) President Obasanjo, who signed the original contract in 1979:

> Just after the handover to President Shagari, a representative of TPE came to meet Obasanjo in his retirement home with the complaint, "Mr President, you did not hand over well". The president asked why he felt that way, to which the man replied that the minister of mines and steel was demanding a bribe. The minister had refused to sign the certificates of completion of jobs, which were needed for payment. But they could not pay any bribe from their contract sum since the payment for the contract was from Russia. "We do not have control over such payment since the bribe payment is not part of the bid". In sum, the project was blocked because of a "lack of enthusiasm for it", which resulted in the project no longer being given sufficient priority. Obasanjo spoke to his successor, Shagari, about it but did not know whether Shagari ever pushed for completion.

Although Buhari wanted to stamp out wastage, he did not dare to stop the Ajaokuta Steel Project and the symbol of industrial development and self-sufficiency that it represented (not to mention the loss of 5000 jobs that it provided). A new agreement for the completion of construction was signed in August 1985, just days before the Buhari regime was overthrown by the Babangida regime, but the schedule continued to be pushed back under Babangida, in 1988, 1989, and 1990, following the departure of Soviet personnel (Matusevich 2003, p. 215).

Whatever the perspectives of the three administrations involved, by 1990, the project had ground to a halt from a lack of both funds and trust (Fig. 5). In the words of Matusevich (2003, p. 189): "The empty concrete blocks of its township (. . .) and the still rolling mills (. . .) stand as silent monuments to the failed ambitions of Nigerian rulers to exorcize by fire and steel the demons of the colonial past. They stand as a silent reminder of the lost grandeur of the Soviet empire, which, terminally ill as it was, tried fitfully to plant its peculiar concept of modernization in an African nation, tried and failed".

4.3 The PPP Revival of 2000–2007

When Olusegun Obasanjo came back for his second term as (this time civilian) president in 1999, the project had been stalled for 10 years. He still believed in its rationale and wanted to revive it but the Soviet Union, its previous partner, was no longer in existence. "I thought the project should be completed by the same people

Fig. 5 Ajaokuta Steel Plant, Zombie of Nigerian Steel Ambitions, in the Summer of 2019 (photo by the authors)

who started it, so I went to see the Russian government. But they said no, and it turned out that the original contractor had been Ukrainian anyway, which now was a separate country! So, I went to the Ukraine, but they were not interested either. That was when I decided that we should find a company from the private sector to do it".

In other words, when all avenues for continuing Ajaokuta as a government project had run out, President Obasanjo turned to a Public Private Partnership (PPP) construct. The Mittal Steel subsidiary, Global Infrastructure Nigeria Ltd (GINL), owned by Pramod Mittal, won a concession (later challenged for corruption accusations, as we see below), in addition to the right of way on the railway; GINL also bought the now-defunct Delta Steel for $30M. The process was handled by the Federal Ministry of Mines and Power rather than the Bureau of Public Enterprise (an institution established by an Act of Parliament to sell government assets or agree to the concession of government property).

GINL was given a 10-year concession for the Ajaokuta Steel Company in 2004. This was converted to 60% equity in May 2007 shortly before the exit of the Obasanjo government. However, a local company, BUA Group, had initially been chosen as the preferred bidder for Delta Steel and continued to agitate for its claim; soon material appeared in various newspapers alleging that the entire concession to GNIL was illegitimate and was robbing the nation via an undervalued transaction. The Yar Adua government established an investigation panel in October 2007 and cancelled the concession agreement in June 2008, alleging that GINL had failed to meet its performance targets and to pay concession fees while undertaking asset stripping. GINL, however, proceeded to international arbitration (Olawale 2013; Okafor 2016) and won the case at the International Arbitration Court in London in 2016. (This settlement foresaw that GINL should be repaid $700M and retain the right to operate the Itakpe mine, which gives us an idea of how much they paid for the concession 12 years earlier.) The parties negotiated but had not found a mutually agreed settlement by 2017 (Udo 2017), although the government claimed that a settlement had been reached, leaving GINL with Itakpe.

In 2019–2020, the government was attempting to get a new concessionaire, who would make the necessary investments. This process is extremely complicated (legally, and in terms of bringing multiple stakeholders on board), and no solution seems currently in sight. According to the Bureau of Public Enterprise in an interview, the key challenge is not a business plan for a reconcession but transparency and credibility (including the understanding of any potentially interested investor that an agreement reached with one administration may be challenged again by the next). Before a final settlement, no contemplation of any revival of Ajaokuta will be possible.

4.4 Conclusions from the Case Example

The case study gives a hint of the complexity of a large public project, where many challenges arise simultaneously, behind which corruption can hide. Nevertheless, the case study highlights that corruption not merely increased budgets (although this was also the case) but also decisively contributed to overruns and delays, apart from the other complexities: bribes and payments had accumulated (very likely already under the Obasanjo military administration, but certainly also) during the Shagari administration, which prompted the Buhari administration to put the project leadership in jail and halt the project. Had the project not possessed such symbolic power, it might have stopped here. But it limped on and was rescued by the civilian President Obasanjo 10 years later, who still believed in it. But he could no longer assemble the same funder and execution consortium and had to revert to a PPP structure, essentially outsourcing the project. This ran again into corruption challenges, as the winner of the bid was challenged for unfair advantage and then asset stripping, which halted the project again, and the project has still not recovered from this second scandal. The case illustrates how corruption delays decisions and forces downstream adjustments that are less effective than if they had to "merely solve the original problems" posed by the project brief.

5 Conclusion

Corruption is a curse of large projects (especially government projects) across the world. We have started out with the observation that many studies of corruption as a "tax on budgets". While this is bad enough (it may be as large as 30% of budgets in large government projects in developing countries), it has been proposed that this does not even capture the worst effects of corruption, which lie in the distortion of project decisions—positioning, structures, funding, emphasis of which kinds of benefits (Kenny (2006) calls this "grand corruption" versus the "petty corruption" of budget inflating bribes).

In this chapter, we have illustrated the distortion effect of corruption in the context of large government projects in Nigeria. We have shown quantitatively, with data across 38 large government projects, that corruption has interaction effects with project management success drivers, which renders these success drivers less effective. In other words, corruption corrodes and weakens management capability in projects. This corrosive effect is more important than the direct effect of corruption of project budgets.

In addition to the statistical analysis across a dataset of large government projects, the chapter also illustrates what corruption looks like when it appears, in one large case example, the Ajaokuta Steel Project in Nigeria. This $5B project has dragged on for 50 years, being delayed and driven into unproductive funding modes and functional subdivisions by multiple complications, not least among which corruption which re-appeared several times over the course of events.

The implications of the, at first glance invisible, corrosive effects of corruption on management success drivers should raise attention and emphasis of policy makers and project owners to corruption. Management literature tends to emphasize the sophistication and effectiveness of management systems for project performance. But management systems are ineffective if governance fails, particularly in the form of corruption. Government megaproject expenditures represent, by some counts, up to 8% of world GDP (Flyvbjerg 2014). Given the size of government project activities, preventing corruption from distorting their effectiveness matters.

Appendix 1: Project sample

Pair	Sector	Completed projects			Abandoned projects		
		Project	Budget $M	Contractor	Project	Budget	Contractor
1	Roads	Lagos-Ibadan Express Road	500	Julius Berger, Reynolds	Lagos-Badagry Express Road	500	China Civil Engg & Constr. Co (CCECC)
2	Bridges	Third Mainland Bridge, Lagos	1000	Julius Berger, Reynolds	Second Niger Bridge	1000	Julius Berger, Reynolds
3	Energy/power	Egbin Power Station	690	Marubeni West Africa	Calabar Power Station	660	Marubeni West Africa
4	Zungeru Hydropower Plant	1000	CNEEC-Sinohydro	Delta State Power Plant	1000	General Electric	
5	Shiroro Hydroelectric Power Station	100	Rockson Engineering Nigeria	Omoku Power Plant Station	100	Rockson Engineering Nigeria	
6	Mambilla Hydroelectric Power	5000	Sinohydro Corporation, China				
6	Steel				Ajaokuta Steel Project, Kogi	5000	Tyajz Prom Export (TPE)
7	Water (dam)	Kanji Dam	250	Balfour Beatty; Nedeco Ita	Otukpo Dam	200	SCC Nigeria
8	ICT (satellite)	Nigeria Satellite 2	300	Surrey Satellite Technology (UK)	Nigeria Satellite 1	300	China Great Wall Industry Corporation

(continued)

Pair	Sector	Completed projects			Abandoned projects		
		Project	Budget $M	Contractor	Project	Budget	Contractor
9	ICT (telecoms)	Airtel Nigeria	1000	Bharti Airtel (India)	Nigerian Telecom. Ltd (NITEL)	1000	Ministry of Communications
10	Sports stadium	Godswill Akpabio International Stadium	100	Julius Berger Nigeria	(Samuel) Ogbemudia Stadium	100	Peculiar Ultimate Concerns Ltd
11	Airport	Abuja International Airport	500	CCEC (China)	Lagos MMA2	500	Bi-Courtney Aviation
12	Yenagoa International Cargo Airport	200	CCEC (China)	Jigawa Airport Project	200	State Ministry of Works	
13	Sea port	Tin Can Island Port, Lagos	250	Port and Terml. Multi Serv.	Calabar Seaport	250	Julius Berger Nigeria
14	Housing	Victoria Garden City (VGC) Housing Estate	1000	HFP Engineering Ltd	Festac Town Federal Housing Estate	1000	Federal Ministry of Housing
15	1004 Housing Estate	200	Zvecan Engineering Nigeria	Abuja Mass Fed. Housing	200	Wengfu (China)	

Pair	Sector	Completed projects			Abandoned projects		
		Project	Budget $M	Contractor	Project	Budget	Contractor
16	Libraries	Olusegun Obasanjo Presidential Library	500	Gitto Costruzioni	Abuja National Library	500	Reynolds Construction
17	Social project	Nigerian Youth Empowerment Scheme (N-Power)	500	Federal Government of Nigeria	Subsidy Reinvestm. and Empowerment Progr. (SURE-P)	500	Federal Government of Nigeria
18	Waste management	Lagos State Waste Management Authority	200	Government of Lagos State	Cleaner Lagos Initiative (Visionscape)	200	Government of Lagos State
19	Health care/hospitals	University College Teaching Hospital (UCH) Ibadan	500	Alexander Gray (UK)	University of Abuja Teaching Hospital (UATH)	500	Mssrs Cochair Technology

Appendix 2: Questionnaire

Numerical questions were asked about planned and actual start and completion dates and planned and actual budgets. All other questions (except Q2a, which has a text answer) are answered in 7-point Likert scales.

1. The project had a well-defined supervision structure (e.g. a combination of clear oversight by a government body with an external execution supervisor).
2. Outline the decision hierarchy structure (e.g. "minister–project officer–supervising consultant–main contractor"). *Likert:* The composition of the supervision structure remained stable throughout.
3. The supervision structure provided oversight on a regular basis throughout the project.
4. The supervision structure provided clear guidance when it came to grey areas.
5. All key decisions were approved by the supervision structure.
6. The supervision structure was regularly kept informed of key aspects of the project.
7. The supervision structure met regularly.
8. The credentials of the members were subject to due diligence prior to membership.
9. The supervision structure regularly uncovered difficulties in the project.
10. The supervision structure regularly uncovered irregularities in the project.
11. The supervision structure provided adequate guidance for resolving problematic aspects of the project.
12. Significant gratification in any form was present in this project.
13. The primary contractor was selected through a selection process appropriate for projects of this scale.
14. The selection process was rigorous and open.
15. The selection process considered contractors' demonstrated experience in similar projects elsewhere.
16. Details regarding planning for the project received wide visibility, for example, through a website.
17. The public were able to ask questions regarding the project.
18. Key stakeholders outside the narrow decision circle had visibility and input before the approval processes of the project.
19. The goals of the project were clearly understood by all parties.
20. The goals were clearly measurable.
21. The prioritization among the most important goals was clear.
22. The project was created with a demonstrated business case defining the goals and public benefits.
23. The benefits of the project to the economy or society were clear and measurable at the start of the project.
24. The project goals and business case were subject to risk scenarios to capture the risks of outcomes.

25. The primary contractor had strong *capability* to deliver a project of similar characteristics and scale.
26. The primary contractor had strong prior *experience* in similar projects with a *track record* of successful delivery of similar projects.
27. The primary contractor and the supervising party had clearly defined roles.
28. The primary contractor and the government's assigned project supervisor (see Question 2) worked together constructively when problems occurred in the execution.
29. *Sub-contractors:* Taken together, the sub-contractors had strong *capability* to deliver a project of similar characteristics and scale.
30. The project had formal plans for managing stakeholders outside the project.
31. The plans were actively used to positively influence stakeholders.
32. Stakeholder views were used to make changes that improved the viability of the project.
33. The project was adequately resourced (in terms of funds) for its initial size.
34. The project funding was renewed/maintained when the project needed the funds to proceed.
35. The project had an adequate supply of skilled staff on the government side.
36. The project had adequate logistical support, for example, for delivery of materials or personnel.
37. The timeline of the project plan was realistic.
38. The project had a well-defined risk plan.
39. The risk plan was comprehensive in the management of risks that did occur.
40. The quality of the risk plan was consistent with similar plans used in projects of this magnitude worldwide.

References

Abimbola A (2015) About 12,000 federal projects abandoned across Nigeria. Premium Times, 16 November 2015 http://www.premiumtimesng.com/news/108450-about-12000-federal-projects-abandoned-across-nigeria.html

Adeyemo AA, Amade B (2016) Corruption and construction projects in Nigeria: manifestations and solutions. PM World J V(X):1–14

Alli-Balogun G (1988) Soviet technical assistance and Nigeria's steel complex. J Mod Afr Stud 26(4):623–637

Amzat A (2018) How Nigerian government, Indians wreck multi-billion-dollar Delta Steel Company, rip off host communities and tax payers. The Guardian Nigeria, 12 February, downloaded from https://guardian.ng/features/how-nigerian-government-indians-wreck-multi-billion-dollar-delta-steel-company-rip-off-host-communities-and-tax-payers/

Cohen MA, Lee HL (1989) Resource deployment analysis of global manufacturing and distribution networks. J Manuf Oper Manag 2:81–104

Elinoff E (2017) Concrete and corruption: materialising power and politics in the Thai Capital. CITY 21(5):587–596. https://doi.org/10.1080/13604813.2017.1374778

Flyvbjerg B (2007) Policy and planning for large-infrastructure projects: problems, causes, cures. Environ Plann B: Plann Des 34:578–597

Flyvbjerg B (2014) What you should know about megaprojects and why: an overview. Proj Manag J 45(2):6–19

Hausman WH, Lee HL, Subramanian U (2013) The impact of logistics performance on trade. Prod Oper Manag 22(2):236–252

Jimoh IF, Loch CH, Sengupta K (2022) How very large government projects are damaging Nigeria and need reform. Palgrave MacMillan, Berlin

Kenny C (2006) Measuring and reducing the impact of corruption in infrastructure. World Bank Policy Research Working Paper 4099, December

Kenny C, Søreide T (2008) Grand corruption in utilities. Public Research Working Paper 4805, World Bank Economics Division, December

Locatelli G, Mariani G, Sainati T, Greco M (2017) Corruption in public projects and megaprojects: there is an elephant in the room! Int J Proj Manag 35:252–268

Loosemore M, Lim B (2015) Interorganizational unfairness in the construction industry. Constr Manag Econ 33(4):310–326

Matusevich M (2003) No easy row for a Russian Hoe: ideology and pragmatism in Nigerian-Soviet Relations, 1960–1991. Africa World Press, Trenton

Okafor P (2016) Ajaokuta Mines: concession back to GHNL, 8 years after without reparation. Vanguard, 11 August, downloaded from https://www.vanguardngr.com/2016/08/ajaokuta-mines-concession-back-to-ghnl-8-years-after-without-reparation/

Olatunji OA (2018) Causations of failure in megaprojects: a case study of the Ajaokuta Steel Plant Project. Front Eng Manag 5(3):334–346

Olawale A (2013) Renationalisation: the taking of Nigeria's Ajaokuta Steel Company from GINL. Lagos Business School Case Study 213-056-1

Olken B (2006) Corruption perceptions vs. corruption reality. NBER Working Paper 12428

Oyeyinka O, Adeloye O (1988) Technological change and project execution in a developing economy: evolution of Ajaokuta Steel Plant in Nigeria. Manuscript Report 187e, International Development Research Centre (IDRC), Canada, April

Reinikka R, Svensson J (2006) Using micro-surveys to measure and explain corruption. World Dev 34(2):359–370

Shleifer A, Vishny RW (1993) Corruption. Q J Econ 108:599–617

Tabish SZS, Jha KN (2011) Analyses and evaluation of irregularities in public procurement in India. Constr Manag Econ 29(3):261–274

Treisman D (2007) What have we learned about the causes of corruption from ten years of cross-national empirical research? Annu Rev Polit Sci 10(1):211–244

Udo B (2017) Ajaokuta belongs to Nigerian Government Despite Concession Dispute – Official. Premium Times, 16 November, downloaded from https://www.premiumtimesng.com/news/headlines/249555-ajaokuta-belongs-nigerian-govt-despite-concession-dispute-official.html

Unongo P (1980) Steel development and Nigeria's power status. Lecture delivered by Paul Unongo at the Nigerian Institute of International Affairs, Victoria Island, Lagos on Thursday 24 July. The Institute, Issue 35 of Lecture Series, ISSN 0331–6262

Service Parts Management: Theoretical Foundations, Practice, and Opportunities

Narendra Agrawal and Vinayak Deshpande

Abstract After sales service is a critical component of any firm's customer acquisition and retention strategy, especially when the products are capital intensive, such as in aerospace and defense, heavy manufacturing, telecommunications, construction equipment, medical devices, process industry, consumer electronics, transportation, and semi-conductor equipment industries. These products are often deployed in mission critical environments, which makes ensuring uptime of these assets critical. Therefore, manufacturers of such products often sell service contracts designed to ensure consistent availability of these assets. Consequently, design and management of the infrastructure needed to deliver such services, also called as the service supply chain, is an extremely important topic for practitioners. Not surprisingly, a significant body of research has emerged in the operations management literature to address the underlying analytical challenges. Distinct attributes of the assets and parts needed to provide service, ways in which demand for service parts occurs and can be satisfied, definition of customer service, and the network of physical locations from where demand can be fulfilled make the underlying analytical problem particularly challenging, and, therefore, exciting for academic researchers. This chapter reviews the key foundational concepts related to the design and management of the inventory strategy needed to provide cost-effective service in spares parts management (SPM) systems. It also provides a brief description of the software solutions provided by some of the major software vendors in the SPM space. It concludes with a brief summary of some of the most exciting trends in this arena that could lead to opportunities for further research by academics and enhancements by industry solutions providers.

N. Agrawal (✉)
Department of Information Systems and Analytics, Leavey School of Business, Santa Clara University, Santa Clara, CA, USA
e-mail: nagrawal@scu.edu

V. Deshpande
Kenan-Flagler Business School, University of North Carolina, Chapel Hill, NC, USA
e-mail: vinayak_deshpande@kenan-flagler.unc.edu

H. Lee et al. (eds.), *Creating Values with Operations and Analytics*, Springer Series in Supply Chain Management 19, https://doi.org/10.1007/978-3-031-08871-1_8

Keywords Spare parts management · Service parts management · Repairable parts management · After sales services · Multi-indentured multi-echelon · Inventory management · Solutions providers

1 Introduction

Over the last several decades, while companies have made impressive strides in the area of supply chain management, the primary focus for many companies has been determining cost-effective ways to get their product into the hands of their customers. The best-in-class companies, on the other hand, have also realized that an equally important business opportunity, and indeed, customer acquisition and retention strategy, is to deeply engage with their customers even as they are realizing value from these products. This engagement is particularly critical for companies that sell capital-intensive products, such as in aerospace and defense (A&D), heavy manufacturing, telecommunications, construction equipment, medical devices, process industry, consumer electronics, transportation, and semi-conductor equipment industries. These products are often deployed in mission critical environments. High capital intensity of the products and the mission critical nature of their application makes ensuring uptime critical, because unavailability of these assets can have significant financial and performance consequences. As a result, provision of after-market services has become an important component of the competitive strategy of these firms. For instance, the aftersales industry in the USA for all vehicles combined is projected to reach $449 billion by 2023 (Automotiveaftermarket.org 2021). In Europe, this figure is expected to reach €247 billion by the same time (Waas et al. 2021). In the A&D industry, after-market services represents nearly 80% of the life-cycle value of an aircraft sale, and gross margins that are 1.4 times that of new equipment (Iyer et al. 2020). Across all the US industrial manufacturers, service margins are nearly 2.5 times that for new products and equipment, even though service revenues are only about 23% of total revenues (Wellener et al. 2020).

From an operational point of view, service parts, or spare parts, are often a key ingredient of the successful delivery of such services. Consider a complex PCB card on an expensive router from its original equipment manufacturer (OEM), Cisco, deployed in the telecommunication network at NASDAQ to facilitate financial transactions (Cohen et al. 2006a). A failure in this card can be disastrous. Indeed, this may be one of hundreds of components within the router that might experience a random failure. Therefore, NASDAQ may have purchased a service contract from Cisco that ensures rapid diagnosis, and potentially a replacement of the failed part within a promised four-hour window. With hundreds of thousands of customers like NASDAQ dispersed all over the globe, Cisco faces a complex and large scaled problem requiring efficient deployment of spare parts and diagnostic equipment and personnel throughout its worldwide network of depots, warehouses and service and repair facilities, called as its service supply chain. Not surprisingly, services account for nearly 27% of annual revenue and yield a healthy 66% gross margin (Cisco's

2020 annual report). Thus, in general, firms must make significant investments in assets that include infrastructure (repair depots, warehouses, communication, and logistics), spare parts inventory and highly trained personnel (customer engineers and repair technicians), collectively referred to as the *service supply chain*. Efficient design and management of assets in the service supply chain is critical for a firm to deliver service to meet customer expectations in a cost effective manner.

There are several reasons why companies are increasingly considering after sales services as a key element of their competitive strategy (Cohen et al. 2006a). First, customers, especially for capital-intensive goods noted above, are demanding that their assets provide greater value, with minimal downtime. This is driven, at least in part, by the competitive pressures faced by these customers in their own respective industries. Newer business models that rely on innovative contractual arrangement such as performance-based contracts (power by the hour) are providing a further impetus for companies to develop their service delivery capability. Second, services offer a sustained, low risk source of revenue stream. While typical business cycles may lead to ups and downs in the volume of purchase of new equipment, assets already owned must continue to generate value. This implies that revenue from services will likely exhibit less volatility. In some industries, such as A&D, it is not unusual for product life cycles to be 25–30 years long. Third, organic growth through R&D driven new products can be an uncertain, expensive, and lengthy process. In contrast, after sales services offer an easier path to new revenue streams. Indeed, companies have found that existing customers who are satisfied with services are a more effective source of additional revenue through cross-selling and up-selling products, than new, first-time customers. Finally, systematic engagement with customer through the service delivery process can lead to deep, customer specific knowledge which is impossible for competitors to possess. Therefore, companies that are good at services are able to gain sustained competitive advantage.

We have three key goals in this chapter. Our first objective is to offer an overview of the key foundational concepts related to the design and management of the inventory strategy needed to provide cost-effective service in spares parts management (SPM) systems. Our description also includes two brief case studies of service supply chains designed and developed to provide service support in the computer and defense industries. We do not intend to provide a comprehensive literature review of this topic, since there are several excellent recent reviews in the published domain. We hope that this chapter will provide a useful starting point for academic researchers as well as industry practitioners, and that they will be able to better appreciate the more detailed survey papers after reading this chapter. We point the interested to readers to reviews and more detailed treatment of this topic provided by Kennedy et al. (2002), Muckstadt (2004), Sherbrooke (2004), Dekker et al. (2013), Basten and van Houtum (2014), Van Houtum and Kranenburg (2015), and Topan et al. (2020). Second, we provide a brief description of the software solutions provided by some of the major software vendors in the SPM space. This section is likely to be particularly relevant to practitioners. Academics will find this section helpful in understanding gaps between academic research and practice. Finally, we conclude with our views on some of the most exciting opportunities for further research by academics and enhancements by industry solutions providers given the recent developments in the global business environment, our ability to solve large-scale optimization problems, and exponential improvements in the computing industry, particularly in the cloud computing infrastructure.

2 Characteristics of Service Parts Management Systems

The challenges faced by managers of service parts inventory are very different from those encountered in finished product and direct material supply systems. There are a number of distinct characteristics that make it especially difficult to provide a high level of customer service at a low cost. These characteristics also present distinct challenges from an analytical modeling point of view. These characteristics are described next.

2.1 Demand Attributes

2.1.1 Demand Source

There are two main triggers that initiate the replacement of a service part; (1) it breaks down unexpectedly, or (2) it reaches a point of planned replacement regardless of its condition. An example of the first case is a starter mechanism in a car that suddenly stops working. An example of the second case is an oil filter that is planned for replacement after a new car has been driven for 5000 miles. Product owners have little control in the first case, and since the cost of delay can be quite high, it is necessary to keep high levels of service parts inventory in the event that a breakdown occurs. The second case, however, is something we often know about in advance or can be predicted with some level of certainty (e.g., based on product age or usage), and hence the appropriate service part can be made available specifically for this purpose at the appropriate time and place. These demands are also referred to preventive and corrective demand. When managing service parts, we often separate these two kinds of demand and when deciding on safety stock levels, we base this decision only on the demand due to random breakdowns.

Since demand is primarily driven by a service event, it is a function of the engineering performance of the part, the size of the installed base of customers who have purchased products that require the part, and the types of service contracts that have been sold to the customer base. Parts that are more reliable generate only occasional demand for replacement parts. This leads to a sparse demand history, which presents challenges in forecasting, as discussed later. Larger the size of the installed base, greater is the demand for parts. If more time sensitive service contracts have been sold, service level requirements are higher to ensure timely repair and replacement of defective or failed parts.

2.1.2 Slow Moving

Many repairable spare parts have extremely low demand (i.e., slow moving), often averaging less than one unit per year. For example, at KLA-Tencor (Chamberlain and Nunes 2004), a leading manufacturer of equipment that is used in semiconductor fabrication plants, 75% of the parts planned had demand of one or less, and 60% of the parts had demand of three or less per year. Such low demand requires very different control methods than those used for high-volume parts, which often turn tens of times a year.

Low demand also makes forecasting challenging, since one has very few observations of historical usage. This is especially true in the initial stage of a part's life cycle, i.e., upon its introduction as a new product, where one needs to rely on engineering (mean time between failure) estimates.

2.1.3 Correlated Demand

Since demand is driven by part failure or planned maintenance, depending upon the event, demand may occur simultaneously for a number of parts or systems. For example, a 30,000-mile checkup of a car will trigger the demand for several parts during the same visit. Therefore, inventory planning methods must explicitly account for this correlation of demand. These correlations are codified in a *service bill-of-materials* or *scheduled maintenance bill-of-materials*, which can be very different from a production bill-of-materials.

2.1.4 Criticality

Criticality refers to the requirement for a part to be functioning in order for the product to be available for use. Typically, there are different degrees of such criticality. A car, for example, is not drivable without a working fuel pump. The car works well enough, however, under most conditions, with a defective right-hand-side wiper blade. Highly critical parts are often characterized by high cost, long repair/procurement lead times and the fact that they are usually repaired rather than being scrapped if they fail. Thus, inventory policies for such parts tend to be very different from parts with low criticality.

2.2 Product/Part Attributes

2.2.1 Repairable Versus Consumable Parts

It is often worthwhile to repair more expensive service parts after a breakdown. For example, a motherboard for a main-frame computer can cost tens of thousands of

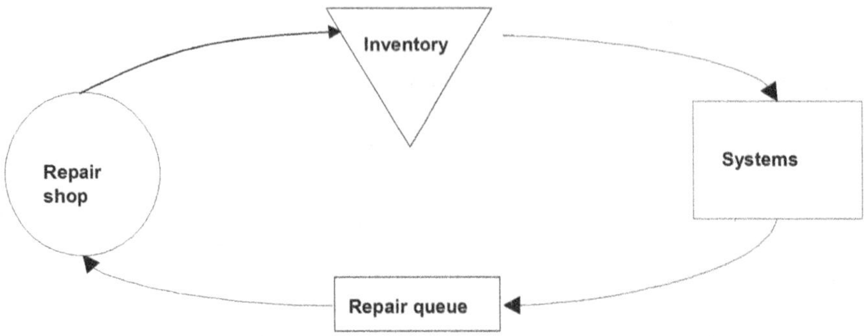

Fig. 1 Closed part cycle for repairables

dollars. If it breaks down, it is replaced by a good motherboard so that the computer is up and running again promptly. But the cause of the breakdown might be just a small chip that costs $10 and is easy to change. By repairing the defective board, one generates a good motherboard that can be used as a service part for potential future breakdowns. Figure 1 illustrates the cycle of repairable service parts.

A broken part goes to the repair queue if it is worth repairing, and otherwise it is scrapped. When the broken part's turn comes, it is repaired and then placed in the inventory of good parts. The inventory of good parts can also be replenished by purchases from the supplier of the part. These good parts are then used to replace parts that break down in a product, which we will henceforth refer to as a *system* (consisting of a collection of parts). Adding to the complexity is the likelihood that sometimes, defective parts are not returned from the field, or parts returned as defective are found to be not so upon inspection.

In comparison, inexpensive parts such as a simple fuse in an electrical system, or a filter in a car, are not repaired, but replaced right away. Such parts are referred to as consumables and managed very differently than repairable parts.

2.2.2 Long and Variable Lead Times

Lead times for service parts, especially for repairable parts, are often very long (e.g., up to 18 months in aerospace and defense) and highly variable. The repair of a high-tech part often needs to take place at a central depot which may be far from the installed base system location. Such repair may require specialized resources, which include extensive testing both before and after the repair itself. The return time delays for defectives, procurement lead times for components used to repair defective parts and the actual repair/testing time all contribute to the overall part lead time.

2.2.3 Large Number of Diverse Parts

The number of parts that must be managed in a service environment can be enormous, often much larger than that in a production environment. The reason for this is that while the production process primarily requires parts and components related to the current generation of product, support must (often mandated by regulation) be offered for a much longer period of time. For example, the service organization of a semi-conductor equipment or telecommunications companies routinely have tens of thousands of active parts in their portfolio. Therefore, multiple generations of products must be supported simultaneously, thereby increasing the total number of parts whose inventory must be managed. When optimizing a system of service parts, one needs to evaluate the parts in *relation to each other*. As we shall see there are significant interactions among all of the parts in terms of the total budget for inventory and the overall system (product) service level. This makes the problem of managing service parts inventory challenging in terms of the underlying mathematics as well as the solution times required to generate an optimal solution.

Further complicating the analysis is the fact that service parts supporting the same system are often very diverse in terms of costs (and other replenishment parameters such as lead times, size, weight, volume, and storage requirements). For example, an F16 fighter jet is supported by parts ranging from fuses that cost virtually nothing to field replaceable units (FRUs), such as the radar system that might cost more than $2,000,000. One will, obviously, make sure not to have an F16 grounded on an aircraft carrier due to the lack of a fuse, while the radar system is so expensive that one may be able to tolerate a lower service level for it at the carrier and stock a limited number at a central depot only. Indeed, service parts management for inventory systems where each part can be optimized *independently* of the other parts are considerably easier to deal with.

2.2.4 Part Chaining

Short product life cycles, especially in technology industries, lead to frequent revisions or upgrade to newer versions of parts and components. This leads to part chains, or a sequence of versions of a component used in a particular product. Therefore, when a service event occurs in the field, it is important to know the exact version of the part that needs replacement. Thus, the replacement part should be either the same version or, if feasible, a newer version, but likely not an older version of the part. In contrast, some parts, especially in the A&D industries, may have very long life cycles depending upon the length of the life cycle of the finished products (e.g., 25–30 years long for Polaris missile systems, or the C-5 strategic transport aircraft first introduced by Lockheed first in 1970 (United States Air Force 2022)). Consequently, for the service organization, it is not enough to know just the number of systems deployed in any region. The exact configuration of each system at each customer location is required, and this makes service delivery systems significantly more information intensive as compared to production systems.

2.2.5 Multiple Indentures

As mentioned previously, assembled systems can be described by a service bill-of-materials (BOM), which specifies how each part is used in putting the final system together. Typically, BOMs are described by multiple levels or indentures, which indicate the hierarchy of part usage. Thus, at the highest level we have the final system. At the next level, we have the major assemblies used to manufacture the system. Each assembly can be broken down into sub-assemblies. This process repeats until we get to the bottom level of components. An investment in service parts could be made at all indenture levels. Having FRUs available leads to faster system restoration. These are the most expensive parts, however. Thus, there is a tradeoff in determining stocking levels across indentures between cost and speed. Overall repair lead times will be determined by the service level of parts at all indenture levels.

2.3 Supply Chain Structure

Service supply chains for large organizations typically tend to be complex multi-echelon systems consisting of a large number of inter-connected locations. At the lowest echelon are the individual forward locations, which could also include customer sites. At the highest level are the central distribution centers that act as an emergency backup and/or replenishment site for its downstream child locations. In between, the network might include additional field or regional stocking locations, as well as repair facilities. The central distribution center locations receive their supply from vendors and/or repair facilities, though other locations can receive such supplies directly from vendors too. Materials flow from the vendor locations ultimately to the customer deployment sites. Reverse material flows occur to support repair of failed items. In this sense, repairable item supply chains tend to be closed loop supply chains. Also, all locations might support each other through *lateral transshipments*, meaning that if one location has excess stock while another has a stock out, the former can *transship* to the latter. Figure 2 illustrates this type of network. The case studies we describe later illustrate the size and complexity of real-world service supply chains.

2.4 Replenishment

2.4.1 Multiple Sources of Replenishment

Parts can be replenished from multiple sources, depending upon costs and customer or contractually specified needs. These sources include:

- Repair facilities, following the completion of repair

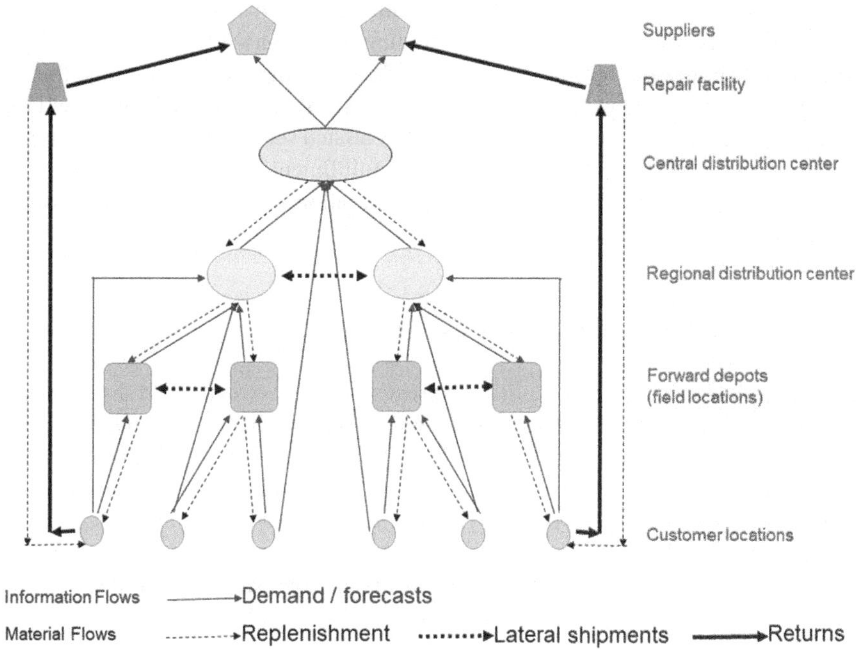

Fig. 2 Schematic example of multi-location service parts network

- Vendor replenishment of consumable items
- New buy, or new purchases of repairable items
- Upstream stocking location
- Lateral stocking location
- Emergency backup location
- Cannibalization: If two systems of the same type are waiting for different types of parts, then one of them can cannibalize the other for parts. For example, if one F16 is waiting for a radar system to become available, while another F16 is waiting for a new catapult mechanism to become available, then the former can get the working radar system from the latter. This reduces the number of systems that are down from two to one. In the military, aircrafts used as a part source through cannibalization are referred to as "hanger queens."
- Substitutability: A higher capability part, or a newer part, can be substituted for a failed part, depending upon feasibility and cost considerations. For example, in case of PC repairs, a 2 TB hard drive can be used as a replacement for a 1 TB hard drive.

2.4.2 Prioritization of Different Customer Segments

In many service support environments, different customers have different priorities and needs for support. For example, a squadron of military aircrafts engaged in combat requires much higher levels of availability than a squadron engaged in training exercises. Similarly, a company trading in foreign exchange futures cannot tolerate downtime for its internet routers while a company with a collection of redundant servers used to support non-mission critical processes will not be willing to pay a premium for rapid repair. Such differentiated service needs can affect both target inventory stocking levels and real-time fulfillment priorities. See Deshpande et al. (2003a,b) for models of service differentiation between different customer segments.

2.4.3 Expediting/Express Shipments

Some suppliers of service parts utilize express shipments, or expedited shipments, in addition to regular shipments, especially in those cases where a customer system is down and is awaiting delivery of a part. Teradyne, for example, offers two classes of repair services to its customers, one with short lead time and the other with long lead time at high and low cost, respectively. Customers will opt for the long delivery time option in cases where they have sufficient on-hand inventory and/or spare system capacity. Options of this type further complicate the analysis since multiple delivery modes have different lead times and could affect stocking levels.

2.4.4 Treatment of Unmet Demand

Unmet demand can be lost for consumable parts that are easily available from a competing supplier, or when third party suppliers can provide feasible substitutes. However, for higher value and capital-intensive repairable items that tend to be designed into the customers' technology roadmaps, unmet demand is usually backordered.

2.5 Financial and Service Parameters and Metrics

2.5.1 Cost Parameters

The key cost parameters relevant to SPM decisions include:

- Purchase cost, which can vary tremendously from a few cents to tens of thousands of dollars,
- Inventory holding cost,
- Repair cost,
- Shipment cost (which are segment specific),
- Expediting cost,
- Shortage, or penalty cost (often contractually specified).

2.5.2 Service Metrics

A variety of service level metrics are used in a service environment, and these are described in more detail in the following section. However, we make two important notes here to identify unique aspects of the service environment. First, while part level metrics are used in practice and are important, such as in finished goods supply chains, the purpose of service parts is to support maintenance and repair of *systems*. So, in the case of a system breakdown all the necessary service parts should be available so that the system can be restored quickly. This ensures that the system will be up and running again with minimal interruptions (downtime). Hence, the relevant service measure is defined at a *system* level, since this is what the customer cares about, e.g., the owner of a car is concerned with the drivability of the vehicle and not the service level of parts at the repair shop. This leads to the need for system availability service metrics that are driven by the level of service for the parts. If, for example, one wants a 95% availability for a particular system (i.e., the product is down no more than 5% of the time awaiting delivery of a part), then one may choose to set service level (fill rate) targets for parts to be on average 95%. This average part fill rate could be realized by setting a lower fill rate for very expensive parts and a much higher fill rate for very inexpensive parts.

Second, we note that the time required to ensure the availability of spare parts is only one component of the overall *job completion time (JCT)* for any service event, since this is what the customer cares about. Industries such as the semi-conductor equipment industry define *machine down awaiting part (MDAP)* as the time spent waiting for parts, but this component of the JCT is relevant only after the customer service engineer (CSE) has diagnosed the issue and order the required parts. Figure 3 illustrates the components of JCT.

3 Repairable Service Parts Management

Repairable service parts are often parts with low demand rates, long "new buy" procurement lead times and high unit costs. Hence it is especially important to manage repairables well. This section, based on Cohen et al. (2004), presents a powerful procedure for optimizing repairable service parts inventory decisions. This procedure is also the foundation for the methods used in more advanced scenarios (e.g., multi-location).

3.1 Fundamentals of Service Parts Modeling

This section provides the foundations for modeling and optimizing service parts systems. We start by considering *a specific* service part stocked at a single location.

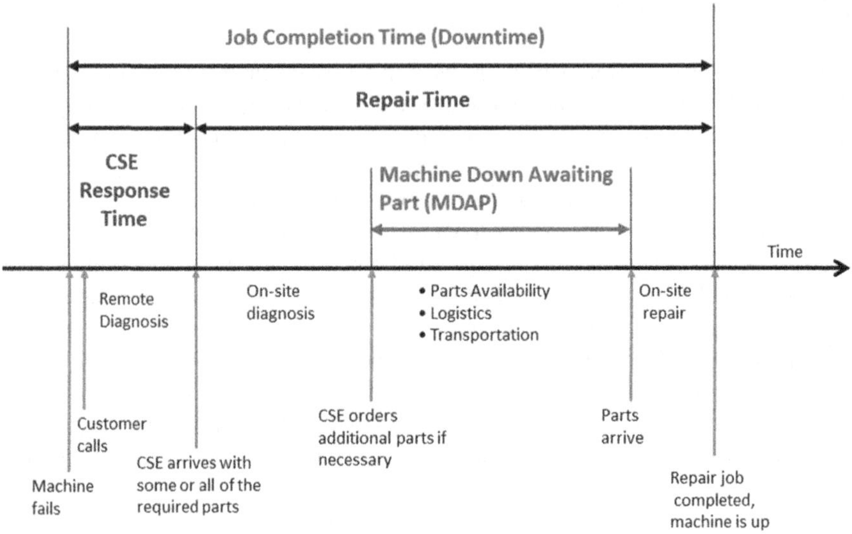

Fig. 3 Components of job completion time. Source: Prof. Morris A. Cohen

3.1.1 Failures of Parts

By failure rate, we mean the rate of failure occurrence. We will characterize here the *failure rate* for each service part. This rate can be measured either by *the number of failures per unit of time or by the time between failures*. We will denote the *average number of failures per year by* λ.

Memoryless Failure Rate

One of the key assumptions in modeling service parts is that of a *memoryless failure rate*. This means that *what will happen in the future does not depend on what happened in the past*, or in other words what has happened does not affect what will happen. While memoryless failure rates are a common assumption in the academic literature there are several reasons in a real-world setting which would not satisfy this assumption.

Empirical research has shown that models that make the memoryless failure rate assumption lead to very reasonable (near optimal) decisions in many real settings. This assumption also simplifies the analysis for repairables. For the remainder of this note we will, therefore, make the memoryless failure rate assumption. A discussion of how big data may help relax this assumption is discussed in the Trends and Research Opportunities section.

Number of Failures in a Time Interval: Poisson Distribution

We consider here the *number of failures* in a given time period, (measured in years). It turns out that the *only* probability distribution for the *number of events (failures)* in a period of time where the events are memoryless is the Poisson distribution. Let $S(t)$ be the number of failures in t years, which are assumed to follow a Poisson distribution. The probability that the number of failures in t years is equal to s is then given by a Poisson distribution with mean λt.

In the management of service parts, we are more interested, however, in *how many spares are needed to avoid a shortage*. The probability that *no more* than s failures will occur during t years gives the foundation for this and can be computed as the cumulative density function (CDF) of the Poisson distribution $\Pr(S(t) \leq s)$.

3.1.2 The Repairables Cycle

Repairable service parts follow a *closed cycle* (Fig. 1). In a *closed* cycle no parts are added to or taken out of the system. If a part fails, it is replaced by a good part from the service parts inventory, if available (otherwise the system waits until a good part becomes available). The failed part is then sent to the repair queue. When its turn comes, it is repaired and then placed in the good parts inventory.

Sometimes there are restrictions on whether a part can be repaired. These restrictions can be physical restrictions (e.g., the part may be too severely damaged to be repaired), or policy restrictions (e.g., maximum number of three repairs is allowed for a *specific* part). In such cases, the cycle will be *open*, meaning that material "leaks" out through disposal at a testing stage and gets resupplied through additional acquisitions. Figure 4 illustrates such a cycle.

Modeling the Repair Process

If part failures are memoryless with an annual rate of λ per year, then the *arrivals* into the repair queue are also memoryless. The repair lead time is defined as the sum of time spent by the failed part to reach the repair depot, the time spent in queue at the repair depot, the time spent in actual repair process, and the time to return the fixed part to the warehouse. It is typically assumed that the repair lead times for parts are independent and identically distributed with a mean of L years. Thus L years is the average time from the part failure until the time the part is placed in the inventory of good parts. Under this assumption, the number of parts in the *repair pipeline* (i.e., parts in transit to the repair shop, parts waiting in the repair queue, and parts in actual repair process) also follows a Poisson distribution. Let R denote the number of units that are in the repair pipeline. Thus R is distributed as a Poisson random variable with mean equal to λL.

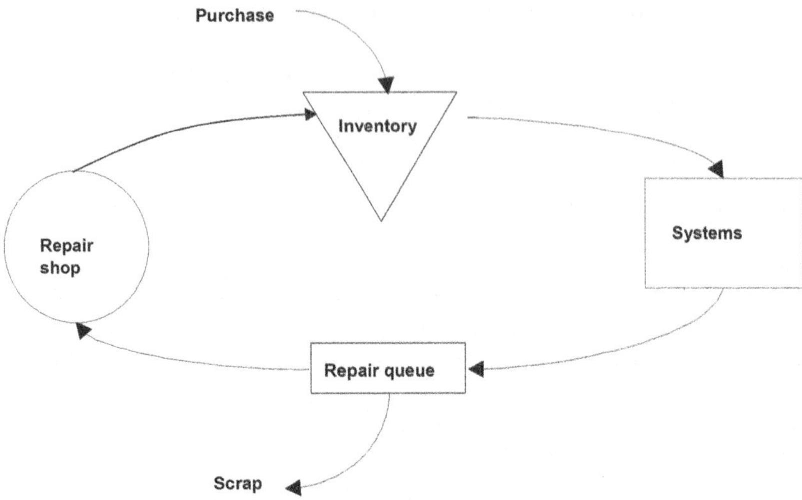

Fig. 4 Open cycle for repairables

The above result is remarkable because the actual shape of the repair lead-time distribution does not matter. Only the mean of the repair lead time is important to measure the repair pipeline. Although in practice repair lead times are often not independent (because of interactions in the repair shop), this approximation has been validated by a number of practitioners (Sherbrooke 2004). This assumption is usually well justified when there exists ample capacity to meet demand for repair.

Note that if not all parts of a specific type are repairable (i.e., a percentage of failed parts are scrapped), then the part repair lead time is a weighted average of the repair and "new buy" procurement lead times.

3.2 Measuring Customer Service

Many alternative measures of customer service can be defined. We will consider here two main types of service measures that are considered especially relevant for service parts management. These two types define *part* and *system* service performance.

3.2.1 Part Service

Service metrics at a *part* level measure (and specify) the service level of parts independently of each other. This is the traditional service approach for tracking customer service in inventory systems, and it applies primarily when the part is a finished product. Part service targets are typically specified for groups of parts, where the groups are made up of similar products. Examples include retailers and mail order companies where a group could be a product family, e.g., men's dress shirts.

The specific service measures that are most often used at a part level are:

(a) **Probability of stockout** This measures the probability that a stockout will occur during a specified time interval at a location when either a customer demands an part or the system generates a replenishment order to be filled from that location. It does not reflect the number of replenishments per year or the size of the stockout. While stockout probability is very easy to compute and to understand, in terms of the underlying mathematics, it does not relate well to the final customer's perception of service quality, especially when it is measured at an internal location (e.g., the central warehouse).

(b) **Fill rate** This measures the expected value of the *percentage of demand* that can be fulfilled directly from available inventory, i.e., off the shelf. This metric is most often used by supply chain managers when they refer to service level. It is defined by the (average) ratio of the quantity shipped to the quantity demanded.

(c) **Backorders** Fill rate only considers if an part is *immediately* available from inventory, i.e., at the point in time when the demand for the part is realized—it does not reflect how long the customer has to wait in case the part is not available. For spare parts this is an important issue, since delay in receiving a part needed for a system repair contributes to the unavailability of the system for customer use (downtime). The backorder rate specifically measures *the average number of parts that systems/customers are waiting to receive*. If, for example, one has no backorders half of the year, a backorder of 1 unit a quarter of the year, and a backorder of 2 units for the remaining quarter of the year, the average number of backorders for the year is 0.75. The problem with the backorder rate is that it is not very intuitive, and hence it is not easy for customers to relate it to their overall service level needs. Another issue is that in some environments excess demands are not backordered at the point where they enter the inventory system. Rather, shortages may be transferred to emergency backup locations (either laterally to other forward locations or vertically to a central warehouse).

(d) **Response time/backorder delay** This is the average amount of time that a customer has to wait for their order to be fulfilled. If the part is available off the shelf, at the point where demand is realized then there is no (or minimal) delay. If the demand order cannot be filled at that location and the demand is either backordered or transferred, then the customer will have to wait until the part arrives.

It should be clear that for a given part, all of the part service metrics introduced here are inter-related and are determined by the interaction between the level of inventory of the part, the process that generates demands and any delays or lags in the system.

3.2.2 System Service

As noted previously, from a customer/system user perspective, service measured at a *system* level is typically more relevant for service parts since the purpose of the after sales service supply chain is to keep a *system* up and running. As we shall see, system service metrics are based on some *combination of part service performance* that is *weighted* by the *importance* of each part to the system.

Different service measures at the system level that are relevant for service parts management include:

(a) **Average fill rate** When measuring fill rate at a system level, one considers the percentage of parts that are required for repair that are available from on the shelf inventory. The system fill rate is then the weighted average of the fill rates for the parts that supports the system, with the weights being the relative demand rates for each part per year.
(b) **Total (system) backorders** The system wide backorders is simply the sum of expected backorders of all parts that are used to support the system.
(c) **Average wait time** As noted before, this consists of the total time the customer has to wait before a failed system is up and running again and is measured in terms of the overall job completion time as well as time spent waiting for the entire collection of parts needed for the service.
(d) **System availability** As we already have noted, the purpose of service parts is to keep systems up and running—in other words as available as possible. It can be proved that the average availability of a system is determined by the total number of backorders. The resulting availability metric is a measure that is both intuitive and directly reflects the customer goal of generating value through the use of the system.

When specifying a target for any service level, the value should be based on:

- The cost of a system being down (e.g., one hour down for a semi-conductor fab can be of enormous cost), and
- The expectations and requirements for availability.

3.2.3 Inventory Position

We define *inventory position* for a specific part as the *total number of parts in the system*. This includes the number of parts on the shelf immediately available for customer use as well as the number currently in repair or in transit minus the number of units backordered. Let s be the target number of units for the inventory position for a specific part type. If there currently is a system that is waiting for this part, it implies that there are no such parts *on the shelf* (otherwise they would have been used to repair the system). Hence, in the case of one or more systems waiting for a specific part (i.e., backorder), it means that more than s units are currently being repaired, or waiting in the repair queue or are in transit. We shall refer to the total number of such units as the number of units "in repair" and denote it by R. If one system is waiting for a specific part, then the number of units in repair of this part is $R = s + 1$, if two systems are waiting for the type of part then $R = s + 2$, and so on.

3.2.4 Probability of No Stockout

Following the previous discussion, the probability of filling a demand for a part is equal to (1—Probability of a stockout) and can be expressed as

$$\begin{aligned} PNS(s) &= \Pr(R = 0) + \Pr(R = 1) + \ldots + \Pr(R = s - 1) \\ &= \Pr(R \leq s - 1)\,. \end{aligned} \tag{1}$$

In order to deal with a *system* of spare parts, we need some more notation. Let n be the *number of spare parts* that supports the system. We index these spare parts by i, so when a variable has subscript i, it means that we are talking about a specific service part out of the total of n service parts.

System fill rate probability is defined as:

$$PNS(s_1, s_2, \ldots, s_n) = \frac{1}{\sum_{i=1}^{n} \lambda_i} \sum_{i=1}^{n} \lambda_i \Pr(R_i \leq s_i - 1)\,, \tag{2}$$

where the probability of not stocking out for each part is weighted by its relative contribution to the total demand for all parts.[1]

3.2.5 Backorders

As has been noted, the expected number of backorders for a part can be expressed as

$$\begin{aligned} BO(s) &= \Pr(R = s + 1) + 2\Pr(R = s + 2) + 3\Pr(R = s + 3) \ldots \\ &= \sum_{j=s}^{\infty} (j - s) \Pr(R = j)\,. \end{aligned} \tag{3}$$

To obtain the expected or average number of backorders, the different realizations of backorder values are weighted by their respective probability. So, the expected number of backorders is 1 times the probability of having 1 number of backorders at any time, plus 2 times the probability of having 2 number of backorders at any time, and so on.

[1] Note that $Fill\ rate = 1 - P\{Stockout\}$ for the special case of a Poisson distribution.

One special case of this expression that is useful, is the expected number of backorders when the inventory stocking level is equal to zero units. This is given by the simple expression

$$BO(0) = \lambda L. \tag{4}$$

The expected number of backorders on a system level is simply the sum of the expected number of backorders of all parts that are supporting the system. Let $BO_i(s_i)$ be the expected backorders for part i when the inventory position is equal to s_i. The systemwide expected backorders is then

$$SBO(s_1, s_2, \ldots, s_n) = \sum_{i=1}^{n} BO_i(s_i). \tag{5}$$

3.2.6 System Availability

Let K be the number of systems being supported, i.e., installed and being used by customers. A simple estimate of the availability due to service parts is then

$$A = \frac{K - SBO}{K}. \tag{6}$$

To summarize, both part and system service metrics are based on management's selection of a vector of target inventory positions $s_1, s_2, \ldots, s_n$. The values for each metric are also affected by the probability distribution for each part at each location (Poisson with mean λ_i and demand lead time L_i). Variation in s_i leads to variation in service metric levels for part i alone. System service metrics on the other hand, are a function of all of the target stocking levels, $s_1, s_2, \ldots, s_n$.

3.3 System Optimization

We are now ready to "put things together." When *optimizing* a *system of service parts*, we seek to allocate the inventory investment so that it leads to the maximum system availability. In other words, we want to spend the next dollar on inventory on the part that provides the highest impact on reducing backorders (which, as noted, can be shown to be equivalent to improving availability).

The overall optimization problem can be stated as following:

Maximize Availability

subject to

Total Inventory Investment $\leq$ Inventory Budget

or,

Minimize Inventory Budget

subject to

Availability $\geq$ Target Availability.

In practice, these optimization problems can be complicated by the existence of additional service constraints (by location, system type, customer, etc.) and additional resource constraints (local budget, cash flow, etc.).

The following steps summarizes the procedure of system optimization:

1. Start with target inventory position of zero for all parts.
2. Calculate expected backorders for each part.
3. Calculate the *reduction in backorders per dollar invested by increasing the inventory position by one unit* for each part.
4. Choose the part with the largest reduction in backorders per dollar invested, and increase the inventory position of this part by one unit. For this part, recalculate the two measures of expected backorders and reduction in backorders per dollar invested caused by increasing the inventory level of this part by one unit.
5. Continue to increase the inventory position of the most promising candidate by one unit until the desired service level (e.g., target availability) is reached or until all of the inventory budget is used up.

Let $\delta_i(s_i)$ be defined as the *reduction in expected backorders for part i when increasing the inventory position from s_i to $s_i + 1$ units*. We then have

$$\delta_i(s_i) = BO_i(s_i + 1) - BO_i(s_i). \tag{7}$$

By writing this out long-hand, we get

$$\begin{aligned}\delta_i(s_i) = &\Pr(R_i = s_i + 2) + 2\Pr(R_i = s_i + 3) + \ldots \\ &- \Pr(R_i = s_i + 1) - 2\Pr(R_i = s_i + 2) - 3\Pr(R_i = s_i + 3) - \ldots\end{aligned} \tag{8}$$

By collecting similar terms, we get

$$\begin{aligned}\delta_i(s_i) &= -\Pr(R_i = s_i + 1) - \Pr(R_i = s_i + 2) - \Pr(R_i = s_i + 2) - \ldots \\ &= -\Pr(R_i \geq s + 1) \\ &= \Pr(R_i \leq s) - 1.\end{aligned}$$

This is a very simple and compact expression for the reduction in expected back orders resulting from increasing the inventory position by one unit for part i.

The measure we are interested in, however, is *reduction in expected back orders per dollar invested in increasing inventory by one unit*. This expression for part i is given by

$$\frac{\delta_i(s_i)}{c_i}. \tag{9}$$

We have now defined all the components required to optimize target inventory levels for a system of service parts at a single stocking location.

3.4 Multi-Echelon Repairable Parts Inventory

In the previous section, we considered repairable parts inventory management at a single location. In this subsection, we consider a system consisting of one central warehouse and multiple forward locations. Demand for repairable parts originates at the forward locations and is satisfied from inventory at the forward location if available. The local warehouse inventory is replenished by the single central warehouse. The central warehouse sends failed parts to either internal or external repair shops. The goal of the system is to find the most cost-effective way of deciding which parts to stock where, and in what quantities, in order to meet some service target such as system backorders or average waiting times. The academic literature dealing with this problem setting usually makes the following assumptions:

- Demand at forward locations that cannot be satisfied from available inventory is backordered till inventory becomes available,
- No lateral transshipments between forward locations, or emergency shipments from the central warehouse, are allowed,
- The transit time from the central warehouse to the forward locations is deterministic, and
- A basestock policy is used for determining the stocking level of each part at each location.

3.4.1 Multi-Echelon Model

Let $i = 1, ..., |I|$ be the set of parts, and let $j = 1, ..., |J|$ be the set of forward locations at which these parts can be stocked. In addition, let $j = 0$ denote the central warehouse. Let the demand for item i at location j be a Poisson process with a constant rate $\lambda_{i,j}$. Let $\lambda_i = \sum_{j=1}^{J} \lambda_{i,j}$ be the total demand at forward locations for part i. The assumption of Poisson demand process is commonly used in academic literature including the well-known METRIC and vari-METRIC type models. The order and shipment time of part i from the central warehouse to the forward location

j is assumed to be deterministic and denoted by $t_{i,j}$. In case the central warehouse is stocked out, then there might be an additional delay due to the wait at the central warehouse which is not reflected in the shipping time $t_{i,j}$. A basestock policy with a basestock level $S_{i,j}$ is used to control inventory of each item i at each location j. This also implies one-for-one replenishments for each repair, i.e., no batching. Finally, it is typically assumed that the central warehouse uses a first-come first-served policy for demand originating from multiple forward locations. Let $\mathbf{S}$ denote the matrix of basestock levels $S_{i,j}$. Let $C_i(\mathbf{S_i})$ denote the expected costs per unit of time for each item i. Then the total average costs $C(\mathbf{S}) = \sum_{\mathbf{i}} \mathbf{C_i}(\mathbf{S_i})$. Also, let $EBO_{i,j}(\mathbf{S})$ represent the expected backorders of item i at location j if basestock levels $\mathbf{S}$ are used. Then typically, the problem is formulated as

$$\min C(\mathbf{S}) \tag{10}$$

$$subject \quad to \quad \sum_i \sum_j EBO_{i,j}(\mathbf{S}) \leq \mathbf{EBO_T}. \tag{11}$$

Solving this problem requires evaluating the average costs $C(\mathbf{S})$ and the expected backorders $EBO_{i,j}(\mathbf{S})$ as functions of the basestock levels at each location. This is typically done recursively by first characterizing the performance metrics at the central warehouse, which then is used to determine the metrics at the forward locations for each part.

The demand process for part i at the central warehouse is the sum of the demand for part i at the forward locations because of the basestock policy followed at the forward locations. Thus, the demand for part i at the central warehouse, $\lambda_{i,0}$ is equal to $\sum_j \lambda_{i,j}$. Let $t_{i,0}$ be the repair lead time for part i at the central warehouse. Then, by Palm's theorem, the number of parts in repair, $X_{i,0}$ of part i at the central warehouse is Poisson distributed with a mean of $\lambda_{i,0}t_{i,0}$. The distribution of the repair pipeline can be used to characterize all performance metrics at the central warehouse. For example, the Backorder distribution, $BO_{i,0}$ of item i at the central warehouse can be characterized by $(X_{i,0} - S_{i,0})^+$, i.e., backorders of part i at the central warehouse is the amount by which the repair pipeline exceeds the basestock level at the central warehouse. Since $X_{i,0}$ is Poisson distributed, the expected backorders of item i at the central warehouse, $EBO_{i,0}$ can be easily calculated.

The next step is to allocate the backordered demands at the central warehouse to the forward locations. Since each backordered demand at the central warehouse stems from forward location j with probability $\lambda_{i,j}/\lambda_{i,0}$, the probability distribution of the number of backorders of forward location j in queue at the central warehouse, $BO^j_{i,0}(S_{i,0})$, has a binomial distribution conditional on the total backorders of part i at the central warehouse $BO_{i,0}(S_{i,0})$. Consequently, one can determine the distribution of the number of parts in the repair pipeline at forward location j, $X_{i,j}(S_{i,0})$. It can be shown that $X_{i,j}(S_{i,0})$ is the sum of two variables, one of which is the number of demands at the forward location during the lead time $D^{\tau}_{i,j}$, and the second one the number of backorders at forward location j at the central warehouse

$BO^j_{i,0}$. Thus, one can write $X_{i,j}(S_{i,0})$ as

$$X_{i,j}(S_{i,0}) = D^{\tau}_{i,j} + BO^j_{i,0}(S_{i,0}). \tag{12}$$

Thus, the distribution of $X_{i,j}(S_{i,0})$ is a convolution of two distributions: the distribution of $D^{\tau}_{i,j}$ is a Poisson distribution with a mean of $\lambda_{i,j}t_{i,j}$ where $t_{i,j}$ is the transit time for part i from the central warehouse to location j, and the distribution of $BO^j_{i,0}(S_{i,0})$, which can be calculated as shown above. The distribution of $X_{i,j}(S_{i,0})$ enables computation of all metrics at the forward location. For example, the backorders of part i at forward location j, $BO_{i,j}(S_{i,0}, S_{i,j})$ can be written as $(X_{i,j}(S_{i,0}) - S_{i,j})^+$.

A key challenge in evaluating the performance metrics using the procedure described above is the computational effort in evaluating the various probability distributions, and particularly the distribution of the repair pipeline, $X_{i,j}$. Several approximations have been proposed in the literature to speed up the computations by approximating the distribution of the repair pipeline. Sherbrooke (1968) developed the METRIC model for multi-echelon evaluation using a single moment approximation of Eq. (12). In this method, one first computes the expected repair pipeline $EX_{i,j}$ by equating it equal to $ED^{\tau}_{i,j} + EBO^j_{i,0}(S_{i,0})$, i.e., by matching the first moment. Then, the distribution of $X_{i,j}$ is assumed to be Poisson with a mean $EX_{i,j}$ as computed by matching the first moment. This significantly speeds up the computation process as it does not require tracking the various discrete probability distributions, but only requires measuring the mean of these distributions for calculating the performance metrics of interest.

Slay (1984) and Graves (1985) developed a more accurate approximation by matching the first two moments of Eq. (12). Thus, both $E(X_{i,j})$ and $Var(X_{i,j})$ are computed by matching the first two moments. If, $Var(X_{i,j}) > E(X_{i,j})$, then one can fit a negative binomial distribution for $x_{i,j}$ using the first two moments. The accuracy of this fit has been shown to be very good since two moments are used in this approximation. Both the one-moment and two-moment approximations significantly ease the computational burden in evaluating the performance metrics of the multi-echelon system, thus enabling the solution to an optimization problem based on these metrics.

A greedy heuristic, similar to the one described for the single echelon model, has been shown to be very effective in solving the multi-echelon model. This requires computing the reduction in backorders, $\Delta_{i,j}EBO_{i,j}(S_{i,j})$ of part i at location j by increasing the basestock level by one unit, as well as the increase in system cost, $\Delta_{i,j}C(\mathbf{S})$, by increasing the basestock level of part i at location j by one unit. Then, one can compute the ratio, $\frac{\Delta_{i,j}EBO_{i,j}(S_{i,j})}{\Delta_{i,j}C(\mathbf{S})}$ to compute the part-location combination that has the "biggest bang for the buck." One can increase basestock levels iteratively using this approach till the service criteria in the constraints of the optimization model are all met. In practice, this analysis is complicated by the potential non-convexity of the objective function or the constraint set, and this requires the use of efficient heuristics to identify solutions close to the global optimal solution.

3.5 *Demand Forecasting for Spare Parts*

Given the attributes of demand for spare parts described previously, analytical forecasting of demand continues to be a significant challenge for academics and practitioners alike. The most commonly prescribed methods for forecasting include time series methods, with several variations, combined with engineering data about part failures, planned and mandated maintenance events, information about installed base and service contracts. Among time series methods, exponential smoothing emerged as an early candidate and found widespread use. Unfortunately, the intermittent nature of demand renders this method inefficient. Therefore, one of the earliest modifications to this method was provided by Croston (1972), which uses exponential smoothing to separately update the estimated demand size and the demand interval (or frequency) whenever a positive demand occurs. Several further modifications have since been proposed (see, for example, Teunter and Duncan 2009). While time series methods are advantageous in that they rely primarily on historical data, these methods must be re-calibrated each time there are major changes in the environment, such as changes to the installed base. Engineering data provides the basis for reliability based forecasting methods. The most recent developments in forecasting rely on the use of Machine Learning and Artificial Intelligence techniques.

4 Case Studies of Industry Applications

4.1 *General Approach in Industry Applications*

Having provided the foundations of the problem and analytical solution methodology that forms the basis of most software systems for practical applications, we briefly describe two case studies of large-scale applications of spare part management systems (other interesting applications can be found in Cohen et al. (2000) and Chamberlain and Nunes 2004). We note that the methodologies discussed earlier are typically embedded in a larger hierarchical framework of decisions. Broadly speaking, there are three primary hierarchies of decisions that are relevant to the service supply chain environment (Cohen et al. 2006b). The first hierarchy is the product hierarchy, which has to do with the multi-indentured nature of the service parts. The second hierarchy is the geographic hierarchy, which has to do with the multi-echelon nature of the service supply chain. The interplay between these two hierarchies ultimately define the most cost-effective way to meet customer service requirements. Understandably, the quickest way to provide customer service is to stock at the highest level of the product hierarchy (e.g., spare Cisco routers for a telecommunication system) at the lowest level of geographic hierarchy (e.g., right at the customer location). The slowest way is just the opposite—stock the lowest level of product hierarchy (components of a router that can be used to replace failed components) furthest away from the demand at the highest level of geographic hierarchy (e.g., central distribution center). The tradeoff is obvious. The first approach is the most responsive, but also the most expensive, while the second approach is the cheapest, but also the least responsive. Mathematical optimization models determine the best combination of asset deployment decisions that leverage these two hierarchies. These decisions are embedded within a chronological planning hierarchy, based on the planning horizon and objectives for the relevant decisions. Design and strategy related decisions about the service business are strategic, and their planning horizon tends to be in years or months. Decisions about positioning of material, human and knowledge resources are the next level of decisions, and made over horizons that span months or weeks. Decision related to redeployment of assets, for example, material flow decisions concerning purchases of additional parts, repairs, replenishment, allocation, and transshipment are made more frequently, on a weekly or daily basis. Lastly, activities in response to actual failure events, dispatch of service engineers, for instance, are made on a daily or hourly basis.

4.1.1 OPTIMIZER: Service Logistics at IBM

Cohen et al. (1990) describe one of the earliest large-scale commercial (non-military) implementation of a scientific approach to management of a multi-echelon service delivery system. The authors designed and implemented a system, called Optimizer, that helped provide management flexibility in setting service level targets for differentiated market segments and improve inventory efficiency and cost control. These objectives were driven by rapid changes in IBM's National Service Division's (NSD) business environment, increasing competition in their market, and growing pressures to decrease inventory investments. NSD was responsible for after sales service support to all of IBM's customers for about 1000 of their products with an installed population exceeding tens of millions. About 15,000 customer engineers (CEs) provided support through a multi-echelon network, aided by a Distribution Operations team that was responsible for transportation, warehousing, and other physical distribution functions, and an Inventory Planning team that was responsible for procuring, planning, and maintaining inventory through the network. Over 200,000 part numbers were managed in the four echelon network consisting of two central warehouses, 21 field distribution centers, 64 parts stations and 15,000 outside locations (unstaffed stocking locations). The number of part-stocking location combinations, referred to as SKUs, were in the millions, and the total inventory investment was valued in billions of dollars.

The objective of the overall problem was to minimize total costs (item costs, regular as well as emergency shipping costs, handling costs, setup costs and inventory holding costs) such that appropriate level of service could be delivered to the various prioritized classes of demand. The model determined optimal (s,S) policies for each SKU. They developed a heuristic method that decomposed the problem by echelon levels and treated the estimated lead time for each echelon as a constant. Although the method relied on heuristics, the resulting benefits from improved forecasting and inventory optimization were substantial. Operational efficiency improvements were pegged at about 20 million dollars per year. Technical details about the methodology can be found in Cohen et al. (1990) and the references therein.

4.1.2 Part-Age Dependent Supply Replenishment Policies at US Coast Guard

Products such as aircraft, ships, automobiles, elevators, engines, etc., all contain parts that may have to be replaced or repaired based on their usage in order to optimize product performance or guarantee safety. The optimal stocking of spare parts and managing the associated repair process constitutes an important logistics function in companies selling/servicing such equipment. Deshpande et al. (2006) use empirical data from the US Coast Guard to identify how part condition information (e.g., accumulated flight hours), obtained from maintenance records, can be used to estimate upcoming demand and thus be used to proactively manage parts inventory. They show that use of their scheme has the potential to decrease inventory costs significantly while improving in-stock availability.

The United States Coast Guard (USCG) has the mission to secure the US Coastline using a combination of air and sea capabilities. The Coast Guard operates 26 air stations located throughout the US borders ranging from Clearwater, Florida to Kodiak, Alaska. Each air-station operates a subset of 10 different aircraft types, with over 200 aircraft across all air stations. When aircraft parts fail, they generate demand for service parts. These service parts are supplied from local inventory (if available), which in turn gets replenished from a single central warehouse facility at Elizabeth City, North Carolina. The total number of individual part numbers managed exceeds 60,000 with a total inventory value of over $700 million.

All repair and supply activities are tracked in great detail by two separate databases—the Aviation Computerized Maintenance System (ACMS) and the Aviation Material Management System (AMMIS). The question explored in this research was the following: "How can USCG benefit from linking the maintenance and the demand databases?". This required the authors to (a) develop an approach to link the databases, and (b) develop an inventory control approach that uses aircraft maintenance information to improve the inventory management of service parts at the USCG.

The authors developed a part age-based inventory policy that classifies parts installed in the field as young or old based on their age relative to a threshold level. The optimal threshold determined through an optimization model that accounts for the marginal costs of shortage and holding, and repair lead time. The state dependent supply policy anticipates the demand for old parts and triggers advance replenishment orders for these parts *before* these old parts actually fail. For young parts, replenishment orders are placed only on actual failures. The arriving replenishments for young and old parts are combined into a common inventory pool at the warehouse, which is used to satisfy demand on a first-come-first-serve basis. If failures of old parts are more predictable, then triggering advance orders for these parts has the potential to decrease expected residence time for parts in the system and thus decrease overall inventory costs.

The impact of this policy was evaluated based on actual demand data for 41 critical parts over a five-year period. Computational results suggest that the proposed policy can lead to significant reduction in inventory cost, as high as 70% for some parts. This is achieved by efficiently matching demand for spare parts with its supply. This analysis suggests that the tools developed can be used for improving the forecasting ability of repair budgets. As much as 52% of the repair budget can be put on a predictable pattern by triggering advance replenishment orders.

5 Leading SPM Solutions Providers

Having discussed the fundamentals of a service supply chain, it should become clear to the reader that elegant and tractable structural properties that are derived and discussed in theoretical research articles are often not directly applicable in practice. More importantly, most real-world applications tend to be much larger in size and scope (number of parts, locations, customers served, suppliers, time period, etc.) and often require solutions in relatively short periods of time (real time in some instances). Thus, the structural complexity, scale, and time requirements render many of the theoretical results and methodologies impractical or ineffective in practice. Nonetheless, these findings provide the basis for heuristics that are often at the core of IT solutions offered by software vendors to design and manage such systems. We are not privy to the exact solution approaches deployed by solutions providers since they tend to be their closely guarded intellectual property. Therefore, we cannot comment on the analytical core of these solutions. However, in the following section, we describe the key capabilities offered by some of the leading providers of SPM solutions.

The leading providers of SPM solutions include PTC, Syncron, Baxter Planning, Oracle and SAP. Of these companies, PTC has the largest annual revenue for SPM related services and leads in terms of its experience and expertise (Blumberg 2020).

In general, most commercial SPM solutions have the following key components:

1. Parts management and grouping: This capability is particularly important in the service business for purposes of forecasting and inventory management. A key element that is distinct in this environment is part chaining, where newer versions of parts replace older ones as product technology evolves. Therefore, it is important to maintain information about such chains, which can get long when products can function for long periods of time. Similarly, in some instances, complicated business rules are used that determine how parts are managed and deployed, so the solutions must allow for the representation of such business rules.

2. Demand forecasting,
3. Inventory planning and optimization,
4. Supply planning (order plan): A significant portion of planners' efforts is spent on decisions that must be made to implement the recommend inventory levels. Such decisions include procurement, shipment modality, lateral shipments, new product buys, last time buys, etc.
5. User interface, reporting and analytics: The ease of use of the solution, customizability, and configurability to fit the unique needs of the business, ability to define and produce meaningful summary and exception reports, KPIs that help in the assessment of the business as well as personnel, etc.

5.1 Baxter

Baxter was founded in 1993 and is based in Austin, Texas. Its SaaS solution offers inventory planning as well as execution capabilities, including features that support logistics network optimization, forecasting, inventory planning, replenishment and redeployment, supply order automation, excess management and planning analytics. Its solution incorporates part, site and customer criticality attributes to meet supply chain total cost objectives. Inventory holding as well as shortage costs at each node in the network are computed, however, the optimization is done sequentially at each echelon, not jointly across all echelons. Similarly, service level targets are not a part of the optimization, though it can be computed. Ease of use and customizability of the user interface, alerts for planners, attribute-based parts classification, rules-based parts grouping, parts chaining and substitution, and forecasting methods that are appropriate for intermittent and low demand parts are strong features of their solution.

5.2 Syncron

Syncron was founded in 1999 and is based in Stockholm, Sweden. Their suite of solutions includes those for parts planning for OEM owned supply chain networks, parts pricing, and uptime management. Their price optimization solution, called Syncron Price, is the key feature of their product suite. This focus, in addition to their Syncron Uptime solution makes them a strong choice for companies interested in offering servitization capabilities. Parts forecasting, planning, and stocking decisions, therefore, are not as well developed. Only basic forecasting and single location inventory optimization capabilities are offered. However, they are well regarded for their user interface, parts grouping and parts relationship features, and inventory management for product locations that span globally.

5.3 Oracle

Oracle is a well-established ERP provider, and Oracle Spares Management is a module within this suite. It became available relatively recently, in 2016. Since their ERP solution was not originally designed with parts planning in mind, their parts grouping and parts relationship capabilities are extremely basic, as are their parts forecasting and multi-echelon inventory optimization capabilities. However, Oracle's Demantra solution can provide a broad array of forecasting techniques. Their Spares Management solution integrates well with their Oracle Field Service solution.

5.4 SAP

SAP, similarly, is also a well-established ERP solutions provider. It offers SPM capabilities through its Extended Service Parts Planning (eSPP) and Integrated Business Planning (IBP) solutions. While these solutions provide basic functionality related to forecasting, parts planning, inventory management and distribution, and some optimization capabilities through IBP, the solution was not developed specifically for the service environment. For instance, forecasting does not address intermittent demand or causal factors, it only uses historical data, which is a significant limitation. Similarly, the architecture does not have robust parts grouping and parts relationship capabilities, and the multi-echelon optimization was developed for finished goods, not service parts. However, SAP's reporting, analytics and data warehousing features are substantial.

5.5 PTC

The Servigistics business unit of PTC is the largest of the software companies that offer a solution for spares parts management (SPM) and leads the field with over 150 clients in industries as diverse as life sciences, industrial products, federal aerospace & defense, electronics and high tech, automotive, and retail and consumer, with industrial products being their largest customer sector. The company based in Boston, MA, offers a range of Augmented Reality, Industrial IoT, Product Lifecycle Management (PLM) and CAD and Service solutions with annual revenues of over $1.5 Billion generated from a global footprint.

A series of mergers between three of the best-in-class solutions of their time, Xelus, Servigistics, and MCA Solutions,[2] has formed the core of their current

[2] Co-founded by Dr. Morris Cohen and Dr. Vipul Agrawal.

SPM solution. Founded by a group of ex Xerox and Kodak employees in the 80s, Xelus was among the earliest companies to develop a comprehensive SPM solution. Their forte was a well-designed planner workflow, with excellent configurability. However, their solution included only basic forecasting capabilities (simple time series methods) and lacked sophisticated inventory optimization methodologies. Servigistics was founded in 1999 and excelled in its robust technology platform that provided a good planning support for global organization with decent forecasting capabilities. However, MIME inventory optimization capabilities were missing. MCA Solutions, also founded in 1999, emerged with the most advanced optimization capabilities, with the first MIME solution motivated by the needs of their clients in the A&D and semi-conductor equipment sectors. However, their solution did not offer compelling tactical planning workflows and required significant customization to fit the clients' unique needs. A merger between the three companies, therefore, made a lot of sense. The resulting solution, branded as Servigistics, provided a much-needed complement to PTC's suite of PLM solutions and leveraged their strength in the IoT arena.

Joint MIME inventory optimization for multiple items, optimization for subsets of parts (parts grouping), flexibility in parts grouping, excellent user interface and convenient customizability, advanced forecasting features that leverage history, installed base, causal, equipment based, and IoT information, extensive planner workflow, and a pricing module integrated with parts planning are among strongest attributes of Servigistics. Their solution also offers the capability to optimize last time buys (LTB) of components, since products often have to be supported for much longer periods of time than the length of time manufacturers actively produce a product before moving on to the next generation of their products.

6 Trends and Research Opportunities

While there is a long history of academic research on service parts management, there are several new exciting developments over the last ten to twenty years that have created significant new opportunities in this arena. These opportunities can be classified into three categories: (1) Globalization; (2) Technology and Big Data; and (3) Modern computing and automation.

6.1 Globalization

Globalization over the past few decades has led to a dynamic business world with increasing risk factors such as supply chain disruptions. From the global chip shortage to a cargo ship stuck in the Suez Canal, recent events have demonstrated the need for agile and robust supply chains. In the service parts management world, these risks have taken additional importance due to the impact that availability of service parts can have on a firm's operations. As a result, service parts supply chains need to become more "agile" and "resilient" in the modern world. *Agility* can be defined as the ability to respond rapidly and cost effectively to short term changes in demand or supply disruptions. *Resilience* is the ability to adapt to structural changes by modifying supply chain strategies, products, and technologies. A recent Gartner report (Geraint and Raman 2021) highlights six strategies for supply chain resilience that includes multi-sourcing, near shoring, network diversification, and inventory and capacity buffers. In order to achieve this goal, planners need tools, which currently do not exist, that can help them anticipate and quantify the impact of future scenarios, evaluate strategies for mitigating risk, and adapt to changes in supply chain structure. Supply chain planners need a way to quantify the impact of both past and future scenarios in order to evaluate risk mitigation strategies, adapt their supply chain structure, and make better decisions. Service parts supply chain planners in the future will increasingly look at "scenario planning" methodology to deliver resiliency and agility in their supply chain. The goal of a scenario plan is not to be able to forecast a future, but to anticipate worst-case, most likely case, and best-case scenarios to stress test the service parts supply chain. Similar to the annual bank stress tests conducted by the Federal Reserve Board to evaluate the financial strength of the banks, firms will likely conduct stress tests of their service parts supply chain to measure the robustness of their operations to unanticipated risk factors. This has also created an opportunity for academic researchers to analyze scientifically sound methods of conducting scenario planning for service supply chains. Gao et al. (2019) use the time-to-recover (TTR) parameters to analyze the risk-exposure index (REI) of supply chains under disruption.

Also, there is an increasing need for research on after sales service supply chains in emerging markets. A recent paper (Kundu and Ramdas 2019) examines to what extent timely after sales service—i.e., fast resolution of repair tasks—impacts technology adoption in emerging markets.

6.2 Technology and Big Data

There has been an explosion in the amount, granularity, variety, and velocity of data that organizations are able to capture. These advances are due to several technologies such as the Internet of Things (IoT), Additive Manufacturing (3D printing) and Blockchain technologies. For example, advances in IoT technology have now made possible actions taken based on real-time sensor readings which has the potential to revolutionize service parts management. As IoT sensors provide more granular and real-time information on the environment and conditions under which a product is operating (e.g., usage, temperature, humidity, etc.), it is now possible to use this detailed information to both anticipate failures that generate demand for spare parts as well as plan for inventory of spare parts. IoT technology will also facilitate predictive maintenance actions in advance of service parts failures, instead of the traditional model of reacting to service parts failures.

However, much more academic research is needed in highlighting what kinds of IoT data will be useful for service parts management, and what should be the frequency and granularity of this IoT data. A recent paper (Saghafian et al. 2022) builds models that allows managers to predict (and influence) the set of other firms with which their sensors will form information links.

Similarly, Additive Manufacturing has the potential to revolutionize the world of service parts management. Additive manufacturing takes the 3-D representation of any object and can build (manufacture) the object by adding one layer at a time. It provides firms the ability to produce spare parts on demand instead of having to stock inventory. The flexibility of 3-D printing technology can help service parts supply chains become much more efficient at low cost because it eliminates the need to stock service parts inventory at multiple locations. Instead of stocking service parts inventory of thousands of expensive parts, a service part can now be quickly printed on failure of a product. This also leads to an opportunity for academic researchers to address questions such as what types of products would benefit the most from 3-D printing technology and what are the best ways to deploy this technology. Song and Zhang (2020) present a general framework to study the design of spare parts logistics in the presence of three-dimensional (3-D) printing technology.

Finally, there has been an explosion in Enterprise software technology that makes data easily accessible across the entire supply chain. As a result, data across divisions and across firms can now be integrated. This can potentially reduce the need for relying on demand forecasts for service parts management and also enable stakeholder coordination. For example, service parts management teams can use data available from marketing such as installed base information and request for quotations (RFQs) in creating a spare parts management plan. Also, the big data revolution has increased the granularity of the data to the transaction level. Since, each transaction can now be easily captured and tracked digitally, one can now build a more accurate representation of supply chain interactions in the service supply chain. Finally, the variety of the data available has also exploded. For example, data from IoT sensors, Marketing, Social Media, etc., can all be integrated to create a better supply chain plan.

Capturing this data, however, is only the first piece to the puzzle. Current planning systems are not able to effectively capitalize on big data, leading many organizations to use ad-hoc methods such as manual interventions and overrides. This has created an opportunity for academics to scientifically understand how this explosion in data can enable effective service parts management.

6.3 Modern Computing and Automation

There has been an explosion in computational power over the last two decades. This has also been partly driven by availability of newer hardware architectures such as Graphic Processing Units (GPUs) and Tensor Processing Units (TPUs).

This has resulted in orders of magnitude increase in computing power which can be used to solve large-scale service parts management problems. There has also been a movement to high performance computing via the cloud that can enable solutions to complex problems. Finally, rapid advances in Machine Learning and Artificial Intelligence techniques in Computer Science has the potential to revolutionize service parts management. For example, Ban and Rudin (2019) explore the Machine Learning approach for solving the classical Newsvendor problem using big data. It will be interesting to see such an approach applied to service parts management.

One area where these developments can have a big impact in service parts management is demand forecasting. The intermittent nature of service parts demand makes the forecasting problem very difficult. The availability of data from different sources can enable better prediction of demand using feature based causal models instead of time series based forecasting models that are commonly embedded in current software systems. Also, machine learning (ML) based models can enable discovery of highly non-linear interactions between causal features that can improve forecasting accuracy. However, much more academic research is needed in this domain to determine conditions and data types for which this is possible. For example, Andersson and Jonsson (2018) explore and propose how product-in-use data can be used in, and improve the performance of, the demand planning process for automotive aftermarket services.

A second area where the development in modern computing will have a big impact is automation of decision support systems for service parts management. The complexity of service parts networks combined with the large number of parts results in a very laborious, time consuming, and expensive process which can be automated through advanced decision support systems. However, this will necessitate development of smart alert generation protocols that detect anomalies and warn the users to intervene when unexpected data is observed by the system. However, there has not been much academic research on Alert Generation algorithms on when an alert should be generated and when human intervention is warranted.

Finally, advances in modern computing may obviate the need to use stylized mathematical models for supply chain planning. The granular representation of real-world data can enable construction of "digital-twins" where one can recreate a parallel universe that represents a service parts supply chain. A digital twin can enable "what-if" analysis where a manager can ask questions such as what would have happened in the past if a different inventory policy was used, or what will happen in the future if a different demand scenario were to unfold. Through accurate computation of key performance indicators (KPIs) that do not rely on stylized models, managers will be able to evaluate supply chain resiliency strategies quickly. Not only is it now possible to run detailed optimization problems that do not rely on large lists of assumptions, but the boost in computational power also unlocks the ability to take a purely data driven approach: a formulation where input data is used to directly drive the end decision (common in machine learning). This also reduces the reliance on forecast accuracy for supply chain planning.

One example of how the existing analytical methodologies can be generalized by leveraging such advances is the relaxation of the assumption of memoryless failures and Poisson demand, which is commonly made in the academic literature but may not hold true in practice. Advances in Big Data and Machine Learning provides opportunities to refine traditional models as discussed below:

(a) **Part failures due to wear and tear** A part is more likely to fail as it gets older and becomes more worn. Consequently, changing a part makes it less likely that this part will fail in the near future. This is often the case for mechanical systems (i.e., non-electronic). The population of installed systems and the service parts included in these systems are often of different ages. Hence, the fact that one part is replaced could affect the *total* demand (failure rate) for *the system*. Data available from sensor technologies and information available about installed base can help refine demand models for service parts management.
(b) **Part Failures due to external events** Some systems are exposed to external forces. One example would be telecommunication centers that are exposed to lightning. During periods with lightning there is a higher probability of parts in a telecommunication center failing than during periods without lightning. To link it to the definition of memoryless failures, let us look at it from a slightly different angle: if a part in a telecommunication system has just failed, it is likely that there is currently lightning in the area, and hence it is more likely that another copy of the same part will fail at a different telecommunication center in the same area. It follows then that what will happen in the future depends on what has (recently) happened. With the advent of big data, causal features such as weather, economic factors, customer usage, etc., can be captured to improve the demand forecast accuracy.
(c) **Demand correlation** Demand for parts is triggered by system failures. Typically, multiple parts will fail together (e.g., a power supply and control boards). In such cases demand for parts are not independent. Both replenishment and repair can also require kits which contain a collection of parts used together. This also leads to correlated demand pattern. Advances in Machine learning and Big Data can help build sophisticated models that capture this demand correlation across parts, customers, and geographies, which can lead to better service parts management solutions.

To summarize, the area of service parts management is ripe for an exponential improvement in performance due to advances in Technology, Big Data, Modern Computing and Machine Learning.

Acknowledgments This chapter is an homage to the substantial body of original and influential research on service supply chains conducted and directed by Prof. Morris Cohen. We were fortunate that we got to work closely with Prof. Cohen first as his doctoral students, and subsequently as collaborators on academic research as well as applied work with companies. We are grateful to have had a first-hand view of the tremendous impact he has had on students, collaborators, academia, and industry.

The first author is also grateful to Dr. Vipul Agrawal (Vice President, Product Management, PTC Servigistics) for many insightful conversations about the exciting world of service supply chains.

References

Andersson J, Jonsson P (2018) Big data in spare parts supply chains: the potential of using product-in-use data in aftermarket demand planning. Int J Phys Distrib Logist Manag 48(5):524–544

Automotiveaftermarket.org (2021) How big is the aftermarket automotive industry?. https://automotiveaftermarket.org/aftermarket-industry-trends/automotive-aftermarket-size/. 14 Oct 2021

Ban GY, Rudin C (2019) The big data newsvendor: practical insights from machine learning. Oper Res 67(1):90–108

Basten RJI, van Houtum GJ (2014) Surveys in Operations Research and Management Science

Blumberg Advisory Group (2020) Spare parts management software: state of the art benchmark evaluation. Blumberg Advisory Group, Warrington

Chamberlain JJ, Nunes J (2004). Service parts management: a real-life success story. Supply Chain Manag Rev 38–44

Cohen M, Kamesam PV, Kleindorfer P, Lee H, Tekerian A (1990) Optimizer: IBM's multi-echelon inventory system for managing service logistics. Interfaces 20(1):65–82

Cohen MA, Lee H, Cull C, Willen D (2000) Supply chain innovation: delivering values in after sales service. Sloan Manag Rev 41(4):93–101

Cohen MA, Deshpande V, Rudi N (2004) Repairable service parts management. In: Teaching note. The Wharton School, University of Pennsylvania

Cohen MA, Agrawal N, Agrawal V (2006a) Winning in the aftermarket. Harvard Business Rev 84(5):129

Cohen MA, Agrawal N, Agrawal V (2006b) Achieving breakthrough service delivery through dynamic asset deployment strategies. Interfaces 36(3):259–271

Croston JD (1972) Forecasting and stock control for intermittent demands. J Oper Res Soc 23(3):289–303

Dekker R, Pinçe Ç, Zuidwijk R, Jalil MN (2013) On the use of installed base information for spare parts logistics: a review of ideas and industry practice. Int J Prod Econ 143(2):536–545

Deshpande V, Cohen MA, Donohue K (2003a). A threshold inventory rationing policy for service-differentiated demand classes. Manag Sci 49(6), 683–703

Deshpande V, Cohen MA, Donohue K (2003b) An empirical study of service differentiation for weapon system service parts. Oper Res 51(4):518–530

Deshpande V, Iyer AV, Cho R (2006) Efficient supply chain management at the US coast guard using part-age dependent supply replenishment policies. Oper Res 54(6):1028–1040

Gao SY, Simchi-Levi D, Teo CP, Yan Z (2019) Disruption risk mitigation in supply chains: the risk exposure index revisited. Oper Res 67(3):831–852

Geraint J, Raman K (2021) Weathering the storm: supply chain resilience in an age of disruption. Gartner Executive Report

Graves SC (1985) A multi-echelon inventory model for a repairable item with one-for-one replenishment. Manag Sci 31(10):1247–1256

Iyer P, Wininger J, Goldberg M (2020) Cracking the services conundrum in aerospace and defense. Bain & Company, Boston

Kennedy WJ, Patterson JW, Fredendall LD (2002). An overview of recent literature on spare parts inventories. Int J Prod Econ 76(2):201–215

Kundu A, Ramdas K (2019) Timely after-sales service and technology adoption: evidence from the off-grid solar market in Uganda. Available at SSRN 3477210

Muckstadt JA (2004) Analysis and algorithms for service parts supply chains. Springer series in operations research and financial engineering. Springer, Berlin

Saghafian S, Tomlin B, Biller S (2022) The internet of things and information fusion: who talks to who? Manuf Serv Oper Manag 24(1):333–351

Sherbrooke CC (1968). METRIC: a multi-echelon technique for recoverable item control. Oper Res 16(1):122–141

Sherbrooke CC (2004) Optimal inventory modeling of systems: multi-echelon techniques, vol. 72. Springer Science & Business Media, Berlin

Slay FM (1984) Vari-metric: an approach to modeling multi-echelon resupply when the demand process is Poisson with a Gamma prior. Report AF301-3, Logistic Management Institute, Washington, DC, 232

Song JS, Zhang Y (2020) Stock or print? Impact of 3-D printing on spare parts logistics. Manag Sci 66(9):3860–3878

Teunter RH, Duncan L (2009) Forecasting intermittent demand: a comparative study. J Oper Res Soc 60(3):321–329

Topan E, Eruguz AS, Ma W, Van Der Heijden MC, Dekker R (2020) A review of operational spare parts service logistics in service control towers. Eur J Oper Res 282(2):401–414

United States Air Force (2022). https://www.amc.af.mil/About-Us/Fact-Sheets/Display/Article/977534/c-5-abc-galaxy-and-c-5m-super-galaxy/. 19 March 2022

Van Houtum GJ, Kranenburg B (2015) Spare parts inventory control under system availability constraints, vol. 227. Springer, Berlin

Waas A, Beck M, Herzberg R, Hauser J, Schlehuber F, Wolk A, Nikolic Z (2021) At the crossroads: the European aftermarket in 2030. Boston Consulting Group, Boston

Wellener P, Lineberger R, Millar K, Bendig O, Hussain A (2020) Aftermarket services: transforming manufacturing in the wake of the COVID-19 pandemic. Deloitte Insights

Playing with DISASTER: A Blockchain-Enabled Supply Chain Simulation Platform for Studying Shortages and the Competition for Scarce Resources

Daniel Hellwig, Kai Wendt, Volodymyr Babich, and Arnd Huchzermeier

Abstract This chapter explores the potential of distributed ledger technology (DLT) in addressing supply chain shortages and competition for scarce resources. Specifically, we assess the effect of strategic information sharing on supply chain efficiency and the creation of virtual markets to improve supply chain performance. To facilitate this research, we designed a simulation platform called DISASTER (DLT In Sourcing And Strategic Trading Experimental Research), which hosts web-based, dynamic, and customizable supply chain simulations that leverage concepts of blockchain technology, and permit capturing of information regarding players' ordering strategies and behavioral traits.

In this chapter, we describe the DISASTER platform and discuss two selected DISASTER simulations that probe supply chain retailers' order behavior: the first investigates the role of information sharing among competing retailers; the second allows for the trading of tokens among competing retailers. In the first simulation, we find that decision makers act more strategically and closer to Nash equilibrium predictions as more information about historical orders of competitors is shared; however, the observed outcome is not invariably an improvement in efficiency as measured by profits across participants. In the second simulation, we observe that initial order quantities remain unchanged as compared to the baseline (non-trading) scenario, despite the possibility to trade on virtual markets; however, over time, more equitable distribution of inventory is achieved, and the supply chain efficiency as measured by profits increases.

Our findings highlight the value of empirical research and management games in shedding light on the role of decision makers' behavioral characteristics and inves-

D. Hellwig · K. Wendt · A. Huchzermeier (✉)
WHU – Otto Beisheim School of Management, Vallendar, Germany
e-mail: Daniel.Hellwig@whu.edu; Kai.Wendt@whu.edu; Arnd.Huchzermeier@whu.edu

V. Babich
McDonough School of Business, Georgetown University, Washington, DC, USA
e-mail: Volodymyr.Babich@georgetown.edu

H. Lee et al. (eds.), *Creating Values with Operations and Analytics*, Springer Series in Supply Chain Management 19, https://doi.org/10.1007/978-3-031-08871-1_9

tigating real-life supply chain challenges and the potential of adopting blockchain-specific capabilities in that space.

Keywords Supply chain shortages · Blockchain technology · Information sharing · Virtual markets · Behavioral operations management

1 Introduction

In a business-as-usual state of the world, supply chains are not typically the center of top-management and popular media attention. However, a stream of recent crises has changed that. The scope, intensity, and duration of supply chain problems are unprecedented and pervasive: shortages, delays, higher prices, and panic buying have affected numerous industries. To list just a few examples, in 2020 and 2021, the world experienced shortages of medical ventilators, personal protective equipment, toilet paper, baker's yeast, pasta, lumber, furniture, pet food, and toys. Consequences of the global microchip shortage are still accruing, but the automotive industry estimates that 2–3 million fewer vehicles were produced in 2021—a total sales loss of $210 billion (AlixPartners 2021; WEF 2021).

Although the centrality of supply chain operations has become increasingly salient to the broader public only recently, the operations management (OM) academic community and practitioners have long argued that supply chain management constitutes a decisive factor in business success (Cohen and Lee 2020). In particular, understanding the value of information sharing has long been a focus of OM research. In the context of the bullwhip effect (BWE), or the demand distortion that travels upstream in supply chains, theoretical and empirical OM literature has shown that sharing demand information can be valuable in reducing the BWE stemming from signal processing causes and in improving supply chain performance (Cohen and Kouvelis 2020). In a similar context, Morris Cohen and colleagues Terwiesch et al. (2005) and Ren et al. (2009) explore the effects on supply chain performance of buyers and sellers being given unreliable information.

Extending ideas in Babich and Hilary (2019, 2020, 2022) and Hellwig et al. (2020), we argue that distributed ledger technology (DLT), specifically, blockchain, can facilitate both the trustless sharing of information in supply chains and the creation of virtual markets to enable a more efficient allocation of scarce supplies. First, blockchain is designed to allow for information sharing among multiple parties while ensuring both trustworthiness and (if needed) anonymity, thereby mitigating key concerns that have thus far limited the willingness of supply chain stakeholders to partake in information sharing. Second, blockchain enables the creation of digital tokens, which can represent unique and secure digital claims on assets and capacities in supply chains. Such tokens enable virtual markets in which supply chain resources can be traded. While the theory and practice of economics and finance highlight the role of markets in achieving efficient resource allocation, such markets have yet to be created and established for all products that flow through supply chains. Indeed, the volume for some products is not sufficient for traditional financial intermediaries to operate respective markets. By eliminating the need for financial intermediaries, blockchain technology can reduce the setup costs for such markets, thus helping to establish markets for less liquid assets. This will allow for the trading of supply chain inventory, thereby yielding a better match between demand and supply in dynamic systems.

To facilitate the investigation of the role of trustless information sharing in supply chains and the creation of virtual markets to improve supply chain performance, we designed a supply chain simulation platform called Distributed ledger technology In Sourcing And Strategic Trading Experience Research (DISASTER). In addition to behavioral experiments, the platform enables classroom and industry learning experiences about challenges arising in real-life supply chain and exploration of the benefits of adopting blockchain technology. Note that it is the concepts rather than the technology of blockchain and digital tokens that are applied in the simulation; nonetheless the functionalities embedded capture key features of how such markets could operate based on blockchain technology in a practical setting.

In this chapter, we describe the DISASTER platform and illustrate its use with two simulations: (i) information sharing among retailers competing for scarce supply and (ii) trading tokens on supplier's capacity between retailers when facing demand uncertainty. In the first simulation, we find that sharing selective competitive information may leave the supply chain worse off; this result is counterintuitive, as supply chain managers are expected to prefer more to less information. In the second simulation, our results demonstrate that initial orders to the supplier remain largely unchanged despite the possibility to trade on virtual markets. This is a surprising finding when compared to the empirical evidence provided by the transshipment literature, which shows that when inventory can be exchanged, post demand realization, orders tend to regress to the mean demand (Katok and Villa 2021). In addition, more than 30% improvement in the evenness of inventory distribution, namely fewer instances of shortages or excess inventory, is achieved, thereby increasing overall supply chain profit by over 20%.

Hereafter, the chapter is organized as follows: in Sect. 2, we introduce the BWE and the role of sharing information about competitors' past orders and blockchain technology in ameliorating supply chain disruptions. Section 3 describes how the virtual markets enabled by blockchain technology can mitigate mismatches between supply and demand. In Sect. 4, we introduce our newly developed platform and illustrate its use with results from two simulation games, and conclude in Sect. 5 with a summary of our contributions and main findings.

2 The Bullwhip Effect and Information Sharing

The BWE describes the phenomenon of greater variance in orders that a company places, as compared with the variance in demand that the company observes. Thus, uncertainty about orders tends to increase as one moves upstream in the supply chain (Lee et al. 1997), making it more difficult to manage supply chains and rising costs. Lee et al. (1997) authored a seminal paper that explains the causes of the BWE and proposes solutions. The authors identified four causes of the BWE: (i) demand signal processing, (ii) rationing games, (iii) order batching, and (iv) price variation. For instance, Baganha and Cohen (1998) discuss empirical observations and results from management games that illustrate the BWE and identify sufficient conditions for multi-echelon inventory policies to reduce this effect. An extensive literature follows this work; for a review, see Wang and Disney (2016).

The management game typically used to illustrate the BWE is the Beer Distribution Game, invented in 1960 by Jay Wright Forrester at MIT and analyzed in detail by Sterman (1989b). This game models operations of a serial supply chain in which, unlike the retailer, players representing other companies (wholesaler, manufacturer, and supplier) have no knowledge of final consumer demand and, moreover, are unable to coordinate their actions with each other—even though their objective is to minimize the total supply chain cost. The Beer Distribution Game is a popular teaching tool and exists in many incarnations; however, it does not permit the analysis of causes of the bullwhip effect that can arise only in non-serial supply chains, such as shortage gaming, which arises when a supplier must decide how to allocate scarce supply among buyers who attempt to manipulate the supplier's decision through their orders. Shortage gaming leads to irrational ordering and buying behaviors and has frequently been observed in global supply chains during the COVID-19 pandemic; the platform we created focuses on that aspect of the BWE.

2.1 Shortage Gaming

Supplier's allocation rules have been extensively researched from a theoretical perspective. For example, Cohen et al. (1986) analyze the optimal order and allocation policies for a multi-echelon inventory system; however, they do not directly link their results to shortages. In subsequent research, Cachon and Lariviere (1999) focus on shortages and show that, in equilibrium, if supply is scarce—and suppliers use the proportional allocation rule—then retailers inflate orders as much as possible.

Experimental research reports human behavior, which can contribute substantially to the BWE, that differs appreciably from theory (Chen et al. 2012; Cui and Zhang 2018). For instance, Croson and Donohue (2006) demonstrate that supply chain inefficiencies, such as the BWE, are present even when operational issues such as supply shortage, demand estimation, and price variation have been eliminated, the reason being that decision makers' suboptimal behavior can be a major driver of suboptimal supply chain performance. In this context, a wide range of behavioral characteristics—divergence in cultural norms, cognitive capacity, and risk preferences as well as biases such as anchoring—have been identified in the field of OM (for an overview, see, e.g., Katok et al. 2018; Fahimnia et al. 2019).

At the same time, managers tasked with decision-making, especially in crisis situations such as facing supply shortages, tend to favor the availability of information because it enables them to calibrate their actions more appropriately. Along these lines, the existing literature stresses that sharing information can facilitate both reducing the BWE and improving supply chain performance (Lotfi et al. 2013; Cohen and Kouvelis 2020). It is noteworthy that the behaviors inducing volatility across supply chains (e.g., decision bias and over-reaction to fluctuations) are also dampened via information-sharing initiatives (Croson and Donohue 2006).

Despite these advantages of information sharing that have been identified in the literature, most practical approaches to alleviating information distortion have been met with limited success, largely because of the desire to maintain a competitive advantage, confidentiality concerns, and questions about the reliability, accuracy, and timing of available information (Lotfi et al. 2013). We propose that blockchain technology can address these concerns and thus facilitate the sharing of information.

2.2 *How Blockchain Can Help*

It is common for organizations to operate their own information technology (IT) systems, which do not directly interface with the IT systems of other companies. Posting data on public outlets raises concerns about sharing strategic secrets, violating customers' privacy, and losing control over the use of that data. In addition, leveraging such data is complicated by reservations regarding their availability and validity, which can arise either from initially incorrect records or from hacking and data manipulation after the fact.

Blockchain technology facilitates the decentralized sharing of information with multiple parties (Hellwig et al. 2020). Tamper-proof permanent recording of data on the blockchain ensures trustworthiness: records cannot be altered, and participants can remain anonymous. The cryptographic mechanisms incorporated in the blockchain protocol help protect this anonymity while simultaneously allowing building a reputation based on participants' behaviors. In addition, fully homomorphic encryption (FHE), which can be added to blockchain solutions, makes it possible to perform computations on encrypted records. This feature enables the derivation of summary statistics from encrypted data which, when decrypted, will match the result as if they had been performed on the non-encrypted data in the first place (Hellwig and Huchzermeier 2022). For instance, the average aggregated data from a group of supply chain parties can be shared without revealing any information about the individual stakeholders to their competition.

These prospects have motivated scholars to investigate the potential of information sharing that leverages blockchain technology to improve supply chain performance (Babich and Hilary 2019). For instance, van Engelenburg et al. (2018) propose a conceptual blockchain architecture to reduce information asymmetry, thereby reducing the BWE while protecting sensitive data. Xue et al. (2020) similarly describe a decentralized blockchain-driven supply chain design to address those untimely and distorted information exchanges that can lead to increased order variance.

Given the advantages offered by blockchain, we hypothesize that using this technology to record and share selected information can improve supply chain performance and reduce the BWE's adverse consequences due to competition among retailers for scarce supply. To assess this proposal, we introduce the supply chain simulation game Information sharing among competitors, which is hosted on our DISASTER platform (Sect. 4.2.1).

3 Virtual Markets

3.1 Market Economics

Matching supply with demand is a challenge that prevails across industries. Even if ample supply is available upstream, stock-outs can occur at the local level because of demand variations and the unequal distribution of inventory. The significance of this issue is amplified when the supply shortages have severe implications. For example, pacemaker producers are scrambling for inventory and seeking priority over other industries in receiving microchips, amidst a global supply shortage of those components, to ensure continued production of their products (Roland 2021).

Markets that facilitate the efficient allocation of resources exist for only a select set of commodities; they do not exist for most goods in supply chains, although there are some approximate solutions: such as pooling inventory in one location and transshipments. Inventory pooling is however usually managed by a central planner in a supply chain, and transshipment strategies are typically restricted—vis-à-vis resolving the mismatch between demand and supply—by terms established prior to the realization of random shocks. Other disadvantages of transshipments, relative to inventory pooling are (i) inefficient operations due to double inventory handling and its accompanying risks, greater lead times, and higher costs; (ii) extensive coordination requirements between shipping and receiving parties; and (iii) the required disclosure of competitive information (e.g., inventory levels). OM research on both topics is voluminous (e.g., for inventory pooling, see Federgruen and Zipkin 1984; Cohen et al. 1986; Deshpande et al. 2003; for transshipments, see Tagaras and Cohen 1992; Rudi et al. 2001; Katok and Villa 2021).

Markets present an opportunity to inject the efficiency of centralized inventory pooling into decentralized supply chain systems. For some products, however, the financial intermediaries that organize commodity exchanges do not find the scale of supply chains large enough to justify the fixed costs of creating and operating such markets. This is where a technology solution, such as blockchain, may be of value. Key questions that arise in this context include how much value such markets can create within the confines of individual supply chains and how will these markets affect incentives and investments as well as physical, financial, and informational flows.

3.2 How Blockchain Can Help

Blockchain enables the creation of digital tokens, which can represent any asset (e.g., currencies, loyalty points, capacities) that are fungible and tradable. Blockchain tokens can be categorized into currencies and tokens. Whereas a currency (e.g., Bitcoin) is usually native to its blockchain, a token leverages an already existing blockchain (e.g., Ethereum) and is built on top of it. Tokens are created via a so-called smart contract, which is a self-executing computer protocol; the process of converting the rights to an asset (e.g., claims on a supplier's capacity) into a digital token is called tokenization.

The combination of blockchain technology's core elements, namely digital tokens paired with a distributed ledger; a decentralized consensus mechanism, which ensures that temporarily divergent versions of the database converge; and cryptographic security measures enable the creation of a decentralized, virtual marketplace. Such features can ensure symmetric information as well as trust in the data and the trading process by providing transparent and valid records of historical transactions (Babich and Hilary 2019). These unique features can be leveraged to create a virtual market for trading tokens, which represent claims on suppliers' capacities among (competing) retailers. The distribution of inventory can thus be optimized prior to physical shipments, thereby facilitating more efficient operations may be achieved as compared with traditional transshipments.

To assess this market's potential for improving supply chain performance and to understand the behavioral implications for decision makers who are exposed to such a market, we leverage the supply chain simulation game Trading tokens among competing retailers that is hosted on the DISASTER platform (Sect. 4.2.2).

4 DISASTER: A Research Platform for Advanced Supply Chain Simulations

Morris Cohen identifies the considerable gap between managers' knowledge and their decisions (INFORMS 2004). Empirical research can shed light on human decision-making behaviors in the context of supply chain management. We therefore introduce purpose-built experimental research and learning platform, DISASTER,[1] that facilitates analyses of how blockchain-enabled information sharing and virtual markets affect supply chains efficiency. Researchers can associate behavioral traits of participants with their performance, allowing these connections to be subsequently analyzed. The DISASTER platform also enables classroom experience that facilitates industry learning about real-life supply chain issues and the potential for blockchain technology applications.

[1] www.disaster-game.com.

This section proceeds as follows. We start by describing the purpose and features of the DISASTER platform. We then describe two simulation games hosted on the platform and conclude by offering an outlook on future developments.

4.1 Purpose

Several platforms and software tools are available in the context of supply chain simulations and games. These can be grouped into two main categories: (i) generic platforms (e.g., z-Tree, oTree, SoPHIELabs) and (ii) supply chain-focused platforms and games (e.g., the Beer Distribution Game, Hunger Chain Game, Flower Game, Fathomd, Newsvendor Game). Existing generic platforms provide an excellent framework for developing simulations, including extensive libraries and communities, and are widely used. However, creating new simulations or customizing existing ones for specific scenarios requires dedicated research resources, a substantial time investment, and coding knowledge. Supply chain-focused platforms and dedicated games cover a wide range of supply chain topics that are well suited to conveying basic concepts and can be easily used in classrooms, but they are limited in their flexibility to adjust for purposes different from those considered in the initial design. (See Appendix A for an overview and assessment of several prominent platforms.)

Although numerous supply chain-focused games exist, none incorporates the features required for our inquiry into the role of blockchain technology for information sharing in supply chains. We have consequently designed a new platform, which has the following functional advantages:

1. Web-based interface; usable from any device with an Internet connection and a browser.
2. Self-contained (e.g., participant links, instructions, quizzes, behavioral questionnaires).
3. Library of ready-to-use "personal traits" questionnaires, including evaluation of its use; this library[2] can be continuously updated and enhanced by all collaborators.
4. Stable and secure data capture; data is saved in real time.
5. Close to zero latency; real-time interactions occur across all user interfaces (UIs), which allows for dynamic and interactive games.

Moreover, the platform differs from existing platforms in terms of the following four attributes:

1. A suite of pre-defined, ready-to-play supply chain simulation games use concepts of blockchain combined with advanced encryption and decryption technologies.

[2] See Appendix C for a list of questions used to assess behavioral characteristics.

2. Plug-and-play approach; UI-based game configuration (e.g., behavioral traits questionnaires, game design, instructions, parameters).
3. Open access of underlying data structure; no alignment with providers is required.
4. No coding skills are needed for adjustments (spreadsheet-based backend).

In short, the DISASTER platform is a new tool with applications in academic research, classroom teaching, and industry learning. The platform has already been successfully used by the authors for research, as well as hundreds of students in courses on operations management and blockchain technology and industry practitioners in Europe and the USA.

4.2 Simulation Games

In what follows, we describe two selected DISASTER games that probe retailers' ordering behaviors. (See Appendix B for a comparison of simulation games that focus on the BWE.) We use these games to illustrate the platform interface and the process of using the platform.

4.2.1 Information Sharing Among Competing Retailers

Description This game aims to research and to demonstrate (i) how using concepts of blockchain technology to record and share select buyer information affects supply chain performance and (ii) the potential of this technology to reduce the BWE's adverse consequences in cases of competition for scarce supplies.

Participants act as retailers in a supply chain that consists of one supplier (played by the system) and multiple retailers (Fig. 1). All retailers have the same demand, cost, and sales price conditions. In every round, participants are randomly matched; all interactions occur through the simulation interface. In each simulation round, participants decide on how many units to order from the supplier, anticipating supply shortages due to the orders of competing retailers while attempting to maximize their own firm's cumulative profit over 30 rounds. (See Appendix D for an example of the simulation instructions.)

Four scenarios are pre-defined, as summarized in Table 1. In the baseline Scenario 1, participants have no information about the order history of other retailers against whom they are playing in each period; these conditions emulate the traditional supply chain set-ups found in today's industries. In the remaining three scenarios, participants observe different levels of information provision/sharing. In Scenario 2, participants observe the average order of both retailers in the previous round; in Scenario 3, they observe the individual orders of both retailers in the previous round; and in Scenario 4, they observe the individual orders of both retailers over all previous rounds.

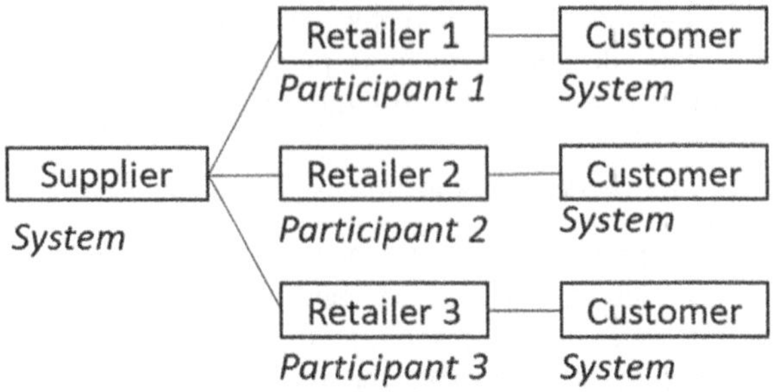

Fig. 1 Supply chain design of the Information sharing among competing retailers game

Table 1 Scenarios of the Information sharing among competing retailers game

Scenario	Information that participants observe	Blockchain application
1 (baseline)	No information about the order history of other retailers	• None (emulating traditional supply chain set-ups)
2	The average order of both retailers in the previous round	• Selected information is recorded on a distributed ledger, thereby building trust by design • Information is anonymized • Fully homomorphic encryption concepts are simulated by sharing aggregated statistics
3	The individual orders of both retailers in the previous round only	• Selected information is recorded on a distributed ledger, thereby building trust by design • Information is anonymized and traceable to individual actors, thereby a reputation is built
4	The individual orders of both retailers in all previous rounds	

This information is provided in a way that blockchain technology would enable in practice. Information is automatically recorded and anonymized, and it is always traceable to the individual entity (i.e., participants carry the history of their past decision even when matched with new players). In addition, features such as fully homographic encryption, which can be combined with blockchain technology—are simulated in the game by displaying the averages of past orders. This approach increases the individual firms' data protection as only aggregated and combined statistics are shown.

The results of each simulation run (e.g., average order per round, order variance, inventory shortages/excess, total profit) are automatically calculated and displayed to the game instructor. At this point, a discussion of how sharing past order information affects supply chain performance can be conducted based on participants' results.

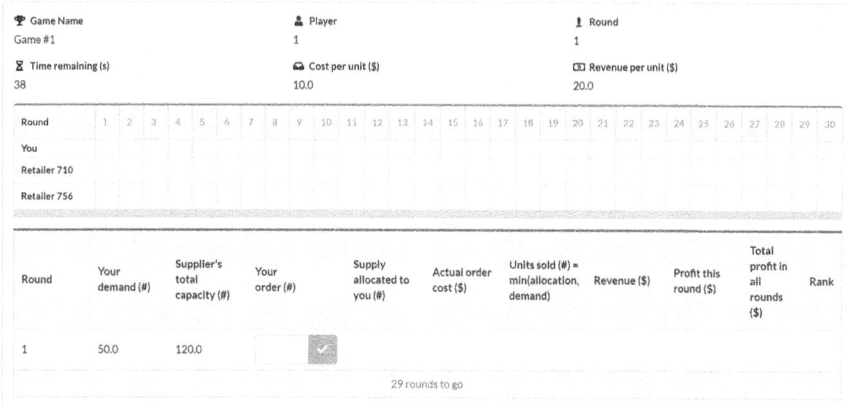

Fig. 2 Interface for order entry in the Information sharing among competing retailers game

User Interface Participants can access the game by clicking on the provided game link, which is automatically sent via a system-generated e-mail once the instructor has initiated the process. If activated, participants can be asked to read the game instructions and complete a readiness quiz prior to entering the simulation interface; following this procedure ensures that everyone understands the game and allows for a smooth simulation experience. Next, participants engage with an intuitive game interface that provides all the necessary information. Figure 2 depicts the scenario in which participants observe the individual orders of both competing retailers.

All displayed game parameters (e.g., number of rounds, time per round, number of players, cost, sales price) can be directly adjusted on the instructor's screen. After completing the game, participants can be asked to fill out a post-game questionnaire for the purpose of gathering additional feedback on the simulation—explicitly asking about the strategies participants applied during the game, testing their understanding of supply chain dynamics, and/or assessing behavioral characteristics through a pre-defined list of well-established questionnaires.

Results We used the DISASTER platform in several OM and blockchain technology courses and collected responses from hundreds of student participants, who were divided into four groups based on the type of historical information available to them when making ordering decisions. Results of these simulation games are shown in Fig. 3, which plots the average order per round placed by the participants. There are four scenarios, as described in Table 1. The control/baseline group (blue line), which has no information about competing retailers' behavior, namely, emulating the traditional supply chain set-ups without the application of blockchain technology demonstrates by far the slowest order inflation over time. When the average order of both retailers in the last round (orange line) or the entire order history (yellow line) is known (simulating the blockchain application in which past order behaviors are automatically recorded, anonymized, and traceable), the graph reveals that orders

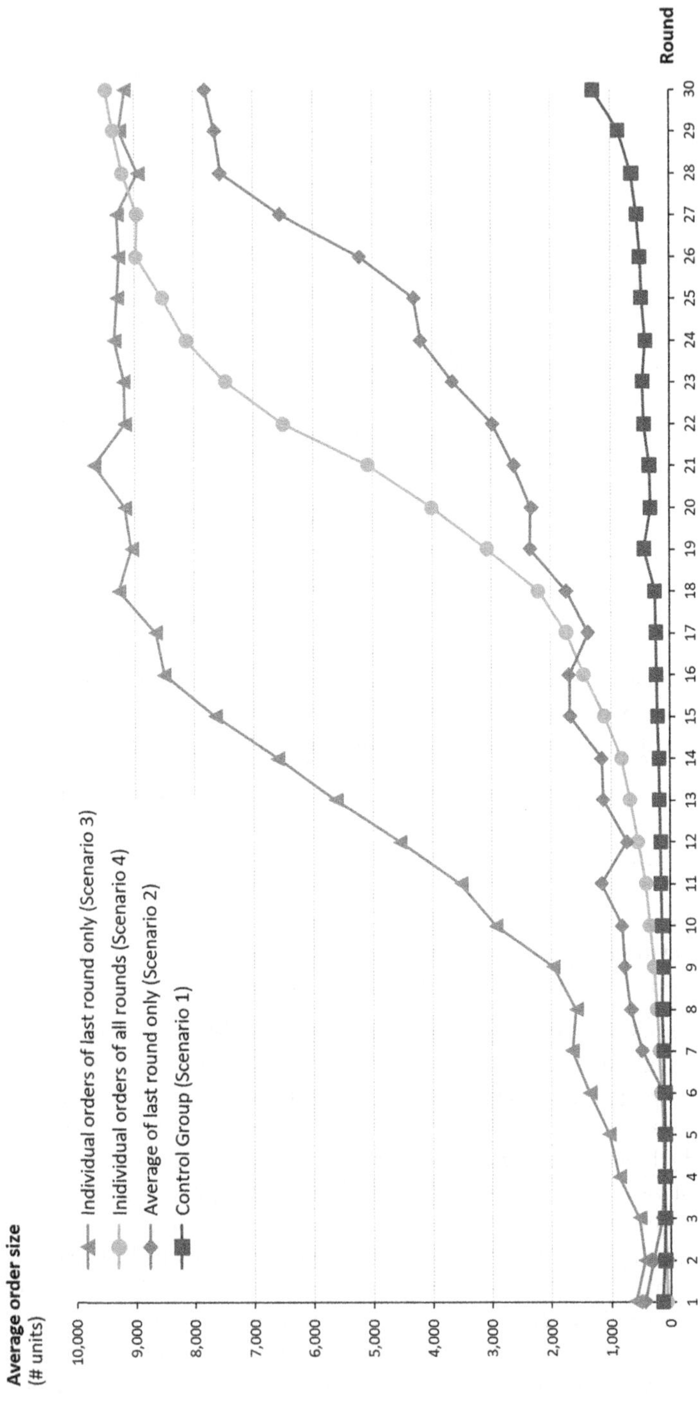

Fig. 3 Simulation results of the Information sharing among competing retailers game

inflate more rapidly. It is interesting that the fastest order inflation converging toward the Nash equilibrium is seen in the scenario under which the two competing retailers' individual orders are shared for only the last round (gray line).

In case of significant order inflation, as observed in scenarios 2–4, there is a disconnect between demand and orders. This is problematic because one would hope that orders not only convey important information to suppliers about downstream demand but also enable them to plan their capacities and resources appropriately. Suppliers often use received orders to allocate their available scarce supplies between customers.

When orders carry no demand information, suppliers are forced to rely on their own (often less accurate) market knowledge and must allocate supplies to customers based on historical and thus potentially outdated metrics. A detailed discussion of the drivers (e.g., behavioral characteristics) leading to such results is beyond the scope of this chapter. Yet the results and implications for academics, practitioners, and policymakers are surprising. The severe consequences of order inflation have been observed in many industries amid the COVID-19 pandemic.

In the absence of concerns such as the reliability, accuracy, and timing of available information, it seems reasonable at first sight to increase information sharing, since managers nearly always prefer more information to less (or no) information. Our results however demonstrate that opposite outcomes can occur: more information sharing does not invariably result in an improvement in efficiency as measured by profits across participants. These insights are relevant for academics, practitioners, and policy makers when designing DLT-based information sharing systems to anticipate potential downsides of sharing information among competing supply chain entities.

4.2.2 Trading Tokens Among Competing Retailers

Description The purpose of this game is to research to what extent demand–supply mismatches can be reduced, and supply chain performance improved, by creating a virtual market among retailers for trading tokens of a supplier's capacity. The tokens represent digital claims on assets and can be enabled by blockchain technology.

Much as in the game described in Sect. 4.2.1, participants act as retailers in a supply chain that consists of one supplier (played by the system) and multiple retailers. All interactions occur through the simulation interface. Two experimental scenarios were played. (For teaching purposes, scenarios can be played consecutively with the same group of participants.) In the baseline Scenario 1, participants must decide how many units to order from the supplier while anticipating uncertain demand and trying to maximize their firm's total profit (i.e., they solve the standard newsvendor problem). In Scenario 2, a virtual market is implemented whose design is based on features offered by blockchain technology. Namely, retailers order tokens of the supplier's capacity (as opposed to units of the product) and then have an opportunity to trade these tokens with each other anonymously while symmetric information as well as trust in the data and the trading process by providing transparent and valid records of historical transactions is ensured. This set-up guarantees that competitive information (e.g., a requested quantity, which may indicate the severeness of a shortage) is not disclosed.

The sequence of events is as follows. At the start, participants decide how many tokens to order from the supplier. All participants know the purchase cost of $10 and the sales price, which is uniformly distributed between $51 and $100. Participants must anticipate uncertain demand, which is uniformly distributed between 0 units and 200 units. All retailers observe identical parameters, but the demand and sales price realizations are independent between retailers and across rounds. That is, retailers act in geographically distant/different markets and have different valuations for goods—a situation commonly observed across industries (as evidenced by different US states' willingness to pay for ventilators depending on the shortage severeness). Once demand has been realized, participants can perform trades with other retailers to buy or sell tokens by specifying the quantity and price; thus, they seek to maximize their respective firm's profits. The simulation lasts for 20 rounds. (See Appendix E for an example of the simulation instructions.)

The results of each simulation run (e.g., supply–demand match, total profits) are automatically calculated and displayed for the instructor. To illustrate the impact of adding the virtual market for trading tokens, results of the two scenarios can be plotted on the same graph.

User Interface This game is embedded in the same framework as the first one. Hence the instructor can again easily adjust game parameters, flexibly modify the game instructions, schedule a readiness quiz, and add post-game questions. The scenario that allows for trading tokens is split into three phases, as we shall describe from the participant's perspective. In the baseline scenario (i.e., standard newsvendor problem), only the first phase is played. The screen for the ordering phase (see Fig. 4) presents an intuitive interface providing all necessary information to place the order to the supplier; it also offers a "decision support calculator."

After placing their initial orders, players enter the trading phase (Fig. 5). In this phase, they submit trade orders to the system.

Finally, in the evaluation phase (Fig. 6), players can observe the outcome of their trading orders and the resulting cash flow.

Results Results from the baseline scenario are in line with the standard newsvendor literature, e.g., Bolton and Katok (2008). More specifically, we observe that (i) orders deviate from optimal solution and exhibit a significant pull-to-center effect and (ii) 30% of participants demonstrate demand-chasing behavior. In the trading scenario, initial orders to the supplier are similar to the baseline (non-trading) scenario. This is surprising given the empirical evidence provided by the transshipment literature indicating that when transshipments are allowed, orders tend to move toward the mean demand (Katok and Villa 2021). Players actively undertake trades with the other participants to increase their own profit, which yields a more than 30% improvement in the evenness of inventory distribution (i.e.,

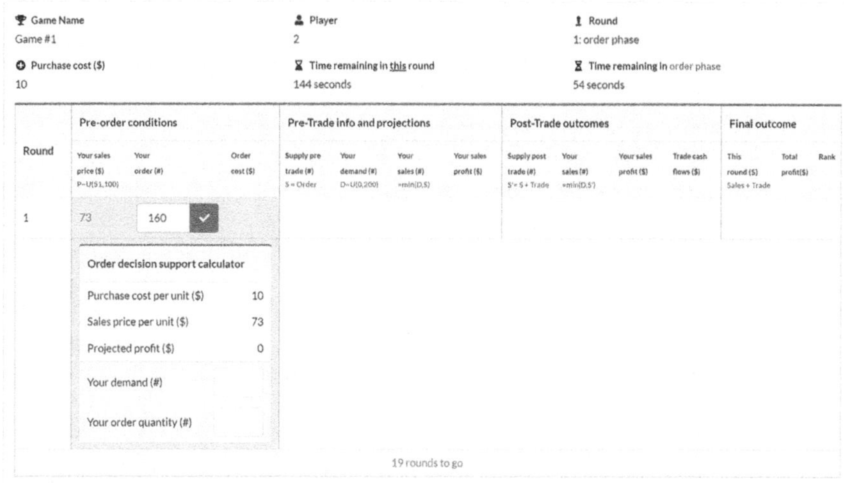

Fig. 4 Interface for initial orders of tokens in the Trading tokens among competing retailers game

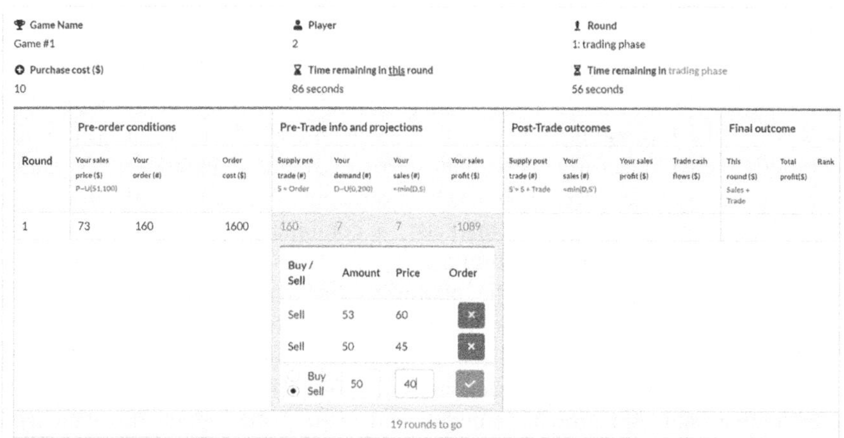

Fig. 5 Interface for trade submissions in the Trading tokens among competing retailers game

fewer instances of shortages or excess inventory) and an overall supply chain profit increase by over 20%. Over time, participants appear to improve their understanding of the market setup; thus, more successful trades tend to be placed toward the end of the simulation.

Our results demonstrate that via blockchain-enabled virtual market, which allows anonymous trading of tokens on supplier's capacity while ensuring symmetric information, trust in the data and transparency can be created and successfully harness the efficiency of centralized inventory pooling.

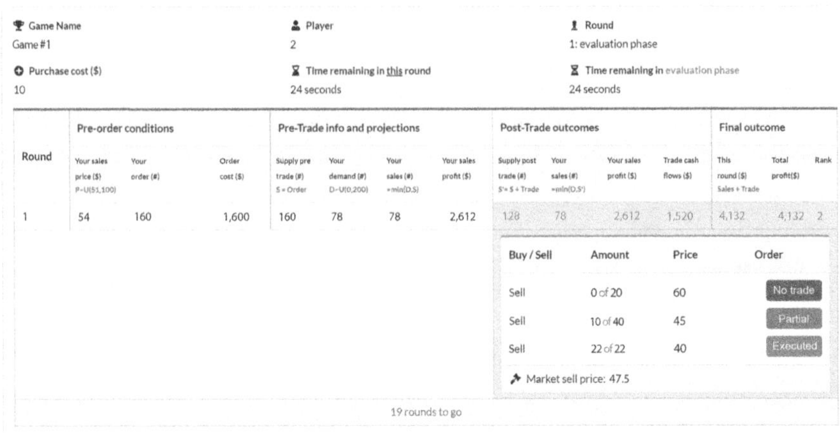

Fig. 6 Interface for review and evaluation in the Trading tokens among competing retailers game

4.3 Ongoing and Planned Enhancements

Two main development streams are ongoing to advance this platform further. First, additional games and scenarios are being developed to increase the number of use cases while leveraging concepts of blockchain and advanced encryption and decryption technologies in supply chains. For example: although the two games described here utilize different blockchain strengths (i.e., advanced information sharing and creation of virtual markets), a combination of both would yield additional intriguing research opportunities.

Second, we are developing the platform's backend. We are working on a blockchain-based data-handling solution (i.e., smart contract) to automate secure user data management and the collection and storage of data for research. This is a common concern for behavioral research simulations. The goal is to create a global, collaborative, and ever-growing simulation data pool that aggregates data from multiple simulations while fully complying with regulations on research on human subjects. That is, we intend to deploy blockchain to collect simulation data, ensuring anonymity and limiting access to participants' identifying information (according to IRB[3] requirements) while allowing participants to withdraw their consent to use the data they generate for research purposes, even after the data have been recorded to comply with GDPR, see GDPR (2022). Such a collaborative approach across institutions will create a powerful database, enabling novel insights for the OM community and beyond.

[3] Institutional Review Board, a committee responsible for the review of research involving human subjects.

A transparent, verifiably anonymous process for collecting user performance data on a blockchain ledger will allow analyses of larger samples than any single researcher can collect, and it will benefit the process of knowledge creation while preserving participants' anonymity and complying with applicable laws and regulations. To facilitate the distribution of rewards for participation in the simulation, an automated reward process is being developed to anonymously pay subjects in cryptocurrency via blockchain. All features are developed to ease usage of the platform by researchers and instructors and to improve the experience of all participants.

5 Conclusion

This chapter describes the potential roles of DLT for addressing supply chain shortages and competition for scarce resources via enhanced information sharing capabilities and controls. We introduce a novel blockchain-enabled supply chain simulation platform called DISASTER that compares favorably with existing solutions owing to several attractive features; these include ready-to-use and highly customizable supply chain simulations that leverage concepts of blockchain and encryption technologies.

By way of demonstration, we describe two simulation games hosted on the DISASTER platform that probe supply chain retailers' order behavior: the first investigates the role of information sharing among competing retailers, specifically during supply chain shortages such as those observed during the COVID-19 pandemic. We find that decision makers act more strategically and more closely to Nash equilibrium predictions when information about historical orders of competitors is shared. The attendant increased order inflation has adverse consequences, such as suppliers' inability to plan capacities or allocate resources appropriately. Whereas more information sharing is commonly desired by managers, especially when concerns such as the reliability, accuracy, and timing of available information are eliminated by a technology such as blockchain, our results demonstrate its potential downsides. The second game enables the study of a virtual market on which tokens of supplier's capacity can be traded among competing retailers. These tokens can be enabled by blockchain technology in practice. We observe that initial order quantities are similar irrespectively of the possibility to trade as well as a markedly more equitable distribution of inventory, resulting in an increase in supply chain efficiency as measured by an increase in total profit across retailers.

Given its easy-to-adjust game set-up and the inclusion of behavioral assessments, the DISASTER platform enables classroom and industry learning experiences about real-life supply chain issues and blockchain technology. More generally, this platform provides insight into how blockchain technology can affect supply chain performance and on the role of decision makers' behavioral characteristics via enhanced information sharing capabilities.

Appendix

A. Comparison of Existing Platforms

	Generic platforms			Supply chain-focused platforms	
	z-Tree	oTree	SoPHIELabs	Fathomd	DISASTER
Description	Software package for programming experiments	Online software for programming experiments	Experiment platform focusing on economic and psychology experiments	Game platform in operations management	Experiment and research platform focusing on advanced supply chain simulations
Offering	Software package to program own experiment	Software platform to develop experiments	Modular-based platform to develop own games	Off-the-shelf operations management games	Off-the-shelf advanced supply chain games leveraging concepts of blockchain and encryption technologies
Access	On request; software to be downloaded	Open source	On request	On request; game usage only	On request; game usage only
Fee model	Free of charge; academia to cite paper, others on request	Free of charge; cite paper	Pay for usage	Subscription fee per student for academia; others on request	Free of charge; cite paper
Data	Self-generated data only	Self-generated data only	Self-generated data only	Self-generated data only	Self-generated data and anonymized data pool
Customization	Requires coding knowledge (C++)	Requires coding knowledge (Python)	Requires coding knowledge (Python)	In collaboration with developers	Freely customizable Excel-based backend; UI changes in collaboration with developers
Features	Library of example games and code snips	Library of basic games and source code; Integration with Amazon Turk	Modular; add-ons and lab management solutions	Library of basic supply chain games	Library of ready-to-use personal traits questionnaires

(continued)

	Generic platforms			Supply chain-focused platforms	
	z-Tree	oTree	SoPHIELabs	Fathomd	DISASTER
Features	Library of example games and code snips	Library of basic games and source code; Integration with Amazon Turk	Modular; add-ons and lab management solutions	Library of basic supply chain games	Library of ready-to-use personal traits questionnaires
Advantages	Widely used; community and manuals available	Large online community (GitHub)	Technical support and training available	Basic supply chain games are ready to play	Advanced supply chain games are ready to play and easy to customize; flexible adjustments of parameters

Note. Information regarding z-Tree is from *Zurich Toolbox for Readymade Economic Experiments*, by z-Tree—Zurich Toolbox for Readymade Economic Experiments (2022) (https://www.ztree.uzh.ch/en.html). Copyright 2021 by University of Zurich. Information regarding oTree is from *oTree*, by oTree (2022) (http://www.otree.org/). Copyright 2022 by oTree team. Information regarding SoPHIELabs is from *SoPHIELabs*, by SoPHIELabs GmbH (2022) (https://www.sophielabs.com/). Copyright 2022 by SoPHIELabs team. Information regarding Fathomd is from *Fathomd*, by Fathomd, Inc. (2022) (https://www.fathomd.com/). Copyright 2022 by Fathomd, Inc.

B. Comparison of BWE Simulation Games

	Beer distribution game	Hunger chain game	Forecast sharing game	DISASTER Game I: Information sharing among competitors	DISASTER Game II: Trading tokens among competing retailers
Concept	Information sharing in serial supply chain	Competition for limited supply	Sharing forecast information between two parties	Information sharing among retailers competing for limited supply	Trading of tokens to match supply and demand under uncertainty
Supply chain design	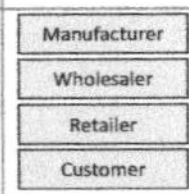	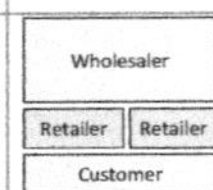	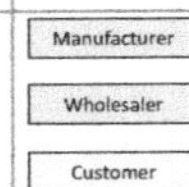	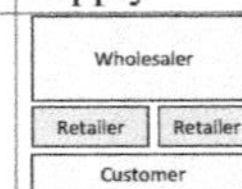	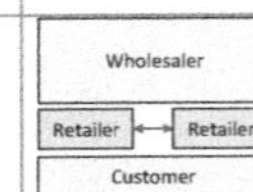
Learning objectives	Experience and understand how lack of information and limited visibility of orders leads to the BWE; learn mitigation strategies for reducing the BWE	Experience and understand the impact of competition for limited supply (panic ordering, hoarding); learn how scarce supply can be allocated fairly	Understand the role of forecast sharing, incentives, contracts, and trust in supply chains	Understand the role, importance, and impact of blockchain-enabled information sharing on supply chain performance when supply is scarce	Understand how the trading of tokens of suppliers' capacity, as enabled by blockchain, can affect supply chain performance under demand uncertainty
Outcomes	Over-reaction to small demand fluctuations, reduced supply chain performance, higher costs	Order inflation and uncoordinated supply chain	Trust and trustworthiness (i.e., limited forecast inflation and limited discounting) lead to improved supply chain performance	Faster order inflation toward Nash equilibrium as information is shared	If trading is enabled, then initial order quantities are reduced and supply chain performance improves

(continued)

	Beer distribution game	Hunger chain game	Forecast sharing game	DISASTER Game I: Information sharing among competitors	DISASTER Game II: Trading tokens among competing retailers
Duration	ca. 1–5 h	ca. 1–2 h	ca. 1–2 h	ca. 1–2 h	ca. 1–2 h
Providers	Multiple	Rutgers Business School	Fathomd	Authors	Authors

Note. Information regarding Beer Distribution Game is from *Flight Simulators for Management Education "The Beer Game,"* by Sterman (1989a) (https://web.mit.edu/jsterman/www/SDG/beergame.html). Information regarding Hunger Chain Game is from *Games and Experiential Learning in Supply Chain Management*, by Zhao (2022) (http://zhao.rutgers.edu/Games-Hunger-Chain.pdf). Information regarding Forecast Sharing Game is from *Fathomd*, by Fathomd, Inc. (2022) (https://www.fathomd.com/). Copyright 2022 by Fathomd, Inc.

↔ Trade ☐ System ☐ Player

C. List of Pre-defined Questions[4] for Eliciting Behavioral Characteristics

Characteristic	Measurement instrument	Reference
Ambiguity aversion	Willingness to pay (WTP) game	Fox and Tversky (1995) and Halevy (2007)
Cognitive abilities	Cognitive Reflection Test (CRT)	Frederick (2005)
Fairness (inequality aversion)	(Hypothetical) Dictator game questionnaire	Forsythe et al. (1994), Fehr and Schmidt (1999) and van Damme et al. (2014)
Loss aversion	Lottery choice task Willingness to accept (WTA) game Willingness to purchase (WTP) game	Kahneman and Tversky (1979), Fehr and Goette (2007) and Gächter et al. (2021)
Positive reciprocity	(Hypothetical) Investment game questionnaire	Berg et al. (1995), Cox (2004), Cooper and Kagel (2016) and Falk et al. (2016)
Negative reciprocity	(Hypothetical) Ultimatum game questionnaire	Forsythe et al. (1994), van Damme et al. (2014) and Falk et al. (2016)
Overconfidence	Questionnaire	Russo and Schoemaker (1992)
Risk preferences	Multiple price list method DOSPERT questionnaire	Holt and Laury (2002) and Blais and Weber (2006)
Trust and trustworthiness	Questionnaire Investment game	Berg et al. (1995), Mayer and Davis (1999) and Falk et al. (2016)

D. Simulation Instructions for the Information Sharing Among Competing Retailers Game (Scenarios 2–4)

Step 1: Past order observation

You can observe the past order(s) of the other two players against whom you are playing in the current round. Similarly, your past order(s) is (are) visible to the players in your group.

Step 2: Order submission

[4] Questions can be added to the underlying spreadsheet with a fast and easy plug-and-play approach

For your order, you can choose an integer number between 0 and 10,000 units.

Once you have submitted your order, you cannot change it.

Step 3: Supplier stock allocation and cost

The supplier has 120 units available in total, which are divided among all three retailers in your group.

The allocation is determined as follows.

(a) The system calculates the total order received from the retailers (i.e., the sum of your order and the orders from the other two retailers).
(b) If the total order is less than or equal to 120, you will receive the number of units you ordered.
(c) If the total order is greater than 120, you will receive:
    Your allocation = (your order/total order) × 120

Please note that you may receive fractions (decimals) of units.

For example,

- If you order 60 units and the total order from all retailers in your group is 110, then you will receive 60 units. The other two retailers will receive 50 units in total.
- If you order 60 units and the total order from all retailers in your group is 150, then you will receive 48 units [=(60 ÷ 150) × 120]. The other two retailers will receive 72 units in total.

The order cost is $10 per unit. The order cost applies only to units you receive. So, for example, if you receive 60 units then your order cost would be $600 but if you receive just 48 units then your order cost would be $480.

Step 4: Sales and revenues

The number of units you sell is equal to the minimum of (i) the demand from your customers (50 units) and (ii) your supply, or the number of units allocated to you by the supplier (as described in Step 3).

Unsold items are discarded at the end of the round; they are not carried over to the next round. Unsatisfied demand is lost and cannot be backlogged to the next round.

For example,

- if the supplier allocated 40 units to you, then your sales are 40 units (=min(40, 50)) and the unsatisfied demand for 10 units is lost at the end of the round;
- if the supplier allocated 52 units to you, then your sales are 50 units (=min(52, 50)) and the leftover 2 units are lost at the end of the round.

Revenue amounts to $20 per unit. Therefore, if your sales are 40 units then your revenue is $800.

Step 5: Profit

Your profit per round = revenue per round – cost per round.

Your total profit over the entire simulation is the sum of profits per round.

E. Simulation Instructions for the Trading Tokens Among Competing Retailers Game

Step 1: Observation of your sales price for the current round

Observe the realization of your sales price, which is randomly drawn from the range of \$51 to \$100 per unit and with an equal likelihood of every integer value (a number without any decimals, such as \$51, \$63, \$95).

The sales price of other retailers is also randomly drawn from the range of \$51 to \$100 per unit.

Sales prices are independent between rounds and across retailers.

Step 2: Submit your order to the supplier

For your order, choose an integer number between 0 and 400 units.

You can use the simulation tool to support your decision on how many tokens to order from the supplier. This tool will provide you with the expected pre-trade profit after you enter your estimated demand and specified order quantity.

Step 3: Demand realization

Your customer demand is randomly drawn from the range of 0 to 200 units, with an equal likelihood of every integer value (a number without any decimals, e.g., 13, 105, 186).

Other players face their own levels of customer demand (i.e., you are not competing for the same customers), which is also randomly drawn from the range of 0 to 200 units.

Customer demands are independent between rounds and across retailers.

Step 4: Cost, sales, and revenue

You can observe your pre-trade profit projection. If you do not submit any trading orders, then that projection would be your final profit in this round. The following text describes how the projected pre-trade profit is calculated.

The order cost is \$10 per token. For instance, if you order 130 tokens then your cost is \$1300.

The number of units you can sell to your customers is equal to the minimum of (i) the demand from your customers (see Step 3) and (ii) how many tokens of the supplier's capacity that you hold (see Step 2). Suppose, for example, that you hold 130 tokens and that your customer demand is 90 units; in that case, your potential sales quantity is 90 units (=min(130, 90)).

Your projected pre-trade revenue is equal to the sales price multiplied by the sales quantity. So if your sales price is \$60 and you sell 90 units, then your projected pre-trade revenue is \$5400.

Finally: Projected pre-trade profit = projected pre-trade revenue – order cost.

Step 5: Perform trades with other retailers in your group

You can change how many tokens you hold by trading with other retailers.

To trade, you specify whether you want to buy or sell tokens, the quantity, and the price. You can sell all tokens that you hold (even if you can then not fulfill your customer demand as the result). You can submit multiple trade orders per round, up to a maximum of five.

At the end of the trading period, the market clears given all orders that the retailers in your group have submitted.

Trading and market-clearing processes (see table below)

A. Sell orders are ranked in price from lowest to highest and buy orders in price from highest to lowest.
B. Units are matched in buy and sell orders whenever the buy price is greater than the sell price of the matched units.
C. The average of the lowest buy price and the highest sell price at which the last match happens is the market-clearing price: all buy orders pay this price and all sell orders receive this price.

Consider the following example. The steps just described are marked by A, B, and C in the table.

Sell orders

	Player	Time	Price per unit	Number of units
	1	10:30:23	$51 (A) ↓	14
(B)	1	10:30:40	$53	21
	1	10:30:15	$56	13
	1	10:30:00	$60	6

Buy orders

Player	Time	Price per unit	Number of units
2	10:30:40	$76 ↑ (A)	19
3	10:30:23	$55	16
2	10:30:00	$54	21
3	10:30:15	$49	9

(C) **Market clearing price = $54 = ($53 + $55) / 2**

After the trading phase is completed, you sell to your customers using the new number of tokens you have.

This marks the end of the round, and the final profits for this round are then calculated. Your total profit over the entire simulation is the sum of profits per round.

Any unsold tokens are voided at the end of the round; they are not carried over to the next round.

Unsatisfied customer demand is lost, and it cannot be backlogged to the next round.

References

AlixPartners (2021) Shortages related to semiconductors to cost the auto industry $210 billion in revenues this year. Retrieved November 5, 2021, from https://www.alixpartners.com/media-center/press-releases/press-release-shortages-related-to-semiconductors-to-cost-the-auto-industry-210-billion-in-revenues-this-year-says-new-alixpartners-forecast/

Babich V, Hilary G (2019) Blockchain and other distributed ledger technologies in operations. Found Trends Technol Inf Oper Manag 12(2–3):152–172. https://doi.org/10.1561/0200000084

Babich V, Hilary G (2020) OM forum—distributed ledgers and operations: what operations management researchers should know about blockchain technology. Manuf Serv Oper Manag 22(2):223–240. https://doi.org/10.1287/msom.2018.0752

Babich V, Hilary G (2022) Tutorial on blockchain applications in supply chains. In: Babich V, Birge J, Hillary G (eds) Innovative technology at the interface of finance and operations. Springer Nature, S.l.

Baganha MP, Cohen MA (1998) The stabilizing effect of inventory in supply chains. Oper Res 46(3):72–83. https://doi.org/10.1287/opre.46.3.S72

Berg J, Dickhaut J, McCabe K (1995) Trust, reciprocity and social history. Games Econ Behav 10(1):122–142. https://doi.org/10.1006/game.1995.1027

Blais AR, Weber EU (2006) A domain-specific risk-taking (DOSPERT) scale for adult populations. Judgm Decis Mak 1(1). https://ssrn.com/abstract=1301089

Bolton GE, Katok E (2008) Learning by doing in the newsvendor problem: a laboratory investigation of the role of experience and feedback. Manuf Serv Oper Manag 10(3):519–538

Cachon GP, Lariviere MA (1999) An equilibrium analysis of linear, proportional, and uniform allocation of scarce capacity. IIE Trans 31:835–849. https://doi.org/10.1023/A:1007670515586

Chen Y, Su X, Zhao X (2012) Modeling bounded rationality in capacity allocation games with the quantal response equilibrium. Manag Sci 58(10):1952–1962. https://doi.org/10.1287/mnsc.1120.1531

Cohen MA, Kouvelis P (2020) Revisit of AAA excellence of global value chains: robustness, resilience and realignment. Prod Oper Manag 30(3):633–643. https://doi.org/10.1111/poms.13305

Cohen MA, Lee HL (2020) Designing the right global supply chain network. Manuf Serv Oper Manag 22(1):15–24. https://doi.org/10.1287/msom.2019.0839

Cohen MA, Kleindorfer PR, Lee HL (1986) Optimal stocking policies for low usage items in multi-echelon inventory systems. Naval Res Logist Q 33(1):17–38. https://doi.org/10.1002/nav.3800330103

Cooper D, Kagel JH (2016) Other regarding preferences: a selective survey of experimental results. In: Kagel J, Roth A (eds) The handbook of experimental economics, vol 2. Princeton University Press

Cox JC (2004) How to identify trust and reciprocity. Games Econ Behav 46(2):260–281. https://doi.org/10.1016/S0899-8256(03)00119-2

Croson R, Donohue K (2006) Behavioral causes of the bullwhip effect and the observed value of inventory information. Manag Sci 52(3):323–336. https://doi.org/10.1287/mnsc.1050.0436

Cui TH, Zhang Y (2018) Cognitive hierarchy in capacity allocation games. Manag Sci 64(3):1250–1270. https://doi.org/10.1287/mnsc.2016.2655

Deshpande V, Cohen MA, Donohue K (2003) A threshold inventory rationing policy for service differentiated demand classes. Manag Sci 49(6):683–703. https://doi.org/10.1287/mnsc.49.6.683.16022

Fahimnia B, Pournader M, Siemsen E, Bendoly E, Wang C (2019) Behavioral operations and supply chain management - a review and literature mapping. Decis Sci 50(6):1127–1183. https://doi.org/10.1111/deci.12369

Falk A, Becker A, Dohmen T, Huffman D, Sunde U (2016) The preference survey module: a validated instrument for measuring risk, time, and social preferences. IZA Discussion Paper 9674. https://doi.org/10.2139/ssrn.2725035

Fathomd (2022) Business Games for better learning. Retrieved December 14, 2021, from https://www.fathomd.com/

Federgruen A, Zipkin P (1984) Approximations of dynamic, multilocation production and inventory problems. Manag Sci 30(1):69–84. https://doi.org/10.1287/mnsc.30.1.69

Fehr E, Goette L (2007) Do workers work more if wages are high? Evidence from a randomized field experiment. Am Econ Rev 97(1):298–317. https://doi.org/10.2139/ssrn.326803

Fehr E, Schmidt KM (1999) A theory of fairness, competition and cooperation. Q J Econ 114(3):817–868. https://doi.org/10.2139/ssrn.106228

Forsythe R, Horowitz JL, Savin NE, Sefton M (1994) Fairness in simple bargaining experiments. Games Econ Behav 6(3):347–369. https://doi.org/10.1006/game.1994.1021

Fox CR, Tversky A (1995) Ambiguity aversion and comparative ignorance. Q J Econ 110(3):585–603. https://doi.org/10.2307/2946693

Frederick S (2005) Cognitive reflection and decision making. J Econ Perspect 19(4):25–42. https://doi.org/10.1257/089533005775196732

Gächter S, Johnson EJ, Herrmann A (2021) Individual-level loss aversion in riskless and risky choices. Theory Decis. https://doi.org/10.1007/s11238-021-09839-8
GDPR (2022) Complete guide to GDPR compliance. Retrieved January 08, 2022, from https://gdpr.eu/
Halevy Y (2007) Ellsberg revisited: an experimental study. Econometrica 75(2):503–536. https://www.jstor.org/stable/4501998
Hellwig DP, Huchzermeier A (2022) Next generation information sharing in a blockchain-enabled supply chain. In: Babich V, Birge J, Hillary G (eds) Innovative technology at the interface of finance and operations. Springer Nature, S.l.
Hellwig DP, Karlic G, Huchzermeier A (2020) Build your own blockchain: a practical guide to distributed ledger technology. Springer Nature, S.l. https://doi.org/10.1007/978-3-030-40142-9
Holt CA, Laury SK (2002) Risk aversion and incentive effects. Am Econ Rev 92(5):1644–1655. https://www.jstor.org/stable/3083270
INFORMS (2004) Morris Cohen, MSOM Fellow, 2004. Retrieved January 22, 2022, from https://connect.informs.org/msom/msom-resources/fellows/cohen
Kahneman D, Tversky A (1979) Prospect theory: an analysis of decision under risk. Econometrica 47(2):263–292. https://doi.org/10.2307/1914185
Katok E, Villa S (2021) Centralized or decentralized transfer prices: a behavioral approach for improving supply chain coordination. Manuf Serv Oper Manag. https://doi.org/10.1287/msom.2020.0957
Katok E, Leider S, Donohue K (2018) The handbook of behavioral operations. Wiley & Sons
Lee HL, Padmanabhan V, Whang S (1997) Information distortion in a supply chain: the bullwhip effect. Manag Sci 43(4):546–558. https://doi.org/10.1287/mnsc.43.4.546
Lotfi Z, Mukhtar M, Sahran S, Zadeh AT (2013) Information sharing in supply chain management. Procedia Technol 11:298–304. https://doi.org/10.1016/j.protcy.2013.12.194
Mayer RC, Davis JH (1999) The effect of the performance appraisal system on trust for management: a field quasi-experiment. J Appl Psychol 84(1):123. https://doi.org/10.1037/0021-9010.84.1.123
oTree (2022) oTree - the most powerful platform for behavioral research and experiments. Retrieved December 14, 2021, from http://www.otree.org/
Ren ZJ, Cohen MA, Ho TH, Terwiesch C (2009) Information sharing in a long-term supply chain relationship: the role of customer review strategy. Oper Res 58(1):81–93. https://doi.org/10.1287/opre.1090.0750
Roland (2021) Pacemaker, ultrasound companies seek priority amid chip shortage. Retrieved October 10, 2021, from https://www.wsj.com/articles/pacemaker-ultrasound-companies-seek-priority-amid-chip-shortage-11633258802
Rudi N, Kapur S, Pyke DF (2001) A two-location inventory with transshipment and a local decision making. Manag Sci 47(12):1668–1680. https://doi.org/10.1287/mnsc.47.12.1668.10235
Russo JE, Schoemaker PJ (1992) Managing overconfidence. Sloan Manag Rev 33(2):7–17
SoPHIELabs (2022) Your partner for online experiments, behavioral research and serious games. Retrieved December 14, 2021, from https://www.sophielabs.com/
Sterman JD (1989a) Teaching takes off flight simulators for management education – "The Beer Game". Retrieved December 16, 2021, from https://web.mit.edu/jsterman/www/SDG/beergame.html
Sterman JD (1989b) Modeling managerial behavior: misperceptions of feedback in a dynamic decision making experiment. Manag Sci 35(3):321–339. https://doi.org/10.1287/mnsc.35.3.321
Tagaras G, Cohen MA (1992) Pooling in two-location inventory systems with non-negligible replenishment lead times. Manag Sci 38(8):1067–1083. https://doi.org/10.1287/mnsc.38.8.1067
Terwiesch C, Ren ZJ, Ho TH, Cohen MA (2005) An empirical analysis of forecast sharing in the semiconductor equipment supply chain. Manag Sci 51(2):208–220. https://doi.org/10.1287/mnsc.1040.0317

van Damme E, Binmore KG, Roth AE, Samuelson L, Winter E, Bolton GE, Ockenfels A, Dufwenberg M, Kirchsteiger G, Gneezy U, Kocher MG, Sutter M, Sanfey AG, Kliemt H, Selten R, Nagel R, Azar OH (2014) How Werner Güth's ultimatum game shaped our understanding of social behavior. J Econ Behav Organ 108:292–318. https://doi.org/10.1016/j.jebo.2014.10.014

van Engelenburg S, Janssen M, Klievink B (2018) A blockchain architecture for reducing the bullwhip effect. In: Shishkov B (ed) Business modeling and software design, vol 319. Springer International Publishing, pp 69–82

Wang X, Disney SM (2016) The bullwhip effect: progress, trends and directions. Eur J Oper Res 250(3):691–701. https://doi.org/10.1016/j.ejor.2015.07.022

WEF (2021) What's the bullwhip effect and how can we avoid crises like the global chip shortage. Retrieved May 20, 2021, from https://www.weforum.org/agenda/2021/05/what-s-the-bullwhip-effect-and-how-can-we-avoid-crises-like-the-global-chip-shortage/

Xue X, Dou J, Shang Y (2020) Blockchain-driven supply chain decentralized operations – information sharing perspective. Bus Process Manag J 27(1):184–203. https://doi.org/10.1108/BPMJ-12-2019-0518

Zhao Y (2022) Games and experiential learning in supply chain management. Retrieved December 16, 2021, from http://zhao.rutgers.edu/Games-Hunger-Chain.pdf

z-Tree - Zurich Toolbox for Readymade Economic Experiments (2022) Zurich toolbox for ready-made economic experiments. Retrieved December 14, 2021, from https://www.ztree.uzh.ch/en.html

Part IV
Practice Research

Operations Management in Semiconductor and Computing Technology Industries: Capacity, Outsourcing, and Production

Shi Chen, Junfei Lei, and Kamran Moinzadeh

Abstract The semiconductor industry has seen some of the most technological achievements in the last century with the most complex supply chains among all modern industries. To address the daunting challenges presented in this industry, operations management (OM) researchers have done numerous studies, which we group into three broad areas: (1) capacity expansion, allocation, and upgrading; (2) outsourcing, contracting, and procurement; (3) production, quality control, and maintenance. In this chapter, we highlight the development of the OM literature on the above three areas with applications to the semiconductor industry. In addition, the most recent information technology advancements, notably cloud computing and cloud-based artificial intelligence, not only have profound impacts on the existing semiconductor supply chains but also give rise to new industries. Hence, through our discussions of the existing studies and future research opportunities, we hope that this chapter will stimulate new research ideas that are either extensions to the previous studies or applications to new operational environments in the semiconductor and computing technology industries.

Keywords Capacity planning · Outsourcing and procurement strategies · Incentives and contracting · Production and maintenance · Semiconductor supply chains · Cloud computing

1 Introduction

The semiconductor and computing technology industries have seen some of the most technological achievements in the last century with the most complex supply chains among all modern industries, as evidenced by the recent global shortage of semiconductor chips that has heavily clobbered many sectors of the economy.

S. Chen (✉) · J. Lei · K. Moinzadeh
Michael G. Foster School of Business, University of Washington, Seattle, WA, USA
e-mail: shichen@uw.edu; jlei@uw.edu; kamran@uw.edu

H. Lee et al. (eds.), *Creating Values with Operations and Analytics*, Springer Series in Supply Chain Management 19, https://doi.org/10.1007/978-3-031-08871-1_10

For instance, the automotive production lines of Tesla and General Motors have been halted, Samsung may postpone launching their new flagship smartphones, and Microsoft has decided to constrain its Surface products throughout 2021 (LaReau 2021; Vakil and Linton 2021). In this section, we first present some background information about the development and new trends in the industry and then describe structures of the semiconductor and computing technology supply chains, followed by a discussion of the major challenges in managing those supply chains.

1.1 The Past and the New Trends

The semiconductor industry has had a global footprint since the 1970s when new products became more and more complex, while consumers became more demanding and price-sensitive. As a result, major original equipment manufacturers (OEMs) switched from in-house production to outsourcing in order to quickly respond to market changes, tightened the product introduction process, and enhanced their market competitiveness. Since then, the entire semiconductor supply chains have gradually shifted from in-house manufacturing to outsourcing to reduce equipment, procurement, and operational costs. A typical example is the change from the integrated device manufacturer (IDM) business model to the fabless–foundry business model starting in the mid-1990s. Under the IDM model, an IDM company (e.g., Intel, Samsung, and SK Hynix) designs and manufactures integrated circuit (IC) products. Under the fabless–foundry business model, however, fabless companies (e.g., AMD, Nvidia, and Qualcomm) focus on designing IC chips and outsource semiconductor fabrication to foundry companies. The foundry companies such as Taiwan Semiconductor Manufacturing Company (TSMC), GlobalFoundries, and United Microelectronics Corporation (UMC) focus on semiconductor fabrication. As a result, the market share of the IDM model shrunk from 85.9% in the first decade of the twenty-first century to less than 60% in 2020 (Malli Mohan 2010; Statista 2021). Nowadays, only a few large IDMs have their fabs since the costs involved in maintaining and operating them are extremely high (Hung et al. 2017).

Outsourcing manufacturing greatly spurred the semiconductor industry's growth due to the following major advantages: (1) Outsourcing to foundry companies significantly lowered the entry barrier to fabless companies as it eliminated heavy investments in building semiconductor fabrication plants. (2) It reduced operational risks as suppliers (i.e., foundry companies) could pool demands from various buyers (i.e., fabless companies). (3) Outsourcing created more flexibility as fabless companies could outsource from multiple foundry companies. (4) It allowed concentrated efforts for each party along the supply chain, thus shortened the cycle time, and improved the efficiency of the whole supply chain. Foundry companies focused on investing in the capacity of mass production and improving product reliability, while fabless companies focused on investing in R&D activities based on market needs. (5) Low-cost manufacturing locations (i.e., developing economics) offered attractive tax rates as well as cheap and skilled labor. As a result, most of the semiconductor supply chains today consist of manufacturing facilities across many countries.

In the last decade, new technological advancements in cloud computing, artificial intelligence, and 5G telecommunication have revolutionized the computing technology industries, which in turn spurred another cycle of sustained growth of the semiconductor industry. According to International Data Corporation (IDC), the semiconductor market is forecasted to reach \$600 billion by 2025, representing a compound annual growth rate (CAGR) of 5.3% through the forecast period, where 5G semiconductor revenue will increase by 128% in particular, with total mobile phone semiconductors expected to grow by 28.5% (IDC 2021). Moreover, according to Gartner, the market size of the worldwide public cloud services is forecasted to grow 23.1% to a total of \$332.3 billion in 2021 (Gartner 2021). Finally, according to another industry report by PWC, artificial intelligence will likely be another catalyst that will drive the decade-long growth cycle for the semiconductor sector, with the market for AI-related semiconductors expected to grow from a current \$6 billion in revenues to more than \$30 billion by 2022, representing a CAGR of almost 50% (PWC 2019).

1.2 Description of Semiconductor and Computing Technology Supply Chains

We now describe typical structures of semiconductor and computing technology supply chains from the upstream semiconductor fabrication equipment suppliers to the downstream end consumers of personal computer products and cloud service providers, as illustrated by Fig. 1.

From the upstream of the supply chain, more than 500 different pieces of equipment are used to convert raw materials (e.g., wafers) into devices, which can

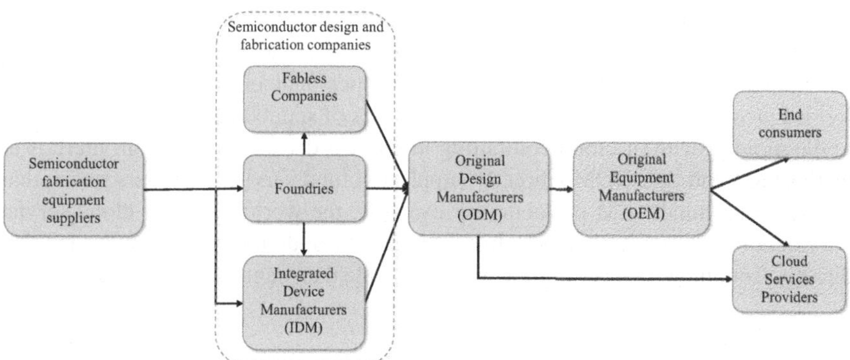

Fig. 1 A typical semiconductor and computing technology supply chain

be classified into three broad categories: fabrication, assembly, and test or back-end equipment. The fabrication equipment is designed to grow (e.g., epitaxial reactors and ion implantation equipment), deposit (e.g., physical or chemical vapor deposition systems), or remove (e.g., photolithography and etching equipment) materials from wafers. Then, wafers will be sent to assembly for further manufacturing, which includes molding, hermetic sealing, die-attach, and lead finish equipment. Finally, the test or back-end equipment is used to test assembled devices, which includes automatic test equipment (ATE), burn-in ovens, UV erase equipment, and vacuum sealers.

The semiconductor design and fabrication companies can be classified into three categories: foundries, fabless companies, and integrated device manufacturers (IDM). Foundries and fabless companies are contractual partners in the semiconductor supply chains, where the former focus on manufacturing and testing physical IC products, while the latter concentrate on designing and developing devices. As mentioned earlier, major foundry companies are TSMC, UMC, and Global Foundries, and major fabless companies include Qualcomm, Nvidia, and AMD. In contrast, IDMs combine functions of foundries and fabless companies as they design, manufacture, and sell integrated circuit products, such as Intel and Samsung. Note that IDMs may also source from foundries to cope with rapid demand growths and reduce unnecessary manufacturing capacity investments.

Original design manufacturers (ODMs) are companies that manufacture labeled products for their downstream clients, for example, the original equipment manufacturers (OEMs), and then the OEMs import finished products to sell them in the end market under their brands. In doing so, the OEMs can concentrate on designing the products. A typical example is the Apple iPhone supply chain, where iPhones are designed by Apple and licensed out to Foxconn for production. The ODM–OEM business model has three significant advantages. First, such a business model reduces production costs as most ODMs are located in countries with low labor costs, tax rates, and transportation costs. Second, the ODM–OEM model allows better resource allocation as the downstream clients (i.e., OEMs) can save manufacturing resources, thereby focusing on new product development and marketing. Third, the ODM–OEM model facilitates economies of scale as the ODMs will mass produce similar products from different clients.

Finally, in addition to end consumers of personal electronic devices, cloud service providers have risen to prominent buyers of semiconductor products thanks to the rapid growth of cloud computing in the last decade. As a result, there is an increasing trend that ODMs directly supply to cloud service providers rather than through traditional OEM partners. For example, the world's leading cloud service providers bought more than $21 billion of server and storage equipment in 2020 directly from the ODMs to build new hyper-scale data centers (Haranas 2020).

1.3 Challenges in the Semiconductor and Computing Technology Supply Chains

In the complex semiconductor and computing technology supply chains, operations and supply chain managers face daunting challenges from demand, yield, and price uncertainties, aggravated by long lead times, short life cycles, and intensive capital requirements of the semiconductor products.

Demands for semiconductor products primarily come from consumer demand for electronic devices (e.g., communication devices and personal computers) and other related commercial goods (e.g., smart chips for vehicles, servers for cloud service providers). However, the short life cycle of semiconductor products limits the accuracy of demand forecasting as drivers of market demand evolve rapidly in the life cycle. Moreover, the same semiconductor components can be assembled in different end products and sold in different markets, while many semiconductor components are substitutable, so demand for one product can change the demands for other products; as a result, demands in the semiconductor supply chains are difficult to forecast (Mönch et al. 2018).

Due to the complexity of the production processes and different quality requirements, outputs ("*yields*") in semiconductor manufacturing may differ from the initial production plan based on input materials. A salient example is the manufacturing of semiconductor chips, where a wafer may yield 10 to 100,000 chips (Han et al. 2012) depending on the specific production process, and the chips will be classified into different grades, depending on specific quality requirements. The high-grade chips can be used to replace the low-grade chips. In other words, a wafer has random yields for a series of chips with different qualities that can be used to assemble different final products.

Finally, the prices of semiconductor components are highly volatile and cyclical. The price uncertainty can be explained from the following three aspects: (1) Prices of semiconductors are closely related to market demand at different stages in the product life cycle. For example, firms may set a relatively high price in the growth stage of the product life cycle to recover initial investments in product development, while the price will decrease rapidly later in the life cycle as the market gradually switches to the next generation of products. (2) Prices of semiconductors are significantly affected by the supply side as well. Due to the long capacity expansion lead times, production capacity is relatively fixed for an extended period of time. To fully utilize production capacity, upstream suppliers (i.e., foundries) often provide discounts to downstream buyers when market demand is low but increase prices when market demand is high.

To address the aforementioned challenges in the semiconductor and computing technology industries, operations management (OM) researchers have done numerous studies, which can be grouped into three broad areas: (1) capacity expansion, allocation, and upgrading; (2) outsourcing, contracting, and procurement; (3) production, quality control, and maintenance. This chapter is not meant to be a comprehensive review of all related studies (as a disclaimer, we admit that it would be impossible to cover all related OM studies given the vast literature on the three areas, and we take the blame for any omission). Rather, our intent is to highlight the development of the OM literature on the three areas with applications to the semiconductor and computing technology industries through discussions of some representative studies. Ultimately, we hope that this chapter could stimulate new research ideas that are either extensions to the previous studies or applications to new operational environments (e.g., cloud computing value chains).

In the rest of this chapter, we will present studies in the aforementioned three areas in order. For each area, we first discuss some representative studies and then dive into details of several influential or recent studies (Arbabian et al. 2021 for Sect. 2, Cohen et al. 2003 and Chen et al. 2021 for Sect. 3, as well as Nahmias and Moinzadeh 1997 and Kim et al. 2010 for Sect. 4).

2 Capacity Expansion, Allocation, and Upgrading

There is a great range of capacity planning problems in the literature on strategic capacity management; the reader is referred to Van Mieghem (2003) for a comprehensive survey of this field. In this section, specific attention is given to studies that are closely related to the capacity planning decisions in the semiconductor and computing technology industries, even though the models and results of many other studies of general capacity management can also be applied to these industries. In other words, our intent is not to cover all relevant studies; rather, we will review early developments and point out new trends through our discussion of some representative studies.

In the rest of this section, we discuss capacity planning problems based on three broad categories: (1) capacity investment and expansion, (2) capacity reservation and allocation, and (3) capacity upgrading and management of obsolescence.

2.1 Capacity Investment and Expansion

Capacity investment and expansion in the semiconductor and computing technology industries are capital-intensive operations with long lead times and significant uncertainties about demand and yield. Efforts to address these daunting challenges have led to a rich literature including Atamtürk and Hochbaum (2001), Karabuk and Wu (2003), Ülkü et al. (2005), Huh et al. (2006), Taylor and Plambeck (2007), Huang and Ahmed (2009), Besanko et al. (2010), Song and Zipkin (2012), Özer and Uncu (2013), Gardete (2016), and Arbabian et al. (2021), among others.

Atamtürk and Hochbaum (2001) present a semiconductor fabrication company's capacity acquisition decision together with production, subcontracting, and inventory control strategies. The objective of their model is to minimize the total cost facing known and non-stationary demand over a finite horizon, and they propose a solution to this problem using math programming. Karabuk and Wu (2003) consider capacity expansion and configuration decisions in the semiconductor industry under high uncertainties from demand and yields. In their model, capacity is defined as the number of wafer starts per week, and the semiconductor company needs to determine the capacity level for each technology at each facility over a finite horizon. They propose a scenario-based, multi-stage stochastic programming model to minimize the total costs associated with capacity acquisition, outsourcing, and adjustment of capacity configuration over a finite horizon. Huang and Ahmed (2009) examine a capacity acquisition problem where multiple types of resources need to be allocated to different tasks, which is motivated by equipment purchase planning in the semiconductor industry. They develop a stochastic integer program where the parameters of the integer program keep evolving according to a discrete-time stochastic process. They solve this problem using scenario tree and multi-stage stochastic integer programming techniques.

There are also some studies of semiconductor companies' capacity planning decisions in a competitive environment. Besanko et al. (2010) consider an infinite-horizon dynamic game between two competing firms. At the beginning of each period, each firm can decide whether to add or withdraw one unit of capacity and then compete with the other firms with the given capacity. Excess demand must be satisfied but at an additional cost. The model is complicated due to the consideration of capacity obsolescence. The authors characterize market and operational characteristics that lead to preemption races or capacity coordination. Motivated by the manufacturing of dynamic random access memory (DRAM), Gardete (2016) develop a model of competition where firms make capacity and production decisions in the presence of demand uncertainty. A key feature of their model is that each firm receives a private signal of the uncertain demand where the signals are correlated, which enables the firms to infer their competitors' demand signals. Their study evaluates the firms' benefits from information sharing in such a competitive environment.

Another relevant stream of research is the optimal timing of a firm's capacity investment and subsequent production decisions, namely, the time-to-market problem. The basic trade-off is as follows: the firm may want to postpone investment in building capacity associated with a new technology or manufacturing process, which can bring benefits such as improved manufacturing yield and quality, but on the other hand, the firm may risk losing market share if competitors enter the market earlier than expected. Ülkü et al. (2005) consider such a capacity planning problem where, due to market uncertainty, the timing of new process adoption and capacity investment is crucial. They find that various factors including competitive intensity, cost and incentive structures, and the rate of forecast updates can significantly affect the optimal time of capacity investment and that the impacts of these factors are different for the OEM and a contract manufacturer. They also show that the OEM can stimulate the contract manufacturer's early investment through a risk-sharing mechanism. Özer and Uncu (2013) examine a sequential, two-stage model to characterize the firm's optimal market-entry and production decisions. In the first stage where the optimal time-to-market decision is made, they show that a threshold policy is optimal. In the second stage where production decisions are made, they prove that the optimal policy is a state-dependent, base-stock policy. Their model can also be used to evaluate the impacts of various market and operational characteristics including the intensity of competition, the rate of forecast updates, and the cost structures on the optimal time-to-market and production decisions.

Over the past decade, technological enhancements led by cloud computing have revolutionized the semiconductor and computing technology industries. The rise of many influential cloud service providers led by AWS, MS Azure, and GCP among others is accompanied by new and challenging capacity planning problems. The capacity of cloud service providers is usually defined by the computing resources including central processing units (CPU), random access memory (RAM), storage disks, and network bandwidths. All of these resources are aggregated in mega data centers around the globe. Hence, the capacity investment and expansion problems specific to the cloud computing industry can be classified into two layers: (1) the higher layer includes the capacity expansion problems associated with building new data centers and (2) the lower layer includes the capacity expansion problems within an existing data center (or a group of connected data centers).

Figure 2 depicts the scope of a typical capacity expansion project of building a new data center, which is based on our professional consulting experience and personal interactions with two leading public cloud service providers in the United States. As Fig. 2 shows, the project spans from buying or leasing land, constructing the buildings (*a.k.a.* "shell"), developing supporting infrastructures and facilities, to installing network and computing equipment. Completion of the entire project usually takes several years or even longer, depending on whether the land and shell are already available when the project starts. Due to the long planning horizon and significant uncertainties in the project completion time and future capacity requirement, a mismanaged capacity expansion project will result in significant

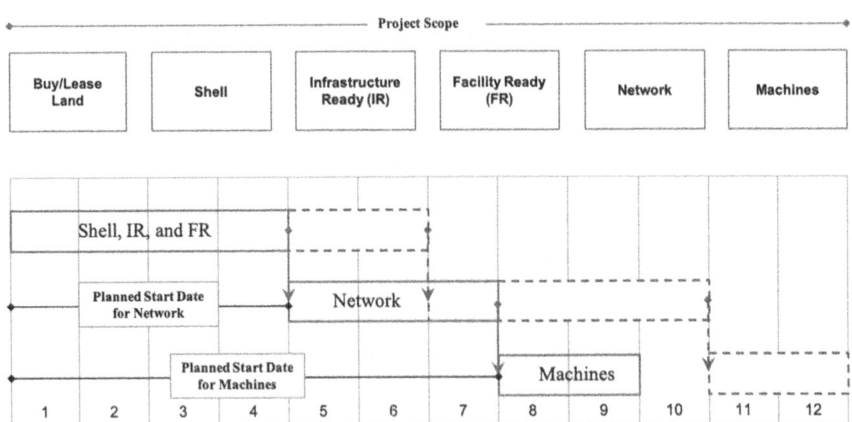

Fig. 2 The scope of a typical capacity expansion project of building a new data center

economic impacts on the cloud service provider. To address this novel capacity expansion problem arising from the cloud computing industry, the following two studies are particularly relevant: Song and Zipkin (2012) and Chen and Lee (2017).

Song and Zipkin (2012) analyze a capacity planning problem based on the well-known newsvendor setting; that is, demand is uncertain and will be realized only at the end of the planning horizon. Unlike the classic newsvendor problem, however, they consider a very long planning horizon such that the firm will receive some partial demand information during the process. In response to the revised demand forecasts, they assume that the firm can either add more capacity or cancel some existing capacity at a certain fee. Interestingly, they find that the formulation of this problem is similar to that of an infinite-horizon, series inventory control model, which enables them to characterize the optimal capacity expansion or cancellation decisions. As can be seen, some key features of the model of Song and Zipkin (2012), including the one-time uncertain demand, partially revealed demand information, and a very long lead time, are applicable to the capacity expansion problem associated with developing a new data center. However, a caveat is that in a data center expansion project, the existing capacity installed based on a previous decision cannot be easily canceled later; for example, once the shell (i.e., the building) is completed, it is impossible to cancel or reduce its capacity. Moreover, Song and Zipkin (2012) do not consider random decision epochs such as the time uncertainties associated with different stages of the data center expansion project.

Chen and Lee (2017) examine a project-based supply chain consisting of a firm that manages the progress of the project and many suppliers each responsible for supplying key equipment or materials for each project stage. Their model is applicable to addressing the time uncertainties in capacity expansion projects of developing new data centers. The fundamental cost trade-offs can be explained by Fig. 2. Suppose that the planned time for completing shell, IR, and FR is four quarters, for network is three quarters, and for installing machines is two quarters. Based on this schedule, the firm may require the network equipment supplier and the machine supplier to deliver at the end of the fourth quarter and the seventh quarter, respectively. However, suppose that the completion of shell, IR, and FR is delayed by two quarters; while the network supplier has been ready for delivery as planned, there will be a holding cost of the network equipment during the delay. Furthermore, suppose that the on-site installation of network is also delayed for one quarter, and then the schedule of installation of machines is pushed further to the end of the tenth quarter. As a result, if the machine supplier has been ready as planned, there will be a holding cost of the machines for three quarters. On the other hand, a project stage can also be finished earlier than planned; in that case, however, the project will be halted if the supplier for the next stage is not ready (as the supplier is aiming at the planned delivery due date). To address such trade-offs, Chen and Lee (2017) develop an analytical model with stochastic activity times and explore the optimal equipment or material delivery schedule to coordinate with the suppliers. As can be seen, however, Chen and Lee (2017) do not consider demand updates featured by Song and Zipkin (2012). Therefore, it will be an interesting future research direction to combine model features of Song and Zipkin (2012) and Chen and Lee (2017) such that the integrated model framework allows partially revealed demand information and stochastic decision epochs, which can better capture the challenges in new data center capacity expansion projects.

Next, let us consider the capacity expansion problems within an existing data center, that is, capacity expansion at the computing resource level. According to our interviews with a leading cloud service provider in the Seattle area, a prominent problem is that capacity expansion of some computing resources, such as CPU and RAM, is usually managed through "bundled" supply packages, for example, pre-configured server clusters. As a result, even though the growth rates of capacity requirements for those computing resources are time-varying and disproportionate, the firm can only deploy new server clusters with a fixed ratio of those computing resources, resulting in a mismatch between demand and supply. To the best of our knowledge, this capacity expansion problem has not been fully explored, although it bears some similarities to the literature on co-production (see, e.g., Bitran and Gilbert 1994, Tomlin and Wang 2008, Bansal and Transchel 2014, and Dong et al. 2014) and the literature on retailing pre-packs (see e.g., Smith and Agrawal 2000). One exception is the work of Arbabian et al. (2021), which directly addresses the capacity expansion problem described above. Given the importance of this problem in the rapidly growing cloud computing industry, below we provide a detailed description of Arbabian et al. (2021).

Arbabian et al. (2021) consider a capacity expansion problem of a firm that faces demand for two types of computing resources, $i \in \{1, 2\}$ (e.g., CPU and RAM), in a finite planning horizon. Suppose that the incremental demand rate for each type of resource is non-negative but is time-dependent; for instance, demand for each type of resource can exhibit an exponential growth with time. Moreover, capacities of the two types of resources are added through deployment of server clusters, which come in a variety of pre-configured packages of the two types of resources. For instance, consider two types of server clusters: CPU-intense and RAM-intense. Hereafter, let us use the terminology *cluster type* j and *cluster* j interchangeably, where $j \in \{1, 2\}$, and note that a unit of a specific cluster type contains a specific ratio of the two capacity attributes.

Let T be the length of the planning horizon, $d_i(t)$ be the incremental demand growth for resource type $i \in \{1, 2\}$, $D_i(a, b)$ be the total demand growth for resource type i in time interval (a, b), and a_{ij} be the capacity units of resource type i in one unit of cluster type $j \in \{1, 2\}$. Furthermore, there is a holding cost including the capital cost and depreciation of the excess capacity, and there is a fixed expansion cost including the shipping, installation, and engineering costs of each expansion. Let c_j be the unit replenishment (purchase) cost of cluster $j \in \{1, 2\}$, h_i be the holding cost rate of excess capacity of resource type $i \in \{1, 2\}$, and A be the fixed expansion cost independent of the size of expansion. Finally, no capacity shortage is allowed; that is, the cost of shortage is exorbitant.

The objective is to determine the best times and quantities of the capacity expansions through deployment of the two cluster types to minimize the total capacity expansion cost over a finite horizon, which consists of the fixed expansion costs, the holding costs of excess capacities, and the purchase costs of server clusters. The authors assume that capacity expansion is immediate, while noting that when lead time for delivery is constant, it can be easily incorporated into the model without affecting the subsequent analysis. In particular, they focus on a class of capacity expansion policies, for which the planning horizon is divided into multiple *capacity expansion cycles (CECs)*, and a CEC is defined as follows: (1) Capacities of the two attributes are added through deployment of the two cluster types such that capacities of both types of resources are leveled (i.e., the excess capacities reach a desired minimum level) at the start and end of each cycle. (2) Capacity expansions are made only when the capacity of at least one type of resource is leveled. (3) Expansions through purchases of the two clusters can be simultaneous or sequential.

The CEC policies have three important characteristics. First, deployment of each cluster type adds to the existing capacities of both attributes, although the ratio of the added capacities is fixed. For example, if the firm purchases Q_1 (or Q_2) unit of cluster type 1 (cluster type 2), this adds $a_{11}Q_1$ ($a_{12}Q_2$) of attribute 1's capacity and $a_{21}Q_1$ ($a_{22}Q_2$) of attribute 2's capacity to the existing capacities. Second, the planning horizon can be divided into multiple CECs with equal or different time intervals. That is, the number of CECs and their durations can be decision variables. Third, if the acquisition of the two cluster types within a CEC is sequential, let us consider the following policy in that cycle. The cycle may contain multiple purchases of a specific cluster type, defined as the *leading cluster*, followed by a single purchase of the other cluster type, defined as the *following cluster*, to level capacities of both attributes at the end of this cycle.

In a finite-horizon problem, a CEC policy as defined above may contain N expansion cycles, where N can be a decision variable. In each expansion cycle $n \in \{1, 2, \ldots, N\}$, there can be multiple replenishment opportunities. If the expansions of the two cluster types are sequential, let m_n denote the number of expansions of the leading cluster, followed by a single replenishment of the other cluster. If the expansions of the two cluster types are simultaneous, let $m_n + 1$ be the number of (joint) expansions of the two cluster types in cycle n. The replenishment pattern may be different from cycle to cycle in a given problem. Depending on times and demand growth rates in the planning horizon, the m_ns can be different for different cycles. Hence, any CEC policy can be characterized by $(N, \vec{M})$, where $\vec{M} = \{m_n; n = 1, 2, \ldots, N\}$. Note that both N and $\vec{M}$ can be decision variables in our model. Furthermore, let T_n be the start time of the n-th cycle (with $T_1 = 0$ and $T_{N+1} = T$), $Q_{k,j,n}$ be the quantity of cluster j in the k-th replenishment ($k = 1, \ldots, m_n + 1$) of the n-th cycle, and $\tau_{k,n}$ be the time of the k-th replenishment in the n-th cycle (with $\tau_{1,n} = T_n$ and $\tau_{m_n+2,n} = T_{n+1}$). An important assumption throughout the paper is as follows:

$$\frac{a_{11}}{a_{21}} \geq \frac{D_1(\tau_{k,n}, \tau_{k+1,n})}{D_2(\tau_{k,n}, \tau_{k+1,n})} \geq \frac{a_{12}}{a_{22}} \text{ for any } k \in \{1, \ldots, m_n\} \text{ of any cycle } n \in \{1, \ldots, N\},$$

which implies that an *attribute-i-intense cluster* is referred to as cluster type i ($i = 1, 2$). This assumption assures that with a combined use of different cluster types, the cloud provider should be able to achieve a balance between supply and demand in each expansion. Otherwise, deployment of those clusters will result in the accumulation of excess capacities of at least one type of resource.

Then, the operating characteristics of the general $(N, \vec{M})$ policies based on sequential and simultaneous expansions can be derived. For ease of exposition, we will show how to derive the total cost within any given CEC with cluster 1 $(j = 1)$ as being the leading cluster. With a slight abuse of notation, for a cycle $n \in \{1, 2, \ldots, N\}$, let m be the number of expansions of the leading cluster (i.e., $m = m_n$). When the leading cluster is employed in the first m expansions, the excess capacity of attribute 2 reduces faster than that of attribute 1 because a_{11}/a_{21} is greater than $D_1(\tau_{k,n}, \tau_{k+1,n})/D_2(\tau_{k,n}, \tau_{k+1,n})$ for any $k \in \{1, 2, \ldots, m\}$, according to the assumption above. As a result, the excess capacity of attribute 1 is always positive when attribute 2's excess capacity reaches zero, upon which the next expansion has to be made. The excess capacity of attribute 1 accumulates until the last expansion, whereby cluster 2 is purchased and employed. At the last expansion, there must be excess capacity of attribute 1 to start with, but then the excess capacity of attribute 1 will deplete faster than that of attribute 2 because a_{12}/a_{22} is smaller than $D_1(\tau_{m+1,n}, T_{n+1})/D_2(\tau_{m+1,n}, T_{n+1})$. Eventually, the capacities of both attributes can be leveled at the same time at the end of this cycle. Thus, for attribute 2, we have

$$a_{21} Q_{k,1,n} = D_2(\tau_{k,n}, \tau_{k+1,n}), \text{ for } k = 1, \ldots, m, \text{ and } a_{22} Q_{m+1,2,n} = D_2(\tau_{m+1,n}, T_{n+1}).$$

For attribute 1, because its capacity should be leveled at the end of the cycle, we have

$$a_{11} \sum_{k=1}^{m} Q_{k,1,n} + a_{12} Q_{m+1,2,n} = D_1(T_n, T_{n+1}).$$

Define $\alpha = a_{11}a_{22} - a_{12}a_{21}$, $F_i(a, b) = \int_a^b D_i(a, t)dt, i \in \{1, 2\}$, and $w_j = h_1 a_{1j} + h_2 a_{2j}$, $j \in \{1, 2\}$.

Then, in a given cycle $[T_n, T_{n+1}]$ with cluster $l \in \{1, 2\}$ as the leading cluster and cluster $f \neq l$ as the following cluster, the total fixed expansion cost will be $A(m + 1)$, the total purchase cost will be $[(c_1 a_{22} - c_2 a_{21}) D_1(T_n, T_{n+1}) + (c_2 a_{11} - c_1 a_{12}) D_2(T_n, T_{n+1})]/\alpha$, and the total holding cost will be

$$\sum_{k=1}^{m} (\tau_{k+1,n} - \tau_{k,n}) \frac{w_l D_f(T_n, \tau_{k+1,n})}{a_{fl}} + \psi_n,$$

where $\psi_n = \sum_{i=1}^{2} h_i[(T_{n+1} - \tau_{m+1,n}) D_i(T_n, T_{n+1}) - F_i(T_n, T_{n+1})]$ is independent of m.

In contrast to the sequential-expansion policy, the cloud provider can employ both cluster types jointly in each expansion. Again, let us consider $m + 1$

expansion opportunities in the n-th CEC with the expansion times $\tau_{k,n}$, where $k \in \{1, 2, \ldots, m+1\}$. Moreover, the cloud provider can achieve a balance between supply and demand in every joint expansion. That is,

$$a_{11} Q_{k,1,n} + a_{12} Q_{k,2,n} = D_1(\tau_{k,n}, \tau_{k+1,n}),\ k = 1, 2, \ldots, m+1.$$

$$a_{21} Q_{k,1,n} + a_{22} Q_{k,2,n} = D_2(\tau_{k,n}, \tau_{k+1,n}),\ k = 1, 2, \ldots, m+1.$$

The total purchase cost will be $c_1 \sum_{k=1}^{m+1} Q_{k,1,n} + c_2 \sum_{k=1}^{m+1} Q_{k,2,n}$, and the total holding cost of attribute $i \in \{1, 2\}$ will be $h_i \left\{\sum_{k=1}^{m+1} \int_{\tau_{k,n}}^{\tau_{k+1,n}} [a_{i1} Q_{k,1,n} + a_{i2} Q_{k,2,n} - D_i(\tau_{k,n}, t)]dt\right\}$. Therefore, in a given cycle $[T_n, T_{n+1}]$, the total purchase cost will be $[(c_1 a_{22} - c_2 a_{21}) D_1(T_n, T_{n+1}) + (c_2 a_{11} - c_1 a_{12}) D_2(T_n, T_{n+1})]/\alpha$, and the total holding cost will be

$$\sum_{i=1}^{2} \left\{ h_i \left[\sum_{k=1}^{m+1} (\tau_{k+1,n} - \tau_{k,n}) D_i(T_n, \tau_{k+1,n}) - F_i(T_n, T_{n+1}) \right] \right\}.$$

Finally, based on the derivations of the total costs in a cycle (for a given sequential- or simultaneous-expansion policy), Arbabian et al. (2021) derive the optimal timing and quantities of expansions in a cycle. Furthermore, to determine the optimal length of the expansion cycles, they provide a dynamic-programming-based algorithm and propose a forward-looking heuristic. The idea of the heuristic is to minimize the total cost rate of each cycle, which is easy to communicate and implement in practice. The heuristic solution can also be used as an excellent starting point for the exact yet tedious dynamic programming solution procedure.

2.2 *Capacity Reservation and Allocation*

Due to long lead times of capacity investment and expansion in the semiconductor and computing technology industries, firms usually need to reserve production capacity from their suppliers. On the other hand, from the perspective of a supplier with a capacity constraint, it is crucial to optimize the overall capacity allocation while dealing with the strategic behavior of the firms due to their misaligned incentives. The interplay between the supplier and the competing firms in the context of semiconductor capacity reservation and allocation has attracted considerable research interests, such as Karabuk and Wu (2003), Erkoc and Wu (2005), Cai and Vairaktarakis (2012), Peng et al. (2012), Wu et al. (2013), Zhang et al. (2017), and Liu et al. (2019), among others.

Karabuk and Wu (2003) examine a capacity allocation problem from the perspective of the headquarter of a semiconductor manufacturer, which needs to allocate production capacity among different product lines. Each product line is managed by a product manager whose incentive is not aligned with the headquarter.

As can be seen, when the product managers have private demand signals, they have a strong incentive to inflate their demand signals in order to obtain a larger expected allocation. To devise an incentive compatible mechanism that induces truth-telling from the product managers, the authors propose an incentive alignment scheme with bonus and charges such that the headquarter can achieve the optimal capacity allocation.

Cai and Vairaktarakis (2012) consider a capacity reservation problem of semiconductor firms competing for limited time slots of a third-party manufacturing facility (e.g., a foundry). On the one hand, each firm books time slots at either the regular or overtime cost rate and incurs a tardiness cost for the delay with respect to a task completion due date; the objective of the firm is to minimize the total of booking, overtime, and tardiness costs. On the other hand, from the third party's perspective, it is challenging to coordinate the firms' production schedules given the capacity constraint. The focus of this study is on mechanism design to achieve a win–win solution for everybody through a cooperative game-theoretical framework; that is, the third party first derives the optimal allocation that maximizes the efficiency of the entire system and then employs a savings sharing mechanism to align incentives of different firms. It is worth noting that the authors illustrate the applicability of the proposed model and solution through two examples: Semiconductor Product Analysis and Design Enhancement (SPADE) in Hong Kong and the supply chain portal of UMC in Taiwan.

Motivated by Intel's equipment capacity planning strategies, Peng et al. (2012) consider a dual-mode framework that consists of three layers of decisions: contract negotiation, capacity reservation, and capacity execution. The framework is named "dual-mode" as the firm can purchase equipment from two suppliers, one with lower cost yet longer lead time (the "base mode") and the other with higher cost yet shorter lead time (the "flexible mode"). The key feature is that the firm can reserve capacity from both supply modes through option contracts before demand is realized and then exercises these options after demand information is updated. They show that such a risk-sharing mechanism can benefit not only the firm but also its suppliers. Similar to Peng et al. (2012), Wu et al. (2013) investigate a semiconductor firm's capacity reservation strategies under a dual-sourcing mode. However, Wu et al. (2013) consider an integrated device manufacturer (IDM) that can either produce in-house or outsource from a third-party manufacturing facility (e.g., a foundry), and they refer to this problem as "horizontal dual sourcing." The focus of their paper, however, is on two types of common contracts: the fixed commitment contracts and the reservation contracts. We will elaborate on their results when discussing the contracting issues in Sect. 3.

Zhang et al. (2017) consider a semiconductor supply chain that consists of a chip manufacturing firm and a set of OEMs. The upstream firm has a fixed capacity to be allocated among the OEMs. Through an analysis of data from the chip manufacturing firm, the authors find that reservations of a larger capacity are not always associated with deeper discounts. The non-monotonic quantity–price relationship is in sharp contrast to the conventional wisdom of quantity-based discounts where a larger quantity always results in a deeper discount. To explore the underlying reason for this observation, the authors develop an analytical model where prices are determined through bilateral negotiations. They show that from the chip manufacturing firm's perspective, accepting reservations from large and small OEMs may be more desirable than accepting reservations from mid-sized OEMs. The reason is that, after satisfying reservations from the mid-sized OEMs, the remaining capacity may be too little to accommodate large reservations on the one hand and too much to accommodate small reservations on the other hand, and thus the chip manufacturing firm may have an incentive to effectively charge a "premium" to the mid-sized OEMs.

Similar to Zhang et al. (2017), Liu et al. (2019) investigate a semiconductor supply chain that consists of a capacity provider and a set of buyers who share the provider's limited capacity. These buyers possess private demand signals about their demand, which will evolve over a finite horizon. The authors propose a multi-period agreement with flexible contract terms that can be adjusted period by period as the buyers' private demand signals update. The focus of their study is on the optimal design of the agreements between the capacity provider and all the buyers to achieve the ex ante efficient capacity investment and the ex post efficient capacity allocation. Properties of the proposed contract will be elaborated later when we discuss the contracting issues (in Sect. 3).

2.3 *Capacity Upgrading and Management of Obsolescence*

Due to the rapid development of new technology and process, capacity upgrading and management of obsolescence are crucial in semiconductor and computing technology supply chains. Some aforementioned studies of capacity investment and expansion have incorporated considerations of capacity obsolescence, such as Besanko et al. (2010), as well as investment in the capacity of a new process with a time-to-market trade-off, such as Ülkü et al. (2005) and Özer and Uncu (2013).

The literature on capacity planning under new product or technology transition is relevant. Motivated by capacity planning strategies of Intel, Li et al. (2014) consider a semiconductor manufacturer's capacity planning problem with two successive generations of products or technologies. The key feature of this problem is that the firm can either invest in the capacity of the new generation or upgrade the installed capacity such that production lines can produce products of both generations. The authors develop an analytical model with an objective of minimizing the total inventory and equipment costs with a chance-constrained service-level constraint in the presence of non-stationary and random demand. They also quantify the benefit from having flexible capacity (i.e., the new or upgraded capacity can produce products of both generations). Moreover, the reader is referred to Li et al. (2013) for a demand forecast model that considers more than two successive generations of product or technology transitions.

Li and Graves (2012) present a model with capacity planning and pricing during a new product or technology transition. They show that product substitution and pricing are effective tools to mitigate supply–demand mismatches during the transition, and they characterize the optimal dynamic pricing strategies for both generations of products. Similarly, Yin et al. (2015) focus on the firm's pricing decisions during the new product or technology transition in the presence of trade-in options. The key feature of their model is the incorporation of product uncertainty and buyers' forward-looking behavior; that is, the additional value of the new product is uncertain due to the risks associated with the new technology, and the strategic buyers' purchase decisions are influenced by their estimation of the new product valuation in the future.

Finally, for a comprehensive discussion of operational problems during new product or technology transitions (not limited to applications to the semiconductor and computing technology industries), the reader is referred to Billington et al. (1998), Lim and Tang (2006), and the references therein.

3 Outsourcing, Contracting, and Procurement Strategies

There is a vast and rich literature on outsourcing and procurement strategies and the associated contracting issues, see, e.g., Tsay et al. (1999) and Cachon (2003) for comprehensive reviews of modeling supply chain contracts. In this section, specific attention is given to studies of this topic that are closely related to the semiconductor and computing technology industries. Our discussion of relevant papers can be divided into two broad categories: (1) contracting in equipment capacity planning and (2) contracting and outsourcing strategies in material procurement.

3.1 Contracting in Equipment Capacity Planning

As noted earlier, some of the aforementioned studies of the capacity planning problems in the semiconductor industry also investigate the incentive issues arising from reservation and allocation of limited capacity, which has led to a stream of literature on the contracting problems associated with capacity planning, such as Erkoc and Wu (2005), Cai and Vairaktarakis (2012), Peng et al. (2012), Wu et al. (2013), and Liu et al. (2019), among others.

Cai and Vairaktarakis (2012) propose a win–win solution for all participants using a cooperative-game approach combined with a truth-telling mechanism. Erkoc and Wu (2005) focus on a capacity reservation contract with a deductible reservation fee, which is conceptually similar to an option contract. That is, the firm can reserve capacity from its supplier through payment of a reservation fee per unit of capacity reserved. Then, when the firm utilizes the reserved capacity to produce the products, the per-unit reservation fee is deducted from the variable production fee, whereas the reservation fee for the excess capacity is unrecoverable. The authors suggest that such a contract is essentially a risk-sharing agreement that can align incentives in semiconductor supply chains.

The contract adopted by Peng et al. (2012) is also an option contract, whereby the semiconductor firm (e.g., Intel) needs to make an upfront payment to its suppliers during the capacity reservation phase, and then the firm can exercise these options after it learns more demand information during the capacity execution phase. Wu et al. (2013) compare two types of contracts: the reservation contract and the fixed commitment contract. The reservation contract is similar to that proposed by Peng et al. (2012) as the IDM is required to pay a fixed reservation fee for capacity reservation and then a variable fee for each unit produced by the foundry. The fixed commitment contract, however, requires the IDM to outsource a fixed fraction of its demand to the foundry. The authors provide conditions under which one type of contract outperforms the other.

Liu et al. (2019) adopt a multi-period mechanism design to achieve ex ante optimal capacity investment and ex post optimal allocation. In addition, the proposed mechanism is expected to satisfy the following constraints: incentive compatibility, interim individual rationality, budget balancing, and efficient investment, such that participation in the agreement is voluntary, all participants are truth-telling, and the mechanism is financially self-sustaining. A salient feature of the proposed mechanism is a "membership-type" contract where each participant is required to pay a "membership fee" to obtain a default capacity in each period such that all participants can trade their default capacity after they learn more demand information at the end of that period.

It is important to note that, due to the long lead times of capacity investment and expansion, the upstream firms in a semiconductor supply chain (e.g., key equipment suppliers) need to make capacity investment decisions, while the design of the product or process is not finalized and demand remains highly uncertain, thus exposing themselves to significant risks of order cancellation or delayed delivery. Hence, incentive misalignment within the supply chain may arise and cause a significant loss of efficiency. Efforts to address this daunting challenge have led to an important stream of literature on examining the supply chain partners' incentives and optimal behavior in such a business environment, such as Cohen et al. (2003), Terwiesch et al. (2005), and Taylor and Plambeck (2007), among others. Given the importance of this problem, below we provide a detailed description of the model and main results of Cohen et al. (2003) to illustrate the key trade-offs.

Cohen et al. (2003) consider a supply chain of customized capital goods, such as semiconductor production equipment, which consists of a buyer and a supplier. To deliver the product to the buyer within a reasonable lead time and avoid high costs of holding inventory, the supplier routinely begins its production based on the buyer's forecasted orders prior to the buyer's firm purchase orders. The forecasted orders are also called "soft orders" as the buyer can revise or even cancel these orders before realization of market demand. The objective of this study is to balance the trade-off between an early start of the order fulfillment process, while facing potential order cancellation and inventory holding costs, and a delayed start until more demand information becomes available, while facing a potential delay cost.

The model setup can be described on a timeline. The supplier receives information of the first soft order (assume an order of unit quantity) at time $t = 0$. The buyer's firm purchase order occurs at some random time, $t = T_N$, with distribution $G(\cdot)$. At time T_N, two scenarios will happen: (1) if the order is cancelled (with probability p), the supplier will not deliver the product and incurs a cost; (2) otherwise, the order is not cancelled (with probability $1 - p$) and will be expected to be delivered before the deadline, RDD_N, which is also random. The supplier determines the production start time, $t_p \geq 0$, after receiving the information of the soft orders. Once the fulfillment process begins at time t_p, it will be delivered to the buyer at time $t_p + LT$, where LT is another random variable representing uncertain production lead time.

From the perspective of the supplier, there are three potential costs associated to market (demand) uncertainty and production lead time uncertainty: (1) If the supplier starts the fulfillment process early, he will incur inventory holding cost. Let h denote the cost incurred by the supplier per unit of time that the product is produced prior to the delivery date RDD_N. Then, the total inventory cost is $h[RDD_N - (t_p + LT)]^+$, where $t_p + LT$ is the time the order is delivered and $(x)^+ = \max(0, x)$. (2) If the supplier starts the fulfillment process late, he incurs a delay cost. Let g denote the unit delay cost, then the total delay cost will be $g[(t_p + LT) - RDD_N]^+$. (3) If the order is cancelled after the supplier starts the production, a unit cancellation cost per time unit, c, is incurred and the total cancellation cost will be $c(T_N - t_p)^+$. Thus, the supplier's expected total cost is given as

$$TC(t_p) = (1-p)h\mathbb{E}[RDD_N - (t_p + LT)]^+ + (1-p)g\mathbb{E}[(t_p + LT) - RDD_N]^+ \\ + pc\mathbb{E}(T_N - t_p)^+.$$

Recall that $T_N \sim G(\cdot)$. Assuming that the random variable $S = RDD_N - LT$ follows a distribution $F(\cdot)$, one can explicitly express $TC(t_p)$. Furthermore, $TC(t_p)$ is convex in the decision variable t_p; thus, there is a unique optimal solution, t_p^*, that minimizes $TC(t_p)$ and satisfies

$$pcG(t_p^*) + (1-p)(g+h)F(t_p^*) = pc + (1-p)h.$$

Given the optimal fulfillment start time, t_p^*, Cohen et al. (2003) estimate cost parameters c, h, and g through industrial data, and they obtain $g = 1.000$, $h = 3.031$, and $c = 2.108$, implying that the holding and cancellation costs are about three and two times higher than the cost of delay, respectively. Furthermore, they fit the arrival time of finalized order to an exponential distribution with parameter α and the requested delivery date, RDD_N, and production lead time, LT, to normal distributions. For the sake of tractability, they assume that the random variable $S = RDD_N - LT$ follows a Weibull $(2, \beta)$ distribution with a constant shift δ to the right and linearize the supplier's expected total cost, under the specific distributions of $F(\cdot)$ and $G(\cdot)$, in the neighborhood of a target starting point τ. The resulting optimal solution t_p^* satisfies the following equation:

$$t_p^* = \frac{\theta_1 e^{-\alpha\tau}(1+\alpha) + \theta_2 e^{-\beta^2(\tau+\delta)^2}(1+2\tau\beta^2) - \theta_3}{\theta_1 \alpha e^{-\alpha\tau} + 2\theta_2\beta^2(\tau+\delta)e^{-\beta^2(\tau+\delta)^2}},$$

where $\theta_1 = pc$, $\theta_2 = (1-p)(g+h)$, and $\theta_3 = (1-p)g$.

The estimation procedure is as follows. Given I observations and J explanatory variables, let $\alpha_i = \exp(\gamma X_i)$ and $\beta_i = \exp(\rho X_i)$, where index i represents the i-th observation, X_i represents a vector including all explanatory variables corresponding to the i-th observation, and γ (ρ) be the estimation parameters. Due to data limitation, the finishing time of each observation is assumed to be normally distributed with mean μ_i and standard deviation σ, $FT_i \sim N(\mu_i, \sigma^2)$. The production lead time, LT_i, is set to $LT_i = \eta Y_i$, where Y_i captures all variables that influence the production lead time. Since the finishing times of two sequential observations are correlated, it is assumed that the joint distribution of FT_i and FT_{i+1} follows a bivariate normal distribution (BVN); that is $(FT_i, FT_{i+1}) \sim BVN(\mu_i, \mu_{i+1}, \sigma^2, \sigma^2, \lambda)$, where λ is the correlation coefficient.

Finally, we would like to comment on two important follow-up works. Terwiesch et al. (2005) empirically analyze the relationship between forecast behavior of a semiconductor equipment buyer and the delivery performance of suppliers. They find evidence that the buyer has a tendency to inflate its forecast when dealing with a supplier of low service level and that the suppliers have a tendency to distrust the buyer's forecast, which in turn results in low service levels. These findings establish the importance of designing certain information sharing agreements within a semiconductor supply chain. Taylor and Plambeck (2007) address a similar problem to that examined by Cohen et al. (2003) while focusing on the optimal design of a relational contract, which provides incentives to both the upstream and downstream firms to participate given the potential for long-term business relationships. Under the relational contract, the supplier chooses to trust the buyer's demand forecast and commits to the capacity level to meet the forecast given that the buyer has an incentive to reveal the true demand forecast and agrees to compensate the supplier for order cancellation after demand is realized. The authors find that the optimal relational contract is complex, so they also propose a simpler contract that can achieve near-optimal performance.

3.2 Contracting and Outsourcing Strategies in Material Procurement

In this subsection, we switch our focus from contracting in capacity planning to contracting and outsourcing strategies in material procurement, especially studies that are closely related to outsourcing and procurement strategies in the semiconductor and computing technology supply chains, such as Wu and Kleindorfer (2005),

Mendelson and Tunca (2007), Wang et al. (2010), Tan et al. (2016), Anderson et al. (2017), Chen et al. (2021), and Dong et al. (2021), among others.

Wang et al. (2010) examine a buying firm's sourcing and supplier reliability improvement strategies in the presence of random capacity and yields. The firm can contract with multiple suppliers while at the same time making efforts to improve the reliability of the suppliers. Through an examination of the firm's optimal sourcing and reliability improvement strategies, the authors find that if the suppliers' reliability heterogeneity is high, dual sourcing is favored over improvement when the random capacity is the major concern, while the opposite is true when the random yield is the major concern. They find anecdotal evidence from a semiconductor firm, Xilinx, which moved away from dual sourcing due to the significant yield performance difference between its two suppliers. Tan et al. (2016) investigate a dynamic procurement planning problem where the buying firm sources from two suppliers with different costs, lead times, capacities, and yields. The authors develop a stochastic inventory model with two re-order points: once the inventory level drops below a re-order point, the firm should place a replenishment order to the respective supplier. In contrast to the conventional wisdom, they find that it can be optimal to allocate a larger fraction of the firm's order to the supplier with a longer lead time, even though this supplier may not have any other advantages over the faster supplier in terms of cost and reliability. Such an observation is due to the consideration of the suppliers' limited and random capacities. In a very recent study, Dong et al. (2021) extend the literature on procurement strategies with random supplier yields to an important direction, whereby the suppliers' random yields can be positively correlated. Based on a dual-sourcing model, they can fully characterize the buying firm's optimal procurement strategy, which indicates that dual souring is less likely as the positive correlation between the suppliers' random yields increases. Their study reveals the key impact of supplier reliability in addition to supplier cost efficiency in the buyer firm's procurement and supplier selection strategies.

In addition to the above literature on a semiconductor firm's outsourcing strategies, there is another important stream of literature that is particularly related to our focus on the semiconductor and computing technology supply chains, i.e., the literature on procurement with spot markets. For instance, Wu and Kleindorfer (2005) propose an integrated model framework where the buying firm can either sign contracts with multiple suppliers in advance or purchase from a spot market. The contracts are capacity options whereby the firm pays a reservation fee per unit of capacity reserved and then an execution fee per unit of capacity utilized. The authors characterize the equilibria of the spot market and the firm's optimal procurement strategy in terms of the contracts and spot transactions. Anderson et al. (2017) examine a similarly structured supply chain that consists of one buying firm and multiple suppliers. Unlike Wu and Kleindorfer (2005), however, Anderson et al. (2017) consider an auction model where the suppliers submit bids to win the buyer's contracts. The suppliers' bids specify the asking prices for their option contracts, which consist of the reservation and execution fees per unit of capacity reserved and utilized, respectively. The buyer needs to determine the optimal portfolio of options in advance and the purchase quantity from the spot market after demand is realized. Their study provides insights into the impacts of different demand characteristics on the buyer's optimal procurement portfolios. In contrast to the two studies mentioned above, Mendelson and Tunca (2007) consider a supply chain that consists of a key supplier and multiple buyers (e.g., manufacturers). Each manufacturer enters a bilateral fixed-price contract with the supplier in advance, and the manufacturers can trade in a spot market after demand uncertainty is resolved. The authors show that the presence of the spot market can benefit the entire supply chain but may make either the supplier or the manufacturers worse off. They also show that the manufacturers will move away from the fixed-price contracts as there are more manufacturers participating and that in the limiting case where there are infinitely many participants, the supply chain can be coordinated.

Recently, Chen et al. (2021) consider a two-stage supply chain consisting of a buyer and a supplier. The supplier procures a key component to manufacture a product, and the buyer orders from the supplier to meet a price-sensitive demand. As the input price of the raw materials is volatile and determined through a spot market, the wholesale price is also volatile. The two parties enter into either a standard contract, where the buyer orders just before the supplier starts production, or a time-flexible contract, where the buyer can lock a wholesale price in advance. Moreover, three selling-price schemes are considered. The efficacy of each of the contracts under the selling pricing schemes is analyzed. A good example of such settings can be found in the rapidly growing cloud computing supply chains, where an ODM can be viewed as the supplier, and an OEM can be viewed as the buyer. The supplier may purchase a commodity-type component (e.g., DRAM) at the spot price as the raw material in the manufacturing of the final product (e.g., a cloud server), which is then sold to the buyer. Given the importance of this problem, below we provide a detailed description of this study to illustrate the basic trade-offs and challenges.

Suppose that the product has to be manufactured by a target time and shipped to the buyer (e.g., the OEM) who sells it to customers (e.g., cloud capacity providers). There is a key component in the product that is traded as a commodity on the spot market (e.g., DRAM) with volatile price. The component plays a major role in forming the final price of the product, and the buyer's market demand is price-sensitive. Prior to manufacturing, the buyer and the supplier have a finite time window, T, referred to as the *price lock-up window*, where the buyer must place his order and the supplier purchases the component for final production. Two procurement contracts between the supplier and the buyer, the *standard* and *time-flexible* procurement contracts, are examined. In the standard procurement contract, the buyer will place the order to the supplier at the end of the lock-up window, T, whereas under the time-flexible procurement contract, the buyer can place the order in advance (i.e., at a time before T) to lock up a favorable wholesale price.

The sequence of events is unfolded as follows. The buyer places an order (and thus locks up a wholesale price) to the supplier during $[0, T]$, and the supplier, after the receipt of the order, procures the component and delivers the order by T. Without loss of generality, assume lead times (delivery of component to the supplier, production and delivery times of supplier) are negligible. Thus, if the buyer places an order at time $t \in [0, T]$, the supplier's procurement occurs during time $\tau \in [t, T]$. The buyer determines the selling price of the final product, and demand will be realized at time T. Specifically, assume that the market demand, D_T, is expressed as: $D_T = D - \alpha P$, where P is the unit selling price of the final product. Suppose that the spot price of the component during the lock-up window, c_t, follows a geometric Brownian motion (GBM):

$$dc_t = c_t(\mu dt + \sigma dW_t), \quad \forall t \in [0, T],$$

Where $\mu \in R$ and $\sigma > 0$ represent the drift and the volatility of the GBM, respectively, and W_t is a Wiener process. Given that the buyer places an order at time $t \in [0, T]$ with spot price c_t, the wholesale price is locked at $W = wc_t$, where $w > 1$. Note that if $t < T$, the fulfillment process follows a time-flexible contract, and when $t = T$, the standard contract is employed. After the receipt of the order, the supplier procures the component needed for the order at $\tau \in [t, T]$ from the spot market at c_τ, stores it until the delivery time T, and thus incurs a holding cost $hc_\tau(T - \tau)$, where h denotes the holding cost rate. Since the price of the final product determines market demand, the pricing scheme employed by the buyer plays an important role. Consider three pricing schemes used frequently in practice: namely, *market-driven*, *cost-plus*, and *profit-max* pricing schemes.

When a *market-driven* pricing scheme is employed, the selling price, P, is determined by the prevailing market price at the end of the lock-up window, T. Thus, $P = (1 + \delta)wc_T = pc_T$, where $\delta > 0$ is the markup rate. Under *cost-plus* pricing scheme, the buyer sets the selling price based on its actual procurement cost; that is, given that the buyer locks up at time t with a spot price wc_t, the selling price will be $P = (1 + \delta)wc_t = pc_t$. Finally, if the *profit-max* pricing scheme is employed, the buyer determines the selling price that maximizes the average total profit based on the locked up wholesale price $W = wc_t$. For the combinations of the two procurement contracts and the three pricing schemes, a unified approach can be applied to analyze the two parties' optimal decisions.

First, let us focus on the buyer's problem. Consider $t \in [0, T]$. The buyer's expected total profit will be $\pi_r(t, c_t) = \mathbb{E}[(P - wc_t)(D - \alpha P)]$, where P is the selling price and wc_t is the locked up wholesale price. Under the market-driven and cost-plus pricing schemes, $P = pc_T$ and $P = pc_t$, respectively. However, if the profit-max scheme is employed, $P = (D + \alpha wc_t)/(2\alpha)$, which is the unique maximizer of the buyer's expected profit given the locked up wholesale price wc_t. If the buyer waits and places the order at a future time, $t + x$, where $x \in [0, T - t]$, its expected total profit will be $\mathbb{E}[\pi_r(t + x, c_{t+x})|c_t]$. Therefore, the buyer should place the order immediately at t, if and only if the expected total profit at t is greater than all expected total profits in the future, $[t, T]$, which implies

$$\pi_r(t, c_t) \geq \mathbb{E}[\pi_r(t + x, c_{t+x})|c_t], \quad \forall x \in [0, T - t].$$

The condition above determines whether the buyer should place the order at the current time, t, during the lock-up window when the input price is c_t.

The supplier's problem can be analyzed in a similar fashion. Suppose the buyer places the order of size Q at the locked up wholesale price W at time t. Then the supplier procures the components needed during $\tau \in [t, T]$. At any point in time, τ, the supplier can either procure the components from the spot market, which results in an expected profit $\pi_s(\tau, c_\tau) = WQ - c_\tau Q - hc_\tau(T - \tau)Q$, or wait and procure at a future time $\tau + x$, which results in an expected total profit of $\mathbb{E}[\pi_s(\tau + x, c_{\tau+x})|c_\tau]$. Then, at any time $\tau \in [t, T]$, the supplier should procure materials required to fulfill the buyer's order immediately if and only if the following relationship holds:

$$\pi_s(\tau, c_\tau) > \mathbb{E}[\pi_s(\tau + x, c_{\tau+x})|c_\tau], \quad \forall x \in [0, T - \tau].$$

Note that under the standard contract whereby all decisions are made at time T, the problem restores to the classical Newsvendor problem with or without pricing. As can be seen, however, analysis under the time-flexible contract is more involved. Chen et al. (2021) find that the buyer's optimal ordering time should be determined by a threshold policy, whereby the threshold is dependent on the drift and volatility of the input price as well as the relative magnitude of these parameters compared to each other. Although the optimality of the threshold policy is somewhat expected, the underlying causes under different pricing schemes are different. Under a market-driven or profit-max pricing scheme, a lower wholesale price is always more desirable, whereas, under the cost-plus pricing scheme, a wholesale price that is closer to a benchmark level is more desirable. Moreover, the supplier's optimal procurement time is either upon the receipt of the order or at the end of the lock-up window. That is, if the input price has a downward trend, the supplier should wait until the end of the lock-up window, but if the input price has an upward trend, the supplier's optimal procurement time should be determined by a comparison between the holding cost rate and the average percentage increase in the input price per time unit. Through a numerical study, it can be shown that the time-flexible contract is a Pareto improvement over the standard contract under the cost-plus or profit-max pricing schemes, whereas the supplier may prefer the standard contract under the market-driven pricing scheme. Furthermore, the two parties' profits are heavily influenced by the input price volatility under the cost-plus or market-driven pricing schemes.

4 Production, Quality Control, and Equipment Maintenance

In this section, we discuss studies that can be classified into two broad categories: (1) production and quality control and (2) equipment maintenance and services. As in the previous sections, our focus is on studies closely related to the semiconductor and computing technology industries.

4.1 Production and Quality Control

Early developments of the literature on production and quality control in the semiconductor industry are mostly motivated by wafer fabrications, such as Lee (1992), Gallego et al. (1993), Ou and Wein (1995), Nahmias and Moinzadeh (1997), and Yao and Zheng (1999), among others.

Lee (1992) examines a lot sizing problem when the manufacturing process can shift from the normal state to an out-of-control state. The firm should take corrective actions once an out-of-control shift is detected, and the firm aims to minimize the total time (processing and rework) in the face of the out-of-control risks. Gallego et al. (1993) consider a lot sizing problem with trial runs of the manufacturing process. If a trial run passes the qualification, the entire batch of the remaining job can be processed, but if the trial run fails, all units in the test batch are lost, and another trial run may be needed. As can be seen, the semiconductor manufacturing firm needs to determine the batch sizes of the trial runs as well as the timing to stop conducting the trial runs (given that all the previous trial runs failed). The authors propose the optimal lot sizing and stopping policy, whereby there is a maximum number of trial runs each with only one unit. Jula and Leachman (2010) investigate a batch-processing and scheduling problem motivated by the burn-in process in the semiconductor industry, which is a key step to test the quality of the assembled integrated circuits under various operating environments (see, e.g., the background information provided in that paper for more details). Given continuous, deterministic, and non-stationary demands for multiple products, the firm needs to determine the batch sizes and processing schedules for different products, while noting that all products must be processed following a common sequence of tasks using the same resources.

A prominent problem in production processes of the semiconductor industry is the random yields of products with different quality levels. Here, it is important to distinguish between two common situations regarding products of inferior quality levels depending on the context of the problem: (1) defective products that must be discarded or sent to rework and (2) products of lower quality that can be sold in a different market segment from that for products of normal quality levels.

With regard to the first situation where defective products must be salvaged, Yao and Zheng (1999) present a production–inspection problem in the semiconductor industry. They consider a two-stage production system with an inspection stage in between. The inspection stage can take batches of completed wafers from the upstream production stage for inspection. Only qualified products can be sent to the downstream production stage. Given the limited capacity of the production and inspection stages, there is a fundamental trade-off as follows. If the inspection policy is too soft, there will be too many flawed products sent to the downstream production stage, but if the inspection is too rigid, then the inspection stage will become the bottleneck. The authors formulate this problem as a Markov decision program (MDP) and show that the optimal production and inspection policies should follow a sequence of threshold policies.

With regard to the second situation where products of different quality levels can be sold to different market segments, Ou and Wein (1995) examine a scheduling problem of a server (e.g., a workstation for wafer fabrication) that can switch among different processes with random yields of multiple product types. Through making dynamic decisions on the adoption of different processes, the firm aims at minimizing the sum of the inventory cost (including work-in-process and finished goods) and the backorder cost. The authors approximate the dynamics of the system using the Brownian motion model and derive a scheduling policy based on the Brownian control problem. Another salient example is Nahmias and Moinzadeh (1997), which considers production environments that have two properties commonly found in semiconductor supply chains: a split in quality levels determined randomly after production and one-way substitution of higher quality products for the lower quality ones. In a recent study, Li et al. (2019) compare two different yield-loss strategies regarding the so-called not-quite-perfect products (NQPP): (1) salvage all NQPP ("scrap") and (2) market the NQPP as a low-end product ("sell"). Given the firm's objective of maximizing the total profit, the authors characterize the firm's optimal yield-loss strategy (whether to scrap or sell) and the optimal pricing decisions given the chosen strategy.

Finally, given the importance of the production environments that are featured by Nahmias and Moinzadeh (1997), we next provide a detailed presentation of the model setup and the main results of their paper. Suppose that the output of the production process is graded into one of the two quality levels. Demand streams for each grade are independent; however, the higher quality level product can be substituted for the lower quality ones, if needed. As mentioned earlier, examples of such processes are abundant in semiconductor and wafer manufacturing. In such industries, these classifications are referred to as *binning*. In particular, the production process of a specific CPU microprocessor may be the same, but the resulting clock speeds of the chip may vary due to imperfections in the production process. Faster chips may be substituted for slower ones if needed in such situations. Specifically, assume that the output of a production process is graded into two quality levels. Denote the higher grade product as grade 1 and the lower grade product as grade 2. Suppose the proportion of the grade 1 product, α, is random, and the proportion of the grade 2 product is $1-\alpha$. Demand for each grade is uniform and constant over time with rates, λ_1 and λ_2, respectively, with $\lambda = \lambda_1 + \lambda_2$ representing the total demand rate. Let $\beta = \lambda_1/\lambda$ be the portion of grade 1's demand. Demand for grade 1 can be only satisfied from its inventory; however, demand for grade 2 can be satisfied not only through its inventory but grade 1's inventory when needed. Furthermore, let A be the set-up cost and h be the unit holding cost rate. Assuming no rationing of inventory, no backorders (i.e., shortage cost is infinite), and that production is instantaneous, the following base-stock production/stocking policy is in effect: *When the inventory of grade 1 is depleted, produce enough to raise the total inventory levels to base-stock level, S.*

Note that the above policy is not necessarily optimal; however, it is practical, implementable, and can be employed as a heuristic policy. Under the proposed policy, define a cycle as the time between placement of two consecutive production runs with no inventory of both products at hand. Note that cycles as defined above are regenerative; furthermore, there can be N $(N \geq 1)$ production runs in each cycle, where N is random and depends on the base-stock level, S, the demand rates, and the successive realization of the grade split, α, in each production run.

Consider a cycle with $N = n$ production runs, and let α_i denote the grade split of the i-th run. Then, for the first run, the lot size is S of which $\alpha_1 S$ is grade 1 and $(1 - \alpha_1)S$ is grade 2. The time required to deplete grade 1 inventory, which triggers the second production run, will be $\alpha_1 S/\lambda_1$. During this time, the total demand rate is λ. Hence, the total consumption during this time will be $\alpha_1 S\lambda/\lambda_1 = \alpha_1 S/\beta$. For the second run under the base-stock level, S, in effect, the lot size will be $\alpha_1 S/\beta$, which produces $\alpha_1\alpha_2 S/\beta$ units of grade 1 that will be consumed in $\alpha_1\alpha_2 S/(\beta\lambda_1)$ time units. In a similar fashion (see Fig. 3), it follows that the size of the i-th production run, q_i, will be $q_i = Y_i/\beta^{i-1}$, where $Y_i = \sum_{j=1}^{i} \alpha_j$. In order to have $N = n$ runs in a cycle, one needs to have grade 2 inventory depleted in the n-th run before grade 1 inventory. This means that for a cycle with $N = n$ runs, $Y_i < \beta_i (i = 1, \cdots, N - 1)$ and $Y_n \geq \beta^n$. Thus,

$$p_n = \Pr(N = n) = \Pr\left\{Y_i < \beta_i (i = 1, \ldots, N - 1) \text{ and } Y_n \geq \beta^n\right\}.$$

While Y_i's are dependent random variables, the distribution of N is independent of S. To obtain an expression for the average total cost rate, $C(S)$, the operating characteristics of the system comprising of the expected cycle time and the expected inventory carried need to be derived.

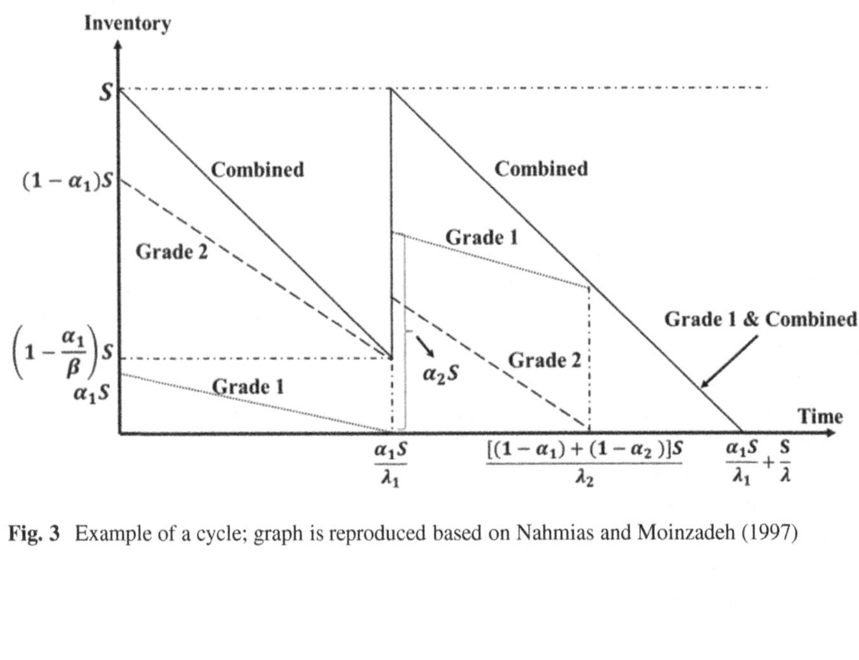

Fig. 3 Example of a cycle; graph is reproduced based on Nahmias and Moinzadeh (1997)

Let T be the cycle time and OH be the total inventory carried in a cycle. From Fig. 3,

$$\begin{aligned} T &= \tfrac{s}{\lambda}\sum_{i=0}^{n-1}\tfrac{Y_i}{\beta^i} \Rightarrow \mathbb{E}(T) = \tfrac{s}{\lambda}\sum_{n=1}^{\infty}\sum_{i=0}^{n-1}\tfrac{\mathbb{E}(Y_i|n)}{\beta^i}p_n \\ &= \tfrac{s}{\lambda}\sum_{i=0}^{\infty}\tfrac{1}{\beta^i}\sum_{n=i+1}^{\infty}\mathbb{E}(Y_i|n)p_n = \tfrac{s}{\lambda}w(\beta,\vec{\alpha}), \end{aligned}$$

where $\vec{\alpha} = (\alpha_1, \alpha_2 \cdots)$ and $w(\beta,\vec{\alpha}) = \sum_{i=0}^{\infty}\frac{1}{\beta^i}\sum_{n=i+1}^{\infty}\mathbb{E}(Y_i|n)p_n$. The average inventory held during a cycle can be obtained by conditioning on $\{N = n\}$. Let OH_i denote the total inventory carried during the i-th production run. From Fig. 3,

$$\begin{aligned} OH_i &= \tfrac{Y_i S}{2\beta^i\lambda}\left[S\left(2-\tfrac{Y_i}{\beta^i}\right)\right] \quad i = 1,\cdots,n-1; \\ OH_n &= \tfrac{S^2}{2\lambda}; \\ OH &= \sum_{i=1}^{n} OH_i = \tfrac{S^2}{2\lambda}\left[2\sum_{i=0}^{n-1}\tfrac{Y_i}{\beta^i} - \sum_{i=0}^{n-1}\tfrac{Y_i^2}{\beta^{2i}}\right]. \end{aligned}$$

Thus,

$$\mathbb{E}(OH) = \frac{S^2}{2\lambda}\left\{2\sum_{i=0}^{\infty}\frac{1}{\beta^i}\sum_{n=i+1}^{\infty}\mathbb{E}_n(Y_i)p_n - \sum_{i=0}^{\infty}\frac{1}{\beta^{2i}}\sum_{n=i+1}^{\infty}\mathbb{E}_n(Y_i^2)p_n\right\} = \frac{S^2}{2\lambda}u(\beta,\vec{\alpha}),$$

where $u(\beta,\vec{\alpha}) = 2\sum_{i=0}^{\infty}\frac{1}{\beta^i}\sum_{n=i+1}^{\infty}\mathbb{E}_n(Y_i)p_n - \sum_{i=0}^{\infty}\frac{1}{\beta^{2i}}\sum_{n=i+1}^{\infty}\mathbb{E}_n(Y_i^2)p_n$.

Since the cycles are regenerative, assuming that the process is stable (the length of the cycles is finite) and by applying Wald's Theorem, the average total cost rate, $C(S)$, is given as

$$\begin{aligned} C(S) &= A\tfrac{\mathbb{E}(N)}{\mathbb{E}(T)} + h\tfrac{\mathbb{E}(OH)}{\mathbb{E}(T)} = A\tfrac{\lambda\mathbb{E}(N)}{w(\beta,\vec{\alpha})S} + h\tfrac{S}{2}\tfrac{u(\beta,\vec{\alpha})}{w(\beta,\vec{\alpha})} \\ &= \tfrac{1}{w(\beta,\vec{\alpha}}\left(A\lambda\tfrac{E(N)}{S} + h\tfrac{u(\beta,\vec{\alpha})}{2}S\right). \end{aligned}$$

Setting $dC(S)/dS = 0$, the optimal base-stock level, S^*, will be

$$S^* = \sqrt{\frac{2A\lambda}{h}} \times \sqrt{\frac{\mathbb{E}(N)}{u(\beta,\vec{\alpha})}}.$$

The above result reveals that the optimal base-stock level is the well-known EOQ scaled by a factor; thus, at the optimal base-stock level, the holding and setup cost rates are equal. Furthermore,

$$C(S^*) = \frac{\sqrt{\mathbb{E}(N)w(\beta,\vec{\alpha})}}{u(\beta,\vec{\alpha})}\sqrt{2A\lambda h}, \text{ and } \frac{C(S)}{C(S^*)} = \frac{1}{2}\left(\frac{S}{S^*} + \frac{S^*}{S}\right).$$

The analysis above holds when the process is stable. Recall that setups occur only when inventory of grade 1 item is depleted. Suppose demand for grade 1 product is large compared to the production yield for grade 1, then inventory of grade 2 item will approach the base-stock level, S, setups will occur frequently, and the cycle becomes infinitely long. Thus, one needs to impose a stability condition for the problem to ensure that this does not happen. When α is constant, the stability condition will be $\alpha \geq \beta = \lambda_1/\lambda$; that is, the proportion of grade 1 produced should be at least as large as the proportion of its demand. When α is lognormal, Nahmias and Moinzadeh (1997) show that the stability condition that guarantees existence of steady state will be $\sqrt{\sigma_\alpha^2 + \mu_\alpha^2} > \beta$, where μ_α and σ_α are the mean and standard deviation of α, respectively. That is, when α is random, the stability condition involves not only the mean but also the variability of the yield. This observation is similar to that of queues where the system is stable when the traffic intensity equals to one in the absence of randomness but becomes unstable when randomness is introduced.

4.2 Equipment Maintenance and Services

In the previous subsection, we have discussed some representative studies of production scheduling problems with random yields of different quality levels. The quality of production outputs is clearly related to the status of manufacturing equipment, of which the performance will deteriorate over time without appropriate maintenance or replacement. In this subsection, we will selectively discuss several representative studies of maintenance scheduling and services.

Sloan and Shanthikumar (2000) consider a semiconductor manufacturing system that produces multiple products through a single machine. The performance of the machine can affect the yields of the products. They optimize the production and maintenance schedules simultaneously and characterize the structural properties of the optimal policy. Berk and Moinzadeh (2000) consider a more general setting where there are multiple identical machines, while the capacity of maintenance resources is limited. They characterize the optimal policy that allows the firm to determine the maintenance schedule for different machines based on their status and ages since the last maintenance. It is worth noting that the problem examined by Berk and Moinzadeh (2000) is motivated by the maintenance scheduling of the plasma etching machines that are crucial for semiconductor fabrications. In a recent study, Jalali et al. (2019) develop a machine-learning-based model to forecast the time-to-failure and health status of the plasma etching machines, which can be employed to enhance the performance of the maintenance scheduling policies.

The body of literature on inventory management of service parts is also relevant. For example, Deshpande et al. (2003) extend the well-known (Q, r) inventory control policy to an environment with two classes of service requests. They propose the so-called (Q, r, K) policy as follows. When the inventory level is above the fixed threshold, K, all requests will be satisfied, while once the inventory level drops below the threshold, the remaining inventory will be used to satisfy requests from the higher-priority class only. Through a numerical study based on characteristics of the operational environment of the semiconductor industry, they find that the performance of the proposed policy is near optimal. Furthermore, they consider various priority rules of clearing the backorders and find it optimal to always clear backorders of the higher-priority class requests first.

Furthermore, since equipment in the semiconductor and computing technology industries are of high technology and capital-intensive, it is popular to outsource the maintenance services to professional service providers. There are important contracting and incentive problems arising from the maintenance services, and there is a stream of literature dedicated to addressing such problems that are applicable to other capital-intensive industries as well. For instance, Guajardo et al. (2012) analyze the relationship between product reliability and the firm's choice between two common types of maintenance service contracts, the time and material contract (T&MC), and the performance-based contract (PBC). Through the development of an econometric model and examination of a proprietary data set, they report that the product reliability is typically 25%–40% higher under PBC as compared to that under T&MC.

Another salient example is Kim et al. (2010). Motivated by the operating environments in the semiconductor industry where the frequency of equipment breakdown is low, while the consequence is serious, they focus on two types of contracts within the class of PBC. While both types of contracts are designed to incentivize the maintenance service provider to increase service capacity and delivery performance, these contracts may result in different optimal behaviors of the service provider. Given the intriguing incentive issues presented in their study, below we provide a detailed description of the model and the main results of Kim et al. (2010) in more detail.

Consider a firm that relies on a mission critical equipment subject to breakdowns that can drastically impact the operations of the firm. Kim et al. (2010) model this problem as a principal-agent problem where an equipment user (e.g., the firm) outsources recovery services to a supplier in case of equipment breakdown. On the one hand, since disruptions occur infrequently, it is expensive for a supplier to commit the necessary resources for the recovery of the equipment as they will be idle most of the time. On the other hand, the user cannot directly write the supplier's capacity investment on restoration service into contract. Suppose that the equipment user is risk-neutral and its objective is to maximize the expected profit subject to a service-time constraint. In particular, the equipment user offers a performance-based contract (PBC) to the supplier, and the supplier, in response, decides how much to invest in service capacity during the contract duration. Since the supplier's investment is unobservable to the user and non-contractible, the user will assess the supplier's performance based on service completion times and make payments based on agreed terms dictated by the PBC. Consider the following two different forms of PBCs: a contract based on the equipment cumulative downtime (referred to as CC) and the other based on the sample average of the downtimes (referred to as AC). In the former, the supplier is penalized for the total equipment downtime during the contractual period, while under the latter, the supplier is penalized for the total equipment downtime divided by the number of disruption occurrences.

Assume that the equipment failures follow a Poisson process with a mean rate λ, and let N denote the total number of equipment failures during the contractual period. Let S_i be the equipment downtime for the i-th failure, and assume that they are independent and identically distributed (i.i.d.) with a rate $1/\mu$. Note that μ represents service capacity invested by the supplier at the beginning of the contract. Assume that the coefficient of variation of S, $v(\mu)$, is concave and decreasing in μ and bounded. Let $\underline{\mu}$ be the supplier's existing capacity. Therefore, the supplier's total investment in capacity expansion will be $c(\mu - \underline{\mu})$, where c is the unit cost of capacity expansion.

Under each of the two types of PBC, the supplier is penalized based on an agreed-upon performance measure, X, at the end of contractual period. Let w be a fixed payment that is independent of the performance measure and p be the penalty rate; then under the PBC, the user will pay the supplier $T = w - pX$, where $X = \sum_{i=1}^{N} S_i$ when the performance measure is based on the cumulative downtime (CC), and $X = \sum_{i=1}^{N} S_i/N$ when the performance measure is based on the sample average of downtime (AC). Unlike the user who is risk-neutral, the supplier is risk-averse with a utility function that follows a mean–variance structure as follows:

$$U(\mu) = \mathbb{E}[T|\lambda, \mu] - \eta\mathbb{V}[T|\lambda, \mu] - c(\mu - \underline{\mu}),$$

where parameter η is the risk aversion coefficient. Note that U is dependent on the specific contract and its payment scheme, X, as $T = w - pX$.

Next, the user's expected profit rate can be written as

$$\Pi = r\left(1 - \mathbb{E}\left[\sum_{i=1}^{N} S_i|\lambda, \mu^*\right]\right) - \mathbb{E}[T|\lambda, \mu^*],$$

where r is the unit profit the user earns when the equipment is operational and $1 - \mathbb{E}\left[\sum_{i=1}^{N} S_i|\lambda, \mu^*\right]$ is the equipment uptime during the contract period. Here, μ^* represents the supplier's optimal capacity investment level under one of the two types of PBC. Thus, the user will select a contract type (CC or AC) based on its anticipation of the supplier's optimal investment response. In addition, the user has a service-time target constraint (STC):

$$\mathbb{E}(S_i|\mu^*) = \frac{1}{\mu^*} < S_I = \frac{1}{\mu_I},$$

which imposes a lower bound on the optimal capacity investment. Furthermore, to ensure that the supplier will participate in the contractual relationship, there is an individual rationality (IR) constraint, $U(\mu^*) \geq \underline{U}$, where $\underline{U}$ denotes the supplier's reservation utility that, without loss of generality, can be normalized to zero.

In an ideal situation when the user can directly write the desired capacity investment μ into the contract, the first-best solution can be easily obtained and can be viewed as an upper-bound benchmark for evaluating performance of the PBC. When the STC constraint is not binding, the optimal capacity is $\mu^{FB} = \sqrt{r\lambda/c}$; otherwise, the optimal capacity is $\mu^{FB} = \mu_I$. In both cases, the user will earn all the surplus and leave zero surplus to the supplier.

When the user cannot directly write the desired capacity into the contract, the supplier's utility function is concave in μ under both CC and AC, so a unique optimal capacity μ^* can be obtained in each case. Furthermore, $\partial\mu^*/\partial\lambda > 0$ under CC, while it is non-monotonic under AC. Under both CC and AC, the user determines the contract terms (w, p) to maximize its expected profit:

$$\max_{w,p} \Pi(w, p) = r\left(1 - \mathbb{E}\left[\sum_{i=1}^{N} S_i|\lambda, \mu^*\right]\right) - \mathbb{E}[T|\lambda, \mu^*],$$

subject to the STC and IR constraints, $\mathbb{E}(S|\mu^*) \leq 1/\mu_I$ and $U(\mu^*) \geq 0$, respectively. It can be shown that when the supplier cannot affect the frequency of equipment disruption (i.e., λ), AC dominates CC from the user's perspective; otherwise, CC outperforms AC. Finally, when the occurrence of equipment failure is sufficiently rare (i.e., when $\lambda \to 0$ such that the equipment failure almost never happens and the STC binds), PBC becomes not so useful in practice as there will be little information about the supplier's performance due to the high reliability of the process.

5 Concluding Remarks

In this chapter, we highlighted the development of OM studies of the semiconductor and computing technology supply chains through discussions of some representative studies in three areas: (1) capacity expansion, allocation, and upgrading; (2) outsourcing, contracting, and procurement; (3) production, quality control, and maintenance services. As can be seen, the OM literature on each of the three areas is rich and impactful. That being said, there is still plenty of room for future OM research in those areas. In particular, the most recent information technology advancements, such as cloud computing and cloud-based artificial intelligence, not only have profound impacts on the existing semiconductor supply chains but also give rise to new industries. Hence, there are research opportunities for not only extending some of the existing studies but also exploring new operations and supply chain management problems in the rising computing technology industries. Through our previous discussions of some representative studies, we have noticed some potential future research directions. Below we provide several remarkable examples.

First, capacity planning problems for new data centers projects exhibit a combination of all key features of capacity planning problems examined in the extant literature: sequential decision-making with information updating, expansion project duration uncertainties, and risks of obsolescence due to new technology transitions. To the best of our knowledge, a general model framework that incorporates all these features is still lacking and thus is worth exploring.

Second, capacity planning problems at the resource level for an existing data center exhibit challenges from the following aspects: "bundled supply" of capacity attributes, multiple classes of demands, as well as time-varying and stochastic demand. Investigation of a general model framework that considers all these aspects is intriguing, and examination of the optimal decisions under the general model is challenging.

Third, as noted earlier, the rise of cloud computing has a profound impact on the organizations of the existing semiconductor supply chains. A salient observation is that the influential new customers—cloud service providers—prefer to contract directly with the ODMs, thus weakening the market and pricing power of the OEMs. Moreover, the development of open-source hardware and knowledge sharing initiatives will enable more ODMs to participate in the computing technology supply chains, thus stimulating competition and driving down procurement costs. The impacts of those initiatives and procurement strategies on the supply chain structures need to be investigated.

Fourth, as the global data centers and the supply chains behind consume a huge amount of energy, there are important research opportunities in capacity planning with a consideration of energy consumption as improvement in capacity utilization is linked to energy savings. Moreover, empirical studies can be done to evaluate the carbon footprints in the semiconductor and computing technology supply chains spanning from wafer manufacturing to data center operations.

Last but not least, there are research opportunities in supply chain resilience, such as dual sourcing, capacity reservation, and spot trading under various risk factors that can cause disruptions to global supply chains, such as sanctions, export restrictions, tariff wars, and the pandemic.

We hope that this paper could be a good starting point for scholars interested in exploring new research directions related to the semiconductor and computing technology industries.

References

Anderson E, Chen B, Shao L (2017) Supplier competition with option contracts for discrete blocks of capacity. Operations Research 65(4):952–967

Arbabian ME, Chen S, Moinzadeh K (2021) Capacity expansions with bundled supplies of attributes: An application to server procurement in cloud computing. Manuf Serv Oper Manag 23(1):191–209

Atamtürk A, Hochbaum DS (2001) Capacity acquisition, subcontracting, and lot sizing. Management Science 47(8):1081–1100

Bansal S, Transchel S (2014) Managing supply risk for vertically differentiated co-products. Production and Operations Management 23(9):1577–1598

Berk E, Moinzadeh K (2000) Analysis of maintenance policies for m machines with deteriorating performance. IIE Transactions 32(5):433–444

Besanko D, Doraszelski U, Lu LX, Satterthwaite M (2010) Lumpy capacity investment and disinvestment dynamics. Operations Research 58(4-part-2):1178–1193

Billington C, Lee HL, Tang CS (1998) Successful strategies for product rollovers. MIT Sloan Manag Rev 39(3):23

Bitran GR, Gilbert SM (1994) Co-production processes with random yields in the semiconductor industry. Operations Research 42(3):476–491

Cachon GP (2003) Supply chain coordination with contracts. Handbooks Oper Res Manag Sci 11:227–339

Cai X, Vairaktarakis GL (2012) Coordination of outsourced operations at a third-party facility subject to booking, overtime, and tardiness costs. Operations Research 60(6):1436–1450

Chen S, Lee H (2017) Incentive alignment and coordination of project supply chains. Management Science 63(4):1011–1025

Chen S, Lei J, Moinzadeh K (2021) When to lock the volatile input price? Procurement of commodity components under different pricing schemes. Manuf Serv Oper Manag (Articles in Advance) 24(2):691–1260

Cohen MA, Ho TH, Ren ZJ, Terwiesch C (2003) Measuring imputed cost in the semiconductor equipment supply chain. Management Science 49(12):1653–1670

Deshpande V, Cohen MA, Donohue K (2003) A threshold inventory rationing policy for service-differentiated demand classes. Management science 49(6):683–703

Dong L, Geng X, Xiao G, Yang N (2021) Procurement strategies with unreliable suppliers under correlated random yields. Manuf Serv Oper Manag 24(1):1–689

Dong L, Kouvelis P, Wu X (2014) The value of operational exibility in the presence of input and output price uncertainties with oil refining applications. Management Science 60(12):2908–2926

Erkoc M, Wu SD (2005) Managing high-tech capacity expansion via reservation contracts. Product Oper Manag 14(2):232–251

Gallego G, Yao DD, Moon I (1993) Optimal control of a manufacturing process that involves trial runs. Management science 39(12):1499–1505

Gardete PM (2016) Competing under asymmetric information: The case of dynamic random access memory manufacturing. Management Science 62(11):3291–3309

Gartner (2021) Gartner forecasts worldwide public cloud end-user spending to grow 23% in 2021, https://www.gartner.com/en/newsroom/press-releases/2021--04-21-gartner-forecasts-worldwide-public-cloud-end-user-spending-to-grow-23-percent-in-2021 (accessed on3/15, 2022)

Guajardo JA, Cohen MA, Kim SH, Netessine S (2012) Impact of performance-based contracting on product reliability: An empirical analysis. Management Science 58(5):961–979

Han G, Dong M, Shao X (2012) Yield management with downward substitution and uncertainty demand in semiconductor manufacturing. Int J Product Res 50(3):743–756

Haranas M (2020) Cloud providers bought $21b in servers and storage from ODMs, https://www.crn.com/news/data-center/cloud-providers-bought-21b-in-servers-and-storage-from-odms (accessed on3/15, 2022)

Huang K, Ahmed S (2009) The value of multistage stochastic programming in capacity planning under uncertainty. Operations Research 57(4):893–904

Huh WT, Roundy RO, Çakanyildirim M (2006) A general strategic capacity planning model under demand uncertainty. Naval Res Logist (NRL) 53(2):137–150

Hung HC, Chiu YC, Wu MC (2017) Analysis of competition between IDM and fabless–foundry business models in the semiconductor industry. IEEE Trans Semicond Manuf 30(3):254–260

IDC (2021) Semiconductor market to grow by 17.3% in 2021 and reach potential overcapacity by 2023, https://www.idc.com/getdoc.jsp?containerid=prap48247621 (accessed on3/15, 2022)

Jalali A, Heistracher C, Schindler A, Haslhofer B, Nemeth T, Glawar R, Sihn W, De Boer P (2019) Predicting time-to-failure of plasma etching equipment using machine learning. 2019 IEEE international conference on prognostics and health management (ICPHM), 1–8 (IEEE)

Jula P, Leachman RC (2010) Coordinated multistage scheduling of parallel batch-processing machines under multiresource constraints. Operations Research 58(4-part-1):933–947

Karabuk S, Wu SD (2003) Coordinating strategic capacity planning in the semiconductor industry. Operations Research 51(6):839–849

Kim SH, Cohen MA, Netessine S, Veeraraghavan S (2010) Contracting for infrequent restoration and recovery of mission-critical systems. Management Science 56(9):1551–1567

LaReau JL (2021) GM to halt production at nearly all North America assembly plants due to new chip problem, https://www.freep.com/story/money/cars/general-motors/2021/09/02/gm-semiconductor-chip-shortage-assembly-plants-close/5694047001/ (accessed on3/15, 2022)

Lee HL (1992) Lot sizing to reduce capacity utilization in a production process with defective items, process corrections, and rework. Management Science 38(9):1314–1328

Li H, Graves SC (2012) Pricing decisions during inter-generational product transition. Product Oper Manag 21(1):14–28

Li H, Armbruster D, Kempf KG (2013) A population-growth model for multiple generations of technology products. Manuf Serv Oper Manag 15(3):343–360

Li H, Graves SC, Huh WT (2014) Optimal capacity conversion for product transitions under high service requirements. Manuf Serv Oper Manag 16(1):46–60

Li R, Xia Y, Yue X (2019) Scrap or sell: the decision on production yield loss. Product Oper Manag 28(6):1486–1502

Lim WS, Tang CS (2006) Optimal product rollover strategies. Eur J Oper Res 174(2):905–922

Liu F, Lewis TR, Song JS, Kuribko N (2019) Long-term partnership for achieving efficient capacity allocation. Operations Research 67(4):984–1001

Malli Mohan K (2010) Outsourcing trends in semiconductor industry. Ph.D. thesis, Massachusetts Institute of Technology

Mendelson H, Tunca TI (2007) Strategic spot trading in supply chains. Management Science 53(5):742–759

Mönch L, Uzsoy R, Fowler JW (2018) A survey of semiconductor supply chain models part I: semiconductor supply chains, strategic network design, and supply chain simulation. Int J Product Res 56(13):4524–4545

Nahmias S, Moinzadeh K (1997) Lot sizing with randomly graded yields. Operations Research 45(6):974–989

Ou J, Wein LM (1995) Dynamic scheduling of a production/inventory system with by-products and random yield. Management Science 41(6):1000–1017

Özer Ö, Uncu O (2013) Competing on time: An integrated framework to optimize dynamic time-to-market and production decisions. Product Oper Manag 22(3):473–488

Peng C, Erhun F, Hertzler EF, Kempf KG (2012) Capacity planning in the semiconductor industry: Dual-mode procurement with options. Manuf Serv Oper Manag 14(2):170–185

PWC (2019) Opportunities for the global semiconductor market, https://www.pwc.com/gx/en/industries/tmt/publications/global-tmt-semiconductor-report-2019.html (accessed on3/15, 2022)

Sloan TW, Shanthikumar JG (2000) Combined production and maintenance scheduling for a multiple-product, single-machine production system. Product Oper Manag 9(4):379–399

Smith SA, Agrawal N (2000) Management of multi-item retail inventory systems with demand substitution. Operations Research 48(1):50–64

Song JS, Zipkin PH (2012) Newsvendor problems with sequentially revealed demand information. Naval Res Logist (NRL) 59(8):601–612

Statista (2021) Share of integrated circuit (IC), integrated device (IDM), and fabless company sales in 2020, by HQ location, https://www.statista.com/statistics/1052972/ic-idm-and-fabless-sales-share-by-headquarter-location-of-company/ (accessed on3/15, 2022)

Tan B, Feng Q, Chen W (2016) Dual sourcing under random supply capacities: The role of the slow supplier. Product Oper Manag 25(7):1232–1244

Taylor TA, Plambeck EL (2007) Supply chain relationships and contracts: The impact of repeated interaction on capacity investment and procurement. Management Science 53(10):1577–1593

Terwiesch C, Ren ZJ, Ho TH, Cohen MA (2005) An empirical analysis of forecast sharing in the semiconductor equipment supply chain. Management Science 51(2):208–220

Tomlin B, Wang Y (2008) Pricing and operational recourse in coproduction systems. Management Science 54(3):522–537

Tsay AA, Nahmias S, Agrawal N (1999) Modeling supply chain contracts: A review. Quant. Models Supply Chain Manag, 299–336

Ülkü S, Toktay LB, Yücesan E (2005) The impact of outsourced manufacturing on timing of entry in uncertain markets. Product Oper Manag 14(3):301–314

Vakil B, Linton T (2021) Why we're in the midst of a global semiconductor shortage, https://hbr.org/2021/02/why-were-in-the-midst-of-a-global-semiconductor-shortage (accessed on3/15, 2022). Harvard Business Review Online

Van Mieghem JA (2003) Commissioned paper: Capacity management, investment, and hedging: Review and recent developments. Manuf Serv Oper Manag 5(4):269–302

Wang Y, Gilland W, Tomlin B (2010) Mitigating supply risk: Dual sourcing or process improvement? Manuf Serv Oper Manag 12(3):489–510

Wu DJ, Kleindorfer PR (2005) Competitive options, supply contracting, and electronic markets. Management Science 51(3):452–466

Wu X, Kouvelis P, Matsuo H (2013) Horizontal capacity coordination for risk management and flexibility: Pay ex ante or commit a fraction of ex post demand? Manuf Serv Oper Manag 15(3):458–472

Yao DD, Zheng S (1999) Sequential inspection under capacity constraints. Operations Research 47(3):410–421

Yin R, Li H, Tang CS (2015) Optimal pricing of two successive-generation products with trade-in options under uncertainty. Decision Sciences 46(3):565–595

Zhang W, Dasu S, Ahmadi R (2017) Higher prices for larger quantities? nonmonotonic price–quantity relations in b2b markets. Management Science 63(7):2108–2126

A Study of the Semiconductor Equipment Supply Chain in the 2000s

Z. Justin Ren

Abstract In 1999–2001, Morris Cohen led a research study of the US semiconductor equipment supply chain, of which the author was a student member. Through extensive field interviews and subsequent data collection, the team was able to empirically test the effectiveness of forecast sharing between a major US semiconductor manufacturer and its largest semiconductor equipment supplier using a novel "imputed cost" approach. This research eventually yielded two empirical papers published in *Management Science* (and a third one in *Operations Research*), which collectively elevated the standards of empirical research in Operations Management.

Keywords Semiconductor · Manufacturing · Supply chain management · Imputed cost · Forecast sharing · Supplier relationship

1 Background

The backdrop was memorable and unique. It was during the heydays of the Internet Boom in the late 1990s. Tech companies were the darlings of the world, as people just started to see the huge potential of the Internet, powered by networks and computers. Hi-tech products such as computers and hand-held devices were in high demand, and as a result, semiconductor companies that supplied all the semiconductor chips in all those devices were in high gear and were facing heavy pressures fulfilling orders on time.

Our research partner (hereafter, we call company CI) was one of the largest semiconductor manufacturing firms in the world, headquartered in Silicon Valley. Sitting at the upstream of the high-tech products supply chain, on the other hand, it was experiencing wide swings in orders from computer manufacturers (As a side

Z. J. Ren (✉)
Operations and Technology Department, Boston University Questrom School of Business, Boston, MA, USA
e-mail: ren@bu.edu

H. Lee et al. (eds.), *Creating Values with Operations and Analytics*, Springer Series in Supply Chain Management 19, https://doi.org/10.1007/978-3-031-08871-1_11

note, it was also the time people started to talk about the now-famous "the Bullwhip Effect" (Lee et al. 1997), discovered by Hau Lee, one of the earliest Ph.D. students of Morris Cohen), and was having difficulty catching up with demand. It was also facing significant challenges with its own equipment suppliers, in that its equipment orders were often being delayed, further exacerbating its own production shortages.

Against this backdrop, we started our study. Our research team was led by Morris, who was then the Panasonic Professor of Manufacturing and Logistics—a title he still holds today—at Wharton's then-called Operations and Information Management (OPIM) Department. I was just a second-year OPIM doctoral student at that time. We were also joined by Teck Ho, then a tenured Marketing faculty at Wharton (who was also a former student of Morris), and Christian Terwiesch, who was a faculty member at Wharton's OPIM Department.

As an inexperienced doctoral student, I had never worked with a large company before. To say that I was a bit nervous was an understatement. But as it turned out, it was the most rewarding learning experience that a doctoral student could ever have. In particular, Morris taught me so much about research and about working with companies that it transformed me from a green hand into a serious operations researcher and, in time, a reasonably good business school professor.

Below is a brief chronology of the study, with a few personal anecdotes and thoughts. What was worth noting was that Morris emphasized fact-gathering and data collection as a starting point. Although we each had a wishlist of topics to study, Morris said: "Let's listen to what they have on their mind." Thus began our field interviews as the first phase of the research process.

2 Phase I: Interviews

We first visited the headquarters of company CI in Santa Clara, and interviewed a few managers in the capital equipment department. Very quickly, a theme emerged: They were all complaining about the delivery delay of their largest equipment supplier (let us call it MT), saying that it was difficult to get their orders delivered on time, and that it was difficult to communicate with MT.

Then we asked the managers to describe their order fulfillment processes with MT. It turned out that there were a number of stages of ordering a piece of equipment, but they could roughly be summarized in the process diagram (Fig. 1), and it started with generating a forecast of an order as follows:

This entire process could take as long as 2–3 years or even longer, which somewhat surprised me. Through more explanation from the manager, it turned

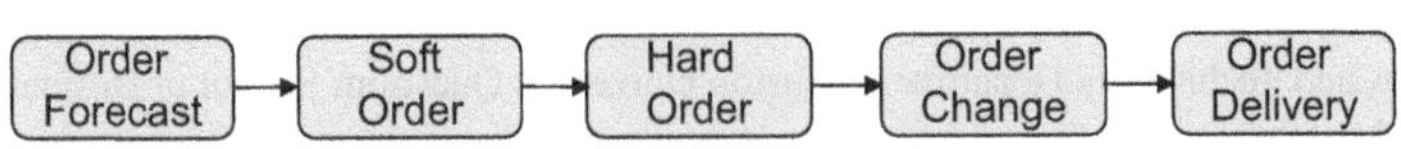

Fig. 1 The entire ordering process starts with forecasts

out that the reason the ordering process took so long had a lot to do with how the semiconductor manufacturing industry evolves and how its supply chain works.

Simply put, semiconductor manufacturing is about packing millions of tiny electronic circuits on a silicon wafer. To be more efficient in manufacturing, one can either use larger silicon wafers or shrink the sizes of circuits (called transistors). It turned out that the semiconductor manufacturers have been doing both since the first semiconductor transistor was made.

Despite the huge capital costs involved, semiconductor manufacturers have been upgrading their manufacturing capacities by using larger and larger wafers to put more of those increasingly smaller but more powerful chips on. The pace of innovation and process improvement was breathtaking (see Fig. 2).

The semiconductor manufacturing processes, however, are complex and slow, not to mention expensive. To make one semiconductor chip, it takes dozens of manufacturing steps, each with a unique machine. Time-wise, it can take as long as 20 weeks to process one single wafer.

The development of semiconductor manufacturing equipment takes even longer, often starting a couple of years before a new semiconductor chip is made. CI, therefore, had to work with its equipment suppliers (in particular, MT as CI's largest equipment supplier) 2–3 years before it could make its next-generation semiconductor processors. In comparison, the personal computer industry has only a 6–9 month window to sell one generation of semiconductor processors. Hence CI had tremendous pressure in getting each generation of manufacturing capacities right because tens of billion dollars of revenue potentials were at stake.

We then traveled to the headquarter of MT in Texas and conducted interviews with some of their managers who were interfacing with CI. When we asked them about the supply relationship between CI and MT, they almost unanimously said that MT was having a hard time fulfilling CI's equipment orders because CI's forecasts were not reliable (recall in Fig. 1 that every order started with a forecast).

With those feedbacks we got from MT we went back to CI and asked its managers about their forecasts. They acknowledged that the uncertain technology roadmap and consumer demand did create some challenges in producing accurate forecasts, but they claimed that sharing forecast information was designed to help its suppliers, because the order fulfillment lead time is long and therefore those forecasts gave the suppliers more time to react and prepare for the eventual orders.

That contradiction in viewpoint between the manufacturer and the supplier piqued our interest, and prompted us to focus on the forecasting aspect of the supply relationship as our next step of the study.

3 Phase II: On-Site Data Collection

I remember Morris, Teck, Christian, and I were sitting at a conference room next to Morris' office discussing next steps. We initially wanted to ask CI to send us some forecasting data so we could better understand how forecast sharing was done

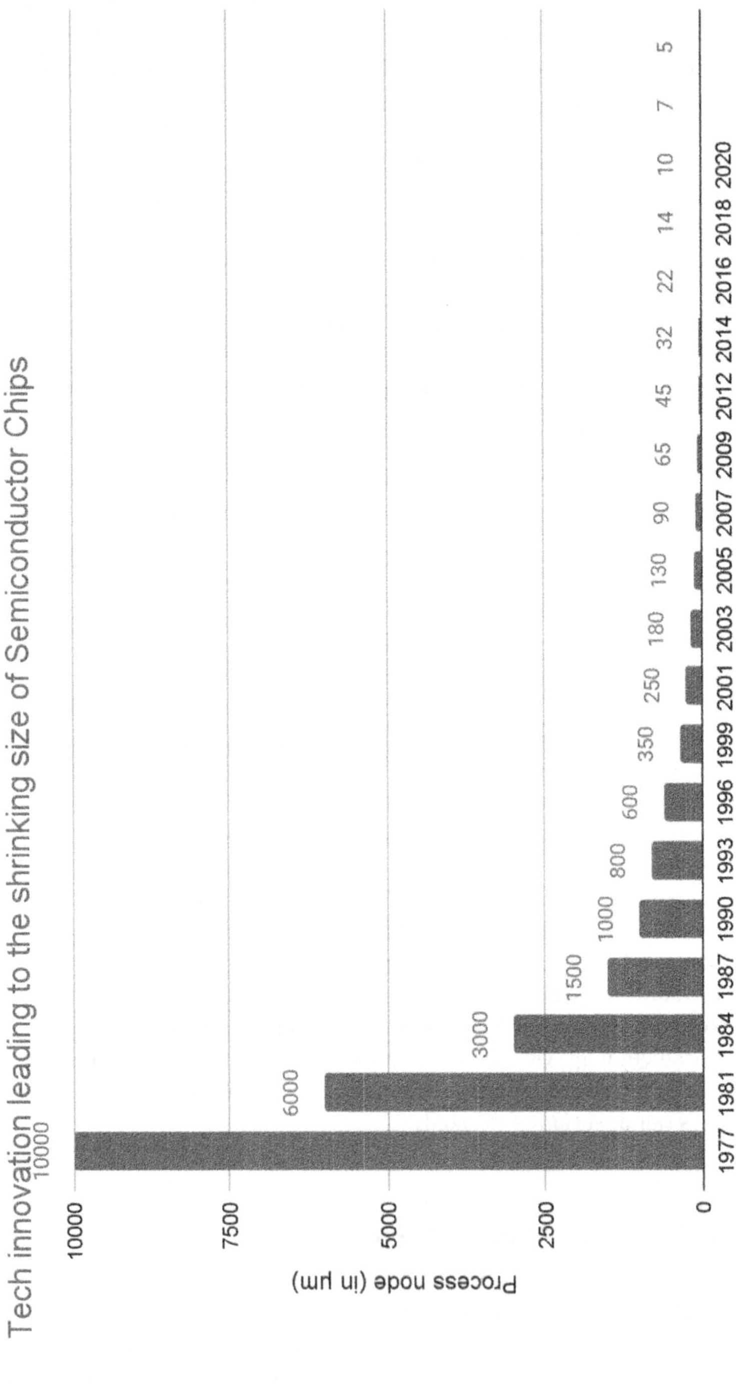

Fig. 2 Tech innovation leads to the shrinking size of semiconductor chips. Source: Graph by author, using data from Wikipedia

between CI and MT, and to what extent such a practice was helping both parties. But very soon, we concluded that to make real progress, it would be far better if I could go to CI in person and spend some time there to see "how sausage was made."

We made the request with CI, and graciously they agreed that I would work as a short-term consultant. The author then spent a 4-month period (July 2000–October 2000) in CI's Capital Equipment Development (CED) group, which was located in Arizona and was the main interface with all of CI's equipment suppliers.

At the site, the author was granted unrestricted access to CED's team and their data, which allowed the author to fully understand the procurement process of CI's capital equipment. A few things that the authors learned there were as follows:

1. Building manufacturing capacity was hugely expensive. The average price of a piece of equipment was $1 million, and it was costing CI more than $1 billion to build a semiconductor fabrication facility ("fab" in shorthand), and it was getting more and more expensive as chips were getting smaller and wafers were getting larger.
2. Technology forecasting was difficult. The longer the horizon, the higher degree of uncertainty. In response, CED used multiple scenarios to prepare for the worst and the best cases and updated its forecasts on a weekly basis based on its most updated intelligence.
3. The two main sources of uncertainty were the timings of technology development and demand for future products. While CED had been very successful in fulfilling its own technology roadmap historically, it was experiencing manufacturing glitches and delays.
4. The CED group had a mandate that its primary mission is to procure enough manufacturing capacity to enable building its latest generation of semiconductor fabs, and to maintain its current semiconductor production.

Also as an aside, I would recommend to any business school doctoral students that they have an immersive industry experience by working on their research sites, from which they would benefit tremendously. For example, I gained a real understanding of the concept of the "culture" of an organization. CED had a rigorous engineer-driven culture, as most of the people working at the group were engineers. When it came to capital equipment planning, the group used quantitative models in forecasting and capacity planning. That meant communications were mostly done with large Excel spreadsheets. Such "institutional knowledge" cannot be easily taught in schools, but is extremely important in understanding how an organization works.

4 Phase III: Data Analysis and the "Aha Moment"

Through the few months on-site, I gained valuable insights into how the whole process of forecast sharing worked. It started with a long-range outlook on how the semiconductor industry would evolve in the coming years and decades. Then those long-range forecasts were translated into mid-range and near-range machine needs and orders. To see why forecasts can be volatile, we can simply look at the basic formula:

Number of machines needed = (total monthly demand) / (machine monthly capacity)

Forecasting total demand was already hard enough. In addition, machine specifications were in flux because of the constant technology development. Dividing the two uncertain quantities, the resulting forecast can be very much unpredictable. But what is crucial here is that this kind of forecasts is very sensitive to the variability in machine capacity.

To see this point, let us do a quick simulation exercise. Assume that total monthly demand is normally distributed with mean 1000 and standard deviation of 1. The intentionally small deviation is meant to minimize the impact of demand volatility. Let us also assume that the machine capacity is random because of technological uncertainty, with a distribution of $N(100, x)$, where x is unknown. So, with slight abuse of notation, the forecast for the total number of machines needed to satisfy demand is:

$$\text{Forecasts of the number of machines needed} = [N\ (1000,\ 1)]\ /\ [N\ (100,\ x)]$$

Now, we gradually increase the value of x, and we can simulate out the statistical distribution of the forecast for the number of machines needed. As one might have expected, the mean of the forecast should be more or less around 10 (i.e., 1000/100). But what about the standard deviation of the forecast? Here is the simulation result (Table 1).

Graphically, it is more telling to see the potentially large impact of uncertainty in machine capacity on forecasts (Fig. 3).

As one can see, forecasts about machine needs can be highly volatile where there is significant uncertainty about the technical capabilities of equipment.

Table 1 Simulation results for the number of machines needed

Standard deviation of machine capacity (x)	Mean of forecast	Standard deviation of forecast
6	10.0	0.6
8	10.1	0.8
10	10.1	1.0
12	10.1	1.3
14	10.2	1.5
16	10.3	1.8
18	10.4	2.1
20	10.5	2.5
22	10.6	2.9
24	10.7	5.6

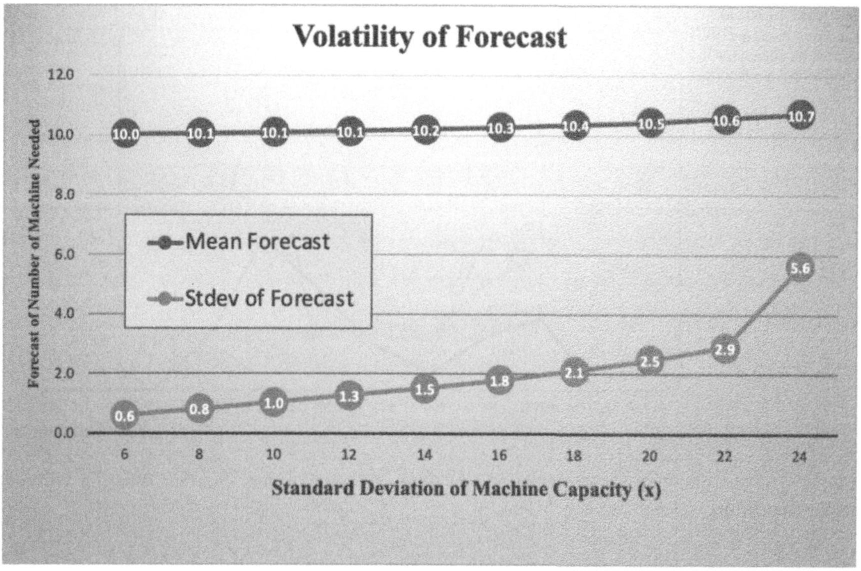

Fig. 3 Uncertainty in machine capacity can be a major driver in forecasts

However, that turned out not to be the main part of the story. If we follow this logic, we should expect that as the uncertainty in equipment capabilities resolves over time, forecasts about machine needs for a particular time should become more reliable, right?

Hoping to see such an improvement in forecasts over time, I spent many days and nights in my cubicle at CI, poring through the countless spreadsheets. One day, in preparation for a weekly call with the research team, I put together all the quarterly forecasts generated by CI and shared with MT as well as their revisions, which resulted in the following now-well-remembered graph (Fig. 4).

In this graph, I plotted a sequence of 7-quarter forecasts, starting with 1999 Q1. For example, in 1999 Q1, a forecast was made for machine demand in 1999 Q1 up to 2000 Q3. In the next quarter 1999 Q2, another forecast was made from 1999 Q2 up to 2000 Q4, while the actual order quantity in 1999 Q2 was realized (which was zero in the figure). Putting those forecasts together, we can see how volatile the forecasts were. But a more intriguing insight emerged as we looked closely at it—the actual orders were almost at the bottom of all forecasts! In other words, there existed a systematic bias in forecasting—CI is over-forecasting!

As an eager doctoral student, I suggested that we write it as an interesting empirical finding, and explained it as a product of CI's engineering-driven culture, and that the company was simply being conservative in its forecasting and procurement.

But Morris saw much deeper. He pointed out that there was a fundamental economic reason. It was in CI's economic interest to over forecast and act conservatively, because the cost of not having enough manufacturing capacity was

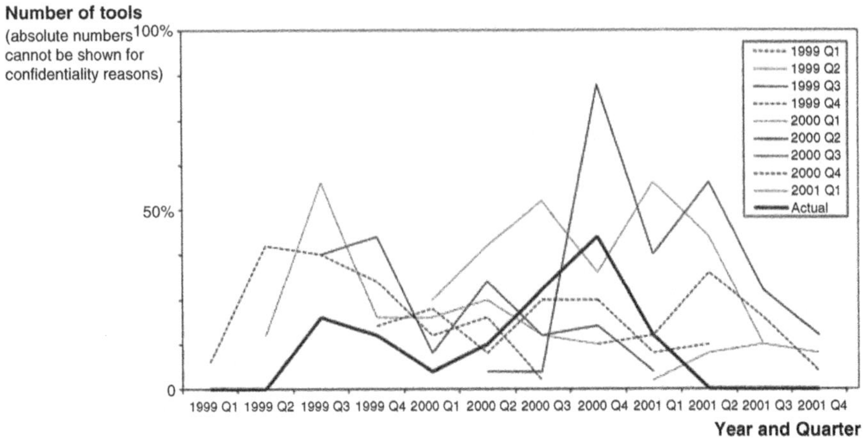

Fig. 4 The aha moment: Order forecasts over time and actual orders. Source: Wharton Working Paper Repository

much greater than the cost of having excess capacity. This was largely due to the very high profit margins of selling semiconductor chips. Now on the receiving end of those volatile forecasts, CI's suppliers must decide *when* to start fulfilling orders based on those forecasts knowing well they could well be canceled or changed. This decision required a trade-off between starting too early, leading to potential holding or cancellation costs, and starting too late, leading to potential delay costs.

Hence, Morris' idea was to tell the story from the cost perspective. He suggested that we employ a newsvendor-type of model in describing the order fulfillment process and then "impute" the overage and underage cost parameters from actual data to describe and explain the supplier's behavior.

This idea of "imputed cost" was quite original, and little did we know at that time that it opened up a new paradigm of empirical research in OM.

5 The First Paper

With this "imputed cost" idea, I went to work. Very quickly I realized how prescient Morris was. Indeed MT's order fulfillment process can be nicely captured with a newsvendor-type of model, but applied in the time domain (instead of the usual inventory setting). For each forecasted order, MT needs to decide on when to start working on a forecasted order. If it starts too early, the order can be finished too early and resulting in excessing holding costs. But if it starts too late, the order will be delivered late and incur delay costs. In addition, the order could be canceled entirely by the customer, resulting in waste.

If the underlying unit holding cost is large relative to the delay cost, then we would observe more late starting times and more late deliveries. If, however, the delay cost dominates, then we would see more early starting times and early deliveries. Thus with this newsvendor-type model, we can back up the implied cost parameters underlying its observed decisions on starting times.

To generalize this idea a bit, an individual or an organization can make a number of decisions which can vary in their settings or magnitude. But as long as they are consistent to the extent that their behaviors and decisions can be explained by a consistent and quantifiable model, then it is usually easier and more insightful to look at the underlying parameters of the model that are driving those behaviors and decisions, instead of trying to explain those decisions themselves.

The challenge here is how to empirically estimate the parameters from real data. I spent many days and nights without progress. Then one late night in my office, I was looking at all the course binders on my shelf, and recalled something I learned in my first class of Mathematical Economics: Taylor expansion. Any function can be approximated, in a certain interval, by a linear function. Why do not I try linearizing this complicated function form, and see what happens?

I got lucky. Our data on the statistical distribution of order lead time fitted quite well with a modified Weibull distribution which has a closed-form distribution function. It also was relatively easy to approximate with the Taylor expansion. The next step was to use the Maximum Likelihood Estimation (MLE) method to estimate the cost parameters in the total likelihood function.

The other challenge that I had to overcome was the fact that order fulfillment times are not independent. This was simply due to the fact that the order fulfillment process at a supplier's facility is a queueing process. If an order was delayed, then those orders behind were most likely delayed as well. To incorporate this dependence, I explicitly introduced a correlation coefficient between the order fulfillment times and worked out the correlated MLE function.

The results were quite shocking. The results showed that MT was acting as if the cost of cancellation to be about two times higher and the holding costs to be about three times higher than the delay cost. In other words, the supplier is very conservative when commencing the order fulfillment. This also meant that the forecast sharing mechanism was not effective at all in facilitating speedy order fulfillment! Initially I thought this could not be true. In fact I had to call a meeting to meet with Morris, Teck, and Christian to ask if this made sense at all. Fortunately they all found the results reasonable, and assured me that I should push forward.

6 The Second Paper

Encouraged by the finding of the first paper (Cohen et al. 2003), we decided to shift our attention from the supplier to the manufacturer and collect more data in order to do a systematic empirical analysis.

Having established the total order time as our key variable of interest in the first paper, we set out and collected data with almost all of CI's suppliers (recall that our first paper is only about one supplier MT). This was exciting because this time, we would have the opportunity to directly test to what extent the over-forecasting behavior we observed in the first study was also existent with other suppliers. If somehow there were some differences across suppliers, then what were the driving factors? More importantly, we would like to see what suppliers were doing as responses to CI's forecasts.

Methodically, we borrowed a few statistical modeling methods that were quite common in other fields (such as bio-statistics and marketing) but were new to the OM field at that time, the most significant of which was using the proportional hazard model in modeling durations of order fulfillment lead time. Again, like what we did in the first paper, we extended the model to incorporate the setting of non-independent observations, which is more appropriate in the manufacturing environment than the typical i.i.d. assumption.

Methodology aside, after implementing the model, we found something interesting. Our data analysis showed that suppliers rationally discounted CI's over-forecasts. The more over-forecasts there were, the worse the delivery performance a supplier gave. We also found that the reverse was true. That is, CI tended to give more phantom orders to a supplier that habitually delayed CI's orders. Such dynamics had the flavor of a Prisoners' Dilemma. There was, however, considerable heterogeneity in supplier performances. We did notice that some suppliers were much better in delivering orders on time than others. In return, CI seemed to be relatively more reliable in their forecasts. In sum, there seemed to be some quid pro quo going on between CI and its suppliers. This paper was completed, submitted, and then accepted in a relatively short amount of time (Terwiesch et al. 2005).

7 The Third Paper

Emboldened by the Prisoners' Dilemma as well as the quid pro quo findings, I proposed to the committee that I write a game-theoretical paper. This was met with some hesitation initially—rightfully so, because through the first two papers, I was building my "brand" as an empirical OM researcher. But Morris gave his full endorsement. "You should write it," he said. "That is the right way. We went in with observations, and formed hypotheses. We then collected data, analyzed them, and had our insights. Now it is time to come up with a theory."

I went to work again. The bar was, as always with theory building in the OM field, very high. Sharing information can be modeled in multiple ways, but because the manufacturer did not commit to any forecasts until they were converted to firm orders, the forecast information shared was merely cheap talk.

Could cheap talk lead to any equilibrium outcome that is better than the one in a prisoners' dilemma? Our third paper explored that possibility. Again we got incredibly lucky. The theory proof was so convoluted that to this day, I am still convinced that there is a missing step somewhere. Nevertheless, the idea was clear. We showed that if the supply relationship was short-term (i.e., spot buy), then the equilibrium was the prisoners' dilemma outcome. The manufacturer over-forecasted, and the supplier under-delivered. However, if the supplier relationship was long-term, then with an appropriately-structured strategy, a cooperative equilibrium could emerge where the manufacturer tells its forecasts truthfully, which is in turn trusted by the supplier. The equilibrium strategy was very much like the "trust but verify" approach we see in practice, but we called it a "multi-period review strategy" in the paper. The strategy was patient in that it reviewed the forecaster each period and did not trigger punishment the first couple of times the supplier believed that the manufacturer was over-forecasting. The manufacturer needed to repeatedly commit non-truthfully behavior in multiple periods in order to fail the review and then receive punishment.

Thus our theoretical paper (Ren et al. 2010) predicted that a communicative supplier relationship could be sustained in a long-term relationship. But sometimes, we could also see supply chain parties engaging in a non-cooperative phase in order to punish over-forecasting. This seemed to fit what we observed in our study pretty well. In fact, I suspect another empirical paper could be written looking at the long-term supply chain relationships across industries to see to what extent they conform to this pattern and what factors can explain the length of each cooperative and non-cooperative phase.

8 Impact

I was extremely fortunate to have worked with Morris, Teck and Christian on this project. We co-wrote three papers together. The first two empirical papers were published in *Management Science*, and the third theoretical one in *Operations Research*.

Over the years, I was told by more than one person that the two empirical papers were considered as the gold standard of OM empirical research of that era. Before our papers were published, empirical research in OM was largely about linear regressions without too much consideration on testing assumptions or on statistical model building. We introduced new ways of thinking as well as new methods of empirical research in Operations Management. We also showed that empirical research can be both rigorous and interesting.

In this impactful research, Morris' leadership and contributions were pivotal and exemplary. Of course, I also had the tremendous fortune to have both Teck and Christian on the team, both of whom are accomplished researchers themselves. They were both brilliant in coming up with ideas, examining details and shepherding the writing, revision, and publication processes of all papers. But without Morris' masterful skills in identifying problems and uncovering crucial insights as well as his patient advising of me as his student, we would not have produced the work that world sees today.

9 Finishing Thoughts

In ancient Chinese proverbs, there is a saying that "A mentor for a day is to be respected as a father for life." Indeed Morris taught me so many things beyond academic research. He showed me how to communicate with people from different backgrounds. He showed me how to prepare for meetings and presentations. He showed me how to work hard and treat people fairly. He also showed me the importance of regular exercise and keeping fit. When we were on business trips together, it seemed that he always had a pair of jogging shoes with him and he would find a place to run wherever we were.

But most importantly, Morris made me a better human being. Once Morris and I had a meeting in his office about how to prepare for a revision to one of our papers. At one point, I realized a limitation of our methodology but I was struggling as to how to admit such a limitation without jeopardizing the prospect of the acceptance of the paper. So I asked Morris: "Here is the problem ... What should I tell the reviewers?"

"Tell the truth." Morris replied.

Seeing that I was hesitating, he asked: "Do you read the Bible?"

"The Bible?" I said.

Looking at my increasingly confused look, he said: "Well, you should. Because it says 'The Truth will set you free.'"

Now, after this many years, Morris would be pleased to know that I not only became a reader of the Bible, but also a believer.

Thank you, Morris.

References

Cohen MA, Ho TH, Ren ZJ, Terwiesch C (2003) Measuring imputed cost in the semiconductor equipment supply chain. Manag Sci 49(12):1653–1670. http://www.jstor.org/stable/4133976

Lee HL, Padmanabhan V, Whang S (1997) Information distortion in a supply chain: the bullwhip effect. Manag Sci 43(4):546–558. http://www.jstor.org/stable/2634565

Ren ZJ, Cohen MA, Ho TH, Terwiesch C (2010) Information sharing in a long-term supply chain relationship: the role of customer review strategy. Oper Res 58(1):81–93. http://www.jstor.org/stable/40605962

Terwiesch C, Ren ZJ, Ho TH, Cohen MA (2005) An empirical analysis of forecast sharing in the semiconductor equipment supply chain. Manag Sci 51(2):208–220. http://www.jstor.org/stable/20110320

Wharton Working Paper Repository. Measuring imputed cost in the semiconductor equipment supply chain. Accessed 20 Aug 2021. https://repository.upenn.edu/cgi/viewcontent.cgi?article=1139&context=oid_papers

Wikipedia. Semiconductor device fabrication. Accessed 20 Aug 2021. https://en.wikipedia.org/wiki/Semiconductor_device_fabrication

Topics in Health Care Operations: Blood Banks, Hospitals and Patients, and Telemedicine

Sergei Savin

Abstract In this chapter, we pursue two main objectives, both related to health care operations. The first objective is to provide an overview of Morris Cohen's main contributions to health care operations research and of the current research trends on the related topics: blood bank inventory management, patient in-hospital flows, and patient choice of hospitals. The second objective is to review recent developments on the adoption of telemedicine, a rapidly growing component of the health care delivery system, and the related research literature in the field of operations.

Keywords Blood banks · Inventory management · Hospital patient flows · Patient decision-making · Telemedicine

1 Introduction

The current list of Morris Cohen's research publications contains well over a hundred papers, and about 10% of them belong to the health care domain. These health care papers dominate Cohen's early career and are focused on the areas of inventory management in blood banks, modeling of hospital patient flows, and patient choice of hospitals. A certain commonality of perspective adopted in these papers stems from the essential feature displayed by many health care systems then and now, namely, their supply-constrained nature. At the center of the research analysis in these papers is the fundamental role played by operational capacity in shaping the cost of service and its quality, and the relative "attractiveness" of service locations in a competitive environment. These issues are reviewed in Sects. 2–4.

This focus on fundamentals created a trailblazing effect on the lines of research that followed. At present, the technology-enabled transformation of the clinical as well as operational aspects of health care places management of constrained

---

S. Savin (✉)
The Wharton School, University of Pennsylvania, Philadelphia, PA, USA
e-mail: savin@wharton.upenn.edu

H. Lee et al. (eds.), *Creating Values with Operations and Analytics*, Springer Series in Supply Chain Management 19, https://doi.org/10.1007/978-3-031-08871-1_12

care capacity at the center of a complex system of interactions involving patients, providers, and payers, burdened with issues such as incentive alignment and information asymmetry. One of the latest additions to this system is a rapidly expanding use of telemedicine and virtually enabled care delivery models, an addition that commenced an intense search for a new balance between the quality, cost, and access to care. In Sect. 5, we focus on the process of telemedicine adoption and the related studies in the domain of health care operations.

2 Inventory Management in Blood Banks

In his review, Pierskalla (2004) outlines the main points in the timeline of the OR/MS community's engagement with the topics of supply chain management in blood bank systems. Starting in the 1960s, this line of research peaked in the 1970s and 1980s, with significant reduction in the volume of publications afterward. Morris Cohen's work on the management of blood bank inventories was part of that peak, resulting in a series of seminal contributions. It takes its roots from his PhD thesis (Cohen 1974) focused on the inventory management of perishable products and written under the supervision of Bill Pierskalla at Northwestern.

Chronologically, Cohen and Pierskalla (1975) constitute the first journal publication on the blood bank management in Morris Cohen's portfolio. The paper looks at the hub-and-spokes supply chain configuration, where a regional blood bank plays the role of the hub and multiple hospital blood banks play the roles of the spokes. The demand process in such a system comes from transfusion needs driven by hospital surgical procedures, and the supply process comes from blood donations at bank locations and from emergency shipments to the hub from outside of the system. Blood is characterized by type and "age," and the paper looks at a problem of controlling the key operational performance indicators and inventory costs for each blood type. For exogenously specified demand and blood donation processes, the management of blood inventory in the system in a stationary setting involves three main levers. The first lever is the ordering policy, represented, in the absence of delays and order costs, by the order up to level S, for the exogenously specified review period. The second lever is the issuing policy that entails the rules for releasing the blood inventory as functions of its age (such as LIFO or FIFO). Finally, the third lever is the "crossmatch" policy, defined by the period of time D (usually expressed in days) during which the available blood is reserved for potential transfusions at a particular hospital, and, therefore, not available to satisfy the demand at other hospitals.

Among the key performance indicators the paper considers, the main ones are "shortages," i.e., the number of inventory units that must be procured through emergency shipments, and the "outdates," i.e., the number of units of inventory disposed of untransfused, due to age expiration. These two performance indicators reflect two types of demand–supply mismatch events. The paper's analysis is based on the data on the "trajectory" of each unit of inventory recorded for a period of three months at the North Suburban Blood Center of Glenview, Illinois. These data were used to infer both the demand and supply processes in the system during this period, which, in turn, allowed for testing, via a simulation, a number of alternative ordering, issuing, and crossmatching policies. The simulation investigates combinations of issuing and crossmatching policies, where LIFO or FIFO on the issuing side is augmented by the crossmatching policies described by $D = 0, 1, \ldots, 7$ days. The simulation results clearly show the dominance of the FIFO approach with respect to the expected values of demand–supply mismatch indicators, with the advantage of FIFO issuing disappearing only for $D = 7$. This crossmatching level, however, is rather impractical since it results in high levels of mismatch indicators, no matter what issuing policy is used.

In addition to the "centralized" setting, where the hub can select a fixed (and small) value of D, the paper also simulates the system's performance in a decentralized setting modeled by D being randomly chosen from a distribution with the mean $D = 4$ and different standard deviations. The "medium" value of mean reflects the setting where the hub provides a broad crossmatching guideline, and the deviations from this guideline by hospital banks are allowed. In this interpretation, the value of the standard deviation of D represents the degree of decentralization in system management. The results of simulating such a decentralized setting show that, while the LIFO policy remains uniformly inadequate, the FIFO policy is severely restrained in its performance by the variability of the crossmatching horizon. The final element of the paper's investigation is the simulation-based optimization of the order up to level S, when the ratio of per-unit "shortage" to "outdate" cost is set at $\$55/\$25 = 2.2$. Note that it is realistic to assume that the shortage cost exceeds the outdate cost, with the former reflecting the phone, emergency transportation, and freezing and thawing expenses, and the latter reflecting the lost cost of processing the unused unit. The results show that, under the FIFO policy, the optimal order up to level remains fairly stable when the crossmatching horizon is varied within a wide range of realistic values (between 2 and 7 days). Based on its analysis, the paper recommends a simple inventory management approach likely to perform well under a wide range of practical settings: the FIFO issuing policy combined with a short crossmatching window, with the optimal order up to level computed analytically, by setting D to 0 and assuming that all issued units are transfused.

Cohen (1976) builds on the earlier work on the perishable inventory (Fries 1975; Nahmias 1975; Nahmias and Pierskalla 1973; Van Zyl 1964) and presents a formal analysis of the single-number order up to policy for perishable, finite-life inventory. In the setting where each unit of inventory has a finite usable life of m time periods, the optimal ordering policy that minimizes the expected sum of (per period) linear ordering, holding, backlog, and spoilage costs is, in general, complex and depends on the available levels of inventory of all different ages. The paper studies the stochastic trajectory of the system under a stationary, single-value order up to policy with the goal of optimizing the above expected cost within this class of ordering polices. The paper, in particular, demonstrates the existence of an invariant distribution for the spoilage process, a key element for the computation of expected cost, and provides a characterization for the expected cost expressions for the case of m = 2.

Cohen (1977) further develops the topic of inventory management for products that undergo deterioration. Perishable products with a maximum usable duration at the center of blood bank inventory management present one such example. Inventory management of decaying products (such as volatile liquids or radioactive materials) represents another variant of the problem of managing inventory whose usable value/quantity changes over time. In particular, Cohen (1977) adds a pricing extension to the problem of managing decaying inventory that is subject to deterministic, price-elastic demand and characterizes the properties of the optimal joint pricing-inventory ordering policy.

While the FIFO inventory issuing discipline is shown in Cohen and Pierskalla (1975) to be dominating the LIFO approach, in some inventory settings involving decaying inventory the issuing policy is controlled by customers. The customers, in the absence of search costs and armed with "expiration date" information, may prefer the "freshest" items in the absence of any discounts related to the age of inventory, thus generating the LIFO dynamics. These assumptions may not correspond to general health care settings and are more characteristic of retail food distribution systems that combine management-controlled inventory ordering and customer-controlled inventory consumption. However, while discussing this line of research, it is important to mention the paper Cohen and Pekelman (1978) that considers stochastic demand and lost sales and analyzes the time evolution of the inventory age distribution under periodic-review ordering and LIFO consumption, as well as the paper Cohen and Pekelman (1979) that extends the inventory analysis to include tax-related considerations.

In Cohen and Pierskalla (1979a) and Cohen and Pierskalla (1979b), the attention is turned to formulating simple and easily implementable decision rules for blood bank managers. In managing blood blank inventory, the challenge is to balance the quality of service outcomes represented by the shortage rate and their efficiency related to the outdates fraction. Both papers focus on settings where both supply and demand are stochastic processes, with supply coming from human donors, and the demand driven by hospital surgical procedures. The objective that the papers adopt is to minimize the expected sum of average shortage and outdate costs for a given set of problem parameters that describe the exogenous processes of demand for and supply of blood, as well as the unit shortage and outdate costs, the chosen crossmatch policy, i.e., the crossmatch release period D, and the ratio of total units of demand that get transfused to the total number of units crossmatched, p. The approach for calculating the optimal order up to level S^* for a given set of problem parameters involves numerical optimization, with the expected cost for each trial order-up-to-level value determined via simulation. This simulation was conducted using the FIFO issuing rule and was based on the extensive data set collected from several blood banks. The optimal decision rule, i.e., the functional dependence of the optimal order up to level and problem parameters, was established using a log-linear regression, with only three factors showing statistically significant contributions: expected daily demand d_M, transfusion-to-crossmatch ratio p, and the crossmatch release period D:

$$S^* = 6.03\,(d_M)^{0.7604}\,(p)^{0.1216}\,(D)^{-0.0677}\,. \tag{1}$$

The prescriptive part of the analysis is appealing from a practical point of view, with the number of factors behind the prescribed optimal policy limited to a small, easily measurable set. In particular, the optimal order up to level was not found to depend on a statistically significant fashion on the details of the blood supply process (such as the age distribution of the blood supply), nor, more importantly, on the ratio of the shortage and outdate costs, as long as it falls within a reasonable range between $\$35/\$25 = 1.4$ and $\$55/\$25 = 2.2$. The paper points out three particularly important observations based on the analysis of the functional dependencies of expected costs on the order up to levels. First, for the realistic ratios of the shortage to outdate costs, the overall cost function is heavily favoring the shortage costs, and the shortage rates achieved under the optimal inventory policies are very low (less than 1%). Second, the expected cost curves are rather "flat" near the optimal order up to levels, indicating that deviations from the optimal policy forced by sudden demand surges or supply shortages will not carry significant penalties. Third, the values of S^*, as indicated by (1), exhibit low sensitivity with respect to the crossmatch policy represented by D. Thus, blood bank managers can focus on reducing D without adjusting the optimal inventory policy. This virtual "decoupling" has significant practical implications, given that D is, on the one hand, one of the most important controls available to blood bank managers, and, on the other hand, one of the most important factors impacting the blood outdate process. Hospital blood banks that rely on a central location for a significant fraction of their blood supply may not be in a position to control its age composition. While the age composition does not have a statistically significant effect on the optimal inventory policy, it does affect the outdate process, with higher average age naturally causing higher outdates. In settings where outdates are treated as one of the key performance indicators, the control of the age of the supply becomes important in its own right. The paper's numerical analysis indicates that the impact of this factor is especially prominent for small banks that are faced with lower daily demand rates: for such locations, the supply should be maintained as fresh as possible.

Cohen et al. (1979) position the analysis of the blood inventory policies within a broad framework of the redesign and management of the US blood management systems under the mandates of the National Blood Policy proposed in 1974 (National Blood Policy 1974). For the system operating in a supply-constrained regime, blood inventory management is identified as a critical process, and the order up to level as a critical factor, within the complex task of managing a multi-echelon supply system distributed over a wide geographical region. Within this system, a hospital blood bank forms the first echelon, with main supply control tasks being crossmatching, as well as the operational, demand forecasting, and inventory ordering policies (e.g., governed by (1)). The second echelon is represented by the community central banks, where the benefits of pooling the supply resources and demands across individual hospitals are accrued. At this level, the blood transshipment policies enter the set of managerial tasks that interact with inventory decisions and directly influence the shortage and outdate outcomes across the community. The regional blood banks form the third echelon of the system, either in the form of an actual blood bank hub that controls the donor recruitment and blood distribution and that is connected to a network of satellite locations with limited (e.g., phlebotomic) functions, or in the form of a purely administrative unit responsible for donor recruitment, blood allocation, compliance, equipment maintenance, and quality control for a network of community central banks. Given a potentially large geographical area of responsibility, the transportation tasks and associated costs may occupy a more salient position in the overall operating cost structure for this echelon. Given the complexity of the overall system and the multitude of decision-making entities, the paper argues for a careful calibration of the new approaches to managing demand and supply matching, and for the evolutionary "step-wise adaptation of the existing system."

Cohen et al. (1980a) focus on the formal analysis of the inventory management problem in periodic-review settings where, in each time period, (1) a fixed fraction of the inventory assigned to demand satisfaction returns back unused, after a fixed time delay, and (2) a fixed fraction of on-hand inventory becomes outdated. These assumptions reflect a wide range of practically important settings, such as systems with a rent/purchase option, standard retail systems where some previously purchased items are returned to inventory, or systems that deal with reparable item inventories. In addition, these settings include blood bank inventory management. The first feature mentioned above may be interpreted as reflecting the impact of crossmatching policies in blood bank settings, where hospital physicians often place orders in a conservative manner, over-ordering by a significant margin. The paper models this feature using two exogenous parameters: the time delay λ reflecting the number of time periods after which the issued inventory returns back and the fraction a of issued inventory that returns. The second "exponential decay" feature is designed to model, in an analytically tractable way, the finite usable life of the inventory: while the inventory in the model has, theoretically, an infinite usable life, only an exogenously specified fraction β of on-hand inventory "survives" in each period. The exponential nature of the inventory decay removes the need to keep track of the actual age of the inventory. The crossmatching feature, however, significantly complicates the analysis of inventory policies, since random demands in each period, even if modeled as i.i.d. random variables, translate, through the "return" process, into a λ-dimensional state of the system. This, in turn, creates a potential "curse-of-dimensionality" issue when searching for the optimal inventory policy. To isolate this challenge, the paper adopts a standard set of assumptions on the remaining part of the problem: in particular, the analysis focuses on the finite-horizon, discounted setting, with stationary demands and costs. Ordering and outdating costs are treated as linear, and shortage and inventory holding costs—as convex functions of inventory, and the lost sales assumption in each time period is adopted. While for $\lambda = 1$ the optimal order policy is described, in each period, by a single "critical number," this may not be the case for $\lambda > 1$. In such settings, however, a single-number policy can serve as a heuristic, and the main focus of the paper is on deriving such a heuristic and evaluating its performance. The premise of the heuristic is an assumption that all inventory remaining in the system at the end of the planning horizon is salvaged at the inventory ordering price: under this assumption, combined with mild conditions on the cost functions, the optimal ordering policy becomes stationary and is characterized by a single order up to level. The effectiveness of this heuristic is demonstrated in a numerical study that compares its performance with that of the optimal policy in settings with $\lambda = 2$.

Cohen et al. (1983) outline an important follow-up on and extension of Cohen and Pierskalla (1979a) and Cohen and Pierskalla (1979b) driven by a technological advance in the field of blood storage: the use of citrate phosphate dextrose adenine as an anticoagulant for the collected blood that leads to an increase of blood shelf life by a factor of 2/3, from 21 to 35 days. The expansion of the simulation–optimization–regression analysis in Cohen and Pierskalla (1979a) and Cohen and Pierskalla (1979b) to include the blood shelf-life duration L results in a new version of the order-up-to-level prescription in (1):

$$S^* = 4.755\,(d_M)^{0.6964}\,(p)^{0.1146}\,(D)^{-0.0453}\,(L)^{0.1332}\,. \tag{2}$$

While the presence of the shelf-life variable affects the estimates for the power coefficients of other variables as compared to (1), the main qualitative features of the optimal order up to level remain unchanged. In particular, the average demand value still dominates other factors in influencing the inventory control policy, with doubling of the demand leading to approximately a 60% increase in the optimal order up to level. Higher shelf life of inventory allows the system to optimally maintain higher inventory levels to further reduce shortages without affecting the outdates. In particular, keeping all other values unchanged, the increase of L from 21 to 35 days leads to about a 7% increase in the value of S^*. The paper provides a separate regression-based analysis of the two key performance indicators, the outdate rate, O_R, and the shortage rate, S_R, adding the deviation of the actual inventory level, S' from the optimal value S^* as an explanatory variable:

$$O_R = 4.11052\left(\frac{(D)^{0.66033}\,(A)^{1.57255}\exp\left(0.00799\left(S' - S^*\right)\right)}{(d_M)^{0.8856}\,(p)^{2.54564}\,(L)^{3.01945}}\right), \tag{3}$$

$$S_R = 0.09629\left(\frac{(D)^{0.05359}\,(A)^{0.57441}\exp\left(0.17356\left(S^* - S'\right)\right)}{(d_M)^{0.34867}\,(p)^{0.43568}\,(L)^{1.09577}}\right), \tag{4}$$

where A is the average age of the supplied blood inventory, expressed in days. These expressions outline the strong impact of shelf life on both types of demand–supply mismatch: if all other parameters are kept unchanged, the increase of L from 21 to 35 reduces the outdate rate by about 79% and the shortage rate—by about 43%. Preserving the stability of the other parameters in the system is indeed required in order to realize the full potential associated with extended shelf life. The paper notes that the initial drop in shortages and outdates may increase tendencies to use higher crossmatching fractions and duration, a higher average age of blood supply, and an increase in tolerance for potential deviations from the optimal order up to policies, all of which can blunt the benefits of an increased L value.

Morris Cohen's foundational work in the area of blood bank inventory management organically combines the focus on tactical inventory issues at a particular blood bank, and strategic issues of interaction among different locations within the same blood supply chain, paving the way for his extensive research on multi-echelon inventory systems in following years.

From a timeline perspective, the papers reviewed here span about a decade, from the mid-1970s to about the mid-1980s. Since then, the nature of managerial challenges associated with blood bank operations evolved to reflect new technological approaches to handling blood products. A more recent review (Beliën and Forcé 2012) provides a description of the main components of the currently used set of blood products (whole blood, red blood cells, blood platelets, blood plasma, and frozen blood), each with its own clinical use, but also with its own shelf life. For example, out of three major "components" obtained by centrifuging whole blood upon its collection (red blood cells, plasma, and blood platelets), plasma has a long shelf life and is considered "non-perishable" (Prastacos 1984), while platelets have a very short shelf life. In connection with the multiple-product nature of blood use, Pierskalla (2004) outlined a "major need for more research in inventory theory for developing and analyzing mathematical models in which a common input source is subdivided into value added components." Beliën and Forcé (2012) outline several new research directions emerged in recent years, in particular, evaluation/best practices research (Heddle et al. 2009; Pereira 2006; Perera et al. 2009; Pitocco and Sexton 2005) as well as research focused on the donor/supply side (Bosnes et al. 2005; Godin et al. 2007; James et al. 1996; Melnik et al. 1995).

3 Modeling Hospital Patient Flows

Hospital care represents the second main direction of health care research Morris Cohen pursued during the 1980s. Cohen et al. (1980b) describe a simulation study of patient flows at a "progressive care" hospital facility where patients are transferred from one facility unit to another as their health state changes: the paper uses as an example a coronary care facility, comprised of coronary care, post-coronary care, intensive care, medical care, surgical, and ambulatory service units. The goal of the analysis is to identify "response functions" that would tie a limited care capacity at each unit to care outcomes. Simulation assumes semi-Markov dynamics for patient trajectories when moving through service units and includes as inputs patient arrival rates and transition matrices between service units, as well as length-of-stay distributions for each service unit. On the output side, the paper looks at three key performance indicators: capacity utilization U for each unit, the fraction of attempted patient transfers into each unit that were blocked due to insufficient capacity (the paper defines a related "service level" S for each unit, i.e., the fraction of time the unit is not blocked), and the proportion, for each unit, of patient days due to "inappropriate" use caused by blocking (the paper results report the complementary fraction corresponding to the appropriate patient-day rate for each unit, P).

The natural requirements for patient care often limit the tolerable duration of delays in settings when a patient must be transferred to a unit that happens to be "full." In cases of such "blocking," hospitals use a variety of approaches to mitigating potential care delays. In addition to the impact of limited care capacity, the paper investigates the effects of two policies used upon blocking: "bumping" and "priority" polices. Under the bumping policy, the incoming patient is always placed in the unit to which the transfer is initiated, and the required care capacity is secured by initiating a transfer out of the unit for a patient with the longest stay. The bumped patient then moves to her "next" unit, and her length of stay there is extended by the remaining duration of stay in the blocked unit; a cascade of "bumps" can occur if the "next" unit is also at capacity. Under the priority policy, the blocked patient is transferred to a non-utilized service unit according to exogenous priority rules governed by medical care standards. Since, in practice, the implied costs of blocking are likely to be shared among the transferred patient and other patients in the service unit to which the transfer is intended, these two blocking rules represent two extremes where these costs are assigned only to one of those parties.

In the simulation study, the capacities of the two most important service units are varied: the number of beds C_1 (with a maximum of 12) and C_2 (with a maximum of 22) in coronary care and post-coronary care units, respectively. The "response functions" for the three key performance indicators (utilization, service level, and appropriate patient-day rates) were calculated under each blocking policy using non-linear regression:

$$U_i = \alpha_i^U - \beta_i^U C_i + \gamma_{ij}^U \left(\frac{1}{C_j}\right), \tag{5}$$

$$S_i = \alpha_i^S - \beta_i^S \left(\frac{1}{C_i}\right) - \gamma_{ij}^S \left(\frac{1}{C_j}\right), \tag{6}$$

$$P_i = \alpha_i^P - \beta_i^P \left(\frac{1}{C_i}\right) - \gamma_{ij}^P \left(\frac{1}{C_j}\right), \tag{7}$$

for service units $i = 1, 2$, $j \neq i$, where all of the estimated coefficients α, β, and γ, if significant at the $p = 0.05$ level, were positive. For example, the results for the utilization rates under the priority policy are

$$U_1 = 0.727 - 0.045C_1 + 3.548\left(\frac{1}{C_2}\right), \tag{8}$$

$$U_2 = 1.081 - 0.027C_2 + 0.401\left(\frac{1}{C_1}\right). \tag{9}$$

Expressions similar to (8)–(9) allow for direct assessments of the impact of adding/removing staffed beds in any care unit or converting beds from one unit to another. While focusing on a specific set of key performance indicators, this analysis enables the decision-makers to make explicit trade-offs between various performance measures, by-passing the difficult task of attaching precise values of implied costs to changes in those measures. Although the derived response functions may not have applicability beyond the specific clinical facility, the used methodology does, allowing the simulation to be harnessed in assessing the impact of various changes in care capacity in systems where patient trajectories involve transfers between different care units.

Cohen et al. (1981) add an important analytical component to the simulation described in Cohen et al. (1980b). At the center of the analysis of this paper is a progressive care system where one of the units has a limited capacity (such as the coronary care unit within the coronary care facility). This focus on a single "bottleneck" within a patient care facility provides an important first-order analysis of the impact of the limited care capacity on utilization of that care unit and on the overall pattern of patient flows within the facility. The approach the paper takes to estimating the utilization of the capacitated unit uses the Erlang loss formula applied to the capacitated unit independently of other units. The mechanism for the estimation stems from the introduction of an extra infinite-capacity care unit that accommodates all patients blocked by a capacitated unit. If patients who leave the capacitated unit never return to it again, the calculation of the blocking probability of the capacitated unit relies on the fact that, under Poisson external arrivals to all units, the capacitated unit functions as an independent $M/G/c$ loss system, where c is the care capacity (e.g., the number of staffed beds) in that unit. The arrival rate to the capacitated unit, γ, is determined as the sum of external arrivals and internal transfers from other units and is given by the solution to the standard service network traffic equations (Kleinrock 1976). Then, if the expected patient stay in the capacitated unit is $\frac{1}{\mu}$, then the blocking probability for that unit is given by the Erlang loss formula:

$$\alpha = \frac{\frac{\left(\frac{\gamma}{\mu}\right)^c}{c!}}{\sum_{k=0}^{c} \frac{\left(\frac{\gamma}{\mu}\right)^k}{k!}}. \tag{10}$$

One of the main results of the paper is to show that, in setting where the patient return to the capacitated unit is possible, (10) can still be used to calculate the blocking probability for the capacitated unit if the patients' length-of-stay times at all units are exponential. Although, for the general semi-Markov patient trajectory model, (10) can only be used as an approximation for this blocking probability, this approximation performs very well in a simulation based on the data collected at a coronary care facility (Kao 1974).

A detailed approach to estimating and validating a semi-Markov model of patient flows within a hospital facility is presented in Weiss et al. (1982). Under semi-

Markov patient flow dynamics, patient transitions between care units are governed only by the unit where a patient is currently located. In addition, the distributional characteristics for patient length of stay at a particular unit are defined only by the nature of that unit as well as that of the next unit on the patient's trajectory, with patient trajectories being independent of each other and of the occupancy states of care units. The paper's approach for creating such a model of patient flows involves an iterative procedure that starts with an initial set of patient groups (e.g., defined based on a set of medical procedures and medical risk levels) and care states/units, estimating the patient flow parameters for this set, and checking if the resulting flow dynamics satisfy, statistically, semi-Markov requirements. If the current model does not fall within the semi-Markov class, changes in the definitions of patient sets and/or care states are implemented, and the statistical tests are repeated on the new iteration of the model. The statistical testing and updating of the model based on a particular set of patient classes and care states involves three main stages. The first stage determines if some patient classes should be combined or divided into sub-classes. In particular, in order to combine two population classes, the statistical similarity tests, such as the Anderson-Goodman test (Anderson and Goodman 1957), must be conducted on the maximum likelihood estimators of between-units transition probability matrices, followed by a test on length-of-stay times for two patient classes, e.g., the Kolmogorov–Smirnov two-sample test. The second stage involves testing the Markovian assumptions for the transition probabilities and the length-of-stay times, with the goal of extending the set of states to ensure the independence of these two characteristics from the "past" state history. Finally, the third stage is designed to test the independence transitions and length-of-stay durations from the occupancy of care units, with a potential removal from the estimation procedure of the data obtained in periods of high unit occupancy. The execution of this iterative approach naturally requires a number of judgment calls on the nature of the patient population groups and care states and potential re-validation of the entire set of statistical tests upon changes in these sets. The paper provides a detailed example of applying this methodology to actual clinical practice using the data from the obstetrics unit of a university teaching hospital.

Cohen et al. (1980b, 1981), and Weiss et al. (1982) played a seminal role in the line of research on strategic planning of hospital capacity and management of in-hospital patient flows. In recent years, in addition to strategic analysis of inpatient bed capacity and staffing decisions (see, e.g., Green and Nguyen 2001, Green 2002, Yankovic and Green 2011), the related lines of research include detailed, "within-day" modeling of inpatient ward dynamics (see Dai and Shi 2021 for the most recent review), interaction between emergency department and inpatient wards (Shi et al. 2015), management of elective surgeries (Bavafa et al. 2019; Jung et al. 2019; Liu et al. 2019), and patient discharges (Bavafa et al. 2021; Chan et al. 2016; Shi et al. 2021).

4 Patient Choice and Hospital Capacity Utilization

In a move from intra-hospital patient dynamics to inter-hospital competition, Cohen and Lee (1984, 1985a), and Cohen and Lee (1985b) focus on an empirical study of the factors influencing patient choice of a hospital facility. This series of papers developed a multinomial-logit approach to describing hospital utilization within a given region in terms of hospital geographical and service features, as well as the socio-economic characteristics of the patient population. In its most general form, the multinomial approach to modeling a choice for a patient located in the geographical location (e.g., a zip code) i of the hospital j among a set of alternatives K uses the "attractiveness" measure V_{ji} (McFadden 1974). Under the assumption that the stochastic component of the attractiveness function is independently Gumbel-distributed, the probability that such a patient chooses hospital j is

$$p_{ji} = \frac{\exp\left(V_{ji}\right)}{\sum_{k \in K} \exp\left(V_{ki}\right)}. \tag{11}$$

The focus of the analysis in all three papers is the structure of the attractiveness functions, with the general functional form given by

$$V_{ji} = f\left(t_{ij}, s_j, b_j, d_{ij}, c_j, e_j\right), \tag{12}$$

where t_{ij} is the travel time between i and j, s_j is the scope of services offered by the hospital j, c_j is the number of licensed beds at hospital j, d_{ij} is the number of physicians with admission privileges at hospital j whom patients from i can access, and c_j and e_j are the location and other factors associated with hospital j (such as teaching status and urban vs. small town vs. rural location). The scope of service characteristics for each hospital included four distinct measures: (1) the number of facilities and services, (2) Guttman's service-mix index (Edwards et al. 1972) that utilizes cumulative scaling, with later-added services representing the higher degree of sophistication in terms of scope of offered services, (3) Berry's grouping that assigns hospitals to different groups based on their "growth" stage (Berry 1973), and (4) a score based on the factor analysis of the first three measures (Cohen and Lee 1984). The model estimation was based on the 1980 data from the state of Rhode Island that included hospital discharge data, the hospital facilities database, a physician information survey, and the data on travel times between different census tracts. A series of regressions reported in Cohen and Lee (1985b) point to the travel time as the most important factor determining patient choice, followed by hospital size and the number of access-providing physicians. The quantitative assessment of a connection between hospital utilization and its size and care capabilities represented an important tool for the situations where hospitals were considering adjustments to their care capacity and/or case mix. Cohen and Lee (1985a) provide an important refinement to these results, reporting, in particular, significant differences in the hospital utilization patterns based on patient gender, age, and income levels.

Cohen and Lee (1984, 1985a), and Cohen and Lee (1985b) were among the first papers to measure the impact of supply-side factors, such as the scope of provided care and licensed bed capacity, in patient choice among hospital facilities. At present, patients often benefit from a substantially expanded information set about the type and the quality of care provided by any particular hospital: for example, in the USA, this type of information set is furnished by the Centers for Medicare and Medicaid Services (Centers for Medicare and Medicaid Services 2021a). This information set expansion resulted in the corresponding expansion in the set of factors that influence patient choice: care quality and ranking (Bundorf et al. 2009; Dranove and Sfekas 2008; Pope 2009; Tay 2003), delays that patients incur while waiting for care (Beukers et al. 2014), and the presence of parking facilities (Smith et al. 2018).

One distinguishing feature of Morris Cohen's research on health care topics is its multi-prone impact that combines influencing the thought process in the community of operations researchers via publications in leading operations outlets with informing the practitioner community through publication outlets more attuned to their interests (such as *Transfusion* and *Medical Care*).

In modern health care systems, detailed data relating to many clinical and operational aspects of care are becoming available to patients, as well as to care providers and payers. On the clinical side, the volume and precision of collected data in diagnostic and care facilities, as well as via the increasingly sophisticated ecosystem of "wearables," ushered in the era of "precision medicine," characterized by individualized approaches to diagnosing and treating patients. On the side of care delivery, precision medicine is being supplemented by an emerging system of individualized, conveniently timed access to the appropriately selected mode of care. A rapid evolution of remote communication technology and infrastructure enabled the creation of new, complex networks of physical and virtual access-to-care points that increase the "on-demand" nature of care provision. One of the important components of the emerging system of care delivery is a shift of some care elements to non-face-to-face channels, a shift that has only accelerated during the COVID-19 pandemic. In the next section, we review the recent trends in the adoption of telemedicine and discuss the related health care operations literature.

5 Telemedicine and Transformation of Health Care Delivery

Telemedicine is commonly defined as a technology-mediated remote modality of patient–provider interactions, such as diagnosis, monitoring, interventions, and care delivery. As with any service innovation, the success of telemedicine depends on the buy-ins from both patients and providers, and, in the case of health care, from the payers.

On the patient side, elimination of the need to be at the provider's location at the time of service reduces the costs associated with accessing care. On the provider's side, the ability to perform certain non-urgent care tasks remotely may free up some care capacity for more complex, "hands-on" tasks. For complex, expert service such as health care, only certain types of service interactions can be conducted remotely without jeopardizing the quality of delivered service (Blumenthal 2020).

The COVID-19 pandemic has led to a fundamental recalibration of the way patients access care around the globe. The telemedicine has seen substantial growth in both developing and developed countries (see, for example, Agarwal et al. 2020, Cui et al. 2020, National Health Service 2021, Peine et al. 2020), and, in the present chapter, we focus on the telemedicine expansion in the US health care markets.

5.1 COVID-19 Pandemic and Explosive Growth of Telemedicine

Pre-COVID-19 surveys conducted by the American Medical Association have already registered a widening interest among physicians in the use of telemedicine tools: the percentage of physicians who reported using tele-visits/virtual visits has increased from 14% to 28% between 2016 and 2019 (American Medical Association Digital Health Research 2020a). However, despite the presence of enabling technological solutions, the adoption of telemedicine has not become widespread until the COVID-19 pandemic: the US Department of Health and Human Services (Bosworth et al. 2020) reported a jump in telehealth visits from 0.1% of all Fee-for-Service Medicare primary care visits in February 2020 to 43.5% in April 2020. The initial rapid expansion of telemedicine services during the pandemic was accompanied by a drop in the overall number of patient–provider interactions (Cohen et al. 2020). McKinsey reports that this initial transient phase has evolved by June 2020 into a phase with greater apparent stability, with 13%–17% of all patient encounters falling within the telemedicine category (Bestsennyy et al. 2021).

This dramatic increase in the use of telemedicine was supported by changes in the Medicare regulatory and reimbursement policies introduced by the Centers for Medicare and Medicaid Services (CMS) as part of the US government response to the COVID-19 Public Health Emergency (PHE). These changes included, in particular, the removal of a number of restrictions on the type of providers, patient location, and the technological means allowed to be used in telemedicine services. In particular, before the pandemic, Medicare compensated physicians for telemedicine services such as "Virtual Check-in" (Centers for Medicare and Medicaid Services 2021b) and "E-visit" (Centers for Medicare and Medicaid Services 2021c). These services had to be initiated by existing patients, provided that patients were located in designated rural areas, and traveled to a health care facility to receive telemedicine services via the approved communication portal. For the duration of the PHE, however, Medicare also allowed qualified non-physician providers to independently bill for patient-initiated "Medicare telehealth visits," irrespective of patient locations, and waived "penalties for HIPAA violations against health care providers that serve patients in good faith through everyday communications technologies, such as FaceTime or Skype." Medicare compensated providers for such telemedicine services at the regular, "in-person" rates, and, further, did not audit submitted claims for the evidence that services were delivered to an existing patient and allowed for reduced or waived cost-sharing for such services (Centers for Medicare and Medicaid Services 2020). In addition, the set of care procedures eligible for Medicare Fee-for-Service reimbursement when delivered remotely was expanded (US Department of Health and Human Services, Health Resources and Services Administration 2021).

The COVID-19 PHE has increased the salience of telemedicine as an important component of the system of health care delivery. The relaxation of the regulatory and financial obstacles to its use has unleashed an intense system-wide experimentation focused on identifying its place in the "new normal" demand–supply match. The initial results of this ongoing process highlighted an expectedly uneven degree of telemedicine adoption across different medical specialties and different patient categories. Chartis Group and Kythera Labs (Chartis Group 2021) report the analysis of the clearinghouse claims vendors data for the period between January 2020 and January 2021. Their analysis indicates that a proportion of telehealth claims, after going through peak values in the initial stages of the COVID-19 pandemic, showed, by January 2021, signs of stabilizing at around 70% for behavioral health specialties, and at around 24%, 17%, and 5% for primary care, medical, and surgical specialties, respectively. Within medical specialties, a substantial dispersion was also observed, with neurology and gastroenterology leading the telemedicine adoption at around 36% and 29%, respectively, and dermatology trailing behind at around 4%. McKinsey analysis (Bestsennyy et al. 2021) confirms this broad dispersion pattern, reporting, for February 2021 that 50% of the psychiatry-related claims and 30% of the substance use disorder claims have the telemedicine designation, with 17% for endocrinology and rheumatology, 13% for gastroenterology, and 8% for dermatology, while the analysis based on consumer report data for January–June 2021 shows that this fraction for "visits with a primary care physician" is 21%. Although these findings are preliminary, they do reflect rather different emerging trajectories for incorporation of the elements of telemedicine into different specialties, with care options related to behavioral health being more "digitally forward" (Chartis Group 2021), while other specialties are finding a more limited use for the telemedicine care modality. Even pre-pandemic, access to quality psychiatric care in the USA was limited: about 44%, 26%, and 10% of the US counties had a practicing psychiatrist, a child and adolescent psychiatrist, and a geriatric psychiatrist, respectively (University of Michigan Behavioral Health Workforce Research Center 2018). The COVID-19 PHE, if anything, made this access issue more urgent, with a wider adoption of telemedicine playing an important role in managing the effects of further reduction of in-person care options.

The estimates for telemedicine adoption in primary care reported in Chartis Group (2021) and Bestsennyy et al. (2021) are broadly consistent with other reported estimates (e.g., 16% in Li et al. 2021 and 17% in athenahealth 2021). It is important to note that, despite the dramatic increase in the use of telemedicine, the overall number of weekly patient visits (in-person as well as "virtual") to a physician practice in July and August 2020 dropped by about 28% as compared to pre-pandemic levels, with the revenues dropping by about 32% (American Medical Association Digital Health Research 2020b). The significant, sustained drop in the overall aggregate patient demand seen by physician practices is also confirmed in Chartis Group (2021).

On the patient side, the level of adoption of telemedicine has been influenced by a number of factors. Patel et al. (2021) analyzed the data for commercially insured and Medicare Advantage enrollees from January to June 2020 and reported varying fractions of tele-visits across patient age categories, with the highest, 39%, in the 20–39 age group, and the lowest, around 25%, in the 65+ age group. These results conform with the findings of the 2020 Kaiser Family Foundation health tracking poll (Kaiser Family Foundation 2020) that showed that 32% of the Americans in the 65+ age group do not have access to the technological solutions required for telemedicine care delivery. The "age split" is also reported in Chartis Group (2021), with the fraction of telemedicine visits in 18–44 and 45–65 age categories being 24% and 19%, respectively, dropping to 14% for patients who are 65+, with the overwhelming majority of telemedicine visits (around 94%) focused on care provision for established (as opposed to new) patients. In addition to the age, socio-economic factors play an important role in shaping patient access to the technology required for telemedicine adoption. For example, the role of household income is highlighted in a recent Pew Research Center survey conducted in January–February 2021: among the US adults living in households with incomes below $30,000, 43% did not have broadband services at home, and 41% did not own a desktop or a laptop (Pew Research Center 2020).

On the provider side, the wider adoption of a new mode for care delivery requires a proper alignment of several enabling elements. During the COVID-19 PHE, provider compensation for telemedicine care is set at levels equivalent to those for in-person visits, and, according to the McKinsey Physician Insights Report, in April 2021 84% of the physicians were offering telemedicine-based care. However, the fraction of physicians ready to continue using virtual visits would drop to 54% if those visits were compensated at a hypothetical 15% discount as compared to in-person visits (Bestsennyy et al. 2021). In its statement for the US House of Representatives hearing "The Future of Telehealth: COVID-19 is Changing the Delivery of Virtual Care," the American Hospital Association (AHA) points out that delivery of care using telemedicine is associated with "substantial upfront and ongoing costs of establishing and maintaining their virtual infrastructure, including secure platforms, licenses, IT support, scheduling, patient education and clinician training," and encourages the US Congress to enable adequate provider compensation for telemedicine care beyond the duration of the COVID-19 PHE (American Hospital Association 2021). The AHA also outlines several main aspects of a flexible approach to regulation and reimbursement of telemedicine care that must be preserved beyond the emergency: coverage and reimbursement for audio-only virtual visits as a way to deliver care to patients who do not have a ready access to broadband and video-conferencing software, relaxation of state licensing rules that would continue to allow physicians from one state to deliver care to patients located in other states, and expansion of the types of providers allowed to deliver telemedicine care. The provider survey conducted by the American Medical Association emphasized the growing importance of two factors identified as requirements for continued adoption of telemedicine care: its coverage in standard malpractice insurance, and demonstration of its efficacy in peer-reviewed publications (American Medical Association Digital Health Research 2020a). On the latter issue, much remains to be done, despite some encouraging "moderate strength" evidence of the positive impact of remote intensive care unit (ICU) consultations, specialty telehealth consultations, telehealth for emergency medical services, and remote consultations for outpatient care (Totten et al. 2019).

At present, the US provider–patient–payer ecosystem continues its search for the precise nature of the "new normal" position of telemedicine in the configuration of care delivery. Although many of the trends described above remain tentative and potentially reversible, the long duration of the COVID-19 PHE has significantly altered the nature of patient–provider care relations by injecting a significant fraction of telemedicine experience. On the patient side, the convenience of this experience has produced expectations of a continued significant presence of this mode of care delivery: according to the McKinsey patient survey, 40% of the patients expect to continue using "telehealth," with the fraction of up to 60% interested in a broader integration of "virtual health" elements in patient care (Bestsennyy et al. 2021). On the payer's side, a significant level of uncertainty exists over the extent to which the extensions to telehealth services compensation will continue beyond the duration of the PHE: a survey of primary care practices by the Urban Institute (Corlette et al. 2021) indicates that full parity between reimbursements for telehealth and in-person visits is not assured going forward, given that "insurers had begun cutting back on the generosity of telehealth reimbursement and re-imposing patient cost-sharing for telehealth visits." A precise cost–benefit analysis between the remote and in-person elements of care delivery may require a focus on the "episode of care" rather than a "patient visit" (Ashwood et al. 2017). At present, CMS proposes to keep the currently used approach until the end of 2022 "to evaluate whether the services should be permanently added to the telehealth list following the COVID-19 PHE" (Centers for Medicare and Medicaid Services 2021d).

Despite the uncertainty in the extent of future reimbursements, there seems to be a growing consensus that telehealth will increase its penetration of the care delivery system, even as the search for a precise delineation between the care elements that can be effectively accomplished remotely and those that must be done in-person continues. The sense of likely growth of the telemedicine component has also been shared by investors: the analysis of the digital health funding by Rock Health shows that the funding secured in the first half of 2021 ($14.7 billion) already surpassed that for the whole of 2020 ($14.6 billion), which itself was almost twice the level of 2019 ($7.7 billion). In terms of value propositions being funded, the top three lists from 2018 and from the first half of 2021 both include biopharma/device research and development, on-demand health care, and fitness and wellness; in terms of clinical lines, mental health held the top funding position during 2018–2021, followed by cardiovascular disease, diabetes, and primary care (Krasniansky et al. 2021). Overall, McKinsey estimates the annual amount of US health care spending that can be "virtualized" as $250 billion (Bestsennyy et al. 2021). The potential pathways for telemedicine expansion go well beyond replacing and/or complimenting in-person office visits within the framework of an existing patient–provider relationship. On the one hand, new opportunities are created for large provider networks to extend their care offerings across new geographies previously served by other providers. On the other hand, telemedicine also creates new cooperation opportunities for provider networks: a 2019 McKinsey survey of 60 CEOs of mid-to-large health care systems describes several examples of partnerships between regional health systems and rural health systems, academic medical centers, and third-party providers of virtual care that create mutually beneficial, telemedicine-enabled integration of primary care, and specialty and sub-specialty care ecosystems (Fowkes et al. 2021).

5.2 Telemedicine in the Health Care Operations Literature

The telemedicine explosion has been a subject of a growing number of operations management studies, and the term "e-visit" has been widely used to characterize the broad range of telemedicine interaction types between patients and physicians. Below we review several emerging directions of operation studies that focus on the impact of telemedicine on the ways health care is delivered: increase in diagnostic and treatment capacity, changes in financial incentives, telemedicine adoption dynamics, and on-demand platforms.

Zhong et al. (2016) focus on assessing the effect of e-visits on physician productivity in primary care. The paper models a single-physician setting and builds an analytical model of an episode of care, where "web services" and e-visits are embedded into the patient care routine. Under the assumption that some web services will result in an e-visit, and some e-visits will be followed up by an office visit, the paper calculates the resulting first two moments of the distribution of the total duration of patient care episode, and the resulting impact on the physician's workload under different care priority policies for office and e-visits. The potential productivity gains stemming from the introduction of non-face-to-face interactions between patients and providers are connected to the fraction of office visits that can be effectively converted into the e-visit mode, and the resulting savings in care capacity.

Green et al. (2021) report the evolution of the fraction of primary care appointments delivered in telehealth mode for two health care provider groups, the Crystal Run Health care (CRH) in New York and the Lehigh Valley Health Network

(LVHN) in Pennsylvania. At CRH, this fraction was around 60–65% at the height of the COVID-19 PHE, dropping to 23% at the end of 2020. For LVHN, the peak values reached 90%, with the average during the pandemic months being 21%. Both provider groups acknowledge that e-visits are associated with substantial provider productivity gains: the LVHN data indicate that, during the period from May 2020 to April 2021, the average in-person visit duration was near 24 min, while the average duration for tele-visits was 16 min. One of the important factors that can further amplify these productivity gains is the reduction in no-shows stemming from a greater convenience of e-visits for patients. Green et al. (2021) use simulation based on the CRH and LVHN data as well as realistic estimates for no-show rates to outline the range of increases in provider daily care capacity and the corresponding increases in patient panel sizes that a primary care provider can manage.

In addition to clinical feasibility and potential productivity gains, the success of telemedicine depends on the acceptance of telemedicine care by physicians and patients based on its socio-economic advantages. Rajan et al. (2019) focus on specialists providing chronic care and model settings where physicians can set the service fee as well as settings where this fee is exogenous and determined by the payer. The paper builds a model where revenue-maximizing providers can choose to offer both in-person and tele-care and set the patient service rates and fees for both types of care, while the utility-maximizing patients choose one of the care options or an "outside" option. From the patient perspective, the main distinctions between the two care options are different utilities of care and the reduced "travel burden" associated with e-visits. While the results of the analysis show that telemedicine is a "win-win" for providers and patients under a broad range of circumstances, they also strike a cautionary note: when the provider can set different prices and service rates for in-person vs. e-visits, the total patient surplus can decrease. Çakıcı and Mills (2020) focus on the place of the tele-triage in the primary care delivery system as a tool for updating patient belief about their health state in the beginning of an episode of an acute (rather than chronic) sickness. The paper models the patient choice of the mode of engagement with the system in the presence of the error-prone tele-triage and argues for the tele-triage co-pay to limit its potential for increasing the overall cost of an episode to the health care system. Ding et al. (2021) explore the operational implications of use of the AI-powered virtual triage tools and outline potential sources of operational inefficiencies associated with their use.

Bavafa et al. (2021) provide a comprehensive look at the adoption of e-visits in primary care in order to identify conditions under which such an adoption would be beneficial to both providers and patients. The paper models the demand for care as an endogenous process, shaped jointly by provider and patient decisions: while providers control the size of their patient panels, and the frequency of scheduled patient office visits intervals, these choices are made within ranges acceptable to patients. Such demand endogeneity plays a crucial role in assessing the impact of e-visit introduction on demand–supply balance at the primary care clinic, as well as the outcomes with a broader societal importance, such as patient health and population care coverage. One of the central tenets of the analysis in Bavafa et al. (2021) is the explicit treatment of provider e-visit compensation as a major factor shaping the system's outcomes, with both "fee-for-service" and "capitation" components considered. One of the paper's main conclusions is that the compensation rates for e-visits and in-person visits should be set as close as possible to ensure that physician revenues and patient panel size increase and that patient health does not worsen.

A separate line of research papers focuses on a new and growing channel of access to care via telehealth technology: on-demand telemedicine platforms. On-demand service platforms have received significant coverage in the operations literature (see, e.g., Cachon et al. 2017, Taylor 2018, and Bai et al. 2019). Liu et al. (2021) point out the main distinction between the Uber-like on-demand service platforms and the on-demand models of health care delivery: in the latter settings, the providers can control the service rate, which, in turn, creates an additional managerial lever for influencing the quality of delivered care. The paper builds a model of an on-demand health care platform by considering interactions between the platform, the care providers/physicians, and the patients. In their model, the platform, anticipating the decisions by providers and patients, either sets a commission rate (a fraction of the service fee patients pay to the providers) or both the commission rate and the service fee. Potential care providers form a finite pool of exogenous size. Each provider, upon observing the financial parameters set by the platform and anticipating patients' actions, makes their decision of whether to join the platform or not (based on their individual reservation profit rate), and, if joining the platform, the rate of service they provide to patients. In addition, if allowed by the platform, each provider determines the service fee they charge to patients. Patients are assumed to arrive according to a Poisson process with an exogenous rate, and the patient care process for each physician is modeled using $M/M/1$ queuing dynamics. A delay-sensitive patient, based on the service fee values and the physician participation and service rate decisions, joins the queue for the provider delivering the highest net utility, if this utility is non-negative (otherwise, a patient selects an outside option with the net utility normalized to 0). One of the main results of the analysis is that, when a platform can only control the operations via a commission rate, it may be inclined to use it as a tool for controlling the supply of care capacity and the competition among physicians by collecting a high commission. On the other hand, a platform that can control both the commission and the service fee will tend to charge lower commissions and set higher fees, leading to increased physician participation and higher quality of delivered care.

Savin et al. (2021) expanded the analysis of on-demand health care platforms by accounting for the multi-specialty nature of health care services. In particular, for a range of medical conditions, patient care can be delivered by a "generalist" physician (a primary care physician or an internist) or by a specialist. In such cases, the ability for patients to select the provider type creates an additional element of interaction among physicians. In modeling the platform operations, Savin et al. (2021) assume that physicians can fall into the generalist or multiple specialist types, and, within a given type, into multiple quality categories (for example, based on academic rank or level of experience), and use the same sequence of events as in Liu et al. (2021). The paper also assumes that the platform sets both the physician compensation rates as well as the patient service fees and that physicians, in addition to their participation decisions, select the daily number of patient appointments of exogenous duration to offer on the platform. In addition, the platform can benefit from pooling of the care capacity across physicians of the same type and rank. The analysis focuses on assessing the effects of the demand interaction on the platform, physicians, and patients. One of the main results of the paper is the demonstration that, although the demand interaction may not benefit both physicians and patients in settings where the platform is not restricted in the way it chooses physician compensation and patient fees, all parties may be better off in settings where the platform applies the same commission rate across all physician types and categories.

6 Discussion

Telemedicine is only one of a number of novel features that appeared on the health care delivery landscape since the 1980s. Rapid technological advances and the collection of increasingly detailed data on the clinical as well as operational aspects of health care are creating favorable conditions for a joint deployment of individualized clinical interventions and individualized, increasingly on-demand, approaches for patients to access care. Health care Analytics (2018) has been established as a major area of research in operations, where precision medicine intersects with precise delivery of care.

Cohen et al. (1980b) open with the following statement: "The rising cost of medical care is viewed by many as the central issue in health care delivery today." More than forty years later, this statement continues to ring true. At the time of that article's publication, the national health expenditures were estimated to be about 8.9% of the US GDP (Statista 2020). In 2019, the American Medical Association (Rama 2019) reported that the national health spending is \$3.8 trillion (\$11, 582 per capita) or 17.7% of GDP in 2019, and with growth projections of 5.5% annually from 2017, this fraction is expected to reach 19.7% of GDP in 2026 (Cuckler et al. 2018). The disruptive influence of technology-based health care innovations enables the diversion of some patient care pathways toward less costly delivery modes. Examples of this phenomenon include the use of a "digital front door" to outpatient care that integrates tools such as e-triage and virtual office visits at the start of a care episode to reduce reliance on hospital EDs, or "hospital-at-home" programs aimed at providing home-based care as a replacement for hospital-based care (US Department of Veterans Affairs 2014). The search for a better place for the US health care system in the space defined by cost–quality–access dimensions (Kissick 1994) continues, and the growing integration of telehealth into the care delivery is likely to play an important role in this search.

References

Agarwal N, Jain P, Pathak R, Gupta R (2020) Telemedicine in India: A tool for transforming health care in the era of COVID-19 pandemic. J Educ Health Promot 9:190. Accessed January 21, 2022. https://doi.org/10.4103/jehp.jehp_472_20

American Hospital Association (2021) AHA statement on the future of telehealth: COVID-19 is changing the delivery of virtual care. Accessed January 21, 2022. https://www.aha.org/2021-03-02-aha-statement-future-telehealth-covid-19-changing-delivery-virtual-care

American Medical Association Digital Health Research (2020a) Physicians' motivations and requirements for adopting digital health. Adoption and attitudinal shifts from 2016 to 2019. Accessed January 21, 2022. https://www.ama-assn.org/system/files/2020-02/ama-digital-health-study.pdf

American Medical Association (2020b) COVID-19 Physician practice financial impact survey results. Accessed January 21, 2022. https://www.ama-assn.org/system/files/2020-10/covid-19-physician-practice-financial-impact-survey-results.pdf

Anderson TW, Goodman LA (1957) Statistical inference about Markov chains. Ann Math Stat 28(1):89–110

Ashwood JS, Mehrotra A, Cowling D, Uscher-Pines L (2017) Direct-to-consumer telehealth may increase access to care but does not decrease spending. Health Affairs 36(3):485–491

athenahealth (2021) athenahealth Telehealth Adoption Report. Accessed January 21, 2022. https://www.athenahealth.com/knowledge-hub/clinical-trends/the-athenahealth-telehealth-insights-dashboard

Bai J, So KC, Tang CS, Chen X, Wang H (2019) Coordinating supply and demand on an on-demand service platform with impatient customers. Manuf Serv Oper Manag 21(3):556–570

Bavafa H, Leys C, Örmeci L, Savin S (2019) Managing portfolio of elective surgical procedures: a multidimensional inverse newsvendor problem. Operations Research 67(6):1543–1563

Bavafa H, Savin S, Terwiesch C (2021) Customizing primary care delivery using e-visits. Product Oper Manag 30(11):4306–4327

Beliën J, Forcé H (2012) Supply chain management of blood products: a literature review. Eur J Oper Res 217(1):1–16

Berry RE (1973) On grouping hospitals for economic analysis. Inquiry 10(4):5–12

Bestsenny O, Gilbert G, Harris A, Rost J (2021) Telehealth: A quarter-trillion-dollar post-COVID-19 reality? Accessed January 21, 2022. https://www.mckinsey.com/industries/healthcare-systems-and-services/our-insights/telehealth-a-quarter-trillion-dollar-post-covid-19-reality

Beukers PDC, Kemp RGM, Varkevisser M (2014) Patient hospital choice for hip replacement: empirical evidence from the Netherlands. Eur J Health Econ 15:927–936

Blumenthal D (2020) Where telemedicine falls short. Harv Bus Rev, June 30 2020. Accessed January 21, 2022. https://hbr.org/2020/06/where-telemedicine-falls-short

Bosnes V, Aldrin M, Heier HE (2005) Predicting blood donor arrival. Transfusion 45(2):162–170

Bosworth A, Ruhter J, Samson LW, Sheingold S, Taplin C, Tarazi W, Zuckerman R (2020) Medicare beneficiary use of telehealth visits: Early data from the start of COVID-19 pandemic. Office of the Assistant Secretary for Planning and Evaluation, US Department of Health and Human Services, Washington, DC. July 28, 2020

Bundorf MK, Chun N, Goda GS, Kessler DP (2009) Do markets respond to quality information? The case of fertility clinics. J Health Econ 28(3):718–727

Cachon G, Daniels K, Lobel R (2017) The role of surge pricing on a service platform with self-scheduling capacity. Manuf Serv Oper Manag 19(3):368–384

Çakıcı ÖE, Mills AF (2020) On the role of teletriage in healthcare demand management. Manuf Serv Oper Manag 23(6):1483–1504

Centers for Medicare and Medicaid Services (2020) Medicare telemedicine health care provider fact sheet. Accessed January 21, 2022. https://www.cms.gov/newsroom/fact-sheets/medicare-telemedicine-health-care-provider-fact-sheet

Centers for Medicare and Medicaid Services (2021a) The hospital compare program. Accessed January 21, 2022. https://www.medicare.gov/care-compare/?providerType=Hospital&redirect=true
Centers for Medicare and Medicaid Services (2021b) Virtual check-ins. Accessed January 21, 2022. https://www.medicare.gov/coverage/virtual-check-ins
Centers for Medicare and Medicaid Services (2021c) E-visits. Accessed January 21, 2022, 2021. https://www.medicare.gov/coverage/e-visits
Centers for Medicare and Medicaid Services (2021d) Calendar Year (CY) 2022 Medicare Physician Fee Schedule Proposed Rule. Accessed January 21, 2022. https://www.cms.gov/newsroom/fact-sheets/calendar-year-cy-2022-medicare-physician-fee-schedule-proposed-rule
Chan CW, Dong J, Green LV (2016). Queues with time-varying arrivals and inspections with applications to hospital discharge policies. Operations Research 65(2):469–495
Chartis Group (2021) Tracking U.S. Telehealth Adoption a Year into the COVID-19 Pandemic. Accessed January 21, 2022. https://www.chartis.com/resources/files/WP_Telehealth-Trend-Analysis_2021-04-28.pdf
Cohen MA (1974) Inventory control for a perishable product: Optimal critical number ordering and applications to blood inventory management. Ph.D. Dissertation, Northwestern University, Evanston, Illinois
Cohen MA (1976) Analysis of single critical number ordering policies for perishable inventories. Operations Research 24(4):726–41
Cohen MA (1977) Joint pricing and ordering policy for exponentially decaying inventory with known demand. Naval Res Logist Quart 24(2):257–68
Cohen MA, Lee HL (1984) Hospital attractiveness as a determinant of regional hospital market shares: A multinomial logit model. In: Brans JP (ed) Operational research, vol 84. Elsevier Science, pp 1032–1046
Cohen MA, Lee HL (1985a) The determinants of spatial distribution of hospital utilization in a region. Medical Care 23(1):27–38
Cohen MA, Lee HL (1985b) A multinomial logit-model for the spatial distribution of hospital utilization. J Bus Econ Stat 3(2):159–168
Cohen MA, Pekelman D (1978) LIFO inventory systems. Management Science 24(11):1150–62
Cohen MA, Pekelman D (1979) Optimal inventory ordering policy with tax payments under FIFO and LIFO accounting systems. Management Science 25(8):729–743
Cohen MA, Pierskalla WP (1975) Management policies for a regional blood bank. Transfusion 15(1):58–67
Cohen MA, Pierskalla WP (1979a) Simulation of blood bank systems. Simuletter 10(4):14–18
Cohen MA, Pierskalla WP (1979b) Target inventory levels for a hospital blood bank or a decentralized regional blood banking system. Transfusion 19(4):444–454
Cohen MA, Pierskalla WP, Sassetti RJ, Consolo J (1979) An overview of a hierarchy of planning models for regional blood bank management. Transfusion 19(5):526–534
Cohen MA, Nahmias S, Pierskalla WP (1980a) A dynamic inventory system with recycling. Naval Res Logist Quart 27(2):196–289
Cohen MA, Hershey JC, Weiss EN (1980b) Analysis of capacity decisions for progressive patient care, hospital facilities. Health Serv Res 15(2):145–160
Cohen MA, Hershey JC, Weiss EN (1981) A stochastic service network model with application to hospital facilities. Operations Research 29(1):1–22
Cohen MA, Pierskalla WP, Sassetti RJ (1983) The impact of adenine and inventory utilization decisions on blood inventory management. Transfusion 23(1):54–58
Cohen O, Fox B, Mills N, Wright P (2020) COVID-19 and commercial pharma: Navigating an uneven recovery. Accessed January 21, 2022. https://www.mckinsey.com/industries/pharmaceuticals-and-medical-products/our-insights/covid-19-and-commercial-pharma-navigating-an-uneven-recovery
Corlette S, Berenson R, Wengle E, Lucia K, Thomas T (2021) Impact of the COVID-19 pandemic on primary care practices. The Urban Institute and the Robert Wood Johnson Foundation.

Accessed January 21, 2022. https://www.rwjf.org/en/library/research/2021/02/impact-of-the-covid-19-pandemic-on-primary-care-practices.html

Cuckler GA, Sisko AM, Poisal JA, Keehan SP, Smith SD, Madison AJ, Wolfe CJ, Hardesty JC (2018) National health expenditure projections, 2019–28: expected rebound in prices drives rising spending growth. Health Affairs 37(3):482–492

Cui F, Ma Q, He X, Zhai Y, Zhao J, Chen B, Sun D, Shi J, Cao M, Wang Z (2020) Implementation and application of telemedicine in China: Cross-sectional study. JMIR mHealth uHealth 8(10):e18426. Accessed January 21, 2022. https://doi.org/10.2196/18426

Dai JG, Shi P (2021) Recent modeling and analytical advances in hospital inpatient flow management. Product Oper Manag 30(6):1838–1862

Ding J, Freeman M, Hasija S (2021) Can AI help improve acute care operations? Investigating the impact of virtual triage technology adoption. INSEAD working paper 2021/11/TOM. Accessed January 21, 2022. https://papers.ssrn.com/sol3/papers.cfm?abstract_id=3806478

Dranove D, Sfekas A (2008) Start spreading the news: A structural estimate of the effects of New York hospital report cards. J Health Econ 27(5):1201–1207

Edwards M, Miller JD, Schumacher R (1972) Classification of community hospitals by scope of services: four indexes. Health Serv Res 7(4):301–313

Fowkes J, Fross C, Gilbert G, Harris A (2021). Virtual health: A look at the next frontier of care delivery. Accessed January 21, 2022. https://www.mckinsey.com/industries/healthcare-systems-and-services/our-insights/virtual-health-a-look-at-the-next-frontier-of-care-delivery

Fries BE (1975) Optimal ordering policy for a perishable commodity with fixed lifetime. Operations Research 23(1):46–61

Godin G, Conner M, Sheeran P, Bélanger-Gravel A, Germain M (2007) Determinants of repeated blood donation among new and experienced blood donors. Transfusion 47(9):1607–1615

Green LV (2002) How many hospital beds? Inquiry 39(4):400–412

Green LV, Nguyen V (2001) Strategies for cutting hospital beds: The impact on patient service. Health Serv Res 36(2):421–442

Green LV, Savin S, Greenberg G, Hines S, Lake D, Minear M, Murphy RX (2021) The role of telehealth in increasing primary care physician capacity. Working Paper

Handbook of Healthcare Analytics: Theoretical Minimum for Conducting 21st Century Research on Healthcare Operations (2018) In: Tayur S, Dai T (eds) Operations research and health care: A handbook of methods and applications. Wiley

Heddle NM, Liu Y, Barty R, Webert KE, Whittaker S, Gagliardi K, Lauzon D, Owens W (2009) Factors affecting the frequency of red blood cell outdates: an approach to establish benchmarking targets. Transfusion 49(2):219–226

James RC, Matthews DE (1996) Analysis of blood donor return behaviour using survival regression methods. Transfusion Medicine 6(1):21–30

Jung KS, Pinedo M, Sriskandarajah C, Tiwari V (2019) Scheduling elective surgeries with emergency patients at shared operating rooms. Product Oper Manag 28(6):1407–1430

Kaiser Family Foundation (2020) Possibilities and limits of telehealth for older adults during the COVID-19 Emergency. Accessed January 21, 2022. https://www.kff.org/policy-watch/possibilities-and-limits-of-telehealth-for-older-adults-during-the-covid-19-emergency/

Kao EPC (1974) Modeling the movement of coronary patients within a hospital by semi-Markov processes. Operations Research 22(4):683–699

Kissick WL (1994) Medicine's dilemmas: Infinite needs versus finite resources. Yale University Press, New Haven, CT

Kleinrock L (1976) Queueing systems. Wiley, New York

Krasniansky A, Zweig M, Evans B (2021) H1 2021 digital health funding: Another blockbuster year…in six months. Accessed January 21, 2022. https://rockhealth.com/reports/h1-2021-digital-health-funding-another-blockbuster-year-in-six-months/

Li KY, Ng S, McCullough J, Zhu Z, Kocher K, Ellimoottil C (2021) Telehealth Use in Michigan During COVID-19. Accessed January 21, 2022. https://ihpi.umich.edu/sites/default/files/2021-03/0216_Primary-Care-Telehealth-Adoption-Brief_FINALv2_0.pdf

Liu N, Truong V, Wang X, Anderson BR (2019) Integrated scheduling and capacity planning with considerations for patients' length-of-stays. Product Oper Manag 28(7):1735–1756

Liu Y, Wang X, Gilbert S, Lai G (2021) Pricing, quality and competition at on-demand healthcare service platforms. Working paper. Accessed January 21, 2022. https://ssrn.com/abstract=3253855

McFadden D (1974) Conditional logit analysis of qualitative choice behavior. In: Zarembka P (ed) Frontiers in econometrics. Academic Press, New York, pp 105–142

Melnyk SA, Pagell M, Jorae G, Sharpe AS (1995) Applying survival analysis to operations management: analyzing the differences in donor classes in the blood donation process. J Oper Manag 13(4):339–356

Nahmias S (1975) A comparison of alternative approximations for ordering perishable inventory. INFOR 13(2):175–184

Nahmias S, Pierskalla WP (1973) Optimal ordering policy for a perishable product that perishes in two periods subject to stochastic demand. Naval Res Logist Quart 20(2):207–229

National Blood Policy (1974) Department of health, education, and welfare, office of the secretary. Accessed January 21, 2022, https://www.govinfo.gov/content/pkg/FR-1974-09-10/pdf/FR-1974-09-10.pdf#page=1

National Health Service (2021) A guide to good practice for digital and data-driven health technologies. Accessed January 21, 2022. https://www.gov.uk/government/publications/code-of-conduct-for-data-driven-health-and-care-technology/initial-code-of-conduct-for-data-driven-health-and-care-technology#principle-1-understand-users-their-needs-and-the-context

Patel SY, Mehrotra A, Huskamp HA, Uscher-Pines L, Ganguli I, Barnett ML (2021) Variation in telemedicine use and outpatient care during the COVID-19 pandemic in the United States. Health Affairs 40(2):349–358

Peine, A, Paffenholz P, Martin L, Wright P, Dohmen S, Marx G, Loosen SH (2020) Telemedicine in Germany during the COVID-19 pandemic: multi-professional national survey. J Med Int Res 22(8):e19745. Accessed January 21, 2022. https://doi.org/10.2196/19745

Pereira A (2006) Economies of scale in blood banking: a study based on data envelopment analysis. Vox Sanguinis 90(4):308–315

Perera G, Hyam C, Taylor C, Chapman JF (2009) Hospital blood inventory practice: the factors affecting stock level and wastage. Transfusion Medicine 19(2):99–104

Pew Research Center (2020) Digital divide persists even as Americans with lower incomes make gains in tech adoption. Accessed January 21, 2022. https://www.pewresearch.org/fact-tank/2021/06/22/digital-divide-persists-even-as-americans-with-lower-incomes-make-gains-in-tech-adoption/

Pierskalla WP (2004) Supply chain management of blood banks. In: Brandeau ML, Sainfort F, Pierskalla WP (eds) Operations research and health care: A handbook of methods and applications. Kluwer Academic Publishers, pp 103–145

Pitocco C, Sexton TR (2005) Alleviating blood shortages in a resource-constrained environment. Transfusion 45(7):1118–1126

Pope D (2009) Reacting to rankings: evidence from "America's Best Hospitals." J Health Econ 28(6):1154–65

Prastacos GP (1984) Blood inventory management: an overview of theory and practice. Management Science 30(7):777–800

Rajan B, Tezcan T, Seidmann A (2019) Service systems with heterogeneous customers: investigating the effect of telemedicine on chronic care. Management Science 65(3):1236–1267

Rama A (2019) National Health Expenditures 2019: Steady Spending Growth Despite Increases in Personal Health Care Expenditures in Advance of the Pandemic. American Medical Association, Policy Research Perspectives. Accessed January 21, 2022. https://www.ama-assn.org/system/files/2021-05/prp-annual-spending-2019.pdf

Savin S, Xu Y, Zhu L (2021) Delivering multi-specialty care via on-demand telemedicine platforms. Working Paper. Accessed January 21, 2022. https://ssrn.com/abstract=3479544

Shi P, Chou MC, Dai JG, Ding D, Sim J (2015) Models and insights for hospital inpatient operations: Time-dependent ED boarding time. Management Science 62(1):1–28
Shi P, Helm J, Deglise-Hawkinson J, Pan J (2021) Timing it right: Balancing inpatient congestion vs. readmission risk at discharge. Operations Research 69(6):1842–1865
Smith H, Currie C, Chaiwuttisak P, Kyprianou A (2018) Patient choice modeling: how do patients choose their hospitals? Health Care Manag Sci 21:259–268
Statista (2020) U.S. national health expenditure as percent of GDP from 1960 to 2020. Accessed January 21, 2022. https://www.statista.com/statistics/184968/us-health-expenditure-as-percent-of-gdp-since-1960/
Tay A (2003) Assessing competition in hospital care markets: the importance of accounting for quality differentiation. Rand J Econ 34(4):786–814
Taylor T (2018) On-demand service platforms. Manuf Serv Oper Manag 20(4):704–720
Totten AM, Hansen RN, Wagner J, Stillman L, Ivlev I, Davis-O'Reilly C, Towle C, Erickson JM, Erten-Lyons D, Fu R, Fann J, Babigumira JB, Palm-Cruz KJ, Avery M, McDonagh MS (2019) Telehealth for acute and chronic care consultations. Comparative effectiveness review no. 216. (Prepared by Pacific Northwest Evidence-based Practice Center under Contract No. 290-2015-00009-I.) AHRQ Publication No. 19-EHC012-EF. Agency for Healthcare Research and Quality, Rockville, MD. Accessed January 21, 2022. https://doi.org/10.23970/AHRQEPCCER216
University of Michigan Behavioral Health Workforce Research Center (2018) Estimating the Distribution of the U.S. Psychiatric Subspecialist Workforce. UMSPH, Ann Arbor, MI. Accessed January 21, 2022. https://www.behavioralhealthworkforce.org/wp-content/uploads/2019/02/Y3-FA2-P2-Psych-Sub_Full-Report-FINAL2.19.2019.pdf
US Department of Veterans Affairs (2014) Hospital at home - an innovative health care model. Accessed January 21, 2022. https://blogs.va.gov/VAntage/17166/hospital-at-home-an-innovative-health-care-model/
US Department of Health and Human Services, Health Resources and Services Administration (2021) Billing and coding medicare fee-for-Service claims. Accessed January 21, 2022. https://telehealth.hhs.gov/providers/billing-and-reimbursement/billing-and-coding-medicare-fee-for-service-claims/#telehealth-codes-covered-by-medicare
Van Zyl G (1964) Inventory control for perishable commodities, Ph.D. Dissertation, University of North Carolina, Chapel Hill
Weiss EN, Cohen MA, Hershey JC (1982) An iterative estimation and validation procedure for specification of semi-Markov models with application to hospital patient flow. Operations Research 30(6):1082–1104
Yankovic N, Green LV (2011) Identifying good nursing levels: a queuing approach. Operations Research 59(4):942–955
Zhong X, Li J, Bain PA, Musa AJ (2016) Electronic visits in primary care: Modeling, analysis, and scheduling policies. IEEE Trans Autom Sci Eng 14(3):1451–1466

Managing Common and Catastrophic Risks in the Airline Industry

David Pyke, Ruixia Shi, Soheil Sibdari, and Wenli Xiao

Abstract This chapter discusses risk management with a focus on the airline industry. The world has become acutely aware of major supply chain disruptions due to the COVID pandemic. Consumers, airline passengers, and companies are scrambling to understand and respond to these events. In that light, we begin the chapter with a brief overview of risk management, highlighting both common and catastrophic risks faced by companies and their supply chains. We then discuss approaches that companies employ to mitigate them. Our primary goal is to explore the risks that airlines face and the approaches they take to manage them, including fuel hedging, capacity management, and ticket pricing. Based on company interviews and our firsthand experience, we note that the airlines typically make these decisions in silos. Therefore, we introduce an analytical model that explicitly integrates them. We derive analytical results and propose directions for future research. We conclude with summary comments about managing risks once the world moves past COVID.

Keywords Supply chain risk management · Airline risk management · Fuel cost · Hedging · Airline pricing · Airline capacity management

1 Introduction

Dr. Morris Cohen has studied risk management in a variety of contexts over many years. From his extensive research on inventory management, and in particular, service parts inventory (Cohen et al. 1986, 1999; Deshpande et al. 2003; Guajardo

D. Pyke (✉) · R. Shi · W. Xiao
Knauss School of Business, University of San Diego, San Diego, CA, USA
e-mail: davidpyke@sandiego.edu; rshi@sandiego.edu; wenlixiao@sandiego.edu

S. Sibdari
Charlton College of Business, University of Massachusetts Dartmouth, North Dartmouth, MA, USA
e-mail: ssibdari@umassd.edu

H. Lee et al. (eds.), *Creating Values with Operations and Analytics*, Springer Series in Supply Chain Management 19, https://doi.org/10.1007/978-3-031-08871-1_13

and Cohen 2018, to cite just a few), to work on operational flexibility and exchange rate risk with Arnd Huchzermeier (Huchzermeier and Cohen 1996), to recent strategic perspectives on disruptive shocks (Cohen and Kouvelis 2021), Dr. Cohen has inspired many students, colleagues, and researchers worldwide to advance this critical area. This chapter builds on Dr. Cohen's research as we examine risk management with a focus on the airline industry. In Sect. 2, we provide a brief overview of risk management, highlighting approaches to managing high probability common risks and low-probability catastrophic risks. Section 3 discusses risks and risk management in the airline industry. In Sect. 4, we introduce an analytical model for coordinated risk management for an airline, and in Sect. 5, we provide summary comments and thoughts about managing risks once the world moves past COVID.

2 Defining and Managing Risk

Risk is often defined as the probability of an event (typically negative) and its impact. Risk management is a process designed to identify potential events that may affect a company or other entity and to manage the risks to be within its risk appetite. Thus, risk management entails event identification, assessing the likelihood and impact of these events, and responding to them. Risk responses may be taken in advance of an event by, for instance, avoiding, reducing, or sharing the risk or by reacting and recovering should adverse events occur.

Figure 1 illustrates risk likelihood and impact and has provided a useful way for companies to categorize the severity of potential adverse events. Abstracting from Fig. 1, one can think of two primary categories of risk—high-probability common risks and low-probability catastrophic risks.

Impact

Likelihood	Negligible	Low	Moderate	Very High	Extreme
Almost certain	Moderate	Major	High	Serve	Severe
Likely	Moderate	Significant	Major	High	Severe
Moderate	Low	Moderate	Significant	Major	High
Unlikely	Very low	Low	Moderate	Significant	Major
Rare	Very low	Very low	Low	Moderate	Significant

Fig. 1 Risk likelihood and impact

Common risks include, for instance, normal fluctuations in currency exchange rates. In the supply chain context, they include moderate delays in shipments and fluctuations in demand. Shipment delays can be due to weather events, such as snowstorms, delays at customs, queues at ports, and so on. Fluctuations in demand can be the result of competitor pricing, promotions, weather, and other underlying randomness in consumer behavior.

There has been extensive research, as well as developments in software and business processes, on managing common supply chain risks. For example, setting inventory levels optimally can both improve service and reduce costs. Dr. Cohen's research has been highly influential in this area. The use of time buffers can help mitigate the impact of shipping delays. These tools can reduce the impact of the relevant risks without changing their likelihood. A potentially more powerful approach is to reduce the variability of demand or lead time by employing advances in supply chain coordination. Sales and Operations Planning (S&OP), for instance, aims to provide the operations and supply chain functions with advanced notice of, say, sales promotions or new major contracts. It also can provide the Sales team with awareness of capacity constraints or inventory shortages. S&OP is a process that is often internal to the firm. Coordination with supply chain partners expands the communication to upstream and downstream companies. Coordinated Planning, Forecasting and Replenishment (CPFR) and Vendor Managed Inventory (VMI) allow firms to plan in advance for promotions, capacity constraints, inventory challenges, and other disruptions. These tools can decrease the likelihood of adverse events by providing early notification.

Low-probability, highly disruptive events are represented toward the right lower corner of Fig. 1. These include extreme weather or geologic events, such as the tsunami that inundated Fukushima, Japan in March of 2011 or the Eyjafjallajökull, Iceland volcano eruption in April of 2010. In both cases, important supply chain participants were affected. It was no surprise that suppliers in the Fukushima area shut down for an extended time. The Eyjafjallajökull eruption, on the other hand, created unanticipated effects. It released huge amounts of ash which soon disrupted 29% of global air traffic. Within days, factories as far away as Cleveland shut down for lack of components. Other catastrophic events in recent memory include the Great Recession of the late 2000s, the Asian financial crisis of the late 1990s, and of course the COVID-19 pandemic.

Perhaps one positive outcome from the COVID pandemic is the increasing awareness among journalists and the broader public about supply chains. Early reporting was frustratingly inaccurate and had glaring gaps. For example, CNN reported on April 29, 2020 that "public, private health labs may *never* be able to meet demand for coronavirus testing over supply chain shortages," (emphasis added) even though no one could figure out the reason for the shortages. One cause was eventually identified as nasal swabs, for which there were only two CDC-approved manufacturers in the world. As it happens, both companies were located in regions severely impacted by COVID, and neither was (not surprisingly) prepared for the dramatic surge in demand. A famous quote is certainly fitting: "*For want of a nail, the shoe was lost. For want of a shoe, the horse was lost. For want of a horse, the rider was lost. For want of a rider, the battle was lost.*" Of course, testing requires many more components than swabs, suggesting numerous potential points of failure for the supply chain. See the Sidebar: components of the Molecular Testing Process for a, perhaps not exhaustive, list of components required.

Sidebar: Components of Molecular Testing Process

Lab Personnel to Prepare Kits
Lab coat
Gloves
Mask

Kit
Box
Foam
Tubes
Swabs

Transport Medium
Hanks Balanced Salt Solution (HBSS) 1X with calcium and magnesium ions
Heat-inactivated fetal bovine serum
Gentamicin sulfate
Amphotericin B

Tester
Sanitizer
Gloves
Gown
Mask
Face shield/protective eyewear

Patient
Sanitizer
Face mask

Lab Tech Taking Sample
Lab coat
Gloves
Mask

Test Prep
Primer/probe mixes
Positive control
Human specimen control
Enzyme master mix
RNA extraction kit

Running the Test
Vortex mixer
Microcentrifuge
Micropipettes
Multichannel micropipettes
Racks for microcentrifuge tubes
Cold blocks
PCR system and software
Extraction system instruments
Molecular grade water
Bleach
DNAZap
RNAse Away
Aerosol barrier pipette tips
Microcentrifuge tubes
PCR reaction plates

Storage
Box
Foam
Cold block
Ice pack
Dry ice if needed for shipping

Reducing the likelihood of these catastrophic events may be impossible. However, it may be feasible to reduce their impact, even though costs may increase in the process. Many companies have developed explicit backup plans that they can deploy if an adverse event occurs. Some firms retain multiple suppliers in different regions, being careful to account for political stability, currency exchange rates, lead times, and shipping lanes. Others maintain excess capacity or inventory. Tesla employs in-house software engineering expertise and uses chips that can perform multiple functions, which has enabled the company to remain somewhat immune from the global shortage of semiconductors during the pandemic. Having visibility to extended layers of the supply chain is valuable as well. Recently, some supply chains have implemented blockchain solutions to enhance visibility and transparency. Finally, it may be possible to buy insurance or to share risk in other ways with supply chain partners. Because the literature on risk management is enormous, we point the reader to one excellent overview, Kouvelis et al. (2012), and the references therein.

3 Risk Management for the Airlines

Airlines face enormous risks that range across both the common and catastrophic categories, some of which mirror those mentioned in the previous section. Their common risks include fluctuations in fuel prices, variations in passenger demand, weather delays, and variable currency exchange rates. A major operational goal of the airlines in managing these risks is achieving and maintaining high load factors. The load factor is the ratio of passenger miles traveled to available seat miles (ASMs), and as such is a measure of capacity utilization. ASM is a measure that counts the total available seats in one mile of flight operation. Because the cost of an additional passenger is very small relative to the incremental revenue, high load factors are critical to airline profitability. In the early 2000s, average load factors for U.S. airlines in the domestic market hovered around 65% to 75%. In the few years before COVID, load factors had increased to around 85%, significantly improving profitability. To achieve these load factors, airlines carefully manage capacity and pricing. Capacity (or ASM) can be managed by adjusting both flight frequency on given routes and aircraft size. Travelers will notice variations in the number of flights per day on a given route, depending on the season, the state of the economy, and other factors. Aircraft size, for this purpose, is defined as the number of seats on the plane. Typically, aircraft manufacturers introduce a base model or platform that can be extended to several new versions. These extensions thus can increase the number of seats without major adjustments to staff training. The Boeing 737-700, for instance, has 137 seats, while the 737-800 has 175, and the 737 Max has 200. Minor adjustments can be made within each model by "upgauging" or adding seats to existing aircraft. Airlines can increase the number of seats on the 737-700 to 143 by installing new seats or decreasing legroom. Major changes to ASM and flight frequency can take months, and of course purchasing new aircraft involves very long lead times. Over the past 18 years, flight frequency for domestic airlines has generally decreased, while aircraft size has trended higher, although with significant short-term variability. Average ASM for these airlines fluctuates but clearly tracks the state of the U.S. economy. (See Pyke and Sibdari 2019.)

Fuel is either the highest or the second highest component of airlines' operational costs, depending on fuel cost fluctuations. Not surprisingly, the average cost per gallon of jet fuel very closely tracks the price of crude oil. In the past two decades, crude oil has increased from $20 per barrel to nearly $140, just prior to the Great

Recession. Oil plummeted in 2008 to around $40 per barrel, before increasing to over $100 as the economy recovered. At this writing, a barrel of West Texas Intermediate is around $77. One approach the airlines have used, with mixed success, in response to these severe fluctuations is hedging fuel costs. Southwest famously hedged around 70% of their fuel consumption prior to 2008, when the spot price was about $100. The financial results were extremely positive, which led other airlines to aggressively hedge fuel costs. Unfortunately, when prices collapsed in 2008, some airlines amassed huge losses because of poor hedging bets. Some airlines abandoned hedging altogether, while others continued, with perhaps more sophistication. The pandemic again dealt a blow to hedging policies, as capacity and oil prices declined sharply. Airlines that locked in a quantity of fuel to purchase at a specified price were faced with the obligation to buy fuel that they did not need. In its 2020 Annual Report, Lufthansa reported that the significant drop in capacity and oil prices due to the pandemic meant that it was over-hedged, and its hedging losses could not be recouped by lower fuel expenses.

Airlines can use a variety of hedging strategies, including futures contracts, call and put options, and swaps. They may also employ a complicated mix of these and other strategies. Each strategy has advantages and disadvantages, depending on the level of risk the airline wishes to accept, the premium built into certain strategies, and the actual market outcome. Some strategies limit the airlines' exposure to higher prices but do not provide benefit should prices decrease. Other strategies allow airlines to have the best of both situations, i.e., paying the market price when prices decrease, and hedging when prices increase, but these strategies come with an upfront premium expense.

For airlines that operate or purchase items globally, currency exchange rate fluctuations can impact profitability. As a result, many hedge relevant currencies. At one global airline, subsidiaries report exposure to 65 foreign currencies. Some of these are hedged using financial instruments, while some are aggregated to create natural hedges. A natural hedge occurs when cash inflows and outflows in different currencies net out and thus reduce exposure. Firms can also manage natural hedges by collecting revenues in the currency they use to pay costs. Residual risk is then managed by using financial hedges.

A powerful tool airlines use to manage load factors and profitability is pricing and revenue management. Revenue management employs sophisticated mathematical algorithms based on the time remaining until a flight's departure date, the open seats on the flight, and the forecast of demand. These algorithms maximize expected revenue, while accounting for possible overbooking and any associated financial penalties and loss of customer goodwill. Prices can change daily and even hourly in some cases.

Before we introduce a model that analyzes three approaches to managing common risks (fuel hedging, capacity management, and pricing), we first briefly discuss low-probability, highly disruptive risks in the airline context. At this writing, the world is entering year 3 of the COVID pandemic, and many people are keenly aware of the catastrophic risks faced by the airlines. While the Fukushima tsunami had a long-term impact on many companies and supply chains, the effect on global airlines was limited. Macroeconomic swings, on the other hand, can profoundly influence airline profitability. The Asian financial crisis, the recession after 9/11 and the tech crash of the early 2000s, and the Great Recession, all led to significant distress for the airlines. In addition, competition on given routes from low-cost airlines can fundamentally alter an airline's profitability. As we have observed recently with COVID, airlines respond to such events by decreasing capacity, canceling aircraft orders, and selectively furloughing or laying off pilots and staff. Furthermore, the industry has experienced many bankruptcies, mergers, and restructurings over the past few decades. Airlines are intentional about outsourcing certain routes to subsidiaries or independent regional airlines. As well, the industry has relied on government bailouts when available. Over the first two years of the pandemic, the U.S. Congress passed several airline relief programs that awarded $54 billion in grants to U.S. airlines, with the condition that they would limit dividends, layoffs, pay increases for senior executives, and stock buybacks. In April of 2020, the government also awarded $10 billion to airports as part of the Coronavirus Aid, Relief, and Economic Security (CARES) Act. The FAA adjusted training requirements, air traffic control tower hours, and requirements for temporary parking for aircraft. Even with these measures, flights may be canceled at an alarming rate. At this writing during the holiday season of 2021, thousands of flights are being canceled because of COVID-related staff shortages (as well as severe winter weather).

As noted above, these actions may limit the impact of catastrophic events, but they cannot change their likelihood. On the other hand, it may be possible for airlines to influence both the likelihood and impact of common risks by employing hedging, capacity management, and revenue management tools. From our experience with airlines and discussions with airline executives, however, it is evident that these three decisions are handled in different departments, with limited communication among them. We are interested in examining the potential improvement in profitability if the airlines made these decisions in an integrated way. We begin to address this issue by introducing an analytical model in the next section.

4 Model for Integrated Risk Management: Maximization of Expected Profit

In this section, we present a stylized model of an airline's decisions on fuel hedging, capacity, and pricing, and we propose an integrated approach that explicitly links the decisions. The airlines make these decisions at different times with respect to a given flight. Hedging decisions are generally made infrequently and are established well in advance of a given flight. Capacity adjustments can be made several months before a flight, but once the flight is posted for passenger booking, airlines are reluctant to change the number of seats. Indeed, they may pay a penalty if a change results in passengers being bumped. Pricing decisions, on the other hand, can be made very frequently and very close the actual flight. Therefore, we consider the three decisions in sequence: percent of fuel to be hedged (h), followed by capacity (k), and finally average price (p), with the objective of maximizing expected profit.

Passenger demand is a function of price, with a random shock to account for underlying demand variability. To facilitate the analysis, we define average price in terms of \$/seat-mile. Capacity is measured by ASM, or the total number of seat miles flown, and the profit function includes a term for the product of capacity, k, and actual fuel cost per seat-mile (CPS). We define the hedging decision, h, as the percentage of total fuel consumption to be hedged. Fuel cost (c) is variable and is measured in \$/seat-mile. As noted above, airlines may use a mix of hedging strategies, some of which build in a premium that accounts for the risk to the other party in the contract. Our stylized model does not attempt to capture the complexity of the possible hedging strategies. Rather, we assume that hedging removes fuel cost uncertainty for the portion of fuel consumption that is hedged, but this requires a premium. We define this premium as a factor, m, and assume that it increases with the standard deviation of c.

Clearly, reality is much more complex than our stylized model, but our ultimate intent is to gain insights that are valuable to airline management and that can lead to a more comprehensive analysis. We first introduce relevant notation, summarized in Table 1, and the objective function. For this model, the objective function maximizes expected profit in a non-competitive context. Later research will address the maximization of a mean–variance formulation, which accounts for risk aversion, as well as a set of numerical results based on representative airline data. To facilitate the current analysis, we rewrite the airline's capacity in terms of a "stocking factor." Finally, we solve the model sequentially by assuming a fixed capacity and hedging percentage and solving for the optimal average price. Given the optimal price, we then solve for the optimal capacity and finally the optimal hedging percentage.

Table 1 Summary of notations

Symbol	Definition
p	Average airfare (decision variable), $\$/seat\ mile$
k	Airline's capacity (decision variable), available seat-miles (ASMs) $ASM = total\ number\ of\ seats * miles\ of\ flight$
h	Percentage of hedging (decision variable)
$D(p) = a - bp + \varepsilon$	Demand, which depends on the airfare and is random
ε	Demand shock that is airfare independent. Let $F(x)$ and $f(x)$ be the distribution and density function of ε, respectively. In addition, let $\bar{F}(x) = 1 - F(x)$. Without loss of generality, we assume that $E(\varepsilon) = 0$. $STD(\varepsilon) = \sigma_d$. The lower and upper limits of the domain for ε are l_d and u_d, respectively
c	Fuel cost ($\$/seat\ mile$). Let $G(x)$ and $g(x)$ be the distribution and density function of c, respectively. $E(c) = \mu_c$ and $STD(c) = \sigma_c$
m	Premium for hedging which increases with σ_c

4.1 Objective Function and Sequence of Events

For a given airfare p, capacity k, percentage of hedging h, realization of ε, and the airline's actual fuel cost per seat-mile (hereafter, CPS for short), the airline's profit is $p\min[a - bp + \varepsilon, k] - kCPS$. Taking the expectation with respect to ε and CPS, we obtain the expected profit of the airline

$$\pi(h, k, p) = pE\ min[a - bp + \varepsilon, k] - k[hm\mu_c + (1 - h)\mu_c]. \tag{1}$$

Note that if $\sigma_c = 0$, then $m = 1$; i.e., if there is no variability, the airline would have no incentive to hedge, and its expected fuel cost would be μ_c. On the other hand, if $\sigma_c > 0$ and a firm offers the airline a no-premium contract (i.e., $m = 1$), the airline could eliminate variability at no cost and therefore would have an incentive to hedge all of its fuel purchases. If $m < 1$, the airlines would have an arbitrage opportunity that does not exist in such contracts. Therefore, in our model, we restrict m to be greater than 1.

The sequence of events is given as follows. First, the airline determines the percentage of hedging, h, to maximize its expected profit. Second, the capacity decision, k, is determined by the airline. And lastly, the airline decides on the price (i.e., airfare) to charge to the consumers. We solve the problem backward (see the analysis below) by first solving for the airfare p, and then the capacity k, and lastly the hedging percentage h.

4.2 Analysis

We present the analysis of solving the game in this subsection. First, we show how the price (i.e., average airfare) is determined.

To facilitate the analysis, we write the airline's capacity k in terms of the airfare p and a *stocking factor* z; specifically, $k = a - bp + z$. The airline's expected profit in Eq. (1) can be written as

$$\begin{aligned}
\pi(h, k, p) &= pE\ min[a - bp + \varepsilon, a - bp + z] - (a - bp + z)[hm\mu_c + (1 - h)\mu_c] \\
&= p(a - bp) + pE\min(\varepsilon, z) - (a - bp + z)[hm\mu_c + (1 - h)\mu_c] \\
&= p(a - bp) + p\left[\int_{l_d}^{z} xf(x)dx + \int_{z}^{u_d} zf(x)dx\right] \\
&\quad -(a - bp + z)[hm\mu_c + (1 - h)\mu_c].
\end{aligned}$$

Let $L(z) = \int_{l_d}^{z} xf(x)dx + \int_{z}^{u_d} zf(x)dx$. The airline's expected profit is

$$\pi(h, k, p) = p(a - bp) + pL(z) - (a - bp + z)[hm\mu_c + (1 - h)\mu_c].$$

Using the first-order condition, we can obtain the optimal value of p, which is

$$p = \frac{a + b[hm\mu_c + (1 - h)\mu_c] + L(z)}{2b}.$$

After obtaining the price p, we are ready to solve for the stocking factor k. Recall that $k = a - bp + z$. To get the optimal k, we need to obtain the optimal z value. Since $p = \frac{a+b[hm\mu_c+(1-h)\mu_c]+L(z)}{2b}$, $p'(z) = L'(z)/2b$. We also know that $L'(z) = \bar{F}(z)$.

Recall that the airline's expected profit is

$$\pi(h, k, p) = p(a - bp) + pL(z) - (a - bp + z)[hm\mu_c + (1 - h)\mu_c].$$

Taking first-order derivative with respect to z, we have

$$\frac{d\pi}{dz} = \{a + b[hm\mu_c + (1 - h)\mu_c] + L(z)\} \frac{\bar{F}(z)}{2b} - [hm\mu_c + (1 - h)\mu_c].$$

Using the first-order condition, the optimal value of z satisfies

$$\{a + b[hm\mu_c + (1 - h)\mu_c] + L(z)\} \bar{F}(z) - 2b[hm\mu_c + (1 - h)\mu_c] = 0. \quad (2)$$

Last, the optimal hedging percentage h can be solved. From Eq. (2), we have

$$hm\mu_c + (1 - h)\mu_c = \frac{[a + L(z)]\bar{F}(z)}{b[1 + F(z)]}. \quad (3)$$

$$p = \frac{a + L(z)}{b[1 + F(z)]}. \quad (4)$$

Using the airline's expected profit of

$$\pi(h, k, p) = p(a - bp) + pL(z) - (a - bp + z)[hm\mu_c + (1 - h)\mu_c],$$

we plug (3) and (4) into (2), to get the airline's expected profit in terms of the stocking factor z as follows:

$$\pi(z) = \frac{a + L(z)}{b[1 + F(z)]} \frac{aF(z) - L(z)}{1 + F(z)} + \frac{a + L(z)}{b[1 + F(z)]} L(z) - \left[\frac{aF(z) - L(z)}{1 + F(z)} + z\right] \frac{[a + L(z)]\bar{F}(z)}{b[1 + F(z)]}.$$

Using the first-order condition, we obtain the optimal z value that satisfies

$$[aF(z) - L(z)][a + L(z)][1 + F(z)]f(z) + zf(z)[a + L(z)][1 + F(z)]^2$$
$$+ \left\{[aF(z) + L(z)]\bar{F}(z) - [1 + F(z)]z\bar{F}(z)\right\}\left\{\bar{F}(z)[1 + F(z)] - [a + L(z)]f(z)\right\} = 0.$$

The following two lemmas characterize the airline's optimal airfare, optimal capacity, and percentage of hedging.

Lemma 1 *(i) The optimal airfare is* $p = \frac{a+L(z)}{b[a+F(z)]}$. *(ii) The airline's optimal capacity is* $k = \frac{aF(z)-L(z)}{1+F(z)} + z$. *(iii) The optimal airfare and airline's capacity are independent of the fuel cost and are solely determined by passenger demand.*

Lemma 2 *(i) The optimal percentage of hedging is* $h = \frac{p\bar{F}(z)-\mu_c}{(m-1)\mu_c}$.

It is a feature of the expected profit formulation that the optimal airfare and capacity are independent of fuel cost. Of course, the optimal percentage of hedging is dependent on fuel cost and the hedging premium. The optimal capacity is a function of passenger demand and the stocking factor, which is analogous to safety stock in an inventory system. However, none of the optimal values include σ_c. As noted above, future research will extend this formulation to account for risk aversion using a mean–variance formulation that, in addition to expected profit, incorporates a negative term with a risk aversion parameter and the variance of profit. Preliminary analytical results suggest that the optimal price, capacity, and hedging percentages each are complex functions of the other two decision variables, as well as the uncertainty in both passenger demand and fuel cost. We anticipate generating insights from the analytical results, in addition to those garnered from numerical results based on representative airline data. The goal is to yield insights into the potential for profit gain from integrating the three decisions, rather than making them in a decentralized way.

5 Summary

Regardless of the overall state of the industry as we emerge from the pandemic, the airlines will continue to face uncertainties in fuel cost and passenger demand. They will manage these mid- and short-term risks by selectively hedging, carefully managing capacity, and dynamically setting prices. We submit that their current decentralized approach to these decisions may be leaving profit on the table and that they will be well served to pursue a more integrated decision process. Enhancing communication and coordination among disparate groups can be extremely challenging. Many companies, for example, struggled to develop effective Sales and Operations Planning (S&OP) processes because of the differing objectives, and longstanding distrust, between sales and operations personnel. Nevertheless, with senior and functional area leadership, S&OP has become a valuable planning tool in numerous companies across a variety of industries. Our goal with this stream of airline research is to identify the potential profit gains from integrating these three key decisions. Such insights could spur senior leaders to undertake and support the hard work of creating effective processes and tools for joint optimization. In order to be convincing to industry leaders, however, it is important that data analyzed in the research be representative. In that light, we note the Bureau of Transportation Statistics, a source of free, massive and valuable databases that is aiding this research.

We close with some comments about leadership in the face of catastrophic risks, both for the airlines and for the broader business and public spheres. As the world recovers from COVID-19, the airlines may face a new normal. The disruption to the industry during the pandemic was unprecedented. By September 2020, passenger demand had declined by up to 75%, and by the end of 2020, it was down by 50%. Industry analysts and insiders suggested that it could take three to five years for the industry to return to normal operations (Calhoun 2020), while some say that it will never return. Whatever the outcome, in responding to this massive disruption, airlines surely will continue to use all the tools at their disposal. Some will not survive, and others will return but with more limited operations. No doubt some will thrive if worldwide demand rebounds, but it will take strong leadership, creativity, and vision to be in that group.

In the broader scope of global supply chains, the massive disruptions due to the pandemic have spurred firms to make some fundamental strategic and tactical shifts. Many have moved manufacturing or suppliers from China to Vietnam, Thailand, India, or other offshore locations. A number of firms have developed domestic or regional suppliers, resulting in reduced lead times but increased costs. The passion for lean supply chains has eased, and firms are more willing to hold additional inventory to buffer for long and uncertain lead times. They are looking carefully at their plans for risk mitigation and recovery, and they are seeking new ways to improve supply chain visibility. In the public sphere, governments are mandating stockpiles of personal protective equipment, ventilators, and other medical supplies. These actions seem wise and are certainly widely supported. Nevertheless, we are wary about the long-term commitment to these policies. Business and government leaders, due to incentives from the financial markets and voters, tend to have a decidedly short-term focus. Will they revert to a myopic focus on cost reduction at the expense of risk reduction? A brief episode from California may be instructive.

Shortly after Hurricane Katrina devastated New Orleans in 2005, then-governor Schwarzenegger announced that the state would invest more than $200 million "in a powerful set of medical weapons to deploy in the case of large-scale emergencies and natural disasters such as earthquakes, fires and pandemics." An impressive initiative followed with the acquisition of three 200-bed mobile hospitals that could be deployed within 72 h on 18-wheelers. These were fully insulated, HVAC-equipped, semi-permanent tents, each containing an emergency room, an intensive care unit, X-ray equipment, an operating room, and surgical wards. They were equipped with ventilators, a full complement of medications, and sleeping quarters for staff. In addition, the state stockpiled medicines and medical gear, including

50 million N95 respirators, 2,400 portable ventilators, and kits to set up 21,000 additional patient beds wherever they were needed. Just a few years later, in 2011, then-governor Jerry Brown came into office facing a $26-billion budget deficit. Among the ensuing cutbacks, the state eliminated the funds to store and maintain the stockpile of supplies and the mobile hospitals. As it happens, the hospitals were never used. Although much of the medical equipment was given to local hospitals and health agencies, the state did not provide any funding to maintain them. Respirators were allowed to expire without being replaced, and the supply of usable N95 respirators decreased to 21 million by the time COVID-19 arrived. The cost to maintain these programs was less than $5.8 million per year, on an annual state budget of about $129 billion. (See Williams et al. 2020.)

Will leaders, both business and government, take a long-term perspective that broadens their goals from a narrow focus on cost reduction? Will they be able to convince shareholders and voters that this perspective is worth the cost? We sincerely hope that our collective memory keeps alive the lessons from the pandemic.

References

Calhoun D (2020) Coronavirus pandemic could force a major U.S. airline out of business says Boeing CEO. NBC News 12 May 2020

Cohen MA, Kouvelis P (2021) Revisit of AAA excellence of global value chains: Robustness, resilience, and realignment. Product Oper Manag 30(3):633–643

Cohen MA, Kleindorfer P, Lee H (1986) Optimal stocking policies for low usage items in multi-echelon inventory systems. Naval Res Logist J 33:17–38

Cohen MA, Zheng Y-S, Wang Y (1999) Identifying opportunities for improving Teradyne's service-parts logistics system. Interfaces 29(4):1–18

Deshpande V, Cohen MA, Donohue K (2003) A threshold inventory rationing policy for service-differentiated demand classes. Management Science 49(6):683–703

Guajardo JA, Cohen MA (2018) Service differentiation & operating segments: A framework and an application to after-sales services. Manuf Serv Oper Manag 20(3):440–454

Huchzermeier A, Cohen MA (1996) Valuing operational flexibility under exchange rate risk. Operations Research 44(1):100–113

Kouvelis P, Dong L, Boyabatli O, Li R (eds) (2012) Handbook of integrated risk management in global supply chains. Wiley

Pyke DF, Sibdari S (2019) Risk management in the airline industry. In: Gong S, Cullinane K (eds) Finance and risk management for international logistics and the supply chain. Elsevier

Williams L, Evans W, Carless W (2020) California once had mobile hospitals and a ventilator stockpile. But it dismantled them. LA Times, 27 March 2020

Understanding Global Supply Chain and Resilience: Theory and Practice

Morris Cohen, Shiliang Cui, Sebastian Doetsch, Ricardo Ernst, Arnd Huchzermeier, Panos Kouvelis, Hau Lee, Hirofumi Matsuo, and Andy Tsay

Abstract This chapter summarizes the last 8 years of collaborative research of a global group of scholars on supply chain management and especially on how companies are dealing with uncertainties and disruptions. Starting with analyzing the factors that drive changes in global supply chain designs, this chapter describes how companies are coping with new types of disruptions such as trade conflicts, natural disasters, and pandemics. Commonly suggested resilience strategies like reshoring or regionalization are de-mystified and discussed based on first-level insights from interviews and survey data. Moreover, we analyzed how companies have handled different types of disruption and the underlying efficiency-resilience trade-offs. The chapter then outlines the different types of complexity and obstacles to supply chain resilience that companies have to overcome based on their individual

M. Cohen (✉)
The Wharton School, University of Pennsylvania, Philadelphia, PA, USA
e-mail: cohen@wharton.upenn.edu

S. Cui · R. Ernst
McDonough School of Business, Georgetown University, Washington, DC, USA
e-mail: shiliang.cui@georgetown.edu; ernstr@georgetown.edu

S. Doetsch · A. Huchzermeier
WHU–Otto Beisheim School of Management, Vallendar, Germany
e-mail: Sebastian.Doetsch@whu.edu; arnd.huchzermeier@whu.edu

P. Kouvelis
Olin Business School, Washington University in St. Louis, St. Louis, MO, USA
e-mail: kouvelis@wustl.edu

H. Lee
Graduate School of Business, Stanford University, Stanford, CA, USA
e-mail: haulee@stanford.edu

H. Matsuo
Institute for International Strategy, Tokyo International University, Kawagoe, Saitama, Japan
e-mail: hmatsuo@tiu.ac.jp

A. Tsay
Leavey School of Business, Santa Clara University, Santa Clara, CA, USA
e-mail: atsay@scu.edu

H. Lee et al. (eds.), *Creating Values with Operations and Analytics*, Springer Series in Supply Chain Management 19, https://doi.org/10.1007/978-3-031-08871-1_14

product characteristics, market environment, and supply chain setup. Finally, the need for measuring resilience is outlined and proposed resilience metrics are discussed.

Keywords Global supply chain design · Supply chain resilience · Resilience metrics · Implementation challenges · Empirical research

1 Introduction: Context and Research Motivation

Globalization of supply chains has increasingly become relevant to policy makers and the public. Advancements in technologies, removal of trade barriers, and growth in supply options from all around the globe have led to complex, multi-tiered supply chains. These global supply chains, which have tended to prioritize cost efficiency, have revealed their limitations in the face of disruptive events that have increased in frequency and severity. Drawing upon a large body of research on global supply chain management, an international group of supply chain scholars came together in 2014 with the goal of understanding how companies were adjusting their global supply chain design and strategies in response to a convergence of major economic, financial, political, and market changes. We started to examine how these factors were driving the redesign of supply chains and the reshaping of operational strategies and have continued to do so. This effort was not a response to any single event. At the time, labor costs appeared to be normalizing across geographies—in particular the US–China wage gap was closing fast. This, together with the strengthening of the Chinese currency, blunted one of the forces that had made China the factory to the world. Around this time frame, a series of systemic shocks disrupted thinking concerning the structure of global supply chains. This change was driven by politicians at the highest levels, who used their bully pulpit to push reshoring initiatives, US–China trade frictions, natural disasters such as Hurricane Harvey, and the global COVID-19 pandemic. Our early work was mostly directed at documenting and understanding adaptations of global supply chain design and strategies that were occurring within this context. The last 2 years have seen increased incidence of "black swan" disruptions of momentous impact, which has led some to argue that these kinds of events will not be so rare going forward. Accordingly, we directed our attention specifically to strategies intended to make global supply chains more resilient. This refocus immediately centered our attention on the tension between long-term efficiency and resilience, which has implications for key attributes of every global supply chain, including technology selection, the approach to outsourcing, the extent of multi-sourcing, and the geographical placement of activities. Our research builds on our team members' collective history of contemplating and contributing to the development of guidelines for global supply chain management, and aims to marry this perspective with data and insights collected, first-hand, from senior supply chain executives from global companies. Specifically, we wanted to understand how senior managers think about these issues, what actions they intend to pursue in the face of recent disruptions, and how they resolve the trade-off between resilience and the usual efficiency goals. Through interviews and surveys that examined real actions taken in response to present events and evolving probability assessments about the future, we built, mostly via an empirically grounded research and analysis approach, a conceptual framework to explain and guide the design of global supply chains at a level of granularity that is necessary to be useful but is lacking in typical studies.

As illustrated by Fig. 1, this chapter gives an overview of how our research evolved over the years (Parts 1 and 2), insights regarding supply chain strategies in different industries (Part 3), and managerial interpretation of our main findings (Part 6). We also outline the limitations of the current research as well as the new issues that emerged (Part 4 and 5) along with future research directions (Part 7).

This chapter addresses the following research questions:

1. What are the factors that will drive changes in global supply chain design and related strategies?
2. Do we expect to see a fundamental shift away from the comparative advantage model that has greatly influenced the design of global supply chains since the early 1990s? Regarding the moment at hand, will disruption risks and trade policies drive widespread reshoring? Will global supply chains evolve into a portfolio of regional supply chains?
3. How do companies design a priori and execute during and after disruptions in order to achieve supply chain resilience? What is the right balance between efficiency and resilience?
4. What explains the diversity of global supply chain designs and resilience strategies observed across industries and among companies in similar industries or even in different business units within a company?
5. How can company managers understand and overcome the specific obstacles to designing and executing profitable and resilient strategies based on lessons from how companies similar to theirs have responded to supply chain challenges?
6. What measures should be used to monitor improvements in resilience?

Answers to these questions were based on a variety of empirical findings derived from a survey, a series of structured interviews from a selected sample of companies that have developed successful global supply chain strategies and interactions with senior supply chain executives in roundtable sessions. The interviews focused on exploring responses to the current crisis as well as developing an understanding of each company's approach to defining their global supply chain strategy. This included a review of the structure and management policies used to drive both efficiency and resiliency. These inputs were all based on actual decisions made by the companies as well as their intentions and plans for the future.

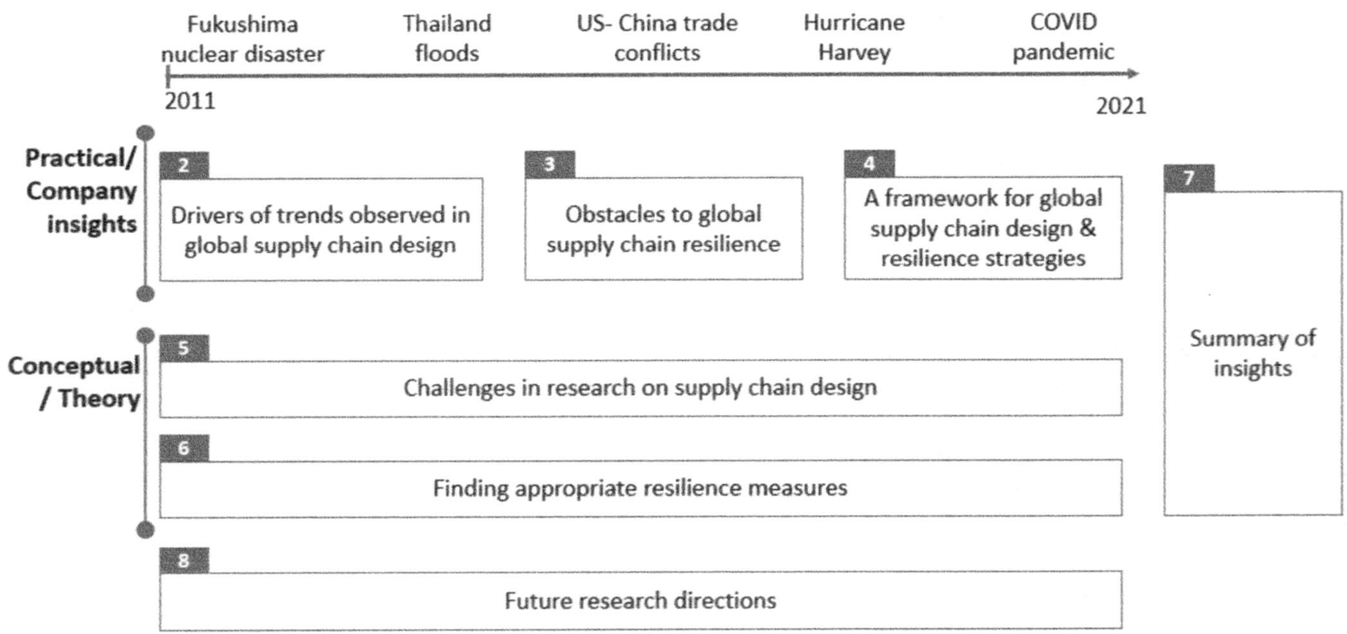

Fig. 1 Structure of this chapter

2 Pre-pandemic Study on Drivers of Trends in Global Supply Chains and Resilience

In a global benchmarking survey of 74 firms conducted in 2015–2016 on production sourcing decisions, we found that companies frequently restructured their global production footprints. The majority of firms engaged in offshoring. Following the 2016 US presidential election, the new administration focused on providing incentives to firms to reshore production activities, mostly from China. In a parallel development, the UK's decision to leave the European Union led politicians to pressure firms not to offshore from the UK. The popular media reported that reshoring to home markets (as defined by the location of the global headquarters or having the closest cultural affinity or heaviest representation in the executive ranks) was occurring. Our research, however, did not find empirical evidence of this occurring at a meaningful scale. In our survey data (85 detailed questionnaires completed by business units in companies regarding actual projects they had undertaken over the preceding 2 years), reshoring occurred rather infrequently, and seldom in response to trade tariffs and political incentives. Increases in capital investments away from Asia and into the USA or Europe were mostly not of a reshoring nature. For instance, we observed that the companies that made facility investments in the US were typically Asian and European firms seeking proximity to the US market or domestic players expanding capacity in their home market (which is not reshoring if this is not replacing supply that formerly came from offshore). None of the US companies in our sample closed a production site in Asia while expanding in the US. China remained the most attractive production location, followed by Eastern Europe and Southern Asia. In many cases, firms largely adhered to the principle of natural hedging, i.e., using a sourcing footprint that roughly matches the geographic footprint of demand. Thus, our findings support the view that the extent of actual reshoring has been exaggerated in press and industry reports (Fratocchi et al. 2014; Dachs et al. 2019).

Some other results of our previous work (see Cohen et al. 2018) point to the following factors to explain changes in global supply chain design:

1. Access to customers, quality, and supply chain performance were the main drivers for increasing production volume in China.
2. Increases in labor costs in China were the prime reason companies left China for lower cost locations.
3. Western Europe found near-shore cost advantages in sourcing from Eastern Europe and China.
4. North America was attractive as a market and attracted new production activity, but not necessarily at North American companies.
5. Multinational production activity in Japan decreased after the 2011 natural disaster.

Shortly thereafter, i.e., during 2017–2018, a major trade war between China and the US erupted. Some firms reacted by moving their operations to Southeast Asia or Mexico. In an effort to diversify sourcing, but recognizing the necessity of using quality Chinese sources, some companies adopted a multi-sourcing strategy termed "China Plus One," i.e., using sources located in China to primarily serve the growing Chinese and Asian markets, while using alternative sources positioned elsewhere to serve other markets. In an executive roundtable we organized in 2018 on the topic of "global operations in turbulent times," senior supply chain executives of world-class global companies confirmed their use of such policies. The discussion in that roundtable and reports describing the last 4 years indicate that US trade tariffs did not work effectively as an incentive for reshoring or for a substantial reduction in sourcing flows from China for most industries. In a few cases, North American companies dealing with retaliatory tariffs in other regions ended up making capacity investments in these regions. Consumers in all regions paid higher prices or even experienced shortages as result of flow adjustments and decreased inventories of some affected goods. The tariff uncertainty led to reluctance for ordering some goods with longer lead times, and when the pandemic hit Western European and US markets, companies were caught with less buffer to absorb the early shock. Moreover, the changes in trade policies had already nudged companies to identity non-China sources that worked well for lower skill or less knowledge-intensive processes with older mature products. While our research group did not pursue a specific study of the impact of trade-tariff factors on global supply chains, some members did explore related issues in recent papers (see Cohen and Lee 2020; Dong and Kouvelis 2020).

3 Obstacles to Global Supply Chain Resilience

While our previous work focused on how global supply chains changed in response to factor changes over a long period (the first 15 years of our new century), the COVID-19 pandemic shifted our emphasis to understanding the resilience of global supply chains in the presence of major unexpected events. In Cohen et al. (2021b), we first address what constitutes supply chain resilience, and then investigate why known resilience strategies are not implemented to the extent expected.

Our first task in the above work was to distinguish between resilience and agility in the context of supply chains. The short-term reaction of companies to major disruptions is to leverage their operational flexibility to address urgent supply shortages or demand surges, consequently surviving or even thriving in the near term. The popular media, consulting reports, and even some academic work, often label this as resiliency. Lee (2004) and Cohen and Kouvelis (2021) argue that agility is the better descriptor in this case. Cohen et al. (2021b) define agility as "the ability to respond rapidly and cost-effectively to short-term changes in demand or supply disruptions." Resilience of supply chains encompasses a longer-term ex-ante behavior. Cohen et al. (2021b) frame resilience as the design and adoption of ex-post recourse actions, which are executed in reaction to the disruptive event. We thus define resilience as "the ability to adapt to structural changes by modifying supply chain, products and technologies strategies." Agility can be achieved through rebalancing asset deployment (such as inventory) to address local shortages, using overtime, or employing expedite shipments. This will solve an immediate problem but will not provide a longer-term solution that requires resiliency. A longer-term strategy to achieve resilience can be based on identifying bottlenecks in the supply chain that lead to long lead times and uncertain supply. Policies to mitigate this problem can be derived from restructuring the supply chain network, i.e., finding different suppliers and sources. This, however, will do little to alleviate a problem in the short-term. Thus, we can only evaluate resilience based on observed performance over long periods and in response to multiple events.

While (supply chain) resilience became the center of conversation as companies around the world responded to COVID-19 and other crises, this attribute generally has not been displayed by many global companies in the last 20 years. We argue that some companies exhibit less resilience than others, not merely because they do not know the recipe for a resilient supply chain. Certainly, many books (Sheffi 2007; Hopp 2011) and articles (e.g., John et al. 2020; Cohen and Kouvelis 2021 and references therein) have discussed aspects of the recipe (e.g., including redundancy in process design, multi-sourcing, and holding inventory and capacity buffers as well as designing products with operational flexibility in mind, by using well-known principles such as component commonality and postponement). This suggests that the basic roadmap to supply chain resiliency is generally understood by managers. So why then is supply chain resilience more the exception than the rule? Cohen et al. (2021b) reported on our investigation of the implementation obstacles that are missing from or are underemphasized in the existing mainstream and academic literature, and which support the conclusion that there is a "knowing-doing gap" (Pfeffer and Sutton 2000).

We identified six obstacles based on interviews of senior supply chain executives:

1. Heterogeneity of supply chains: Companies may have different supply chains for each product group, which makes a one-size-fits-all resilience strategy inappropriate.
2. Fragmentation of the decision-making architecture: Multiple supply chain actors need to be coordinated (meaning through both synchronization of action and incentive alignment) to achieve supply chain resilience. Complexity and conflicts of interest can quickly arise without deliberate efforts to counteract them.
3. Accentuated efficiency and resilience trade-offs: The best compromise between cost efficiency and resilience is not easy to achieve even in a simple setting, let alone in one which contains multiple divisions and functions within a company that may have disparate priorities.
4. Resource limitations: All companies have limited resources (e.g., cash) and thus have to prioritize activities (e.g., moving sales online) that enable survival through COVID-19 or any other crisis at hand. This can cause de-prioritization of efforts to enhance resilience, which oftentimes require big upfront investments whose ROI might not be realized for a long time, if ever.

5. Existing factor market limitations: A company's options for resilience are constrained by the technical and business capabilities of its supply base.
6. Lack of needed supply chain financing and insufficient government incentives: A supply chain is only as strong as its weakest link. A company may therefore need to provide financial support to its supply chain partners. The required capital can be a barrier to implementation.

Our discussion with executives from companies from different industries made it clear that the nature of their product markets, technological sophistication of their products, operation of their supplier networks, production process complexity, and logistics and distribution aspects of their businesses all heavily influence which obstacles assume priority in their environment. Highly sophisticated product companies that are at the forefront of technology often struggle more with limitations in accessing factor markets for required source materials, high-quality suppliers and elite engineering talent. One example from our interviews would be a leading US company that focuses on storage and network technology, e.g., servers. Similar to many other information technology companies, it has outsourced most of its production and thus inherits the constraints of its contract manufacturers, which strongly limit the footprint of choices. Such companies are limited in the execution of a diverse manufacturing footprint and the use of multi-sourcing by the tremendous amount of financial resources and management development efforts required in their industry. Often the solution comes from using new technologies to redesign products, through increasing the product integrality, changing the scale and level of automation of production processes for creating mix flexibility, and/or making investments to increase ownership and control of their supply chains. But this "design-for-resilience" rethinking of products and processes in technology uncertainty environments is often perceived as risky long-term thinking by executives, and thus is often abandoned for easier to execute acquisition and consolidation strategies, which are favored by financial shareholders and markets.

Companies with highly diverse product portfolios to serve multiple product markets with different priorities, typically are exposed to the complex portfolio of loosely coordinated and conflicting priority supply chain processes that are present in their environment. They often end up with complex multi-tier networks of transactional suppliers, limited deep-tier visibility, and confusing global organizational structures. Companies such as Unilever, Colgate, or Nike fall into this category. Their presence in environments with weak infrastructure and supporting regulations via deep-tier suppliers is motivated by the promise of cheaper materials and low-cost labor. This logic of efficiency has motivated the modular nature of their products, with a large portion of them outsourced. This results in multi-tier networks of deep-tier, potentially problematic suppliers. For these chains, efficiency is the competitive imperative, and their shareholders view resilience strategies, such as excess capacities and buffer inventories, as wasteful investments and a bad use of working capital. The most successful among them try to reduce product and process complexity and design better-coordinated supply chain processes within a hierarchical supply chain organization (with some centralized processes that leverage scale and global access, and some independence of activities reflecting efficiency and responsiveness trade-offs of their product markets).

One example for a successful hierarchical structuring of a very diversified product portfolio of about 1 million SKUs from over 20,000 suppliers is Emerson, a US company that manufactures products and provides engineering services for a wide range of industrial, commercial, and consumer markets. Their first-level corporate strategy is designed to set guidelines and standards across all business units, e.g., for contracts, dual sourcing or go-to-market strategies. They also leverage commodities where scale matters, e.g., steel, electronics, and use an internal, centrally operated logistics network. Management of their business units is achieved by controlling outcomes in terms of performance metrics such as lead time and customer service. Whenever possible, in terms of access to materials and suppliers, these companies revert to shortening their supply chains by reducing lead times through market-focused regional strategies. For these companies, their complex supplier network with limited ensuing visibility of often smaller and under-resourced suppliers requires attention to systematic supply risk management. But the complexity, continuous long-term commitment and resource intensity of risk management programs can result in paralysis, and abandoned or short-term, ill-fated projects. Resilience is discussed immediately after a disruptive event, but as soon as some recovery is achieved, efficiency becomes the immediate priority. Of course, these limitations can be observed in any company with poor management, but we suggest that they are especially relevant for the class of companies with diverse product portfolios.

4 A Framework for Global Supply Chain Resilience Strategies

Our research then shifted into learning from the pandemic crisis by reviewing the response of world-class supply chains. We also compared the measures used to increase resilience in practice with what the deductive analytical literature prescribes. We found a theory-practice gap that suggests that the widely accepted concepts of a "customized supply chain," meaning a supply chain that is "custom-tailored" for the business, and "supply chain resilience" are not sufficient on their own. Therefore, we introduce the concept of "Bespoke Supply Chain Resilience" which is based on the fact that different customized supply chains have different resilience requirements and therefore require different strategies to achieve resilience. Companies with a portfolio of supply chains therefore need to identify multiple supply chain specific resilience solutions that account for the different constraints and trade-offs they are facing. For example, for a company such as Henkel, which operates three different business units with three different supply chains, there is no single company-wide resilience strategy. Rather there is one strategy for their adhesives business and another for their beauty care business, where rapid changes are needed to achieve resilience.

Our intention in this section is not to review the methodology used to build a comprehensive conceptual framework of the resilience lessons, but rather to demonstrate how executives can use the framework for developing supply chain strategies that will be effective in the face of future disruptions. There is a long history of developing normative models for supply chain design based on analytic optimization models (see relevant references in Cohen et al. 2018). These models mostly focus on supporting optimal production network configurations associated with global sourcing for an after-tax profit-optimizing firm over a long planning horizon. However, there is a lot less research and understanding of how companies should adjust in the short-to-medium term, to changes in major factors, such as labor rates in different countries, exchange rates, trade policies, and, with increasing significance over the last 10 years, as well as to major disruptions (e.g., earthquakes, tsunamis, major industrial accidents, and an unprecedented pandemic).

In Cohen et al. (2021a), we developed an empirically grounded analysis of global supply chain resilience, based on interviews of senior supply chain executives across major companies in different industries. We applied a granular unit of analysis based on product groups or business units within the companies. This allowed us to identify patterns of resilience strategies for supply chains across multiple companies and industries. This led to our "Bespoke Supply Chain Resilience" framework for clustering supply chains along two dimensions, which we referred to as the "Triple-P SC framework" (see Fig. 2). This framework represents the current thinking of supply chain executives that we observed and was compared to approaches proposed in the SC and OM literature. This led to the definition of three archetypes, i.e.,

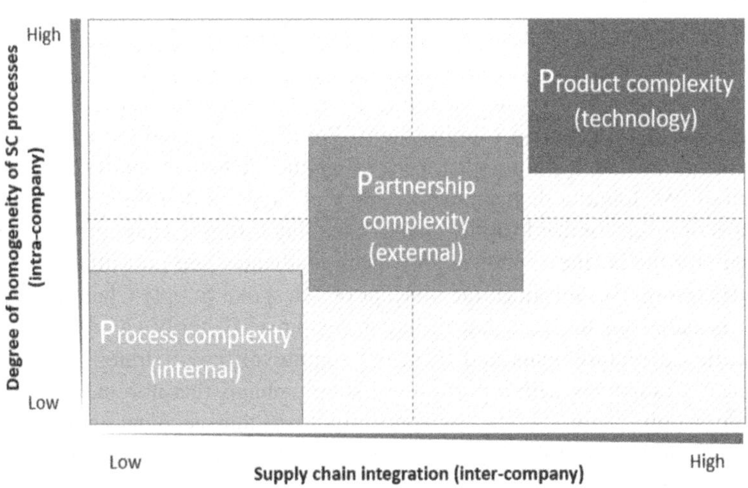

Fig. 2 Triple-P supply chain resilience archetypes

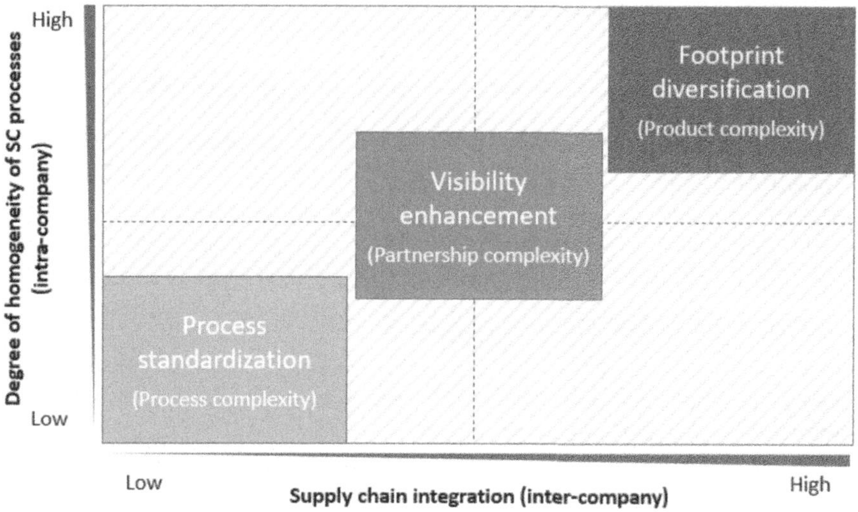

Fig. 3 Common resilience strategies based on Triple-P archetype classification

typical supply chain designs that emerged from a cluster analysis of 26 supply chains. The corresponding common resilience strategies are indicated in Fig. 3.

Our analysis revealed two main dimensions for clustering supply chains across companies and industries based on their responses to uncertainty. These two dimensions, which we refer to as "major influencers of resilience strategy," are *Homogeneity of internal supply chain processes* and *Integration with other actors in their supply chains*. In our clustering analysis, we defined four stages of SC process homogeneity (sorted from low to high homogeneity) and five degrees of supply chain integration (sorted from low to high integration). This resulted in the positioning illustrated in Fig. 2 based on the scatter plot of Fig. 4 (refer to Cohen et al. 2021a, b, for more details).

With respect to product architecture, we identified the following operational features: product complexity, homogeneity of product portfolio, degree of product modularity, and level of product customization. With respect to the supply chain process, we identified the following features: availability of potential suppliers, level of pull (vs. push), length of lead time, and degree of (manufacturing) outsourcing. Analysis of all of the supply chains in our sample showed that we could use these operational attributes to define the three supply chain "archetypes" to enhance our understanding of observed resilience strategies.

To further narrow the list of attributes, we noted that "availability of potential suppliers" and "homogeneity of product portfolio" were the two most distinguishing attributes, followed by "product complexity," "lead time," and "level of pull."

Companies that have homogeneous portfolios of high complexity products (mostly industrial, and often with B2B transactions), and with limited availability of select skills suppliers, design global supply chains using "one-size-fits-all" (usually

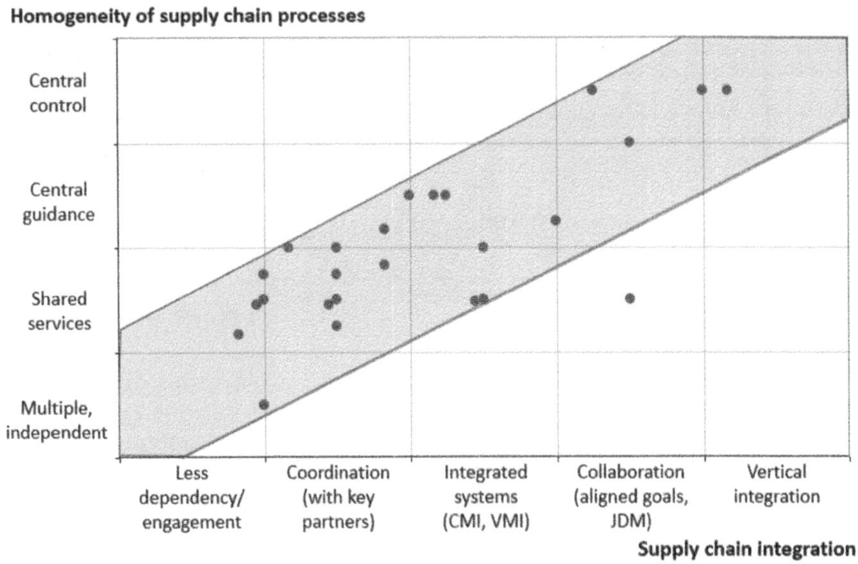

Fig. 4 Plot of supply chains with respect to two main influencers of resilience

based on high quality, high service, and emphasizing technology leadership) for all products. The vertical integration of a significant block of the required activities reduces the risk of dependence upon a small number of capable suppliers and limits dangerous knowledge spillover risks. These companies occupy one end of the diagonal in our framework.

Examples for this type of companies are ASML, Infineon, HP Enterprise. We refer to this archetype as the "Product (complexity) archetype." The other extreme in our diagonal in Fig. 4 represents companies with very diverse portfolios of more common usage (mostly consumer), and less technologically sophisticated products, but operating with a large pool of globally available efficient suppliers, often through transactional relationships. These companies have to deal with the inherent complexity of diverse products with very different competitive priority markets, and with the need to maintain multiple product finishing and market-end delivery processes to achieve the demand fulfillment priorities. Examples for this supply chain archetype are P&G, Colgate, Nestlé, or Würth. In a typically complex portfolio of both functional and innovative products, and with the need to build the portfolio of efficient and responsive chains for different product markets, these companies end up creating a loosely connected portfolio of heterogeneous supply chains. These chains rely extensively for sourcing and distribution on a large number of transactional partners using a multi-tiered structure that inhibits limited visibility to deeper tiers. The complexity of the portfolio of supply chain processes they manage creates chaotic supply and distribution networks whose usage necessitates a high level of planning. The pursuit of execution efficiency, while balancing the flexibility needs for shifts among products as demand preferences change, is often the Achilles heel for these companies. They are the "Process (complexity) archetype" residing at the other end of the diagonal.

The companies in the middle of the diagonal face moderate levels of challenges due to product complexity and the availability of supply options. Their product portfolios are reasonably complex, with many different products but of standardized variety or with customization options. The technological complexity is not as high, but with some engineering skill complexity, making qualified suppliers reasonably available in most locations. Typical examples for this type of companies are car manufacturers such as Daimler or General Motors or producers of industrial and consumer products such as Emerson, Cisco, or Panasonic. Logistic and customer response metrics drive these companies closer to their end-product markets. Their supply chains reflect a balance of outsourced and in-house production. Their supply chains are characterized by multi-tier supply networks with large transactional suppliers operating on a global scale, but with fewer qualified "premium" partners for the higher quality engineered components needed by their products. These companies shift into a role of a supply chain integrator in fulfilling regional demand. For example, BMW, the German premium car manufacturer, operates a carefully coordinated mix of efficient and responsive processes, that shares efficiency and scale-driven processes (commodity procurement, some distribution and logistics assets, etc.), and allows for end-market differentiated processes that are relatively close to the customer. This positions BMW and other similar businesses in the middle of the "supply chain process heterogeneity" dimension. They often own their assembly and finishing/customization processes and position them near their end markets. They also shop globally for lean, qualified quality, low-labor-cost production partners and low-cost commodity procurement. These practices correspond to a position near the middle of the vertical integration/extent of outsourcing dimension. We refer to these lean supply chain integrators as the "Partner (complexity) archetype."

Our "Triple-P" framework not only uses operational attributes of product and process complexity to help executives characterize their business units, but also suggests directions for global supply chain redesign.

The 26 supply chains which we analyzed are all on the diagonal and were chosen because they belong to companies that have a leading position in their respective industries. As supply chain resilience is difficult to measure and it is still too early to see the long-term effects of some strategies, we cannot empirically prove that a supply chain needs to be on the diagonal to be successful. However, being off the diagonal means that a company is vertically integrated for multiple independent supply chains (bottom right corner), which is difficult to achieve in terms of investment and complexity. Alternatively, a company that has only one supply chain setup for all its SKUs while having loose relationships with other supply chain actors, even though only a part of the value creation is done in-house, would be position in the top left corner. This positioning makes it difficult for a company to maintain a competitive advantage as the setup does not work for complex production processes, IP protection, or exploiting economies of scope. Small companies with niche products might be in this situation. Therefore, we believe that companies that operate supply chains off the diagonal will need to have a good reason for doing so.

Pursuing the goal of residing on the diagonal compels companies to rethink the structure of their supply chain processes. In particular, they must determine their degree of heterogeneity, i.e., where they land along the continuum defined by the options of multiple independent supply chains, shared services, central guidance, or one size-fits-all. This analysis may also stimulate a rethinking of the extent of outsourcing/vertical integration. This requires determination of where they land among options that include an arm's length relationship with suppliers, coordination with key partners, investing in highly integrated systems with partners, active aligned collaboration of strategic partners, and ownership investments in vertical integration. The framework allows for a design of a global supply chain to balance the trade-off between efficiency and resilience through the choices regarding the extent of ownership of activities (vertical integration) and organizational structure and planning processes (heterogeneity of supply chain processes).

At the same time, organizations can use the "Triple-P" framework (which we also refer to as the "Bespoke Supply Chain Resiliency" framework) in their efforts to build resilience. For this purpose, we identified obstacles to implementation that are peculiar to each identified archetype. The major obstacles for the "Product complexity" archetype unsurprisingly relate to factor market limitations, due to the highly specialized facilities and skill sets, which increase the degree of difficulty for diversifying the production footprint. Infineon, the German semiconductor company, is a company with this archetype. Adding production capacity involves high upfront investments and takes 6–12 months with existing buildings or up to 3 years for a greenfield factory. Moreover, access to a pool of highly skilled employees and talent is needed.

Furthermore, the "Process complexity" archetype suffers from the organizational complexity of diverse supply chain processes and the challenges of managing multi-tiered supplier tree structure with limited visibility and control in the deeper tiers. Such organizations need to effectively balance continuously shifting efficiency and resilience trade-offs. Their complex supplier portfolios often involve sourcing from environments with weak infrastructure and loose regulations (e.g., vis-à-vis treatment of workers and the natural environment), often with small-and-medium size suppliers needing assistance with financing and process improvements. For example, the apparel business unit of Nike operates in a fragmented supplier market with many smaller specialized factories due to the great variety of materials and clothes. Due to the pandemic-related drastic demand drop for apparel in 2020, Nike developed a grading framework to decide which suppliers they are able to "save" through prioritization of the remaining orders and supply chain financing.

Finally, the "Partner complexity" archetype may have to overcome the obstacles faced by both the "Product complexity" and "Process complexity" archetypes that present at more modest intensities. The resources available to support their needs for some owned facilities close to their customers limits the extent of regionalization. Reliance on highly qualified mid-tier partners demands their attention to careful selection, qualification, and integrated planning. At the same time, product portfolios that mix engineered-to-order and consumer products can stretch their organizational support for supply chain processes. However, the key challenges for these supply chain integrators are partner relationship management and the need for deep visibility into their supply and logistics resources. For example, BMW uses a supply chain and logistics platform to monitor all materials and suppliers in lower tiers to do fast root cause analysis, quickly escalate potential disruptions, and initiate countermeasures. The platform is run by a cross-functional team of procurement and logistics experts and helps BMW to use its competitive power to influence the decisions of their suppliers when issues occur. Moreover, BMW also collaborated with key suppliers during the COVID-pandemic through worker sharing concepts to keep the lines of their suppliers running.

Executives that understand the Triple-P framework (Fig. 2) will know how operational attributes position a business within a cluster (Product, Partner, or Process archetype), obtain a path to enhance resilience, and identify implementation obstacles peculiar to each cluster. We summarize the nature of the solutions we propose (Fig. 3) as follows:

"Product complexity" organizations have to deal with the challenges of major design and manufacturing facilities' footprint diversification. The challenges are financial investment, skilled labor requirements, and supplier network availability in support of geographic diversification. As a result, digitalization of their supply chains and automation has a high priority. At the same time, they must pursue public (potentially government based) and private partnerships to create the needed diversified network.

"Process complexity" organizations have to address the complexity of their portfolio and processes. Their resilience depends on reduction of this complexity. We refer to this as an effort of "standardization," but note that it is far from the usual levels of expected lean standardization. It is imperative for them to rethink their complex multi-tier supplier structures and reassess where the search for low cost has compromised visibility and response flexibility. While the necessity of complexity driven by their diverse product markets will remain, these organizations have to find ways to support their planning processes through investments in integration technologies, financing support of their suppliers, and ESG initiatives in developing country sourcing locations.

"Partner complexity" organizations have to mix the above solutions for the two extreme archetypes. While the complexity of their product portfolio needs to be reassessed, their multi-tier structure and number of suppliers also requires careful revisiting. Emphasis on creating the right "premium" tier partners with aligned incentives, collaboration processes and end-to-end visibility across carefully orchestrated supply chains is what we refer as the "visibility enhancement" solution. In this case current digitalization technologies will drive investments for these organizations, and the pursuit of ESG initiatives will allow them to both narrow and select the qualified partners they need. Moreover, similar to the "product complexity" businesses, they will be challenged in expanding their owned facility footprint in pursuit of intended regionalization strategies.

5 Challenges for Research on Global Supply Chain and Resilience

With the disruptions caused by either natural disasters such as the COVID-19 pandemic or earthquakes, or geo-political frictions such as tariff wars and trade policy disagreements, the general public's awareness of the impact of such disruptions on supply chains for goods and services has increased significantly. This has led to a steady stream of academic and industry reports on operations strategies and supply chain redesigns that promise to enhance resilience.

While we welcome the increased interest, we note that many of these studies have severe limitations in their research design and analysis. In this section, we discuss some common pitfalls and limitations. This section is meant to encourage future research by suggesting how it can become more credible and therefore more impactful.

Most studies have been based on questionnaires completed by industry practitioners (Cohen et al. 2022). For online surveys, a response count in the hundreds or even thousands is not uncommon. However, the robust volume of responses might not provide meaningful information if the surveys are not designed properly. Below are issues specific to this domain.

The most critical detail to get right is the unit of analysis in these surveys. A large global company may have multiple product groups or divisions that have very different product and operating characteristics and therefore may utilize a portfolio of disparate supply chain strategies. When a representative of such a company participates in a survey, we do not know if this individual is answering for one specific, perhaps dominant, product, or instead has in mind some "composite" of all the company's supply chains. The survey's instructions must make clear the unit of analysis. Our resilience strategy research (Cohen et al. 2021a) is based on product group level data, and we clarified the unit of analysis upfront with the interviewees.

A common question in many of these surveys was on how companies would change the design of their supply chain, possibly through reshoring or more diversified sourcing. The respondents might be reporting on intent at that point in time, which might not translate into real action. For example, we have seen study results reporting that a certain fraction of the respondents adopted reshoring, when the data actually indicate that a different fraction of the respondents were *intending* to reshore. Sections 3 and 4 articulate obstacles that prevent companies from implementing their desired supply chain strategies, so we also do not know if a respondent is describing the supply chain his/her company aspires to or the one that is actually in place.

Some surveys try to capture the decision process or the logic behind certain decisions. A response would be meaningful only if the respondent was very close to the decision, or perhaps was a very senior executive with ownership of the decision. Yet we have seen surveys being completed by mid-level managers who might not have a complete perspective, making their responses somewhat speculative. To overcome this issue, in our data collection documented in Cohen et al. (2021a), we interviewed only top-level supply chain executives well-positioned to discuss the topics at hand.

To the extent possible, surveys should obtain information about the operating characteristics of each respondent's organization and product offerings. For example, what is his/her position in the supply chain being described? What is the extent of vertical integration versus outsourcing? (This question is more involved than might be apparent at first glance, as many functions are involved in operating a supply chain, and each one can separately be performed in-house, outsourced, or somewhere in between.) What does the company's supply base look like? What is the company's distribution channel strategy? What is the product mix that flows through the supply chain in question? We have seen studies in which all the responses were aggregated into summary results, without concern for the kinds of operating characteristics mentioned above. Our "Triple-P" framework explicitly factors the operating characteristics, e.g., for example, "Availability of potential suppliers" and "Homogeneity of product portfolio," into the choice of resilience strategy (Cohen et al. 2021a).

The previous point cautions against over-aggregation of the response data. We also advise care in the choice of how to segment the data for analysis and reporting. For instance, one common approach is to present results by industry, which is not without merit. However, some companies can be difficult to place into a single industry categorization. Beyond that, a company's product groups can be quite disparate, requiring different supply chain strategies. Even if you accept the placement of Nike into the sports apparel category, Nike's shoe, clothing, sports equipment, and electronics businesses face very different challenges and constraints. In terms of survey design this is really a manifestation of the "unit of analysis" issue discussed earlier.

Moreover, surveys should not ask yes-no questions (e.g., do you reshore or not?) without specifying how much reshoring is needed for the answer to be yes. And then you would want to capture the amount of reshoring respondent by respondent so you can aggregate properly. For example, when a survey says 10% of the respondents were reshoring, we do not know if this set of companies reshored just a small fraction of their manufacturing, or reshored a substantial fraction. Unless a survey was designed to get to that level of detail, the 10% figure is not very useful.

Most studies build up to a denouement that takes the form of a list of recommendations. We do not disagree with the vast majority of the individual recommendations we have seen, but find them problematic when presented as a list without prioritization that is tailored to the individual case, given that some of the recommendations might directly conflict with others. For example, we have seen recommendations that call for both reducing risk exposure by reshoring and diversified sourcing. Of course, customized advice can be offered only if the survey collected sufficiently detailed information from each respondent, but attempting to do goes beyond the scope and purpose of a survey.

We also note that actual performance outcomes of recommended or adopted strategies are rarely documented. In some cases, the questions in the survey were not sufficiently detailed to perform a deeper analysis. For example, simply asking whether your inventory increased or decreased due to your actions has limited value. An increase in inventory could indicate positive or negative performance depending on the underlying reason (good planning and strong relationships with suppliers enabled preferential access to materials during a shortage, versus mis-forecasting that leads to overstock of the wrong items).

6 Finding Appropriate Resilience Measures

The old saw "What you can't measure you can't improve" certainly applies to the pursuit of supply chain resilience. While the literature fully comprehends traditional process improvement and agility measures, there is a need for well thought-out supply chain resilience metrics that take the long-term perspective appropriate for assessing resiliency.

The supply chain function uses metrics that are mostly operational (e.g., On-Time-In-Full order deliveries (OTIF), fill rates), along with some asset-turn measures that link to financial performance (e.g., inventory turns). Traditional metrics are meant for short-term evaluations (e.g., how good is your customer service, what is the lead time to customers, how much is spent to expedite shipments). Investments to improve these metrics can produce results quickly (e.g., centralization of inventory would reduce inventory through pooling, design for postponement can reduce inventory while improving customer service, using digital technologies to improve forecasting can improve SC metrics). However, investments in resilience may require a longer time horizon to show positive impact. Further, in as much as investing in resilience is analogous to buying insurance, the costs might be ongoing with no guarantee ever being offset by a positive payoff. But if the catastrophic event ever does happen, you would be glad to have made that investment.

This section describes the measures supporting our Triple-P framework for achieving "bespoke resiliency" in global supply chains. These measures focus on three stages of the chronology, including the last category, which is the necessary postmortem that we feel has received inadequate attention in the discussion of resilience:

"Ex-ante agility planning" measures, which identify key vulnerabilities, and ensure the right asset investments and operational hedges are in place to guard against anticipated future disruptions.

"Agility of actual response" measures, which gauge the effectiveness in monitoring the arrival of a disruption and the agility of response.

"Exhibited true resilience" measures, characterizing the totality of recovery in terms of financial performance, customer service, time to stabilize organizational processes, and growth over competitors across potentially multiple disruptive events and for longer horizon (3–5 years).

What is frequently recommended by the literature, and what might be easier to put in place, is what we refer to as "agility" planning metrics (some others call these "resilience" or "contingency response" metrics, but they do not fit our definition of resilience in Part 2) such as the following: Time-to-Recovery (TTR), Time-to-Survive (TTS), and Expected Profit Loss (EPL)(Simchi-Levi et al. 2015, 2018). We can assess these at every node in the supply chain, where a node could be a process or facility or other key asset. These measures are easier to compute when the scope is internal to the measuring party, and more difficult when examining external suppliers and service providers. The assessment should ask the following questions:

If a disruptive event takes out one of the nodes, how long will it take for the node to recover to different levels of operational capacity (with 100% recovery used to measure TTR)?

For how long do the existing operational hedges (mostly redundant capacity or inventory buffers within the supply chain) allow the supply chain to continue serving customers (TTS)?

And, if fully serving customers is not possible, how much is the expected profit loss (EPL) (includes both short-term and long-term)?

We highly recommend using these agility-planning metrics across the supply chain to quickly identify and prioritize the vulnerabilities. This will drive preemptive actions to increase redundancy, such as inventory and capacity buffer increases, multi-sourcing, or footprint diversification, as well as modifying product designs and/or product line.

After the recovery from the disruptive event, "agility of actual response" measures will reveal failures in planning processes, partner inadequacy, and ineffective investments and operational hedges. These metrics should be monitored and aggregated over time, such as the "time of sustained shortages."

When reported to an organization's leadership and investors, measures of exhibited true resilience can motivate and justify the long-term investments in resiliency that can support long-term profitability, better servicing of customers, and market share growth.

Our Triple-P "bespoke resiliency" framework can help with the implementation of resilience metrics in the following areas:

1. An organization's position relative to the diagonal in Fig. 4 helps identify organizations to use as benchmarks vis-a-vis relevant "agility response metrics."
2. Just as the resilience strategies reflect whether a supply chain's major complexity is in process, partnerships, or product, so should the performance metrics. When process complexity dominates, measuring and controlling the complexity of the processes, becomes important. For example, measuring product modularity, the percentage of standardized components, or the percentage of multi-purpose of production facilities are metrics that are especially helpful for this type of supply chain. When partnership complexity dominates, attention turns to measures related to the effective shifting of sourcing to key premium supply partners, especially ones that encourage effective collaboration with these partners on

scenario planning and risk management. Examples would be supply chain visibility metrics that measure the quantity and quality of information sharing across tiers, e.g., up- and downstream inventory levels. Finally, when product complexity dominates, the key measures will reflect access to critical input materials, manufacturability of the product designs, and degree of diversification of the facilities' footprint. An example of such a metric is the percentage of dual sourcing or dual site sourcing of critical supplies.

7 Summary of Our Research Insights

Our group of supply chain scholars embarked on a research path to understand how the last 10 years have shaped global supply chains. This section summarizes our main learnings.

1. Is reshoring of production activities happening in North America and Western Europe? If so, what has been the role of trade and political changes of the last decade?

   Our work published in Cohen et al. (2018) offers the answer. While investment activity in manufacturing in these markets has increased, the primary investors are foreign firms are also seeking proximity to customers in these attractive markets. For Western European and North American firms, even import tariffs on raw materials or finished goods did not stimulate substantial reshoring activity, and in a few cases, the increased sourcing costs and/or retaliatory tariffs drove companies to expand in their foreign-based competitors' territories.
2. How have trade tariffs and the COVID-19 pandemic affected attitudes regarding China as a sourcing location?

   Global supply chain managers realized the significant risks due to their extensive dependence on China. Recent times have seen cost increases due to trade tariffs and expensive logistics (on top of the ongoing erosion of China's ability to provide a seemingly endless supply of inexpensive labor), leading to shortages and longer lead times resulting from COVID's impacts on China's ports and manufacturing facilities. For some industries (e.g., apparel, toys), finding alternative sourcing locations is rather easy and often multi-sourcing has already started. But for others, China's available production capacity, ability to ramp to volume for new products, and their multi-tier-deep ecosystem of qualified suppliers erect formidable barriers to switching to new sources in the short-term. The "China Plus One" compromise sourcing strategy has been a goal for some time for certain industries, but progress has been slowed as COVID's impact was obviously not limited to China.
3. To what extent do companies prioritize resilience in designing and executing their supply chain strategies? Do we see active commitment to resilience after 2019?

   The increased frequency of disruptive events combined with increased severity of the last 10 years (2011 Japanese earthquake and tsunami, 2011 Thailand flooding, 2017 Hurricane Harvey, etc., and the COVID-19 pandemic being an event of unprecedented magnitude) has sensitized companies and managers to disruption risks. Many organizations remain in a survival and short-term response mode as of this writing, measuring any reasonable response as a success with the usual measures of agility (TTR and profit loss). However, in our framing, resilience involves thinking about the long term, and using lessons of past events to inform strategies and resource investments that will prepare their supply chains to survive and even thrive in the face of knowable and unknowable future shocks. We have empirically identified substantial obstacles to enhancing resilience, even though in many cases the roadmap to that destination is readily available and well understood. After the recovery from a disruptive event, managers and financial markets prefer to think about the next quarter's performance. We hear a lot about resilience, but we often do not see the actions needed to build the necessary redundancy and operational flexibility. These actions are perceived to be too "expensive" in the eyes of investors and markets.

4. What is our advice to supply chain managers about building resilience for the current uncertainty-fraught environment?

   Our research is very clear in eschewing a "one-size-fits-all" answer. Modern supply chains are diverse and complex, and each supply chain's product, process and organizational attributes will dictate its resilience strategies. The mapping articulated by our "bespoke resiliency" Triple-P framework is a key contribution of our empirical research. Thus, our advice to managers is to use the framework as follows:

   (a) Position your supply chain along the dimensions of "supply chain process heterogeneity" and "degree of vertical integration." This will affiliate your supply chain with one of three archetypes: Product complexity, Partner complexity, and Process complexity.
   (b) Assess the gap between your current supply chain and the recommendations of our framework for the archetype. This analysis might call for greater standardization of processes, gaining better control through increased ownership of activities, or working more closely with trusted partners.
   (c) Based on your positioning, understand the main obstacles for achieving resilience. Then study the best practices for increasing resilience of this archetype. Some adaptation for your environment will be necessary.
   (d) To monitor the progress towards resilience, use the metrics described in our Sect. 5.

Consulting reports tend to write their recommendations at an industry level and suggest that companies should emulate the approaches of the "Top 25" world-class companies as distilled into a list of 10–15 points. This perhaps caters to the tendency of top executives to prefer uniformity of practices and measures. But this is not consistent with what our research leads us to recommend. Global companies typically manage a complex portfolio of products and serve a diversity of markets, requiring that different business units and their managers pursue resilience in a bespoke fashion.

5. Are lean production and supply chain practices inappropriate when resilience is a priority? Should companies increase inventories and install excess (i.e., underutilized) capacity to prepare for future disruptions?

In the eyes of the media and popular press, the supply chain failures during the COVID-19 pandemic are an indictment of lean principles and practices. This viewpoint at best lacks nuance and may also simply misunderstand lean production. Our Triple-P framework argues that lean practices actually enhance resilience for at least two of the archetypes. This is not an issue for the Product complexity archetype. For the Product complexity archetype, resilience is built into the product design, automation of processes, excess capacity that is funded by high margins, and strong relationships with a small circle of qualified suppliers. The need for inventories is primarily at the input material level, and global access to these inventories might be constrained in some disruptions.

For the Partnership complexity archetype, which relies on a few key partners for success in general, resilience comes from strengthening these relationships, visibility into partner operations, and coordination in responding to any disruption. High interdependency, short lead time, a committed relationship with keiretsu suppliers are actually key elements of the Toyota Production System that is known more broadly as lean production. Toyota and its suppliers problem-solve cooperatively during stable times and crisis times alike. After 2011's devastating Japanese earthquake, tsunami, and brush with nuclear disaster, which disabled almost 90% of production capacity at car companies like Toyota and Nissan, Toyota was able to fully recover in unexpected ways in less than 3 months. The current pandemic has caused shortages in semiconductor chips that have become critical components in automobiles, but these companies have thus far derived some level of protection from their proactive planning and strong partnerships with suppliers. Lean processes, continuously improved, supported by a culture of attention to quality and deep commitment to relationship with suppliers, have proven to be resilient.

The same holds true for the Process complexity archetype. Some of their products are functional, and true lean supply chains, with characteristics to the above, will quickly recover without huge buffer inventories. Buffers buy short-term agility, but visibility and collaborative problem-solving buy future resilience. The implementation challenges for this archetype are: suppliers are smaller and less visible, frequently undercapitalized and located in areas with weak infrastructure. A larger number of suppliers in diversified locations may be necessary. It is important to help the existing suppliers finance their inventories and allocate business or even provide infusions of capital to sustain the suppliers through the difficult disruption periods. These gestures build trust and loyalty that translate into supply chain resilience. Lean supply chains do tend to lack flexibility in shifting among products. Moreover, lean does not necessarily advocate for extremely focused efficiency by product, and practicing lean practices such as "heijunka" improve mix flexibility. Lean principles adapted to the needs of the different archetypes can achieve efficiency, quick response in delivery, and fast recovery from crises. This is true resilience.

8 Future Research Directions

We outline some open questions in this exciting and timely area of supply chain resilience that we hope that our community will address.

1. Empirical validation of our Bespoke Resiliency Triple-P framework

   Our framework suggests multiple hypotheses concerning the relationship between operational attributes and effective resilience strategies. We hope these hypotheses can be verified through study of a larger data sets of company operating data. This will entail fleshing out ex-post resilience measures that reflect ex-post performance of companies over longer periods (5–10 years) and using them to objectively assess actions intended to enhance resilience as well as operational and financial performance.
2. Empirical validation that processes and supply chains which operated according to true lean principles are resilient.

   We can make an anecdotal case that lean practices implemented for reasons of competitiveness and profitability have also enhanced resilience (which should not be surprising if resilience is in fact critical to long-term competitive and profitability). Central to that is understanding that lean does not see the capacity and inventory levels as decision variables to be lowered to make the financials look good, but rather as outcomes whose correct levels will naturally move lower as organizational processes and problem-solving capabilities improve. That is, lean is not about choosing to reduce capacity and inventory levels, but rather improving the system so that lower levels of these resources are the right outcome.
3. How will design-for-resilience be affected by near-future challenges and opportunities in global supply chains?
4. Almost all agree that digitization (through technologies such as IoT, blockchains, robotics, machine learning, 3D printing, etc.), ESG requirements and realities (sustainability concerns, climate change, labor conditions, safety regulations, etc.), and an environment with increased political risks will force executives to rethink their global supply chain strategies. Modelling and optimization approaches for capturing global supply chain resilience are necessary

We argued that the best way to make global supply chain decisions that effectively capture relevant objective trade-offs, reflect different cost and exchange rate scenarios, include logistic and other constraints (labor availability, supplier locations, etc.), is to formulate optimization models capturing such issues (see Cohen and Lee 1989; Huchzermeier and Cohen 1996; Kouvelis et al. 2013). But what is the best way to capture this longer-term perspective of resilience suggested by our recent work, in structured mathematical programming formulations? Resilience is not the responsibility of a single firm, or even of the traditional linear supply chain for a product group. Resilience depends on other supplier and distribution partners in complex dynamic networks. It often involves unexpected and hidden bottlenecks beyond the control of the firm or the supply chain (ports, trucking and shipping regional capacities, limited resources on a global scale for certain inputs, etc.), and all such concerns have to be captured in a longer time horizon with considerable uncertainty.

The frameworks introduced by our research and described in this chapter offer suggestions for directions for companies to pursue in the pursuit of resiliency. Further research is required to understand the impact of the strategies that are adopted.

References

Cohen MA, Kouvelis P (2021) Revisit of AAA excellence of global value chains: Robustness, resilience, and realignment. Prod Oper Manag 30(3):633–643

Cohen MA, Lee HL (1989) Resource deployment analysis of global manufacturing and distribution networks. J Manuf Oper Manag 2(2):81–104

Cohen MA, Lee HL (2020) Designing the right global supply chain network. Manuf Serv Oper Manag 22(1):15–24

Cohen MA, Cui S, Ernst R, Huchzermeier A, Kouvelis P, Lee HL (2018) Benchmarking global production sourcing decisions: Where and why firms offshore and reshore. Manuf Serv Oper Manag 20(3):389–402

Cohen MA, Cui S, Doetsch S, Ernst R, Huchzermeier A, Kouvelis P, Lee HL, Matsuo H, Tsay AA (2021a) Bespoke supply chain resilience. Stanford University Graduate School of Business Research Paper. https://ssrn.com/abstract=3873941

Cohen MA, Cui S, Doetsch S, Ernst R, Huchzermeier A, Kouvelis P, Lee HL, Matsuo H, Tsay AA (2021b) Putting supply chain resilience theory into practice. Manag Bus Rev. https://doi.org/10.2139/ssrn.3742616. https://ssrn.com/abstract=3742616

Cohen MA, Cui S, Doetsch S, Ernst R, Huchzermeier A, Kouvelis P (2022) Maximizing learning from surveys on supply chain agility and resilience. Why Operational Context Matters: Realizing the Full Potential of Supply Chain Resilience Surveys https://ssrn.com/abstract=4074109 or http://dx.doi.org/10.2139/ssrn.4074109 Forthcoming Supply Chain Management Review

Dachs B, Kinkel S, Jäger A (2019) Bringing it all back home? Backshoring of manufacturing activities and the adoption of Industry 4.0 technologies. J World Bus 54(6):101017

Dong L, Kouvelis P (2020) Impact of tariffs on global supply chain network configuration: Models, predictions, and future research. Manuf Serv Oper Manag 22(1):25–35

Fratocchi L, Di Mauro C, Barbieri P, Nassimbeni G, Zanoni A (2014) When manufacturing moves back: concepts and questions. J Purch Supply Manag 20:54–59

Hopp WJ (2011) Supply chain science. Waveland, Long Grove, IL

Huchzermeier A, Cohen MA (1996) Valuing operational flexibility under exchange rate risk. Oper Res 44(1):100–113

John G, Manenti P, Watt S, Raman K (2020) Future of supply chain: crisis shapes the profession: supply chain executive report. Gartner. https://www.gartner.com/en/documents/3994949/supply-chain-executive-report-future-of-supply-chain-cri. Accessed 15 Feb 2022

Kouvelis P, Munson CL, Yang S (2013) Robust structural equations for designing and monitoring strategic international facility networks. Prod Oper Manag 22(3):535–554

Lee H (2004) The triple-A supply chain. Harv Bus Rev 82:102–112, 157

Pfeffer J, Sutton RI (2000) The knowing-doing gap: How smart companies turn knowledge into action. Harvard Business School Press, Boston, MA

Sheffi Y (2007) The resilient enterprise: Overcoming vulnerability for competitive advantage. MIT Press, Cambridge, MA

Simchi-Levi D, Schmidt W, Wei Y, Zhang PY, Combs K, Ge Y, Gusikhin O, Sanders M, Zhang D (2015) Identifying risks and mitigating disruptions in the automotive supply chain. Interfaces 45(5):375–390

Simchi-Levi D, Wang H, Wei Y (2018) Increasing supply chain robustness through process flexibility and inventory. Prod Oper Manag 27(8):1476

The manufacturer's authorised representative in the EU is Springer Nature Customer Service Centre GmbH, Europaplatz 3, 69115 Heidelberg, Germany. If you have any concerns regarding our products, please contact ProductSafety@springernature.com

Printed and bound by CPI Group (UK) Ltd, Croydon, CR0 4YY
28/09/2026
02224070-0009